SAP Intelligent RPA for Developers

Automate business processes using SAP Intelligent RPA
and learn the migration path to SAP Process Automation

Vishwas Madhuvarshi

Vijaya Kumar Ganugula

BIRMINGHAM—MUMBAI

SAP Intelligent RPA for Developers

Copyright © 2022 Packt Publishing

Associate Group Product Manager: Richa Tripathi

Senior Editor: Rohit Singh

Content Development Editor: Tiksha Lad

Technical Editor: Pradeep Sahu

Copy Editor: Safis Editing

Project Coordinator: Deeksha Thakkar

Proofreader: Safis Editing

Indexer: Tejal Daruwale Soni

Production Designer: Vijay Kamble

Marketing Coordinator: Deepak Kumar

First published: May 2022

Production reference: 1050522

Published by Packt Publishing Ltd.

Livery Place

35 Livery Street

Birmingham

B3 2PB, UK.

ISBN 978-1-80107-919-8

www.packt.com

To dear Shama, Anushka, Alisha, the late Mrs. Kanta Devi, and Prof. C. B. Arya for helping me become who I am today.

– Vishwas Madhuvarshi

To my daughter Samhita for being an inspiration and encouraging me to write a book.

– Vijaya Kumar Ganugula

Contributors

About the authors

Vishwas Madhuvarshi has been developing software for more than 20 years and has seen the industry as a developer, project manager, and director. He is currently a global director of emerging technologies and works across the complete hyperautomation toolchain – ranging from RPA, user experience, business process automation, and blockchain to AI/ML – in SAP practice. He has been instrumental in setting up the company's RPA and process mining practices. While this is his first book, Vishwas has written several whitepapers on RPA and user experience. He is from Delhi, India, and currently lives in Houston, USA. You can reach Vishwas on LinkedIn, vishwasmadhuvarshi.

Vijaya Kumar Ganugula has been working in the IT industry since 2000. He is an RPA delivery lead, working on a variety of automation projects using most of the leading RPA tools on the market. Vijaya is currently working as a deputy general manager at HCL Technologies Ltd focusing on automation solutions for clients spread across geographies and business lines. His team is one of the early attendees of the official training on SAP Intelligent RPA and has been working with SAP Intelligent RPA since 2019.

I would like to thank my loving and patient wife, Haritha, and my daughter, Samhita, for their continued support, patience, and encouragement throughout the long process of writing this book.

About the reviewers

Maria Victoria Bonzon has 5 years of experience working at SAP, with 2 of them as part of the UX and Mobility Consulting team for Latin America. As an industrial engineer, process optimization has always been of interest to her and she believes that intelligent technologies are an excellent tool for that. She has a particular interest in RPA due to the high potential to improve processes with a low **Total Cost of Ownership (TCO)**.

On a professional level, she is someone who is constantly looking for new challenges and willing to overcome them. She wishes to keep dreaming big and following her goals with passion and consistency.

Marek Benda is a senior ABAP developer with over 17 years of experience, who has been dedicated to SAP Intelligent RPA since its first release a few years ago. He currently works as a systems architect and developer on several SAP Intelligent RPA projects.

Table of Contents

3

Installing SAP Intelligent RPA On-Premise Components

4

Setting Up SAP Intelligent RPA On-Premise Components

5

An Overview of Desktop Studio

6

An Overview of Desktop Agent

Part 2: Installing and Setting Up SAP Intelligent RPA

7

An Overview of Cloud Studio

8

An Introduction to SAP Spotlight and Signavio

Part 3: Developing Bots with Desktop Studio

9

Desktop Studio Perspectives

10
Creating and Managing Projects

11
An Introduction to Technology Connectors

12
Capturing and Declaring Applications, Pages, and Items

13

Designing Scenarios

14

Advanced Criteria Definition

15

Controlling Workflows and Scenarios

16

Designing Custom Pages with UI Designer

Part 4: Generating and Updating the JavaScript Code

17

Generating Code

18

An Introduction to Desktop SDK

19

SDK Extension Libraries

20

Managing Environment Variables

Part 5: Building and Running Projects

21

Building Projects

22

Deploying Projects

23
Debugging Projects

Part 6: Orchestrating Workflows with Cloud Studio

24
Development Using Cloud Studio

25
Reusability of Packages Across Multiple Solutions

26

An Introduction to Process Recorder

Part 7: SAP Intelligent RPA Store, Roadmap, and SAP BTP Automation Services

27

SAP Intelligent RPA Store

28

SAP Intelligent RPA – Future Roadmap and Automation-Related Services

Assessments

Index

Other Books You May Enjoy

Preface

SAP is the market leader in enterprise application software. With nearly 440,000 customers worldwide, 77% of the world's transaction revenue touches an SAP system. SAP has made automation a key pillar across its product suite and counts on SAP Intelligent **Robotic Process Automation (RPA)** to automate repetitive work and integrate automation capabilities across SAP and non-SAP systems. This book provides end-to-end coverage of business process automation using SAP Intelligent RPA.

You will learn about various building blocks of the SAP Intelligent RPA solution, follow many step-by-step tutorials on creating bots from initial application declaration to workflow design and deployment, and make bots run in attended and unattended modes. You will also learn about SAP Intelligent RPA 2.0 components such as the low-code Cloud Studio and an updated runtime to create and execute your bots.

By the end of this book, you will be able to create bots capable of interacting with SAP and non-SAP systems. In addition, you will understand the efficient management of these bots and various SAP Cloud Platform services that complement SAP Intelligent RPA. Finally, you will also learn some of the lessons that we as authors of this book learned while delivering SAP Intelligent RPA projects.

Who this book is for

This book is for developers and business users interested in learning SAP Intelligent RPA for the automation of non-value-add, monotonous, and error-prone work. SAP Intelligent RPA offers three modes of development—no-code, low-code, and pro-code. Business users can use the no-code development mode with no technical knowledge assumed. A rudimentary understanding of JavaScript is helpful for business users but is essential for developers who want to engage in pro-code development to address complex challenges.

Access to the SAP Business Technology Platform trial system would be necessary as you progress through the book. Although you can wait to set the system up when needed, we recommend setting it up now by using this link, `https://www.sap.com/products/business-technology-platform/trial.html` and exploring the available functionalities as and when possible.

What this book covers

Chapter 1, SAP Intelligent RPA Architecture and Components, explains the overall architecture of SAP Intelligent RPA along with their dependency on other components in using the SAP Intelligent RPA. You will understand the options available to develop and deploy the automation solutions and which component is relevant for any step in automation solution development.

Chapter 2, An Overview of SAP Intelligent RPA Cloud Factory, gives an introduction to SAP Cloud Factory, which centrally manages all common resources related to SAP Intelligent RPA. This chapter introduces terminology and usage of the Cloud Factory and explains Environments, Agents and Agent Groups, Packages, Jobs, and Triggers.

Chapter 3, Installing SAP Intelligent RPA On-Premise Components, explains the system requirements for installing and running the Desktop Studio and Desktop Agent, and installation procedures. It also explains installing third-party dependencies.

Chapter 4, Setting Up SAP Intelligent RPA On-Premise Components, includes an explanation of various topics required to complete the setup and before running the automation solutions, which includes security within SAP Intelligent RPA, authorization, roles, and authentication.

Chapter 5, An Overview of Desktop Studio, includes a short introduction to Desktop Studio perspectives to familiarize you with the terminology.

Chapter 6, An Overview of Desktop Agent, gives an introduction to Desktop Agent, explains the role of Desktop Agent during the automation process, how Desktop Agent is launched, and how to connect Desktop Agent to Cloud Factory.

Chapter 7, An Overview of Cloud Studio, explains the Cloud Studio and its usage, differentiating the Desktop Studio from Cloud Studio, and different options available in Cloud Studio to import packages, create workflows, and export projects.

Chapter 8, An Introduction to SAP Spotlight and Signavio, introduces a couple of additional tools from SAP that can help ease understanding the process and orchestrate an automation solution.

Chapter 9, Desktop Studio Perspectives, is an extension of *Chapter 4, Setting Up SAP Intelligent RPA On-Premise Components*, which includes a very detailed explanation of the Desktop Studio, different perspectives, and usage while developing an automation solution.

Chapter 10, Creating and Managing Projects, covers a detailed explanation of projects, including how to create projects, structuring projects, project properties, dependencies, and maintaining versions.

Chapter 11, An Introduction to Technology Connectors, gives an introduction to eight connectors available in SAP Intelligent RPA, including a detailed explanation of the Web, UI Automation, SAP GUI, SAPUI5, and Win32 connectors, along with usage examples on when to use which connector for capturing screens.

Chapter 12, Capturing and Declaring Applications, Pages, and Items, introduces us to SAP Intelligent RPA terminology used for automating applications. It has a detailed explanation of how to capture different types (Windows Desktop applications, and web applications) of applications, capturing and defining pages, and subpages within applications. The chapter also shows how to identify the controls within the page and defines the criteria for identifying these.

Chapter 13, Designing Scenarios, covers creating workflows and adding activities such as set or get values from UI components/controls, or performing actions on controls such as clicking a button.

Chapter 14, Advanced Criteria Definition, covers extending the criteria definitions learned in *Chapter 12, Capturing and Declaring Applications, Pages, and Items*; this chapter covers advanced declaration techniques provided by SAP Intelligent RPA that are used to identify pages and controls uniquely in complex applications.

Chapter 15, Controlling Workflows and Scenarios, explains how to includes loops to process a list of data and control the flow based on data, that is, to include conditional flow in the workflows.

Chapter 16, Designing Custom Pages with UI Designer, includes a detailed explanation of the UI Designer perspective and how to create custom pages and use them in a workflow.

Chapter 17, Generating Code, provides a detailed explanation of building the automation project and where to look for compilation errors while building the project. This chapter also covers how the generated project source code is organized.

Chapter 18, An Introduction to SDK Reference Guide, covers the SDK and different libraries available in the SDK that are useful while developing an automation solution.

Chapter 19, SDK Extension Libraries, is a continuation of the previous chapter, where a detailed explanation of SDK extensions is covered. This includes integrations with Office apps such as Outlook, Excel, and so on, PDF integration, and other specific technologies, such as SAP extensions.

Chapter 20, Managing Environment Variables, covers the usage of environment variables, how to create them in the Cloud Factory, and reading and using them in workflows.

Chapter 21, Building Projects, explains how a project is built for testing or deployment and probable issues and resolutions faced during building the project.

Chapter 22, Deploying Projects, covers how a project is deployed to the Cloud Factory and different options available for controlling the deployments targeted to specific groups based on either users or business areas.

Chapter 23, Debugging Projects, targets developers involved in automation solution development. This chapter includes a detailed explanation of the Debug perspective. It covers the steps to follow to check the state of the pages, screens, and controls, and identify and monitor the changes to variables and controls.

Chapter 24, Development Using Cloud Studio, provides a detailed explanation of how the Cloud Studio is used for developing automation solutions and how the Cloud Studio can be used like Desktop Studio for the development of automation solutions.

Chapter 25, Reusability of Packages Across Multiple Solutions, covers how to manage solution components and reuse them across automation solutions.

Chapter 26, An Introduction to Process Recorder, gives an introduction to process Recorder and how it can be used to accelerate the development process.

Chapter 27, SAP Intelligent RPA Store, explains the usage of SAP Intelligent RPA Store and how to download the predefined solutions and adopt them by updating as per business requirements to increase automation productivity.

Chapter 28, SAP Intelligent RPA – Future Roadmap and Automation-Related Services, discusses SAP Intelligent RPA's future roadmap as well as a list of automation-related services available in SAP **Business Technology Platform** (**BTP**).

Any errata related to this book can be found at the following link: `https://github.com/PacktPublishing/SAP-Intelligent-RPA-for-Developers`.

Download the color images

We also provide a PDF file that has color images of the screenshots and diagrams used in this book. You can download it here:

`https://static.packt-cdn.com/downloads/9781801079198_ColorImages.pdf`

Conventions used

There are a number of text conventions used throughout this book.

`Code in text`: Indicates code words in text, database table names, folder names, filenames, file extensions, pathnames, dummy URLs, user input, and Twitter handles. Here is an example: "Since this is an SAP page, we will be using the keys defined under `SAPScripting` and not `e.key.Enter`, which can be used for non-SAP pages."

A block of code is set as follows:

```
<VariableSizedWrapGrid Orientation="Horizontal"
 MaximumRowsOrColumns="3" ItemHeight="200" ItemWidth="200">
    <Rectangle Fill="Red" />
    <Rectangle Fill="Blue" />
    <Rectangle Fill="Green" />
    <Rectangle Fill="Yellow" />
</VariableSizedWrapGrid>
```

Bold: Indicates a new term, an important word, or words that you see onscreen. For instance, words in menus or dialog boxes appear in **bold**. Here is an example: "Right-click on the **GLOBAL** node in the **Workflow** perspective and select the **New Workflow...** option from the context menu."

> **Tips or important notes**
> Appear like this.

Get in touch

Feedback from our readers is always welcome.

General feedback: If you have questions about any aspect of this book, email us at `customercare@packtpub.com` and mention the book title in the subject of your message.

Errata: Although we have taken every care to ensure the accuracy of our content, mistakes do happen. If you have found a mistake in this book, we would be grateful if you would report this to us. Please visit `www.packtpub.com/support/errata` and fill in the form.

Piracy: If you come across any illegal copies of our works in any form on the internet, we would be grateful if you would provide us with the location address or website name. Please contact us at copyright@packt.com with a link to the material.

If you are interested in becoming an author: If there is a topic that you have expertise in and you are interested in either writing or contributing to a book, please visit authors.packtpub.com.

Share Your Thoughts

Once you've read *SAP Intelligent RPA for Developers*, we'd love to hear your thoughts! Scan the QR code below to go straight to the Amazon review page for this book and share your feedback.

https://packt.link/r/1801079196

Your review is important to us and the tech community and will help us make sure we're delivering excellent quality content.

Prologue – SAP Process Automation Service

Just before this book was published, we learned that the SAP Intelligent RPA service might soon be discontinued in its current form. While the news came as a shock, we talked with the SAP team to understand the way forward. As a result, we learned that while the SAP Intelligent RPA and Workflow Management services may be discontinued soon, they will become part of a new service, **SAP Process Automation (SPA)**. This information quelled the initial shock, but several additional questions came up overall. In this prologue, we will try to answer those questions under the following topics:

- Understanding the SPA service

- Transitioning to SPA from SAP Intelligent RPA

- Where to begin and look for help when needed

Understanding the SPA service

SPA is a new SAP service that intends to combine two existing services, SAP Intelligent RPA and Workflow Management, to offer automation developers a full suite of tools in one place. Within the SPA service, we still have the option of creating either automation or a workflow or creating an end-to-end process. However, all these options are available under a single service now. If your license for SAP Intelligent RPA or Workflow Management is valid for more time, you can still keep using those services for that duration.

Our core concern is to help you transition from SAP Intelligent RPA to SPA. Therefore, we will touch upon only the relevant parts of the service. Let's see how SPA looks and how we can create automations using this new service.

Check out the following screenshot:

Figure Prologue.1 – SAP Process Automation

Let's discuss the nine areas of interest shown in the preceding screenshot:

1. **Lobby**: This is the landing page of the SPA service, shown in the preceding screenshot. The one significant difference from SAP Intelligent RPA that you will also see here is a link to **My Inbox** (**5**).

2. **Store**: This tab leads to the pre-built content for SPA. Here, you will see the content for live processes (workflows) in addition to process automation content. **Store** is slightly different from the SAP Intelligent RPA store, and there are no bots built using Desktop Studio. Here is a screenshot of it:

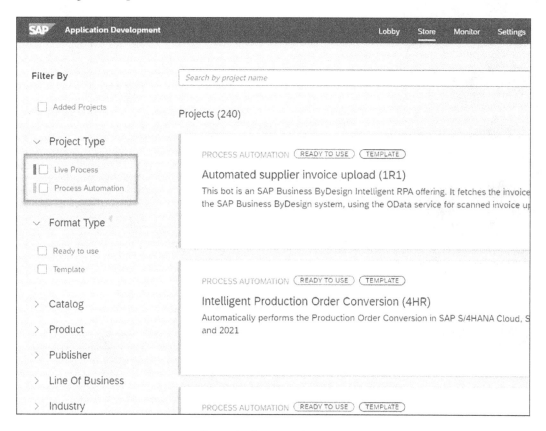

Figure Prologue.2 – SPA store

3. **Monitor**: You can manage and monitor all your processes and workflow instances from this tab.

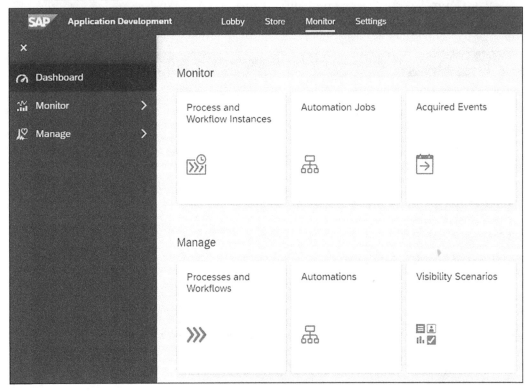

Figure Prologue.3 – Monitor tab

4. **Settings**: You can manage agents, backend configurations, destinations, and several other settings from this tab.

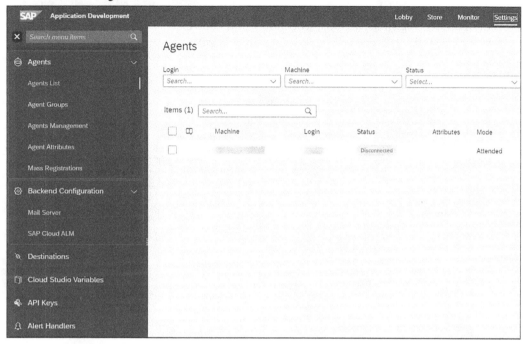

Figure Prologue.4 – Settings

5. **My Inbox**: **My Inbox** opens up in a new tab and shows all tasks assigned to the logged-in user. Since we have no running automations yet, our list is empty.

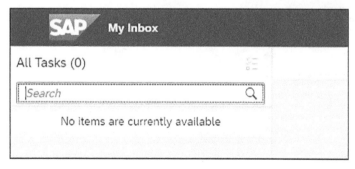

Figure Prologue.5 – My Inbox

6. **Create a Process**: This link leads you to an interface similar to the Workflow Management service. After providing the project and process names, you can create an end-to-end process using various constituents, such as forms, approvals, automations, decisions, actions, workflows, and controls.

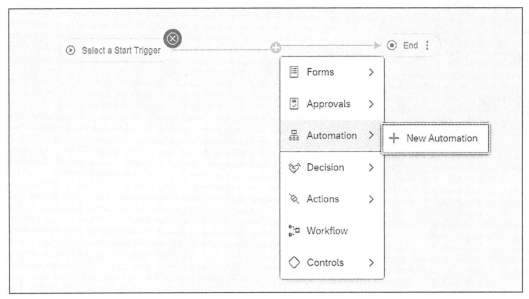

Figure Prologue.6 – Create a Process

7. **Create a Form**: As the name suggests, this link leads you to a form editor where you can create a custom form for your scenario.

8. **Create an Automation**: As Intelligent RPA developers, this link is the most relevant to us. This link leads us to a project creation screen.

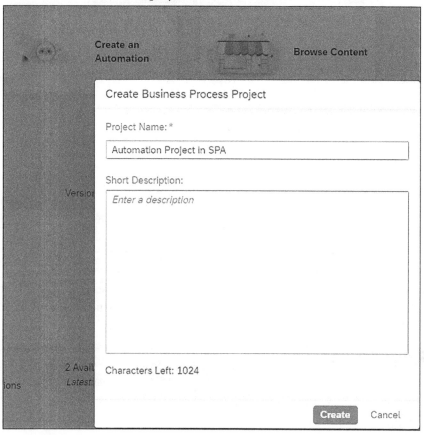

Figure Prologue.7 – Automation project creation in SPA

Once the project is created, the next screen for **Create Automation** pops up.

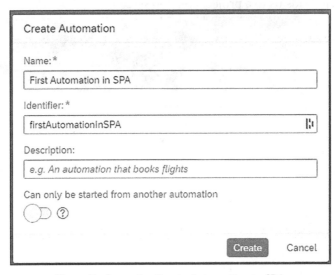

Figure Prologue.8 – Create Automation in SPA

Once you have provided the necessary information on this screen, you will see the familiar editor from SAP Intelligent RPA with all the constituents exactly as you would be used to.

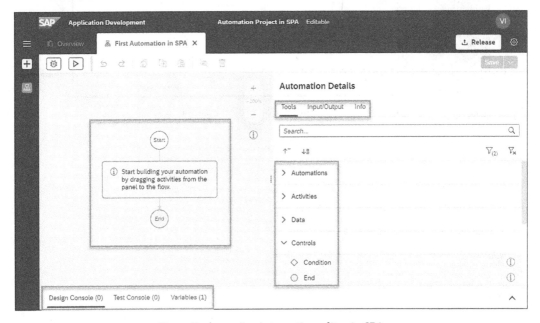

Figure Prologue.9 – Automation editor in SPA

Since we are at the beginning of the book, these images may not mean much to you now. It would be safe to say that even if SAP Process Automation Service replaces the SAP Intelligent RPA service in the future, you will still be able to use your learnings from this book in the new service.

9. **Browse Content**: This link leads you to the **Store** tab (**2**).

Transitioning to SPA from SAP Intelligent RPA

Transitioning from the SAP Intelligent RPA service to SPA raises the following two questions:

- How long can I continue working on the SAP Intelligent RPA service?

  We have been told that customers can keep using the SAP Intelligent RPA service until the end of their license validity. However, license renewal may or may not be available after the license validity expiration.

- Can I migrate my current SAP Intelligent RPA projects to the SPA service?

  Yes. With some limitations, you can now migrate your SAP Intelligent RPA projects to SAP Process Automation. For details, please check here, `https://blogs.sap.com/2022/04/20/move-now-import-your-sap-intelligent-rpa-projects-into-sap-process-automation/`.

  So, you can create new automations, import pre-built automations from the store, and migrate your SAP Intelligent RPA projects to SAP Process Automation. Keep following the SPA roadmap at `https://roadmaps.sap.com/board?PRODUCT=73554900100800003832&range=CURRENT-LAST#Q2%202022` to understand the updates to the migrate feature.

Where to begin and look for help when needed

While the SAP team has shared that the SAP Intelligent RPA and Workflow Management services may be retiring, these services have not been listed under the **RETIRING SOON** section. So, we can keep using these services for some more time:

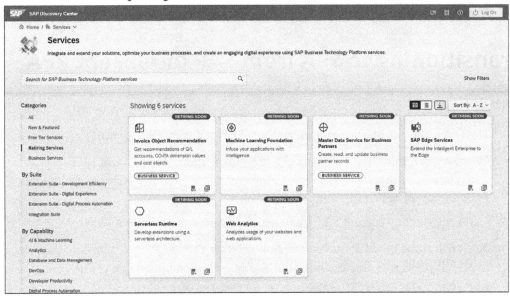

Figure Prologue.10 – Services retiring soon

However, preparing for the eventual shift from SAP Intelligent RPA to SPA would be a wise move on your part to be ready for the transition. To experience SPA, now a part of SAP's new free tier, follow this blog by Sebastian Schroetel: `https://blogs.sap.com/2022/03/30/sap-process-automation-free-tier-is-out-create-your-own-automations/`. To start building projects in the SPA service, you can follow this seven-part series of blogs by Murali Shanmugham: `https://blogs.sap.com/2022/02/20/getting-started-with-sap-process-automation-the-new-no-code-experience-for-automation-part-1/`. You can also find answers to most of your questions at SAP's help page for SPA at `https://help.sap.com/docs/PROCESS_AUTOMATION`.

Summary

In this prologue, we discussed SAP's proposed transition from SAP Intelligent RPA to SPA. As we understand it, there is no direct impact on your ongoing SAP Intelligent RPA projects, and there is now a straightforward migration path for SAP Intelligent RPA projects to SPA. Also, all your learnings from this book will remain applicable to the new SPA service. Now, let's begin learning about SAP Intelligent RPA.

Part 1: Introduction to SAP Intelligent Robotic Process Automation

This is an introductory part of the book in which you will be familiarized with the products and different components available in SAP Intelligent **Robotic Process Automation (RPA)**. You will also get an understanding of the brief history of SAP Intelligent RPA and how it has evolved into a reliable product for all automation needs of any organization or business area. This section also explains how to install and set up SAP Intelligent RPA and where to get the installable files. You will see a list of prerequisites before starting the installation and how to set up different third-party tools used by SAP Intelligent RPA for various development activities.

This section comprises the following chapters:

- *Chapter 1, SAP Intelligent RPA Architecture and Components*
- *Chapter 2, An Overview of SAP Intelligent RPA Cloud Factory*
- *Chapter 3, Installing SAP Intelligent RPA On-Premise Components*
- *Chapter 4, Setting Up SAP Intelligent RPA On-Premise Components*
- *Chapter 5, An Overview of Desktop Studio*
- *Chapter 6, An Overview of Desktop Agent*

1
SAP Intelligent RPA Architecture and Components

This chapter aims to provide you with an introduction to SAP **Intelligent Robotic Process Automation (IRPA)** and how you can use it to help your organization achieve its automation objectives. We will discuss a brief history of SAP Intelligent RPA, its components, and how they relate to each other. After this quick introduction, we will talk about all the available resources in your learning journey and where to seek help when you need it. Finally, we will address why you should learn SAP Intelligent RPA and why your organization should use it.

In this chapter, we will cover the following topics:

- A brief history of SAP Intelligent RPA
- The core components of SAP Intelligent RPA
- The relationship between Intelligent RPA components
- Where to find help when needed
- Why should you learn and use SAP Intelligent RPA

By the end of this chapter, you will understand SAP Intelligent RPA and why an individual or an organization should use it. You will also gain knowledge of how to use SAP Intelligent RPA.

Let's begin with understanding a bit of the history of SAP Intelligent RPA.

Technical requirements

- For the instructions and code in this chapter, you just need an internet connection.

A brief history of SAP Intelligent RPA

SAP acquired Contextor SAS – a Europe-based firm specializing in delivering RPA solutions – in November 2018 and renamed it SAP Intelligent RPA soon after. However, Contextor had been delivering RPA solutions in Europe since 2003 and involved in research and development specific to RPA since 2000.

Why is this important?

It is necessary to understand that SAP Intelligent RPA is based on an RPA platform with a deep foundation and solution maturity spanning nearly 2 decades. Any RPA solution can offer the expected functionalities, but solution maturity takes time, and SAP Intelligent RPA has gone through that process.

The solution that SAP launched in 2018 as SAP Intelligent RPA is now renamed SAP Intelligent RPA 1.0, and a new version, SAP Intelligent RPA 2.0, has been launched recently. SAP started offering pre-built bots for Intelligent RPA as SAP Best Practice content in 2019 and changed the delivery model through the Intelligent RPA Store some time back. We will briefly discuss all core components in this chapter while leaving detailed discussions about each of them to later chapters in the book. For now, we will move on to discuss SAP Intelligent RPA's core components.

The core components of SAP Intelligent RPA

Six core components spread equally on cloud and on-premises make up the SAP Intelligent RPA platform. They are primarily categorized as cloud and on-premises components. Let's discuss each of these components in the following sections.

Cloud components

We can classify the following three components as cloud components:

Figure 1.1 – The cloud components of SAP Intelligent RPA

As the name suggests, cloud components reside in the cloud, specifically in the SAP **Business Technology Platform** (**BTP**), previously known as the SAP Cloud Platform. The three cloud components are Cloud Factory, Cloud Studio, and the Store, each discussed in the following subsections.

Cloud Factory

Cloud Factory – also known as Intelligent RPA Factory – serves as the orchestration and monitoring center of SAP Intelligent RPA. It hosts resource management tools and monitors job execution, displays logs, and historical job data. Cloud Factory is where the registration of desktop agents and the creation of agent groups take place. It also provides the apps for configuring a dedicated mail server and integration with the SAP **Application Lifecycle Management** (**ALM**) tool.

Cloud Studio

Cloud Studio is the newest entrant to the SAP Intelligent RPA toolset and is the main constituent and development tool of Intelligent RPA 2.0. SAP Intelligent RPA provides three modes of developing RPA bots – **Low Code** (**LC**), **No Code** (**NC**), and **Pro Code** (**PC**). Cloud Studio is currently aligned with NC and LC modes of automation development but will soon also offer PC mode. Using Cloud Studio, you can create new projects or assemble, test, and validate new and existing projects.

Store

The Intelligent RPA Store is the online catalog and delivery platform for all SAP's predefined content, including bots for business and learning, built using Cloud Studio and Desktop Studio. SAP clients can use these bots as a starting point to develop custom bots specific to their business case, saving both time and money in the process. Bot Store also lists all the SAP Intelligent RPA SDKs. You can search for desired content on parameters such as `design tool`, `catalog`, `category`, `application`, `edition`, `line of business`, and `industry` using the store. At the time of this writing, the Store lists 353 SAP packages. In the beginning, SAP delivered Intelligent RPA content through the SAP Best Practices channel but switched to the Store in 2020. You can access the Store from Cloud Factory or directly via this URL: `https://store.irpa.cfapps.eu10.hana.ondemand.com/#/home`.

Let's now discuss the on-premises components.

On-premises components

The remaining three components are classified as on-premises components, as shown in the following diagram:

Figure 1.2 – On-premises components

We will talk about each component in detail next.

The Desktop Agent

The Desktop Agent is a small software component that is essential on a workstation or server that is running automations. Desktop agents leverage user sessions to carry out automations by connecting with and invoking the actions on the components (Microsoft Outlook, Microsoft Excel, the web browser, and so on) involved in the automation scenario. The desktop agent connects with Cloud Factory using a WebSocket connection (persistent and bidirectional) and runs both attended and unattended automations.

Desktop Studio

Desktop Studio is a software component installed on a developer's workstation and is the **Integrated Development Environment** (**IDE**) for developing all aspects of process automation. Desktop Studio's various development perspectives provide tools for application capture, code editing, workflow design, and user interface design. Desktop Studio is associated with LC and PC modes of automation development.

The browser extension

The browser extension is the software module that gets installed along with other on-premises components and is responsible for the automation scenarios associated with a web browser.

Having learned about the different components that constitute SAP Intelligent RPA, we'll next learn about how they interact with each other.

The relationship between Intelligent RPA components

While all components of SAP Intelligent RPA are not equal and every member does not interact with every other component directly, there are numerous connections and interdependencies that drive the bot building and execution processes. Let's take each element one by one and discuss the following aspects:

- The primary users of the component
- Interaction with other components
- Maintenance of the component

The following diagram describes all these aspects visually, but we will elaborate on these aspects as we go along:

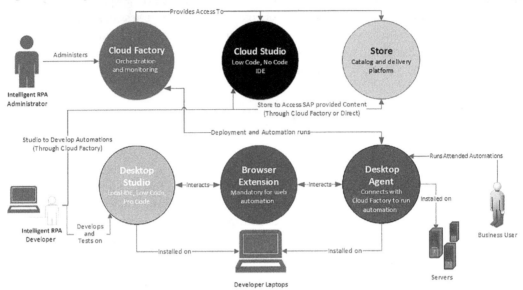

Figure 1.3 – A flowchart showing interactions between Intelligent RPA components

Let's see how this interaction works:

1. **Cloud Factory**: Administrators are Cloud Factory's primary users, but developers also utilize Cloud Factory as the landing page for accessing Cloud Studio and the Store. Business users usually never need to access Cloud Factory directly. Cloud Factory is the de facto control center of the Intelligent RPA platform and hence connects with many components. Cloud Studio can only be accessed through Cloud Factory, while a user needs to access the Store from Cloud Factory to use any pre-built content. Cloud Factory and desktop agents interact to make unattended packages available at scheduled times and run automations in attended mode. SAP maintains and keeps updating Cloud Factory frequently:

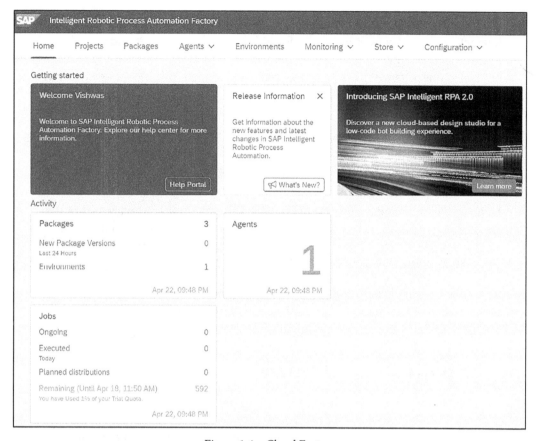

Figure 1.4 – Cloud Factory

2. **Cloud Studio**: Developers are the primary users of Cloud Studio. Administrators also have access to the studio, but they do not need it for their function. Cloud Studio connects with the factory to deploy generated projects, and a developer can access the local filesystem to upload any available files or desktop packages. The maintenance of Cloud Studio is owned by SAP.

3. **Store**: Business users and developers are the Store's primary consumers to find predefined content relevant for their intended automations. The Store is connected to Cloud Factory but can also be accessed directly with a public URL. The Store is maintained by SAP and keeps getting new content regularly.

4. **Desktop Studio**: Developers are the primary users of Desktop Studio. The studio interacts with the browser extension for web application capture, and with the operating system and various applications on its host system to build automations, but it also interacts with the Desktop Agent for debugging. While newer versions of the studio are provided by SAP, it is a developer's or IT team's responsibility to keep the studio current.

5. **Browser extension**: Post-installation, no user needs to interact with the browser extension, except for maintenance directly. However, the browser extension interacts with Desktop Studio and the Desktop Agent for application capture and execution.

6. **Desktop Agent**: Besides business users, Cloud Factory is the primary user of the Desktop Agent. While business users use the Desktop Agent to run automations in attended mode, Cloud Factory interacts with the Desktop Agent to run unattended automations as per the schedule.

Now that we have learned about the various components of SAP Intelligent RPA and how they interact to create automations, let's understand why it is important to consider using SAP Intelligent RPA as your primary automation platform.

Why SAP Intelligent RPA?

With over 400,000 customers worldwide and 77% of the world's transaction revenue going through an SAP system (see `https://www.sap.com/about/company.html` for more details), SAP is the undisputed leader in the **Enterprise Resource Planning** (**ERP**) space. Hyperautomation – a synergistic combination of advanced technologies such as artificial intelligence and machine learning with RPA, workflow, and **Business Process Management** (**BPM**) solutions – has featured in Gartner's *Top 10 Strategic Technology Trends* for 2020 and 2021.

SAP Intelligent RPA appeals to this large SAP customer base due to the native integrations, continuous product improvements, and SAP's plan to provide embedded automation inside SAP S/4HANA and other cloud **Line of Business** (**LoB**) products, which started in 2021 (see `https://roadmaps.sap.com/board?PRODUCT=73 554900100800002142&range=CURRENT-LAST#Q2%202021` for more details). Moreover, SAP Intelligent RPA delivers the benefits of hyperautomation by its unique placement alongside the complementing services of AI, ML, workflow, and BPM within SAP Business Technology Platform (previously known as SAP Cloud Platform), where SAP Intelligent RPA also resides.

This unique combination makes SAP Intelligent RPA the desired automation platform. It ensures that developers learning this platform will benefit from the vast customer base and continuous product improvements.

Where to find help when needed

SAP Intelligent RPA is a vast topic and is growing at a rapid pace. While we will bring you the core knowledge to begin your journey as a successful Intelligent RPA developer, we highly recommend supplementing your reading at the following places:

- SAP Blogs (`https://blogs.sap.com/tags/73554900100800002142/`) is a great place to learn all things about SAP Intelligent RPA. Use the **CATEGORIES** selection (technical articles, product information, and so on) to limit the blog posts to your area of interest.

- The SAP Intelligent RPA community (`https://answers.sap.com/tags/73554900100800002142`) is the place to ask questions and learn from the questions that others have asked.

- The SAP Intelligent RPA Store (`https://store.irpa.cfapps.eu10.hana.ondemand.com/#/explore/order=last-updated%2Cdesc`) is the place to see all the bots that are available to you as a developer. There are also many packages labeled as learning that you should use in your learning journey.

- The SAP Intelligent RPA website (`https://help.sap.com/viewer/product/IRPA/Cloud/en-US`) is an excellent place to begin if you have any questions.

- The SAP Intelligent RPA YouTube channel (`https://www.youtube.com/channel/UCkJEtt4vQqJ_HJ7DxiR19qw`) is a good source for overview videos, tutorials, demos, and webinars. While this channel is now renamed to SAP Process Automation, you can still find several videos related to SAP Intelligent RPA.

- You can access various SAP Intelligent RPA-relevant courses on the openSAP website (`https://open.sap.com/courses?q=RPA`).

Summary

In this chapter, we learned about the brief history of SAP Intelligent RPA, the core components of SAP Intelligent RPA, and how these components interact with each other. We also discussed why learning SAP Intelligent RPA is beneficial for developers like you. You now have a basic understanding of SAP Intelligent RPA. We will learn about arguably the most important component of SAP Intelligent RPA – Cloud Factory – in the next chapter.

Questions

Here are some questions for you to test your knowledge. The answers to these questions can be found at the back of the book in the section named *Assessments*:

1. Which SAP Intelligent RPA component is the main constituent of SAP Intelligent RPA 2.0?

2. What options do you find under the **Configuration** tab of Cloud Factory?

3. Which SAP Intelligent RPA IDE offers the NC mode of development?

2

An Overview of SAP Intelligent RPA Cloud Factory

This chapter introduces SAP Cloud Factory, a cloud-based application to centrally manage all common resources related to SAP Intelligent RPA. We will discuss the terminology associated with Cloud Factory and briefly discuss monitoring options and the alert framework. As we go along, we will create an environment, add an agent, import a package from the Store, and schedule its execution.

When you access SAP Intelligent RPA Cloud Factory, you will see a page similar to the following. We will discuss the tabs marked **1** to **6** in the following screenshot in this chapter:

Figure 2.1 – Cloud Factory landing page

In this chapter, we will cover the following topics:

- Environments
- Agents and agent groups
- Projects and packages
- Triggers
- Monitoring
- Configuration

By the end of this chapter, you will understand the functionalities in Cloud Factory and how to use them effectively.

Let's begin with the first topic: environments.

Technical requirements

- An internet connection
- Access to the SAP Business Technology Platform trial system (https://www.sap.com/cmp/td/sap-cloud-platform-trial.html)
- A subscription to the SAP Intelligent RPA trial version (https://help.sap.com/viewer/82d5a2499d8449dda691bb4d5b3d7949/Cloud/en-US)
- An agent installed on your workstation and registered with your Intelligent RPA tenant (feel free to skip to *Chapter 6, An Overview of Desktop Agent*, for installation instructions before coming back)

Environments

Organizations running SAP tend to have a three-system landscape. These systems are usually called development, test, and production (there can also be two-, four-, or five-system landscapes, but an SAP landscape with three systems is most common). A transport mechanism exists to move the code and related artifacts (dependencies) only in one direction (development → test → production). An environment serves a similar purpose in SAP Intelligent RPA. While SAP servers are usually physical, the Intelligent RPA environment is a logical entity and serves as an encompassing unit for all the project's runtime resources.

Here is how we can create a **Dev** environment named `irpa_book`:

1. First, click on the **+ New Environment** button, as shown:

Figure 2.2 – Creating an environment – 1

2. In the next option box, enter the details as shown in the following screenshot. It is recommended to assign the same names to your landscape environments with various types. So, `irpa_book` of type **Dev**, `irpa_book` of type **Test**, and `irpa_book` of type **Prod** should form the Intelligent RPA landscape for your client project. For our use case, only one environment of type **Dev** would work just fine.

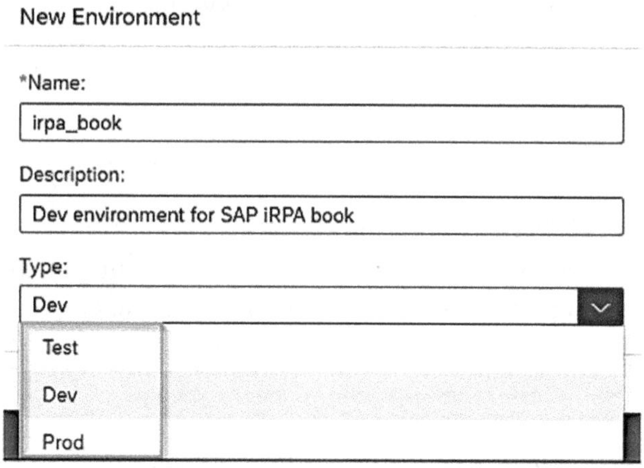

New Environment

*Name:

irpa_book

Description:

Dev environment for SAP iRPA book

Type:

Dev

Test

Dev

Prod

Figure 2.3 – Creating an environment – 2

3. Click on **Create**, and you'll have your environment ready.

Once created, you can share this environment with eligible users, edit it, or delete it. You can share the environment with a user, group, or anyone and assign them one of the following privileges:

- **Manage**: Can modify and share the environment
- **Edit**: Can modify the environment's content but cannot share
- **Read**: Can read the environment's content
- **View job data**: Can only view jobs' data

As shown in the following screenshot, you can also add packages, triggers, agents, variables (small data elements that store values of the text type and credentials locally), API keys, and alert handlers to your newly created environment or act on existing ones.

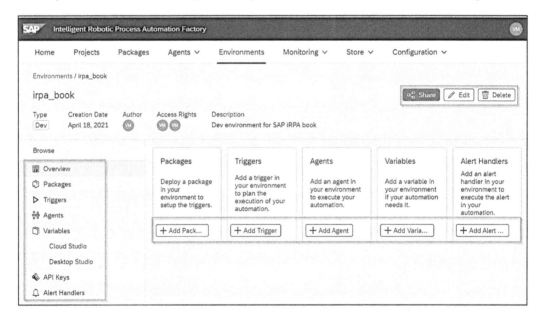

Figure 2.4 – Available actions for an environment

At the bottom of the **Environments** tab, you will find an environment console that displays any errors, warnings, or informational messages for that environment.

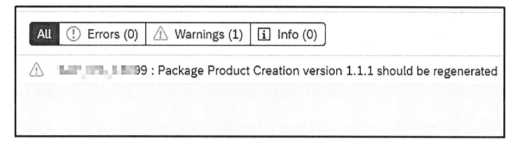

Figure 2.5 – Environment console

When working on a development project, this console is the place to look for any errors, warnings, or information.

Agents and agent groups

An agent (Desktop Agent) is a mandatory software component installed on computers designated to run automations. It uses the context of a user session to execute automation scenarios. For unattended scenarios – with no user interaction – Cloud Factory initiates the automations. A user usually starts the attended scenarios through an agent.

Once you add the name and domain of your tenant from Desktop Agent, the agent shows up under the **Agents** tab. From here, you can add this agent to the environment using the **+ Add Agent** button, as shown here:

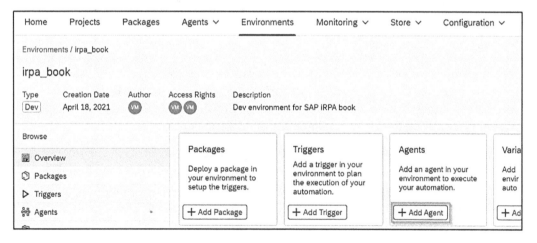

Figure 2.6 – Adding an agent to an environment

Once added, just like an environment, you can share, edit, or delete the agent.

Under the **Agents** tab, you can see all the agents available in Cloud Factory, their status, their mode (attended or unattended), the product version, and other relevant information.

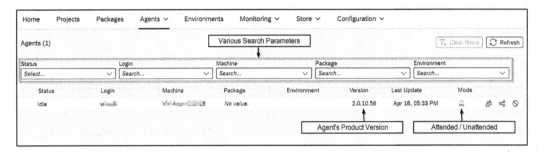

Figure 2.7 – Agents tab

An agent can be in one of these statuses:

- **Disconnected**
- **Preparing** (in the process of connecting)
- **Idle** (connected, no project)
- **Starting** (project loading)
- **Ready** (connected and project loaded)
- **Paused**
- **Running**
- **Busy** (maintenance state)

An **agent group** is a collection of agents that you can manage collectively. For example, suppose you need to run an automation scenario simultaneously on tens or hundreds of computers. In that case, an agent group will come in handy to deploy automation scenarios, control the executions, and monitor them for the outcomes.

An agent group can be of the **Machine** or **Login** type. **Machine** refers to the **device name** of the computer that will act as an execution system for automations (you can find it at **Windows Settings | System | About | Device Specifications | Device Name**). In contrast, **Login** refers to your login name on that computer. To create an agent group quickly, you can create a CSV file with information about all the agents and import this file to make the group.

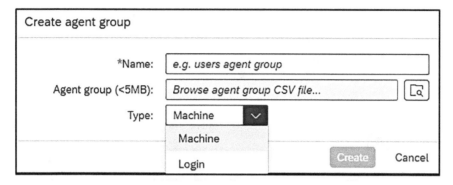

Figure 2.8 – Creating an agent group

The CSV file format and the steps to create an agent group are not discussed here but can be found at `https://help.sap.com/viewer/c836fab4182e45548b6c6c6d0 d0a9146/Cloud/en-US/94e58952326c4cb48215a25096f7b892.html`.

The **Agents** tab also contains **Alerts** and **Registrations**. **Alerts** refers to the email messages you can configure in certain events, such as agent deletion, a lost connection to an agent, a connection closed by an agent, or no eligible agent available for distribution of the automation. **Alerts** requires the configuration of a mail server.

Registrations refers to the generation of a registration token for mass registration of agents. This token can be downloaded on the workstations designated to run automations, and registrations of agents can be sped up using the command line or registry editor. Both **Alerts** and **Registrations** are beyond the scope of this book.

Let's move on to projects and packages.

Projects and packages

A project is a design-time object, while a package is an immutable, deployable entity created from a project. While you can *create a new project from scratch*, there is no way to create a new package. A new package can be generated from a project.

Figure 2.9 – Creating a new project

Also, a previously exported package can be imported or a pre-built package can be acquired from the Store.

Figure 2.10 – Importing a package

A project can have various constituents, such as captured applications, automations involving the applications, processes made of various automations, imported files, data types, and alerts.

A package can have various life cycle states, such as preview (default, first state for a package), released (only released packages can be added to a production environment), deprecated (state before package deletion), and decommissioned (set for automatic deletion). Packages follow semantic versioning (more information at https://semver.org/), and versions take the form of Major.Minor.Patch (for example, 2.1.1). The major version constitutes breaking changes. The minor version refers to additive, backward-compatible changes, while the patch comprises backward-compatible bug fixes. As a package is immutable, you need to save it as a project to make any changes.

Let's import a package from the Store. To do so, perform the following steps:

1. Go to the **Store** tab and search for the Hello World package.

2. Select the one for Cloud Studio and click on **Get** on the next screen.

    After a few seconds, the package's status on the **Acquisitions** tab will change to **Success**, and at this time, you can see the Hello World package under the **Packages** tab. However, you will notice that two other Core SDK and Excel SDK packages have also shown up as these were listed as dependencies for Hello World.

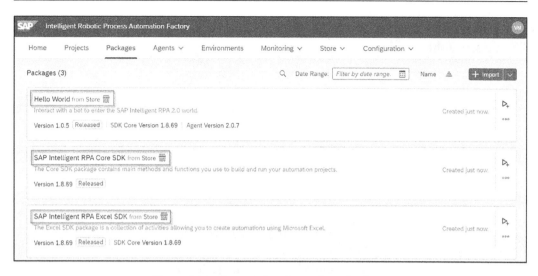

Figure 2.11 – Imported packages from the Store

Open these packages and see all the actions that you can take. We will add a trigger to this package in the next section, but try to take other actions and see whether there are any surprises, especially in the decommission step.

Triggers

A trigger makes a package in an environment available to run in response to a specific event. You can add a trigger from inside an environment or from a package. In both cases, you'll arrive at the same window. Within an environment, use the + **Add Trigger** button to create a new trigger.

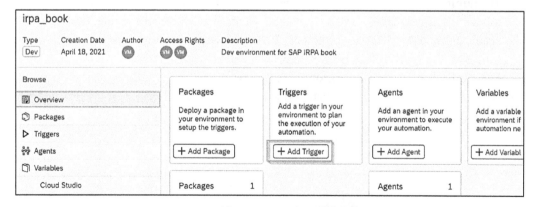

Figure 2.12 – Adding a trigger from an environment

You can also initiate the addition of a trigger from a package, as highlighted in the following screenshot:

Figure 2.13 – Adding a trigger from a package

There are three types of triggers:

- **Attended**: An attended trigger makes the package available to assigned agents during the specified period. A user can run the job manually during that time window. While creating an attended trigger, you need to provide the following information:

1. A name
2. An optional description
3. Desktop package to be deployed
4. Date range (when the package will be available)
5. Time zone
6. Time
7. Window (days of the week and time)

   The numbers in the preceding list correspond to the following screenshot. The following trigger makes the NewLaunch1 package available to assigned desktop agents on April 18, 2021, and April 25, 2021. This package is available for running from Monday to Thursday from 8:00 A.M. to 5:00 P.M. and from 8:00 A.M. to 12:00 P.M. on Friday. For an automation project created in Cloud Studio, a project pane artifact is necessary to create an attended trigger.

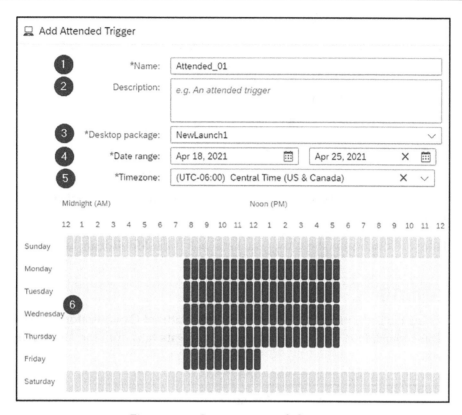

Figure 2.14 – Creating an attended trigger

- **Scheduled**: A scheduled trigger makes the package available during the given time window, but the agent runs the automation as per the schedule defined. To ensure that the bot runs as scheduled, Desktop Agent must be connected with Cloud Factory. Should you face any problems when the bot runs in scheduled mode, check the SAP troubleshooting documentation at `https://help.sap.com/doc/0ff61ed2d1334ed7804f77cd38cb708e/Cloud/en-US/a0b24deefff14ba9b7cb32b38b9793d5.pdf`. Besides the field we saw for an attended trigger, the following additional fields are needed for a scheduled trigger:

  - **Recurrence**: How often the trigger is activated. Specify in minutes, hours, days, weeks, or months.

  - **Jobs expire after**: A job that is not distributed before or is not responding after the defined time window expires would be canceled.

  - **New job**: If deactivated, a new job will not be added until the previous one on the same trigger has finished execution.

Refer to the following screenshot for these:

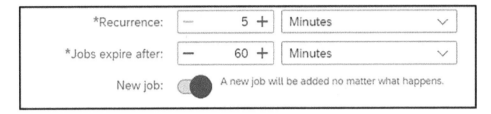

Figure 2.15 – Additional fields for a scheduled trigger

- **API**: An API trigger makes your automation available to external applications for execution.

This concludes our discussion about triggers. Let's look at the **Monitoring** tab next.

Monitoring

The **Monitoring** tab is the place to look for the overall status of Cloud Factory. You can access the **Dashboard**, **Jobs**, **Logs**, **Consumption**, and **Data** tabs from the **Monitoring** tab, as shown:

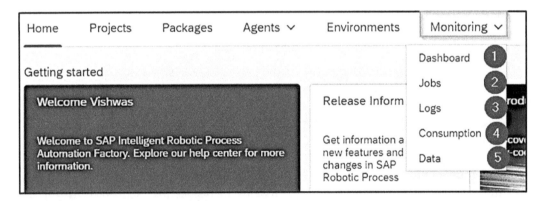

Figure 2.16 – Monitoring tab

Here are the details of each tab:

- **Dashboard**: This tab shows environments with distributions (planned distributions signify the unattended tasks ready to be executed), ongoing jobs (the number of ongoing jobs), agents (the number of agents and their status), history (job history), and jobs executed **Today** (the number of jobs completed on that particular current day) in **Last 7 days**, or **Last 30 days**).

- **Jobs**: Here, you can see the information about individual jobs, their status, trigger, duration, and so on. Use the filter at the top to find the jobs during a date range, automation package, job status, and so on. **Flat mode** lists all the jobs even if they are children of another job.

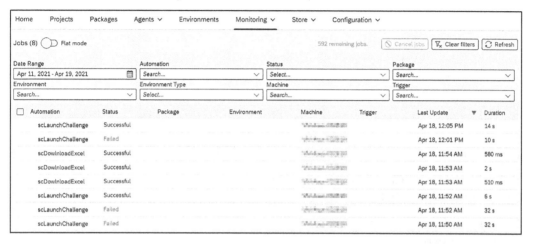

Figure 2.17 – List of jobs

- **Logs**: This tab gives you visibility of all event logs centrally. You can filter the logs using various available criteria.

- **Consumption**: This tab shows you the number of monthly job runs for the past 13 months graphically.

- **Data**: From this tab, you can download records of historical job data, alert logs, distribution, and business activity data in CSV format. Once downloaded, you can use this data to study any patterns.

With this, we conclude the discussion about the **Monitoring** tab. Let's discuss the **Configuration** tab next.

Configuration

If you plan to use alerts (not necessary now but recommended for client projects), you can configure an email server under the **Configuration** tab. See detailed steps in the blog at `https://blogs.sap.com/2020/11/04/how-to-configure-mail-server-in-sap-intelligent-robotic-process-automation-cloud-factory/`.

SAP Cloud **Application Lifecycle Management** (**ALM**) is a cloud counterpart of SAP Solution Manager. Both these solutions help with the application life cycle management of products. If your company subscribes to SAP Cloud ALM, you can integrate your Intelligent RPA instance from here.

Summary

In this chapter, we learned about SAP Intelligent RPA Cloud Factory, the central point of management for all common resources. We started our discussion with environments and the roles they play in SAP Intelligent RPA. We learned about the three types of environments and all the artifacts that they can contain. We moved on to discuss agents and agent groups, and then discovered that while agents are mandatory for the workstation executing our automation packages, agent groups give us a mechanism to manage many agents together.

We also talked about projects and packages and understood the relationship between the two. Triggers of various types were discussed next, and we learned about three kinds of triggers: attended, scheduled, and API. Under **Monitoring**, we discussed different options available to keep a watch on our Intelligent RPA Cloud Factory status.

Now it is your turn. Go and try out various options available under Cloud Factory. We will discuss Desktop Studio in the next chapter.

Questions

Here are some questions for you to test your knowledge. The answers to these questions can be found at the back of the book in the section named *Assessments*:

1. Can you explain the difference between a project and a package?
2. Which types of triggers are available under SAP Intelligent RPA?
3. You have installed an agent on your workstation, but it is not visible in Cloud Factory. What could be the reason?
4. Which types of variables can you add to an environment?
5. What does the consumption page show under the **Monitoring** tab?
6. What kinds of logs can you download from the logs page under the **Monitoring** tab?

3
Installing SAP Intelligent RPA On-Premise Components

In the previous chapters, we learned about the architecture and core components of SAP Intelligent RPA and understood the central role that the SAP Intelligent RPA cloud factory plays. It is now time to focus on the on-premise setup of the SAP Intelligent RPA components. You will recall that three pieces – Desktop Studio, Desktop Agent, and the browser extension – make up this setup.

In this and the following chapter, we will install all these components along with the essential support structure. Web browser configuration and Desktop Agent tenant registration will follow next before verifying the installation of all these components. Once you go through this installation process, you will have a powerful suite of tools at hand to start automating business processes.

We will discuss the following topics in the sections that follow:

- Supported operating systems

- Minimum system and network requirements

- Supported browsers

- Supported technologies for automation

- Installing SAP Intelligent RPA on-premise components

- Installing remote tools for Visual Studio

- Installing a source code comparison tool

- Supported languages

Let's begin with understanding the supported operating systems.

Technical requirements

- System administrator rights on your computer

- Microsoft Internet Explorer 11

- Microsoft .NET Framework 4.7.2, available here: `https://dotnet.microsoft.com/download/dotnet-framework/net472`

- Microsoft Visual C++ 2013 Redistributable Package x86, available here: `https://www.microsoft.com/en-us/download/details.aspx?id=40784`

- Remote Tools for Visual Studio 2019 – described later in this chapter

- Access to a trial account of SAP BTP – follow this guide to get one: `https://developers.sap.com/tutorials/hcp-create-trial-account.html`

- Access to a trial account of SAP Intelligent RPA – follow this guide to get one: `https://help.sap.com/viewer/82d5a2499d8449dda691bb4d5b3d7949/Cloud/en-US`

Supported operating systems

At the time of writing this chapter, only the **Windows operating system** supports the installation of SAP Intelligent RPA components. While you can install SAP Intelligent RPA components on a desktop running Windows 8.1 or Windows 10, Windows 10 (64-bit) is the recommended version. If you need to install SAP Intelligent RPA components on a server, Windows Server 2016 (64-bit) is the recommended version, but you can also use Windows Server 2012 R2 (64-bit).

If you cannot access a physical machine running the aforesaid operating systems or cannot get the administrator rights on your computer, consider using cloud-based virtual machines for your learning. For example, AWS, GCP, and Azure offer a free tier that you could use to begin your Intelligent RPA learning.

Now that we have established the necessity of a computer running the Windows operating system, let's discuss the minimum configuration for this computer to be used as a development system for SAP Intelligent RPA.

Minimum system and network requirements

We have clubbed the minimum requirements for using the Desktop Agent, Desktop Studio, Cloud Studio, and SAP Intelligent RPA factory under the following hardware and software categories. While installing all the listed software is mandatory for the proper functioning of installed Intelligent RPA components, you can rest assured that you won't need to worry about hardware compatibility as long as you have a relatively new—post-2012—desktop.

Desktop Agent		
Hardware		**Software**
Screen Resolution	1024*768	Microsoft .NET Framework 4.7
CPU	Single Core	Internet connection to SAP BTP
Memory	1 GB of free memory	Microsoft Internet Explorer 11
Disk Space	1 GB of free space	
Desktop Studio		
Hardware		**Software**
Screen Resolution	1920*1080	Microsoft .NET Framework 4.7
CPU	Dual Core	Internet connection to SAP BTP
Memory	2 GB of free memory	Supported browser (discussed further)
Disk Space	1 GB of free space	Microsoft Visual C++ 2013 Redistributable Package x86
		Remote Tools Visual Studio 2019 for remote debugging
		Java JRE 8 (included in the setup, no additional setup required)
		Node.js (included in the setup, no additional setup required)
		Three-way Diff Tool through command line
Cloud Studio		
Hardware		**Software**
Screen Resolution	1920*1080	Microsoft .NET Framework 4.7
CPU	Dual Core	Internet connection to SAP BTP
Memory	2 GB of free memory	Supported browser and browser extensions (discussed further)
Disk Space	1 GB of free space	Microsoft Visual C++ 2013 Redistributable Package x86
SAP iRPA Factory		
Hardware		**Software**
Screen Resolution	1024*768	Internet connection to SAP BTP
		Supported browser (discussed further)

Figure 3.1 – Minimum requirements

As this information changes periodically, please always check for the latest information at `https://help.sap.com/viewer/6b9c8e86a0be43539b670de962834562/Cloud/en-US/0061438816a34fa78b77c99852318c70.html`.

Next, let's take a look at the supported browsers.

Supported browsers

While the latest Google Chrome and Microsoft Edge browsers—V90 or greater—support most SAP Intelligent RPA components, as of the writing of this book, web view control of MS Internet Explorer 11 is required for the Desktop Agent. This requirement will soon become obsolete with the upcoming updates but till then, install both IE11 and either Google Chrome or Microsoft Edge.

Supported technologies for automation

A business process usually goes across various technology components such as web applications, MS Office, Windows-based applications, and so on. As expected, the automation project to automate that business process must interact with all these components.

SAP Intelligent RPA supports the following technologies for automation:

Desktop Agent and Desktop Studio		
Type of Software	**What is supported**	**Additional information**
Windows-based application	WIN driver	WinDriver gives full access to a Windows application. UIAutomation gives a significant subset but it is restricted to the user interface.
	UIAutomation	
Java-based application	Swing (JRE/JDK 8)	
SAP	SAP GUI for Windows 7.40 or greater	
	SAP S/4HANA on-premise edition 1809 or greater	
Web application	WebPage (HTML4/HTML5)	
	WebService (REST calls, SOAP calls)	
Terminal-based application (HLLAPI)	IBM Personal Communications 14.x (third-party software component)	Direct access to mainframe applications (3270, zOS...) is managed by HLLAPI channel through a third-party software component.
Surface Automation/OCR	Recommended if the application you want to automate can't be automated using any of the other technology connectors previously described	
Microsoft Office	Version 2013	Access to Microsoft Office (Excel, Word, Outlook) is available through the corresponding Activities in Desktop Studio.
	Version 2016	
Cloud Studio		
Type of Software	**What is supported**	**Additional information**
Windows-based application	UIAutomation	
SAP	SAP GUI for Windows 7.40 or greater	
	SAP S/4HANA on-premise edition 1809 or greater	
Web application	WebPage (HTML4/HTML5)	
	WebService (REST calls, SOAP calls)	
Microsoft Office	Version 2013	Access to Microsoft Office (Excel, Word, Outlook) is available through the corresponding Activities in Cloud Studio.
	Version 2016	
	Version 2019	

Figure 3.2 – Supported technologies

As this information changes frequently, please always check for the latest information at `https://help.sap.com/viewer/6b9c8e86a0be43539b670de962834562/Cloud/en-US/0061438816a34fa78b77c99852318c70.html`.

After establishing the requirements for SAP Intelligent RPA on-premise components, let's now begin the process of installation.

Installing SAP Intelligent RPA on-premise components

You can download the required setup files for SAP Intelligent RPA from the following two locations. Both options will lead you to download a standard Windows MSI installer. We used the SAP software downloads option:

- **SAP software downloads**: `http://help.sap.com/disclaimer?site=https://launchpad.support.sap.com/#/softwarecenter/template/products/_APP=00200682500000001943&_EVENT=DISPHIER&HEADER=Y&FUNCTIONBAR=N&EVENT=TREE&NE=NAVIGATE&ENR=73555000100200010391&V=MAINT`

    - Use this link if you have an SAP S-ID.

    - Choose the download link with the highest patch level:

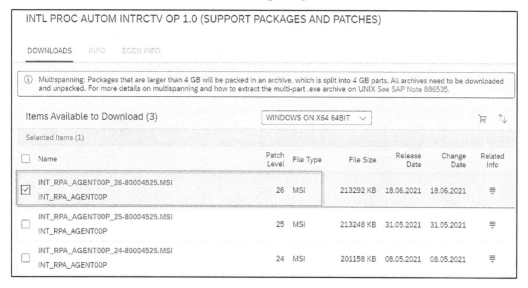

Figure 3.3 – Download SAP Intelligent RPA components

- **SAP development tools**: `https://tools.hana.ondemand.com/#cloud`

  - Use this link if you do not have an S-ID for SAP.

  - Go to the bottom of the page to find the download links. Choose the one with the highest version:

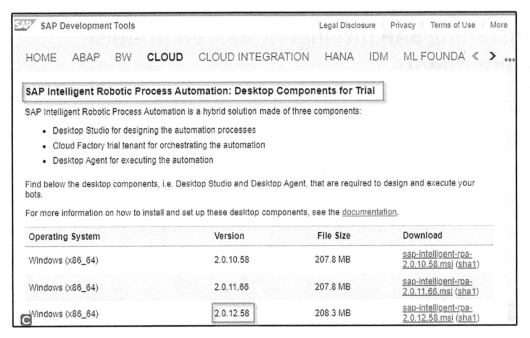

Figure 3.4 – Download SAP Intelligent RPA components

Note

As the SAP Intelligent RPA on-premise component installer automatically installs the web browser extension for Google Chrome, please close all the Chrome tabs before starting the installation process.

Installation procedure

Let's begin the installation process as follows:

1. Launch the MSI file to begin execution to display the following screen:

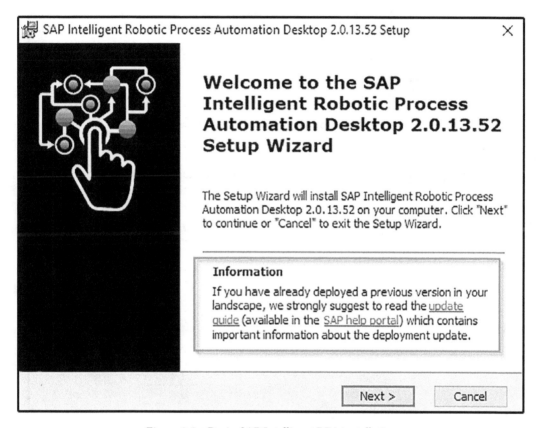

Figure 3.5 – Begin SAP Intelligent RPA installation

While we are installing version 2.0.13.52, the version and the deployment process may differ slightly depending upon your installation time. If you have already deployed a previous version of SAP Intelligent RPA on your computer, please ensure to read the **update guide** (See **Information** in the preceding screenshot).

2. Select **Next**, and choose the components to install. While the Desktop Agent
    installation is enabled by default, let's also select to install the Desktop Studio and
    SDK for learning purposes. Our selection will allow us to fully use SAP Intelligent
    RPA to develop, orchestrate, and execute automation projects.

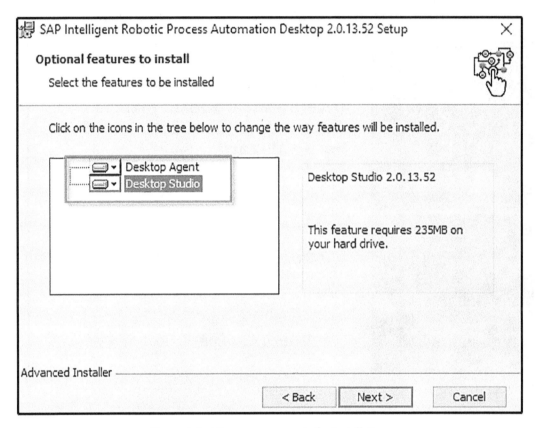

Figure 3.6 – Choose components for installation

3. Select **Next**. You can use the proposed installation folder or choose another location using the **Browse...** function. We will stay with the proposed location.

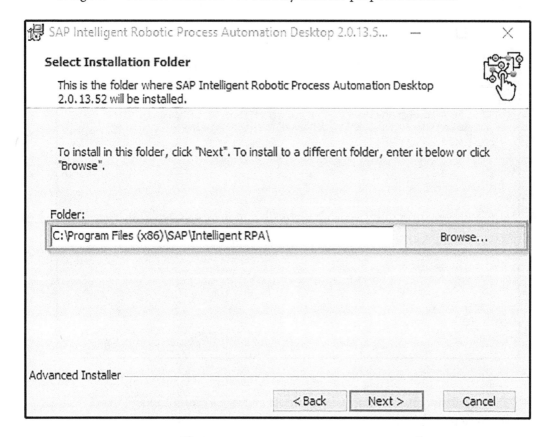

Figure 3.7 – Select installation folder

4.   Select **Next** and then **Install** to begin the installation process.

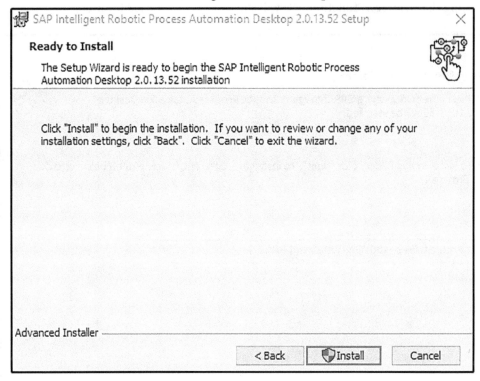

Figure 3.8 – Start installation

The installation process may take a minute or more to complete and may seek your approval to make changes to the computer.

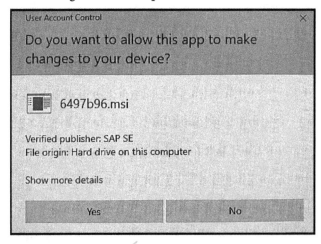

Figure 3.9 UAC approval

5. Select **Finish** to complete the installation process. We will carry on with the Desktop Agent tenant registration in the next chapter. For now, let's continue installing the required on-premise components for Desktop Studio.

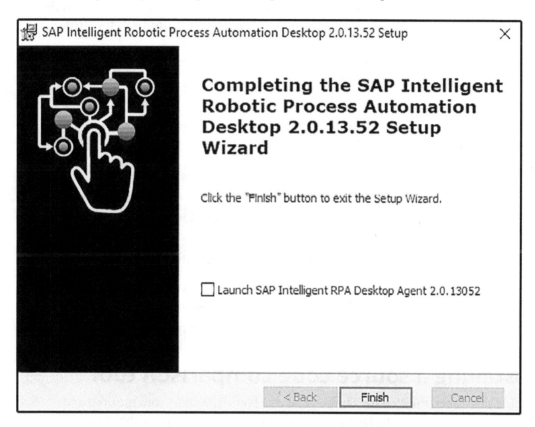

Figure 3.10 – Finish installation

Next, let's install the remote tools for Visual Studio, a prerequisite for completion of installation.

Installing Remote Tools for Visual Studio

Before we start installing the final components of SAP Intelligent RPA, please ensure that you meet all the technical requirements described at the beginning of this chapter.

Installation procedure

Here are the steps to install remote tools:

1. Go to `https://visualstudio.microsoft.com/downloads/`, open the **Tools for Visual Studio 2019** section, and download **Remote Tools for Visual Studio 2019**.

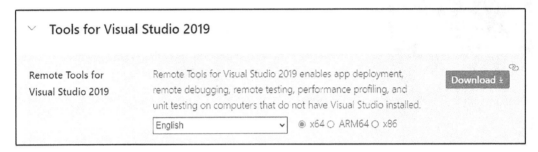

Figure 3.11 – Download Remote Tools for Visual Studio 2019

2. Double-click on the saved executable file to start the installation. Next, agree to the license terms and conditions and click **Install** to begin the installation.

    The installation process may take a minute or more to complete and may seek your approval to make changes to the computer. Click on **Close** to exit the setup wizard.

Let's continue the installation process with a source code comparison tool.

Installing a source code comparison tool

Behind the scenes, the Desktop Studio generates JavaScript code from the drag-and-drop workflow components. However, as a developer, you can replace the generated scripts or add custom code manually. These manual activities require code comparison and merging. While it is possible to do a manual comparison, source code comparison tools can do the same comparison swiftly and without the usual errors associated with monotonous human activities. For this reason, we recommend you install either KDiff3 or the Beyond Compare tool. Either one of these tools is sufficient, but as SAP uses KDiff3 in all examples and tutorials, we will show how to install this tool. If you'd prefer Beyond Compare, please follow a similar process.

The procedure to install the KDiff3 tool is as follows.

Installation procedure

Perform the following steps for the installation:

1. Go to `https://download.kde.org/stable/kdiff3/?C=M;O=D` and download the latest executable file:

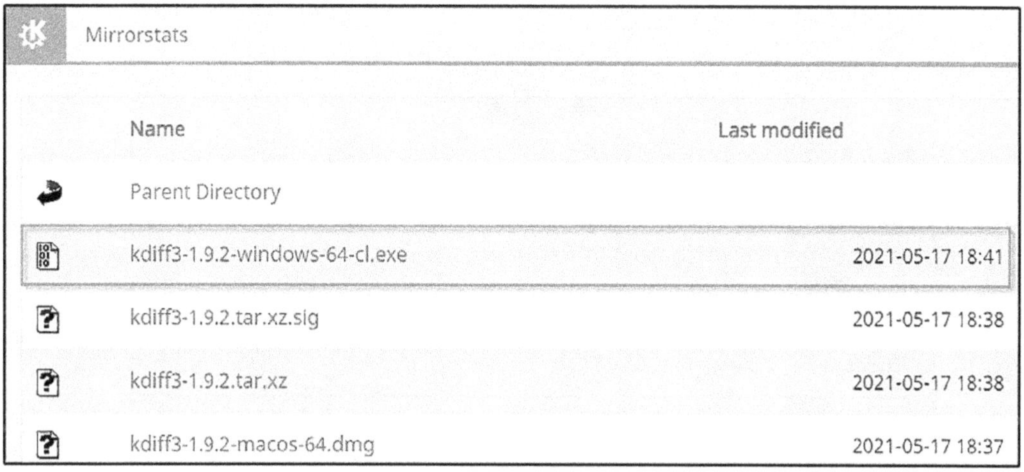

	Name	Last modified
	Mirrorstats	
	Parent Directory	
	kdiff3-1.9.2-windows-64-cl.exe	2021-05-17 18:41
	kdiff3-1.9.2.tar.xz.sig	2021-05-17 18:38
	kdiff3-1.9.2.tar.xz	2021-05-17 18:38
	kdiff3-1.9.2-macos-64.dmg	2021-05-17 18:37

Figure 3.12 – Download KDiff3

2. Double-click on the saved executable file to start the installation. Next, provide your approval to make changes to the computer and click **Next**.

3. Choose **Install for anyone using this computer** or **Install just for me**. We chose the first option. Click **Next**.

4. Choose the install location for KDiff3 and click **Next**. We went with the default location.

5. Choose the start menu folder and click **Install**. Click **Finish** to complete setup.

6. Open the Desktop Studio, navigate to **File** and click **Settings**.

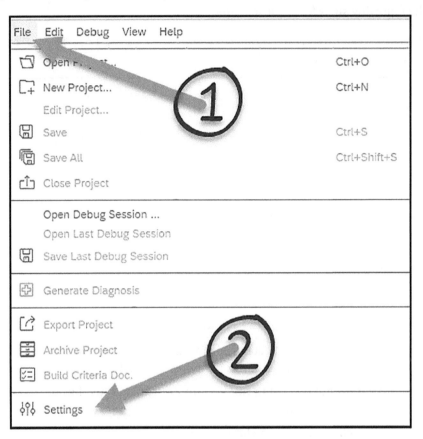

Figure 3.13 – Open Settings

7. On the **Settings** screen, select the **Workflow** tab and scroll down to the bottom.

8. Then, under the section **Merge | Merge tool**, navigate to the installation path for KDiff3, `C:\Program Files\KDiff3\bin\kdiff3.exe` in our case.

9. Then, under the section **Merge | Merge Command Line**, select **kdiff3**. Finally, click **Save** as shown in the following screenshot and restart Desktop Studio:

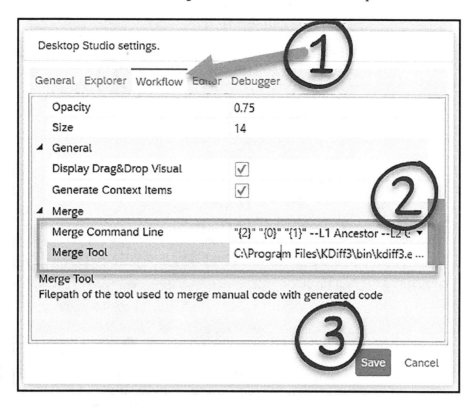

Figure 3.14 – Set KDiff3 as a merge tool

Now that we have completed the installation process, let's see which languages are supported by SAP Intelligent RPA Desktop Studio.

Supported languages

The Desktop Studio supports several languages and you can choose any of these as the user-interface language for the Studio.

To choose your preferred language, navigate to **File** and click **Settings**. Next, select **General** and navigate to the section **Misc**. Here you can select the language of your choice. You will need to restart the Desktop Studio for the language to take effect.

This is shown in the following screenshot:

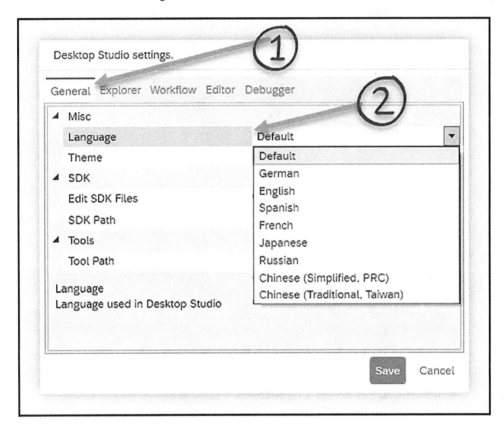

Figure 3.15 – Misc settings window

This concludes our discussion about the supported languages.

Summary

Desktop Studio, Desktop Agent, and the browser extension are the three core components of SAP Intelligent RPA's on-premise setup. In this chapter, we began the installation process and reached nearly midway. We will conclude and verify the installation process in the following chapter. After that, you will have access to a complete SAP Intelligent RPA setup to start creating automations on-premise or in the cloud.

We touched upon nearly all the pieces of the SAP Intelligent RPA on-premise setup and have gained a deeper understanding of the components, such as Remote Tools for Visual Studio and the source code comparison tool KDiff3. While we have completed the initial installation, we will complete the process in the next chapter by registering the Desktop Agent with a tenant, configuring web browsers, and finally, verifying that the installation is complete. Before we conclude this chapter, let's see how well you understand the SAP Intelligent RPA installation requirements.

Questions

Here are some questions for you to test your knowledge. The answers to these questions can be found at the back of the book in the section named *Assessments*:

1. Which of the following operating systems support the installation of SAP Intelligent RPA?

    1. Microsoft Windows

    2. Linux

    3. macOS

    4. Ubuntu

2. If you have Google Chrome or the Microsoft Edge browser installed, why do you still need IE11?

3. While language selection for the Desktop Studio is helpful, is it possible to interact with websites and applications running languages apart from English?

4
Setting Up SAP Intelligent RPA On-Premise Components

While we started installing SAP Intelligent RPA components in the previous chapter, the finalization and verification of this setup is the goal of the current chapter. Desktop Studio and Agent are now installed, but we must register Desktop Agent with our Intelligent RPA tenant to use this setup productively. To use the browser extension effectively, we need to configure the web browsers. Finally, a confirmation that everything works as expected will round off this chapter and give us a functional SAP Intelligent RPA setup.

To understand how this works, we will examine the following topics in this chapter:

- Registering the Desktop Agent tenant
- Configuring web browsers
- Verifying the installation of on-premise components

By the time you finish this chapter, you will have all the necessary tools, both on-premise and cloud-based, to start creating the brilliant automations you have been dreaming about.

Let's start with Desktop Agent tenant registration first.

Technical requirements

- System administrator rights on your computer

- Microsoft Internet Explorer 11 or the latest version of Chrome

- The completed installation of SAP Intelligent RPA on-premise components from the previous chapter

- Access to a trial account for SAP BTP – follow this guide to set this up: `https://developers.sap.com/tutorials/hcp-create-trial-account.html`

- Access to a trial account for SAP Intelligent RPA – follow this guide to get access: `https://help.sap.com/viewer/82d5a2499d8449dda691bb4d5b3d7949/Cloud/en-US`

Registering the Desktop Agent tenant

As discussed in earlier chapters, business users and the Cloud Factory both use Desktop Agent to run automations. While registering Desktop Agent with an Intelligent RPA tenant is mandatory for automation executions, it is a straightforward one-time process for each tenant.

Procedure for registering

Perform the following steps to register Desktop Agent with the Intelligent RPA tenant:

1. Locate the SAP Intelligent RPA Factory tenant URL from your BTP trial account. To do so, log in to your BTP trial account, navigate to the subaccount with the SAP Intelligent RPA subscription (**1**), click on **Instances and Subscriptions** (**2**), and then click on the **SAP Intelligent Robotic Process Automation Trial** link (**3**). Refer to the following screenshot for help:

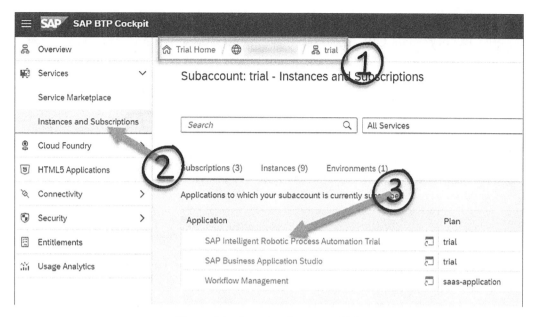

Figure 4.1 – Locating the tenant URL

SAP Intelligent RPA Factory will open up in a new tab. Copy the URL up to and including `hana.ondemand.com/`. We will use this URL in the steps ahead.

2. If not already running, start Desktop Agent from either the **Start** menu or by navigating to your installation folder.

3. Click on the ellipses (**1**) and then on **Tenants** (**2**), as shown in the following screenshot:

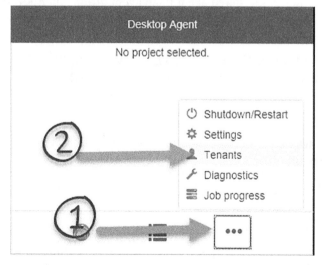

Figure 4.2 – Start of tenant registration

4. Next, enter a name of your choice in the **Name** field, and insert your SAP Intelligent RPA Factory tenant URL (up to and including hana.ondemand.com/) from *step 1* under **Domain**. Then, click **Save** to finish the tenant registration process:

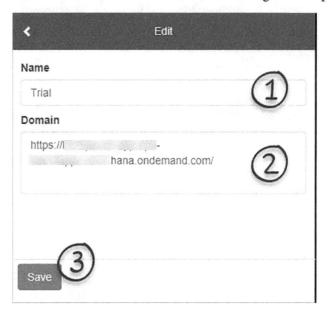

Figure 4.3 – Finishing the tenant registration

5. A login window will open. Log in to your SAP Intelligent RPA Factory tenant with your username or email and password.

6. To declare your newly registered agent in an agent group, open SAP Intelligent RPA Factory, go to the **Agents** tab and click **Agent Groups**. If an agent group does not exist, create a new one.

7. Select the desired **Agent Group**, create a new node by clicking **+** (**Add node**), and enter a name and label for the node. Depending on whether the agent group is of type **Machine** or **Login**, the name should be the same as your **Machine ID** or the **Login ID** that you plan to use:

   - To get the machine ID, execute the hostname command in Command Prompt and use the output.

   - For your login ID, use the login ID that you plan to use to log in to the machine running Desktop Agent.

   With this step, we complete the tenant registration.

Let's continue the process of setting up SAP Intelligent RPA on-premise components with the configuration of our web browsers in the next section.

Configuring the web browser extension

While the Desktop Studio installation process *installs* the web browser extension for Google Chrome, Internet Explorer, and Microsoft Edge, you are still required to *enable* that extension for your browser.

First, let's see the process for all three browsers listed here. Follow the appropriate procedure for the browser that you plan to use.

Google Chrome

Here is how we configure the extension for Chrome:

1. Open Google Chrome and type `chrome://extensions/` in the address bar to go to **Extensions**, then find **SAP Intelligent RPA Extension**.

2. Click the toggle button to activate the extension as shown in the following screenshot:

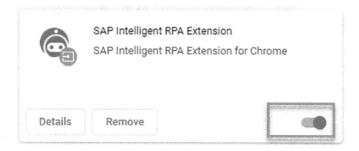

Figure 4.4 – Activating the extension in Google Chrome

> **Note**
>
> Optional: if you need to access HTML files locally, click **Details** on the **SAP Intelligent RPA** tile. Then enable the **Allow access to file URLs** option.

Microsoft Internet Explorer

We configure the extension in Internet Explorer as follows:

1. Open Internet Explorer and go to **Tools |Manage Add-ons**, select the **CxWebBho3 Class** add-on, and click **Enable**, as follows:

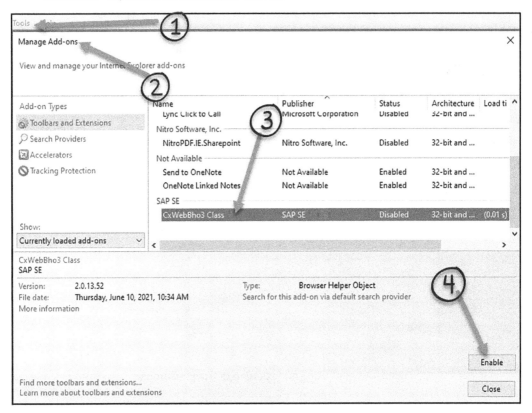

Figure 4.5 – Activating the extension in Internet Explorer

2. Next, select **Tools | Internet Options | Advanced**. Here we have two sections with the following options:

    ▪   In the **Browsing** section, ensure that the **Enable third-party browser extensions*** setting option is enabled.

    ▪   In the **Security** section, ensure that the following options are enabled:

        ◆   **Allow active content from CDs to run on My Computer***

        ◆   **Allow active content to run in files on My Computers***

        ◆   **Use TLS 1.2**

Then click on **Apply**.

3. After this, select **Tools | Internet Options | Security**:

    -   Click **Internet | Custom level**.

    -   Ensure that the **Active Scripting** option under **Settings | Scripting** is enabled.

    Click **OK** to apply these changes.

4. Click **Apply** and **OK** to exit **Internet Options** and close **Internet Explorer**.

Microsoft Edge

Configure the extension in Microsoft Edge as follows:

1. To ensure that you have the Chromium-based version of Microsoft Edge, type `edge://settings/help` in the address bar and ensure that you have version 86 or above. This is how you can check it:

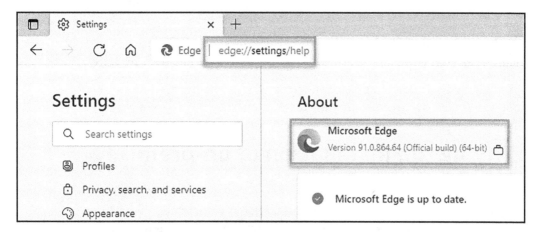

Figure 4.6 – Checking the Microsoft Edge version

Opening this link will automatically check for updates. If the version is up to date, you will see **Microsoft Edge is up to date**. If an update is available, it will start downloading automatically. Restart the browser once updated.

2. Type edge://extensions/ to go to the list of installed extensions and click the toggle on for **SAP Intelligent RPA Extension**:

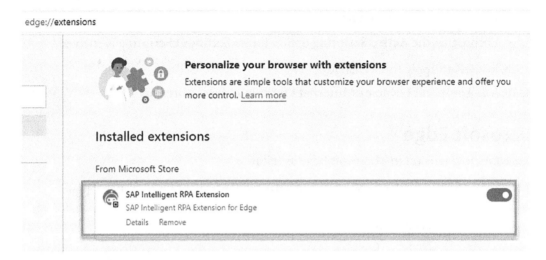

Figure 4.7 – Enable the SAP Intelligent RPA extension

You have now configured the SAP Intelligent RPA extension in Microsoft Edge.

With this activity, we have completed the setup of SAP Intelligent RPA on-premise components. Now it is time to verify the installation.

Verifying the installation of on-premise components

Finally, now is the time to verify that our installation is complete and everything is working as it should. To check this, we will perform the following few steps:

1. Start Desktop Studio and create a new project using the **File | New Project** menu. Create the project as shown:

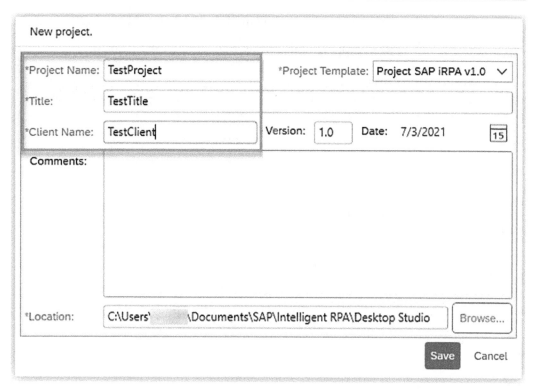

Figure 4.8 – Create a new project for setup verification

2. Click **Save**. Build the project using **Debug | Build**.

3. Check the output panel. An output of **Build done : 0 error(s), 0 warning(s)** verifies a successful setup, as shown here:

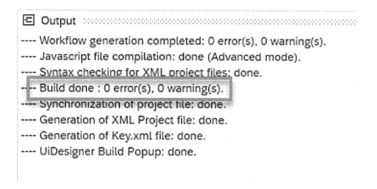

Figure 4.9 – A successful build to verify the setup

4. Press *F5* to launch Desktop Agent in debug mode or via **Debug | Debug (F5)**.

    If **Desktop Debugger** opens, then this verifies a successful installation of Desktop Agent:

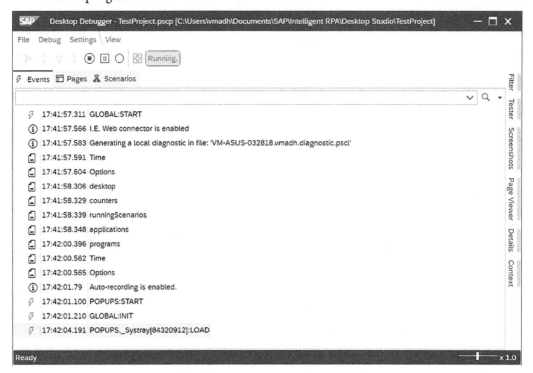

Figure 4.10 – Desktop Debugger verifies the Desktop Agent setup

We have now confirmed the successful installation of our on-premise setup for SAP Intelligent RPA and are all set to explore the individual components in the following chapters.

Summary

You have now registered Desktop Agent with your SAP Intelligent RPA tenant, configured the web browser extension, and verified the successful installation of all on-premise components for SAP Intelligent RPA. These steps conclude our setup process, and you now have access to a complete SAP Intelligent RPA setup. The following few chapters will familiarize you with the functionality of both Desktop Studio and Cloud Studio, along with Desktop Agent. With this knowledge, you are ready to create your automations on-premise or in the cloud.

As technology tends to change swiftly, the instructions in this chapter may not match your onscreen components. If so, search for the latest version of the **SAP Intelligent RPA Installation Guide** to find what may have changed in recent versions of SAP Intelligent RPA.

With the installation completed, we are now ready to learn about Desktop Studio and all the possibilities it brings in the next chapter.

Questions

Here are some questions for you to test your knowledge. The answers to these questions can be found at the back of the book in the section named *Assessments*:

1. To register Desktop Agent with your Intelligent RPA tenant, you copied the SAP Intelligent RPA Factory URL in the following format and used it in the **Domain** field, but the registration did not go through. What could the reason be?

   ```
   https://XXXtrial.app.irpatrial.cfapps.XX10.hana.ondemand.
     com/#/home
   ```

2. Besides developing RPA applications, you also build websites and have some local copies of your sites on your laptop. Even though your SAP Intelligent RPA installation was successful, you cannot access your local URLs. What could the reason be?

3. While creating a new project as part of the *Verifying the installation of on-premise components* section, the default selection for the project template was **project SAP Intelligent RPA version 1.0**. What are the other options, and when should you use them?

5
An Overview of Desktop Studio

Developing automation is like building Lego® structures. You envision a design, identify and gather the necessary pieces, join them together, check whether the result matches your vision, make minor adjustments if required, and the structure is ready.

To develop automation, we go through similar steps. Envision an automated business process, identify the applications and capture them, connect those applications and develop them further, test the result and make minor tweaks, and the automation is ready.

This chapter will discuss Desktop Studio, the on-premises **Integrated Development Environment (IDE)** that you can use to create all aspects of process automation. This chapter will help you understand the various building blocks of desktop studio and their roles in the automation creation cycle.

In this chapter, we will cover the following topics:

- Introduction to perspectives in Desktop Studio
- Introduction to the Explorer perspective – capturing applications
- Introduction to the Workflow perspective – connecting applications to create automation
- Introduction to the Editor perspective – developing automation further

- Introduction to the Debug perspective – testing automation and making tweaks

- Introduction to the UI Designer perspective – developing visual add-ons (optional)

By the end of this chapter, you will have an understanding of the automation creation process and the Desktop Studio perspectives to help you achieve the steps of the process.

Let us begin with getting introduced to some perspectives in Desktop Studio

Technical requirements

- An internet connection

- Access to the SAP Business Technology Platform trial system (`https://www.sap.com/cmp/td/sap-cloud-platform-trial.html`)

- A subscription to the SAP Intelligent RPA trial version (`https://help.sap.com/viewer/82d5a2499d8449dda691bb4d5b3d7949/Cloud/en-US`)

- Desktop Studio installed on your workstation

- Recommended: I'm using the **Automatic Creation of Sales Order Requests from Unstructured Data (5LT)** package from the Intelligent RPA store to show various perspectives in this chapter. If possible, download this package from the store and open it in your Desktop Studio to follow along.

Introduction to perspectives in Desktop Studio

Desktop Studio provides perspectives to carry out various development tasks associated with creating automations. A perspective essentially is a collection of tools and windows dedicated to carrying out a development task. The left-hand side of the following screenshot shows the five perspectives available to a developer:

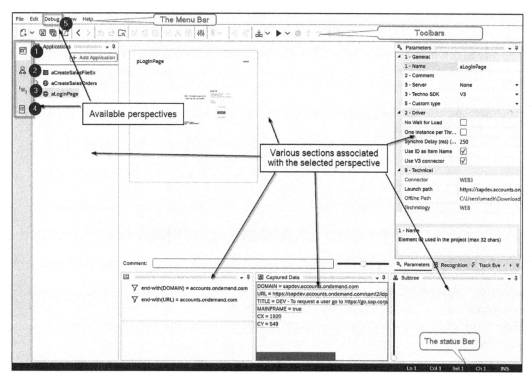

Figure 5.1 – Desktop Studio perspectives

Let's look at the perspectives shown:

- The **Explorer** perspective (**1**) is selected, and all the sections associated with this perspective are visible.

- The **Workflow** perspective (**2**).

- The **Editor** perspective (**3**).

- The **UI Designer** perspective (**4**).

- The **Debug** menu with the debug option (*F5*), which leads to the debug perspective (**5**).

The screenshot also shows the common elements available from all perspectives:

- **The menu bar**: The top-level menus do not change with perspectives, but the options within the menus vary. Try various menus for perspectives and note the changes.

- **Toolbars**: All the tools won't be available simultaneously; available tools change with perspectives.

- **The status bar**: Primarily used in the **Editor** perspective.

Let's now take a closer look at various sections of the **Explorer** perspective.

Introduction to the Explorer perspective – capturing applications

We use the **Explorer** perspective to **capture applications**. Capturing applications records the screenshots and internal structures of the applications and stores them for later – even offline – use. Once we have captured the applications, the next step is to help Desktop Studio recognize various application elements. The following screenshot divides the **Explorer** perspective into six broad areas:

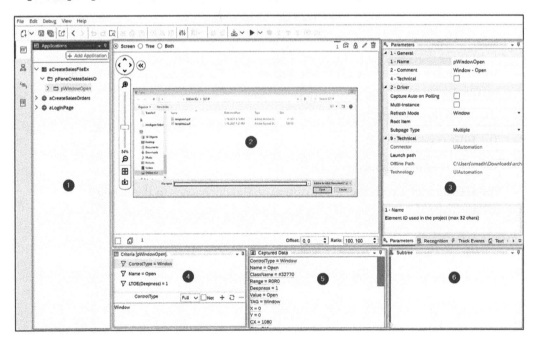

Figure 5.2 – The Explorer perspective

Let's study these areas next:

1. **The project tree**: The project tree displays the application, application pages, and page elements hierarchically. Pages and page elements are color-coded based upon their recognition status: green if the criteria exists to identify the element uniquely, red if the item cannot be uniquely identified with the given criteria, and black if you have not attempted the recognition on the element yet. Each tree node has a context menu with node-specific functions. We use **Add Application** in the top-right corner to capture a new application. In the preceding screenshot, you will notice three applications. The top-most application is expanded while the bottom two are not.

2. **The capture panel**: While you can move around, hide, or unhide every other panel in the Explorer perspective, the capture panel always stays put and helps us identify various application components. Based on the project tree's selection, the capture panel either shows an **Application View** or a **Page View**. The preceding screenshot shows the page view as we have selected a page component, pWindowOpen. The application view will display one thumbnail for each page in the application. You will be able to update the page comments and zoom-in or zoom-out page thumbnails using the slider. The page view in the following screenshot has several options worth discussing:

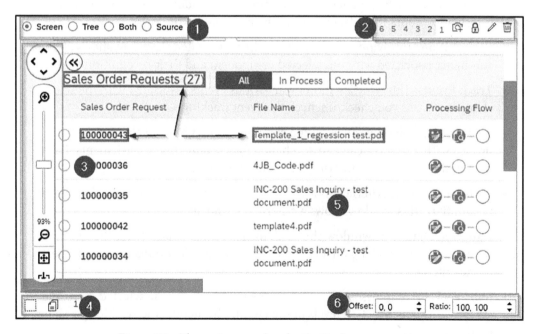

Figure 5.3 – The capture panel under the Explorer perspective

The display selector (**1**) lets you choose what you want to see in the display panel (**5**). The capture toolbar (**2**) shows various capture options. Numbers **1**-**6** in this toolbar show the number of captures available for the selected page; currently, capture **1** is selected. The camera icon makes a new capture, while the lock icon locks/unlocks the selected capture during the recognition process. You can also edit or delete the selected capture. The resize panel (**3**) helps you zoom in or out of the screen. In the picture, we have it at 93% to show all the components legibly. You can also move the image around using the arrows at the top of this panel. The action toolbar (**4**) helps you copy the image to the clipboard or display an image selector to be more selective with the image. The display panel (**5**) shows the selected page capture from the capture tool bar (**2**) in the format selected in the display selector (**1**). You can choose to see just the screen (current selection), the DOM tree, both, screen and the DOM tree or the application source. Many green boxes – depicting declared elements – in the display panel (**5**) can be identified by arrows pointing to them. If these green boxes do not cover the items correctly, you can use the correction toolbar (**6**) to adjust them.

3.   Panels (**3**) to (**6**) in *Figure 5.3* can show any of the following tool windows:

- **Parameters**: Shows the parameters associated with the selected element in the project tree and a help panel at the bottom of the window that shows contextual information about the selected row in the parameters window.

- **Recognition**: This window gets active at the page or item level and shows all the sub-items associated with the selected component and their recognition status.

- **Track Events**: This window shows you various events associated with the selected element and lets you check/uncheck the event tracking.

- **Text**: The text window shows all the components that have a value for the **Text** property. This window can come in handy for selecting invisible elements. Each item in this window comes with the applicable context menu.

- **Criteria**: With the criteria window, you can view and edit the criteria for element recognition. This window shows a criteria tree and an editing panel.

- **Captured Data**: This window shows all the properties available for the selected element. Double-clicking on any property in this window transfers that property to the criteria.

- **Subtree**: Subtree shows a subsection of the DOM tree for the selected item. The subtree can show you 3-10 levels of the DOM. This depth is selectable by a slider on the left.

You can show or hide any of these windows from the **View | Tool Windows** path. With this, we conclude our discussion of the Explorer perspective (capture applications) and we will move to the Workflow perspective (connect applications).

Introduction to the Workflow perspective – connecting applications to create automation

We use the Workflow perspective to **connect applications**, resulting in automation workflows. We captured these applications utilizing the Explorer perspective. As depicted in the following screenshot, the Workflow perspective consists of four major areas:

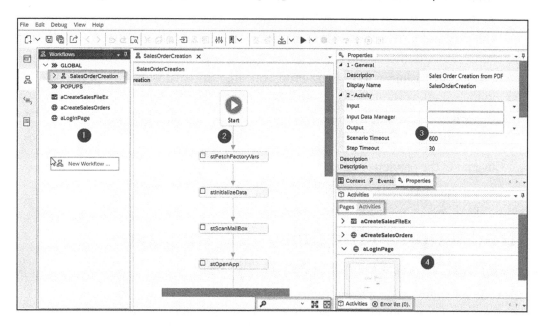

Figure 5.4 – The Workflow perspective

Let's talk about those areas in detail:

1. **The Workflows window**: The **Workflows** window shows all the workflows from your current project. You can see one workflow in the screenshot under **GLOBAL**. This workflow has been selected and is open in the workspace panel (**2**). At generation time, your workflows get converted to JavaScript code. By default, each generated script becomes part of the global scope. To create a new workflow, right-click anywhere in the window.

2. **The workspace**: You develop workflows in the workspace by adding activities and pages to the selected workflow. To build a new workflow, you can drag and drop **pages** and **activities** from the tool panels and connect them. At the bottom of the workspace, you will find options to zoom in and out, expand the workflow to fit to screen, and see an overview of a long workflow that is hard to fit on screen.

3. **Tool panels**: These panels house many subwindows that can be moved around as desired. We have the following windows in the screenshot:

   - **Context**: This shows the data context associated with the project. You can create folders and items under context to store and retrieve the required application data.

   - **Events**: You can design functional events using the **Events** window.

   - **Activities** (visible in bottom panel): Using the **Activities** window, you can drag and drop pages from the declared applications and available activities to the workspace (**2**).

   - **Properties** (visible in top panel): Properties are associated with the selected object in the workflow window (**1**) or workspace panel (**2**).

   - **Error list**: This window shows errors generated at the time of the workflow build process.

4. Covered in the previous point.

With this, we will move on to the next perspective.

Introduction to the Editor perspective – developing automation further

While code generation takes place automatically during workflow creation, the editor perspective helps us **develop the automation scripts** further at the code level. The Editor perspective is similar to the other editors, such as Visual Studio Code, BlueJ, or Eclipse, that you may have used in your development career and provides comparable features. Some of these features are listed here:

- Code autocomplete
- Syntax highlighting
- In-built quick help (*F1*)
- **Go to Workflow** (takes you to the relevant node in the Workflow perspective)
- **Show in Code Map** (shows a navigate code map with the selected code snippet highlighted)
- **Show in Page Viewer**

The major components of the Editor perspective are shown in the following screenshot:

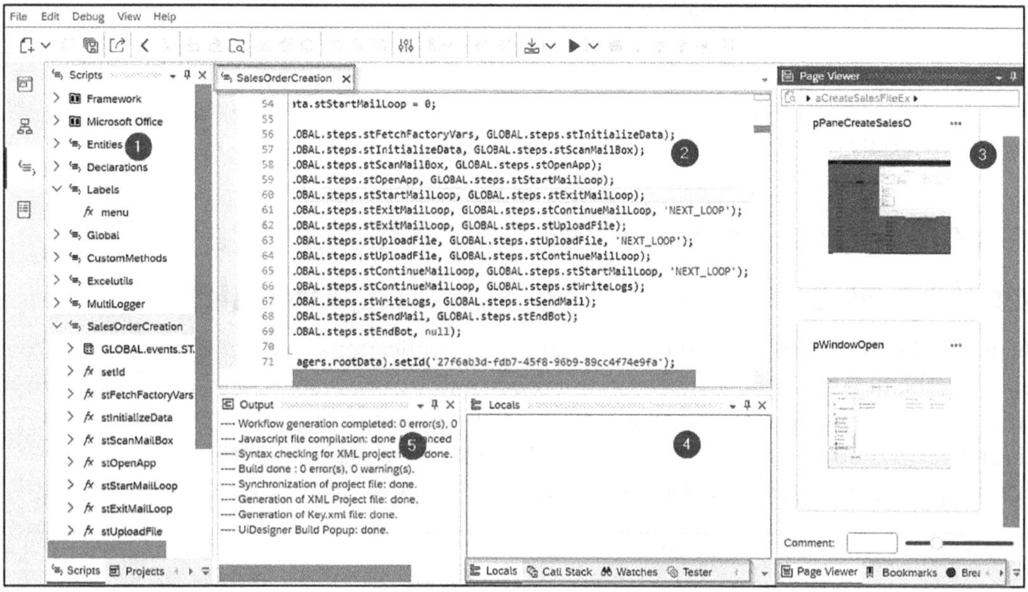

Figure 5.5 – The Editor perspective

The key components of this perspective are as follows:

1. **The script tree**: Lists all the script files included in the current project. From here, you can open any script to work.

2. **The document editor**: This is the central component of the Editor perspective that is used to edit selected scripts.

3. **Tool windows (3, 4**, and **5**): You can move these tool windows around as desired. Some of the tools available are as follows:

   - **Page viewer**: Displays a captured page.

   - **Bookmarks**: You can set bookmarks in the code to go back and forth. This tool lists all the bookmarks.

   - **Breakpoints**: Lists all the code breakpoints.

   - **To-do lists**: All the set reminders in the code are listed here.

   - **Code Map**: Displays the code structure of the script being edited.

   - **Find Results**: Search results following a "Find all" search.

   - **Error List**: Results of code compilation are listed here.

   - **Locals**: Used in debugging.

- **Call stack**: Used in debugging.

- **Watches**: Used in debugging.

As a developer, it will be best for you to learn about this perspective by going around and using the available options. This perspective should be similar to the other IDEs that you would have used so far. When stuck, press *F1* to open the in-place quick guide.

Introduction to the Debug perspective – testing automation and making tweaks

We use the Debug perspective to test and debug the applications. When we launch the debugger, the desktop agent switches to test mode and we can test various workflows from there. The Debug perspective can run in pop-up or embedded mode. You can control this and various other options from the **View | Manage Debugging Options** popup. The various options available in the Debug perspective are shown in the following screenshot:

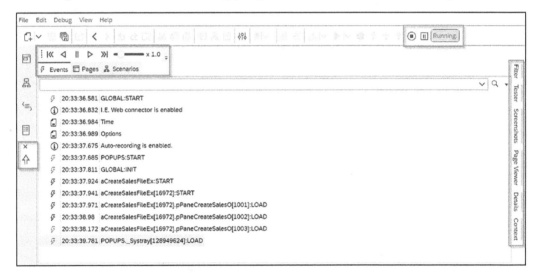

Figure 5.6 – The Debug perspective

We have explained those options briefly here, but a detailed explanation is left for the later chapters and your research:

- The **Events** view (current selection): Shows all the events with a timestamp and type of event (left-most icon).

- The **Pages** view: To display the recognized and yet to be recognized pages.

- The **Scenarios** view: To show the automation scenario currently being executed.

This view has several levels of displays and options to hide and show various data elements.

- The **Tester** view: To run quick validation tests.

- The **Filter** view: To show/hide specific applications and events.

- The **Screenshots** view: To show the screenshots captured during execution. Screenshot functionality can be switched on/off as desired.

- The **Page viewer**: This shows the screenshots of the captured pages.

- The **Details** view: This shows further information for the selected items.

- The **Context** view: This shows the current value of context items.

Let's now continue our discussion of the last perspective.

Introduction to the UI Designer perspective – developing visual add-ons (optional)

We use the UI Designer perspective to design and insert user interaction in a business scenario where the functionality is desired but not provided by the base application. We can modify the base application or use any other technology to develop these **user interfaces** (**UIs**) and use those UIs in our workflow. For this reason, we rarely use this perspective, but it is available and can be used when needed. Let's study the various components of the UI Designer perspective in the following screenshot:

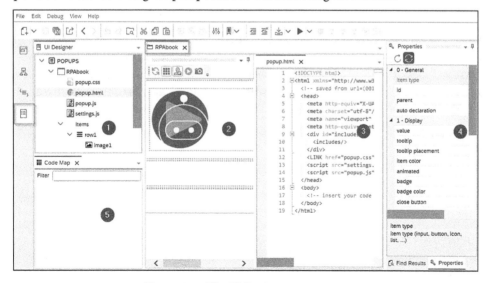

Figure 5.7 – The UI Designer perspective

The components are as follows:

1. **The resource tree**: Lists all components associated with the popup in the pop-up editor (**2**)

2. **Popup editor**: The graphical UI designer to edit your popup

3. **Code editor**: To edit the code base directly for minute details

4. **Tool windows**: (**4**) and (**5**) consolidate various tools that we can move around. You will find the following tools here:

   - **Properties**: The current selection in (**4**) shows properties associated with the selected items in the resource tree (**1**).

   - **Find results**: To search a string in the current code editor.

   - **Code map**: Shows the code structure of the script.

With this, we conclude our discussion of all the perspectives in Desktop Studio.

Summary

We learned about Desktop Studio in this chapter. We started with a bigger picture of the studio and then delved deeper to discuss each perspective briefly. We used a package from the SAP Intelligent RPA store and used it to explore various perspectives, namely, Explorer, Workflow, Editor, Debug, and UI Designer. With this knowledge, you are ready to develop automations using the Desktop Studio that we will address in the upcoming chapters.

Now you know about two of the most important components of SAP Intelligent RPA: the cloud factory and the Desktop Studio. If you haven't already done so, I recommend you download Desktop Studio and get a subscription to the SAP Intelligent RPA trial version. Then you will be in an excellent position to explore various options in these two components. Spend some time learning these components in more detail. We will discuss the Desktop Agent in the next chapter.

Questions

Here are some questions for you to test your knowledge. The answers to these questions can be found at the back of the book in the section named *Assessments*:

1. Which perspective would you use to capture applications?
2. How do you access the **Debug** perspective?
3. Are you likely to use the UI Designer perspective for a scheduled (unattended) automation?
4. What is the core purpose of the Workflow perspective?
5. What similarities do you find in the IDEs that you have used and the Editor perspective?

6
An Overview of Desktop Agent

As discussed in *Chapter 1, SAP Intelligent RPA Architecture and Components*, a Desktop Agent is a small on-premise component of SAP Intelligent RPA that we need to install on any workstation running automation. The core responsibilities of Desktop Agents are twofold. On the one hand, they maintain a persistent communication channel (using the WebSocket protocol) with Cloud Factory to run automations and report back the execution status. On the other hand, they interact with various desktop applications to run the automation.

In this chapter, we will cover the following topics:

- How Desktop Agent works
- Exploring the Desktop Agent tabs
- Common issues and their resolutions

By the end of this chapter, you will be able to understand the basic functioning and more nuanced aspects of using a Desktop Agent.

Let's begin with the first topic on the working of the Desktop Agent.

Technical requirements

- An internet connection

- Access to SAP Business Technology Platform trial version (`https://www.sap.com/cmp/td/sap-cloud-platform-trial.html`)

- Subscription to SAP Intelligent RPA trial version (`https://help.sap.com/viewer/82d5a2499d8449dda691bb4d5b3d7949/Cloud/en-US`)

How Desktop Agent works

As shown in the following image, the Desktop Agent connects with **Cloud Factory** and various application connectors to carry out its functions:

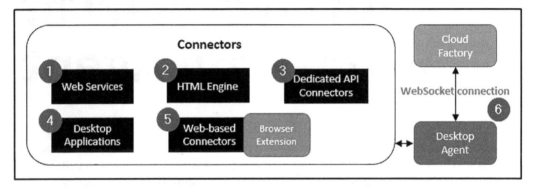

Figure 6.1 – How Desktop Agent Works

Let's discuss these connections briefly (note that at the time of writing, the Desktop Agent was available *only for Windows OS*):

1. **Web services**: This connects with various web applications/services like ServiceNow, AWS, and SAP Business Technology Platform using APIs.

2. **HTML engine**: This is to display popups and custom forms, and is used to customize web interfaces at runtime.

> **Note**
>
> To make it easier to use your automation, you can insert certain elements on the web pages using SDK classes and functions. It is an exciting feature but is beyond the scope of this book. See a demo at `https://www.youtube.com/watch?v=2H6oQdPVpvM` and feel free to explore it further at `https://help.sap.com/viewer/dbe2687952b8433a953c6b6305429122/Cloud/en-US/6cd85f3984084ddb8b92d34cec750229.html`.

3. **Dedicated API connectors**: These are for applications like Microsoft Office© and the SAP GUI.

4. **Desktop applications**: This is to connect with the Windows OS and native Windows applications.

5. **Web-based connectors**: This is for connecting with web browsers and all the applications accessed through them.

6. **WebSocket connection**: WebSocket is a persistent, full-duplex, bidirectional connection operating over HTTP that facilitates messaging between a client and server.

The Desktop Agent is part of the default installation for SAP Intelligent RPA on-premise components. If you have already installed SAP Intelligent RPA Desktop Studio, then you have the Desktop Agent installed. If not, please go back to *Chapter 3*, *Installing SAP Intelligent RPA On-Premise Components*, for installation instructions.

Now that we have the Desktop Agent installed, let's explore the Desktop Agent's tabs and their respective functionalities.

Exploring the Desktop Agent tabs

At installation, the Desktop Agent is configured to start at Windows logon. If you have the Desktop Agent installed, it will appear in your system tray.

As shown in the following screenshot, the Desktop Agent has three tabs:

Figure 6.2 – Desktop Agent for Windows

From the preceding screenshot, we can observe the following:

- **About**: Shows information about Desktop Agent's current status, version, user, and machine.

- **Projects**: Shows all the projects available and the selected mode (interactive/background). In *attended mode*, you can click the **Start** button for a project to begin execution.

- **More Actions**: This tab shows many sub-actions. Let's look at them all:

    - **Shutdown/Restart**: This is self-explanatory.

    - **Settings**: This is for language selection and a checkbox to automatically start the agent at Windows logon. Select this checkbox for unattended mode.

    - **Tenants**: This is for registration with your Intelligent RPA tenants. You can store more than one tenant, but only one can be active. You need to enter a name and the SAP Intelligent RPA Factory tenant URL you want to connect. To register, get your Factory URL, remove #/home, and enter the remaining URL into the field marked **Domain**. Click **Save**.

    - **Job progress**: You can see the status of a running job here.

After learning about the tabs of the Desktop Agent, let's now discuss some common issues related to the Desktop Agent encountered by SAP Intelligent RPA developers.

Common issues and their resolutions

Here are some common issues related to the Desktop Agent that you may come across sooner or later:

- **WebSocket connection closed**: This sometimes happens in unattended mode. Jobs will show up in a failed status because the Intelligent RPA Factory and agent are unable to connect. Usually, an agent restart fixes the issue temporarily, but a deeper discussion may be needed with your web security team to address the root cause.

- **System reboot during unattended mode**: As the agent starts at Windows logon, you can store your Windows credentials in the Desktop Agent and ensure that the agent will load after a reboot. You can find more information on this at https://help.sap.com/viewer/9a34587e2f8b478b9b8a0e158f2b9215/Cloud/en-US/da0cc503387c4781ab684beb94618a4b.html.

- **Server busy error**: There could be several reasons for you encountering a server busy popup that interrupts your automation process. Going through the following blog can help you troubleshoot the issue: `https://blogs.sap.com/2021/05/10/how-to-handle-a-server-busy-popup/`.

- Search the following SAP notes at `https://support.sap.com/en/index.html` for more common issues pertaining to the Desktop Agent:

  - `2796483`: `Agent <your agent> already connected error` when attempting to log in to the Desktop Agent.

  - `2796491`: Nothing happens when launching a scheduled scenario.

  - `2796377`: The Desktop Agent icon does not appear in the Windows System Tray.

  - `2798996`: The error `CCtxtRun2Dlg::OnGoToSocket: SetIpaSocket failed` occurs when downloading a package from the Factory.

  - `2796396`: No registry key, bad value, can't find a JSON file.

  - `2981018`: How to fix agent connection issues happening during Cloud Factory update

  - A problem restarting the agent: Type `services` in the command window and ensure that **SAP Intelligent RPA Desktop Service** is running.

As an Intelligent RPA developer, you may encounter other issues not listed here, but these are the most common issues and can be used as a quick reference list to begin your troubleshooting.

Summary

In this chapter, we learned about the Desktop Agent, the on-premise counterpart of Cloud Factory. We discussed the architecture, connectors, and tabs of the Desktop Agent. We also discussed some common issues that we can encounter during projects. You have now learned about both ends of SAP Intelligent RPA: Cloud Factory and the Desktop Agent. This knowledge puts you in a position to explore various possibilities at both ends.

Explore away. We will discuss a fascinating topic, the cloud studio, in the next chapter.

Questions

Here are some questions for you to test your knowledge. The answers to these questions can be found at the back of the book in the section named *Assessments*:

1. What are the additional steps to install the Desktop Agent on macOS and Linux?

2. Which connector do you require for interacting with Microsoft Outlook?

3. Is Italian an available language under the settings?

Part 2: Installing and Setting Up SAP Intelligent RPA

This section sets the basis for SAP Intelligent RPA 2.0, where the focus is changing from development using on-premises to cloud development using Cloud Studio. This section also introduces tools for process discovery and modeling tools that are useful while automating a business process.

This section comprises the following chapters:

- *Chapter 7, An Overview of Cloud Studio*
- *Chapter 8, An Introduction to SAP Spotlight and Signavio*

7
An Overview of Cloud Studio

This chapter introduces you to the core **Intelligent Robotic Process Automation 2.0 (Intelligent RPA 2.0)** constituent and the future of **SAP** Intelligent RPA bot development, **SAP Intelligent RPA Cloud Studio**. We will discuss the essential components of Cloud Studio in this chapter and will develop an entire project later, in *Chapter 24, Development Using Cloud Studio*. We hope this chapter excites you enough to start trying out Cloud Studio as you go through development exercises using Desktop Studio in the following chapters.

In this chapter, we will cover the following topics:

- Cloud Studio's place in the SAP Intelligent RPA world
- Designing automation solutions with Cloud Studio
- Reusing packages from Desktop Studio in Cloud Studio
- Deploying packages and projects from Cloud Studio

By the end of this chapter, you will understand the core components and capabilities of Cloud Studio.

Let's begin with understanding Cloud Studio in SAP Intelligent RPA.

Technical requirements

- An internet connection.

- Access to the **SAP Business Technology Platform** (**SAP BTP**) trial system
  (`https://www.sap.com/cmp/td/sap-cloud-platform-trial.html`).

- Subscription to SAP Intelligent RPA trial version (`https://help.sap.com/`
  `viewer/82d5a2499d8449dda691bb4d5b3d7949/Cloud/en-US`).

- The **RPA Challenge** package from the Intelligent RPA store. Get this package
  from the store, select **Save as... New Project**, and open it in Cloud Studio to follow
  along. To learn how to get a store package, please refer to *Chapter 27, SAP Intelligent
  RPA Store.*

Cloud Studio's place in the SAP Intelligent RPA world

SAP is slowly but surely transitioning to be a cloud company. From the core ERP
components to supporting solutions, most components are on a path to transition to
the cloud. The on-premise SAP Intelligent RPA components either already have a cloud
counterpart or there is a clear plan to have one.

> **Note**
>
> SAP Intelligent RPA Cloud Studio is currently the cloud counterpart to SAP
> Intelligent RPA Desktop Studio and provides comparable services in slightly
> differing ways. It is conceivable and recommended to use SAP Intelligent RPA
> Cloud Studio for new automation. However, given the existence of several SAP
> and customer automation built using Desktop Studio, you must know SAP
> Desktop Studio too, at least for a few more years.

While you can create artifacts such as processes and user tasks only with Cloud Studio,
the development process on both platforms is similar. We will explain some variations in
this and the following chapters. All your learnings from Desktop Studio development will
apply to Cloud Studio, with some variations. Let's now see how we use Cloud Studio for
the creation of automation.

Designing automation solutions with Cloud Studio

Just as with Desktop Studio, developing automation using SAP Intelligent RPA Cloud Studio is like building LEGO® structures. As shown in the following screenshot, you can create seven types of artifacts in Cloud Studio:

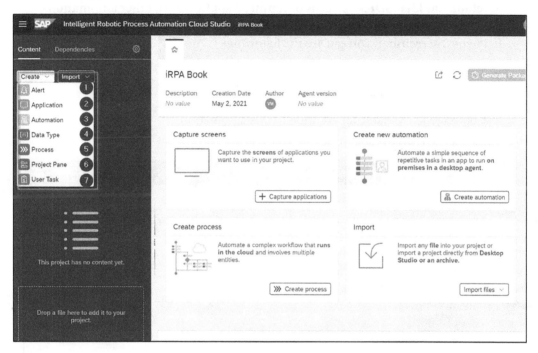

Figure 7.1 – Artifacts in Cloud Studio

We will discuss each of these artifacts briefly, as follows:

1. **Alert**: You will recall our brief discussion of alerts and registrations in *Chapter 2, An Overview of SAP Intelligent RPA Cloud Factory*. Those alerts helped you send out email messages on predefined events related to desktop agents and distribution lists. Cloud Studio alerts enable you to define business events such as `shipment_delayed` or `payments_overdue` as alerts where your business stakeholders need to be notified. You can then use these alerts in your automation using a `Raise Alert` activity. To react to these alerts, you need to create **Alert Handlers** under **Environments** in Cloud Factory.

2. **Application**: Going back to our LEGO® analogy, captured applications correspond to the building blocks of automation. We use application artifacts to capture applications running on your workstation and recognize **user interface (UI)** elements from these applications for later use in automation. This artifact is comparable to the output of the **Explorer** perspective of Desktop Studio.

3. **Automation**: An automation is an ordered flow of activities from various **software development kits (SDKs)**, screens of **captured applications**, **other automations**, **data types**—custom or from the SDKs—and multiple **controls** added to the project. In the next screenshot, you can see the following:

    1. Two **Automations**

    2. Open **Run RPA Challenge** automation

    3. Components available for addition to this automation

    Have a closer look here:

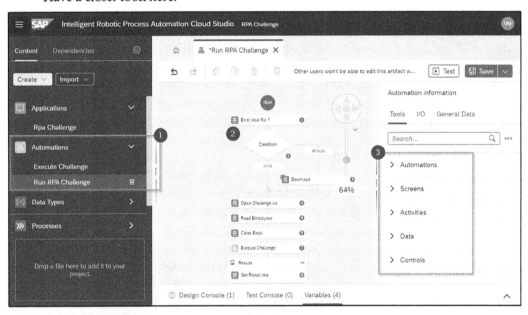

Figure 7.2 – Automation components

4. **Data Type**: Cloud Studio makes three basic data types available to you—**String**, **Number**, and **Boolean**. If you need to represent a **complex data structure** such as **Person** in the **RPA Challenge** project, you can combine these basic data types in any way you choose. Besides the basic data types and custom data structures you create, you will see numerous other data structures under the **Data** tab. These data structures are part of the SDKs added to the project.

5. **Process**: Gartner included *hyperautomation* under the *Top 10 Strategic Technology Trends for 2020 and 2021*, describing it as a combination of several technologies such as RPA, **artificial intelligence/machine learning** (**AI/ML**), and intelligent business process management software. In Cloud Studio, a **process** combines Intelligent RPA and SAP workflow artifacts, resulting in a hyperautomation running on the SAP BTP. To build a process, we use components called **Skills**. Besides the automation built using Cloud Studio, there are three types of skills available, as follows:

   - **Scenarios**: Designed with Desktop Studio and reused. We will discuss more on this in the next section, *Reusing packages from Desktop Studio in Cloud Studio*.

   - **User Tasks**: We will discuss user tasks in the following paragraphs in this section.

   - **Processes**: A process can use another process as a subprocess.

6. **Project Pane**: This is an interesting and currently required, but seemingly unnecessary, artifact for attended automations. Essentially, you use **Project Pane** to create a preview of the **Desktop Agent**'s **system tray** (**systray**). You can choose a project label to show in the systray. It is conceivable that a checkbox and an input field against automations in Cloud Studio indicating the intent to deliver them in **Systray** for attended automation may someday remove the need for **Project Pane**.

7. **User Task**: A **User Task** temporarily pauses the automation/process and hands over control to a user to provide input or make a decision. A user task is sent to the inbox of a workflow participant (user) for taking the indicated action.

Now that you know the artifacts available for creation in Cloud Studio, let's see how you can utilize your packages from Desktop Studio in Cloud Studio.

Reusing packages from Desktop Studio in Cloud Studio

You can reuse all the development work you did in Desktop Studio in your Cloud Studio projects. To do so, you would need to import your Desktop packages to Cloud Studio as scenarios.

In Cloud Studio parlance, a **scenario** is a reusable collection of several steps. If you come from the SAP ABAP background, a scenario is like a **Function Module**.

For JavaScript developers, you can think of a scenario as a **function**. A productive project of some complexity will usually have several scenarios. When you export a project as a package from Desktop Studio, Desktop Studio scenarios are compiled and exported as a part.

The following screenshot shows that we imported into Cloud Studio the **Automatic Creation of Sales Order Requests from Unstructured Data (5LT)** store package that we compiled and exported from Desktop Studio earlier.

(**1**) shows imported **Desktop Packages**, (**2**) shows available **Scenarios** within this package, and (**3**) shows the switch to make these scenarios available as a skill in the processes that we plan to create:

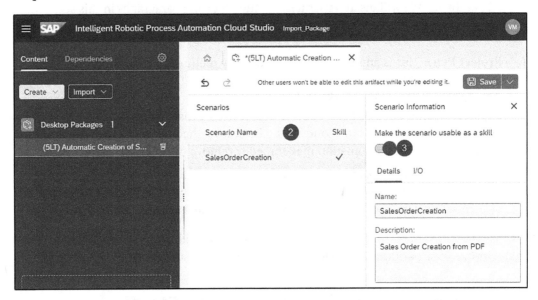

Figure 7.3 – Importing Desktop packages

After a few years of Intelligent RPA development, your team should have developed a package of matured utilities usable in every Intelligent RPA project. It would be sensible to import that package to every Intelligent RPA project to save time and effort.

While designing a Desktop scenario, if you defined the scenario-specific **input/output (I/O)** data types, these data types will be created in Cloud Studio when you import the scenario. Let's now find out about the process of taking Cloud Studio projects to Cloud Factory and various environments.

Deploying packages and projects from Cloud Studio

Once your project is complete, you can generate a package from this project to deploy it to your current environment. Should you want to migrate your project to a different environment for *further development* (*sandbox to development*), project export is an option. Similarly, for transporting your project in the landscape (*development to QA to production*), consider exporting a package. Let's study both these options next.

From Cloud Studio, you can generate a package and export a project or package. As shown in the following screenshot, once your project is complete, you can click **Generate Package** (**2**) to make it available in Cloud Factory for deployment. Once done, you can add this package to the environment of your choice and assign triggers to run automation jobs:

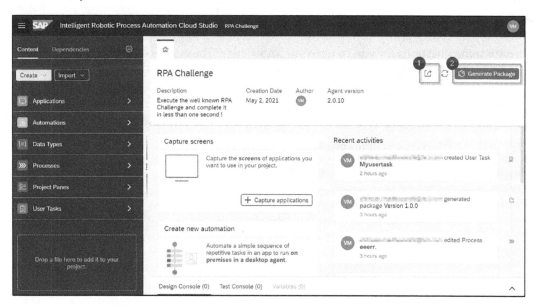

Figure 7.4 – Exporting a project or generating a package

To transport your project to another environment (*development to QA or QA to production*), you can export a project or a package (**1**). Once you click the **Export** icon, you will get a warning to export the dependencies separately. The export is downloaded to your workstation as a `.zip` archive. You can import this `.zip` archive along with the dependency archives to the target environment.

This brings us to the conclusion of our discussion about Cloud Studio.

Summary

We began by evaluating the place of Cloud Studio in the SAP Intelligent RPA world, addressing the need for understanding both Cloud Studio and Desktop Studio to be a successful SAP Intelligent RPA developer. We discussed the artifacts available for creation in Cloud Studio before understanding how to use a Desktop Studio package within your Cloud Studio automation. An analysis of how to export projects and generate packages from Cloud Studio brought us to the end of the chapter.

You have now learned about all the components of SAP Intelligent RPA and how SAP Intelligent RPA interacts with other SAP BTP services such as Workflow Management. The stage is now set for learning development skills on these components in the next section of the book. In the next chapter, we will continue this exciting discussion by introducing you to some fantastic new members of the SAP family.

Questions

Here are some questions for you to test your knowledge. The answers to these questions can be found at the back of the book in the *Assessments* section:

1. Can you use Cloud Studio offline?
2. Can you use the SAP Workflow Management service from Desktop Studio?
3. What are the types of skills available for building a process?
4. Can a package contain more than one scenario?

8

An Introduction to SAP Spotlight and Signavio

While progressive and ambitious developers know their tools of choice thoroughly, they also deeply understand the environment that these tools operate in. As an experienced developer, your customers will often ask you about where to begin their automation journey. To answer this question, you can look back at your own experience or search online to see what the industry is doing and guide your customers accordingly. The problem with this approach is that even from the same sector, these experiences are still second-hand and may not apply to your customer fully. Fortunately, business process intelligence tools can peer deep into your customer's IT landscape and generate a report indicating the processes that are prime candidates for optimization or automation. SAP Spotlight and Signavio are the tools that can help you with this requirement. SAP Spotlight has been divided in two products now—**Process Discovery** and **Process Insights**. Process Discovery is a free tool to provide one-time insights into your business processes whereas Process Insights is a paid tool, similar to Process Discovery but for the continuous monitoring of your processes. While the information in this chapter is still relevant, you can read more about SAP Process Discovery at `http://www.sap.com/process-discovery` and SAP Process Insights at `https://www.sap.com/products/process-insights.html`.

It is acceptable if you skip this chapter now and return to it after a while. However, I recommend that you understand these tools well enough to speak about them, as this knowledge could take you from a great developer to a trusted advisor.

We will briefly discuss the following topics in the sections that follow:

- Introduction to SAP Spotlight
- Introduction to Signavio

By the end of this chapter, you will understand SAP Spotlight and Signavio enough to hold introductory discussions with your clients and will have access to learning tools to further your skills.

Let's begin with the first topic of getting introduced to SAP Spotlight.

Technical requirements

- For this chapter, all you need is an internet connection.

Introducing SAP Spotlight

Let's break our discussion about Spotlight into two logical sections. In the first section, we will focus on SAP Spotlight and why you should consider using it. We will discuss how to use a Spotlight report, the various sections of the report, and the areas you should focus on during your process discovery journey in the second section.

Let's now understand what SAP Spotlight is and why you should use it.

What is SAP Spotlight?

SAP Spotlight is a process discovery tool that graphically maps business processes within your SAP ERP 6.0 systems using the digital footprints (transaction logs) that every business process run invariably creates. Once the mapping is complete, SAP Spotlight compares the efficiency of your mapped business process with the target process efficiency. It arrives at target efficiency using some predefined KPIs and all comparable process maps created for various other SAP customers.

SAP Spotlight is a cloud-based system. Hence, no on-premises installation is required. To access the free **Process Discovery for SAP S/4HANA Transformation** offering for your organization, you need to follow a four-step process:

1. Extract data.
2. Initiate your request.
3. Confirm request.
4. Receive results from SAP.

You can find details about these steps in a how-to guide at www.s4hana.com. You will also find sample PDF reports, an online live sample report, and frequently asked questions about Spotlight reports.

How to use a Spotlight report

A Spotlight report is a complex document depicting various lines of business and end-to-end processes. Our core focus is on identifying the automation opportunities using this report. There are various other outcomes that you can derive from this report, but that discussion is beyond the scope of this book. If interested, you can find many resources and a sample report at www.s4hana.com.

SAP provides two reports, one in PDF format and another online. Once you get your report from SAP, log in to the provided link to explore the report. For now, consider using the demo report available at the following link:

```
https://demo.spotlight.cloud.sap/project/61097292-78fc-
4aee-a96f-ffc2ca8403aa/analysis/88333874-5ad8-4325-a412-
85b1be235556
```

At login, you will see the landing page shown in the following screenshot. Click on the **Reports** link:

Figure 8.1 – Spotlight landing page

You will reach the **Reports** page. Scroll down to the bottom till you see the **Process Automation** link, as shown in the following screenshot. Click on this link:

Figure 8.2 – Process Automation

The next page will list all the automation opportunities assigned to various ways of automation that SAP offers. Look for the ones tagged with **iRPA Bot Store**. Selecting any of these links will take you to the pre-built bots in the SAP Bot store. Refer to the following screenshot:

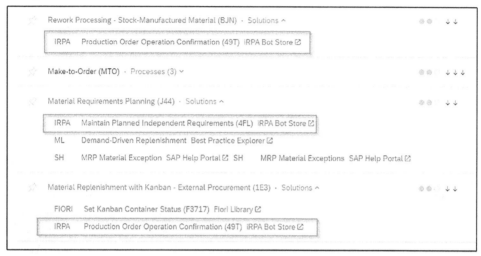

Figure 8.3 – iRPA opportunities

If you want to see all these opportunities listed in one place, select **Recommendations** on the vertical menu and choose lines of business that interest you. As shown in the following screenshot, you should see all SAP iRPA opportunities in one place:

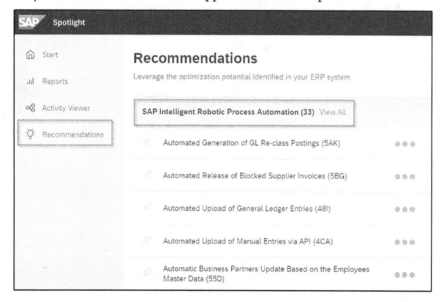

Figure 8.4 – Automations recommendations

This brings us to the end of our Spotlight discussion. In the next section, we will look at the functionalities that Signavio offers.

Introducing Signavio

Signavio offers a collection of products branded as the Signavio Business Transformation Suite. Unlike Spotlight, the Signavio suite is a commercial offering, and you need to license it for commercial use. However, for learning purposes, Signavio offers a 30-day free trial at `https://www.signavio.com/`.

Let's discuss the products that make up this suite.

SAP Process Manager by Signavio

Process Manager is a web-based, graphical process modeling tool that uses **Business Process Modeling Notation** (**BPMN**) to model business processes. A BPMN model uses a small set of visual elements including events, activities, gateways, flows, data, artifacts, and swimlanes. BPMN-based process models exist at three levels—from level 1 (high level) to level 3 (detailed modeling)—and you can model at all these levels using SAP Process Manager by Signavio. An example BPMN process model showing events, swimlanes, gateways, and flows is as follows:

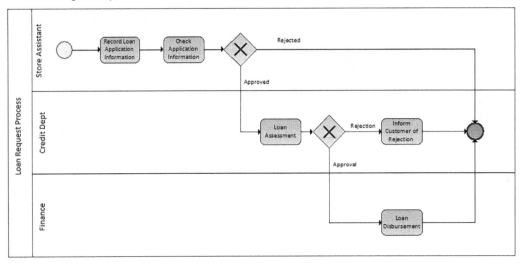

Figure 8.5 – A process model using BPMN (https://upload.wikimedia.org/wikipedia/commons/4/4f/BPMN_Process_jpeg.png by Iancpierce / CC BY-SA 4.0)

You can build a similar process model with SAP Signavio Process Manager using the core BPMN elements and elements with added information specific to your organization.

SAP Process Intelligence by Signavio

Process Intelligence, or process mining, is a technology that uses "event log" data generated by business processes and maps it graphically to show all the paths that a business process takes. *For business process mining, we are most interested in this product.*

As seen in the following figure, the business process follows more than one path:

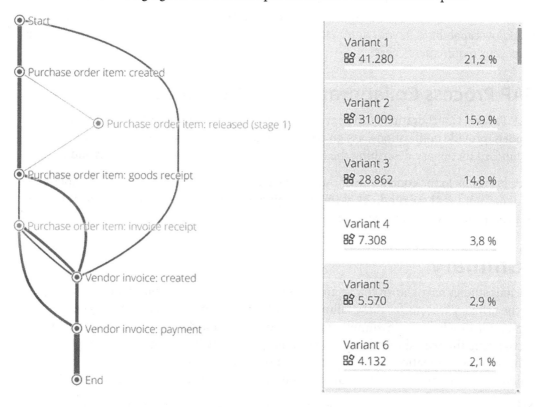

Figure 8.6 – Process Intelligence by Signavio

The tool models the most-used path with the thickest line while modeling lesser-used variants in reducing degrees of thickness. You can also see details about six variants and the percent usage associated with each of them on the right side.

This model provides us with inputs to optimize this process by reducing or eliminating undesired variants and gives us invaluable information about the variant to automate to provide the best ROI to our customers.

SAP Workflow Accelerator by Signavio

SAP Workflow Accelerator (**SWA**) is a workflow modeler and runtime engine broadly comparable to the workflow capability of the **SAP Workflow Management** (**SWM**) service available on SAP **Business Technology Platform** (**BTP**). SAP has recently clubbed SAP Intelligent RPA and SAP Workflow Management services under **SAP Process Automation** (**SPA**) on BTP. Also, since Cloud Studio comes with built-in integration to the workflow service, you may derive more value from using SPA when you require workflow capabilities in your automations. Evaluate both services and choose the one that suits your requirements best.

SAP Process Collaboration Hub by Signavio

SAP Process Collaboration Hub provides teams with a central place to share process models, provide notifications, assign tasks, provide an event newsfeed, and share a standard dictionary describing the terms associated with business processes and models.

This brings us to the conclusion of our Signavio and Spotlight discussion. Even though you may not use these products at the beginning of your RPA career, having an awareness of these products will serve you well.

Summary

Various studies have shown that as many as 60% of RPA projects end up in failure. One of the primary reasons for these failures tends to be selecting the candidate processes for automation based on assumptions instead of irrefutable data points. We started by recognizing the crucial role that process mining tools play in determining the right processes for automation. Then, we discussed two SAP platforms—one free and one paid—that you can use to help your clients find the optimal automation candidates.

Now you know enough about SAP Spotlight and SAP Signavio to have initial discussions with your clients. We recommend you continue your learning journey of these platforms at `https://help.sap.com/viewer/product/SPOTLIGHT/CLOUD/en-US` and `www.signavio.com`.

In the next chapter, we will pick up our discussion about Desktop Studio and discuss various perspectives that this multifaceted tool offers. You may want to refresh your knowledge of Desktop Studio by re-reading *Chapter 5, An Overview of Desktop Studio*, before continuing with the next chapter.

Questions

Here are some questions for you to test your knowledge. The answers to these questions can be found at the back of the book in the section named *Assessments*:

1. For generating a Spotlight report, which landscape server should you use for data extraction?

2. Does a Spotlight report provide process automation opportunities only for SAP iRPA?

3. Who can initiate a request for an SAP Spotlight report?

4. Which four products make up the Signavio suite?   .

Part 3: Developing Bots with Desktop Studio

This section includes a detailed explanation of Desktop Studio, different perspectives, and its usage while developing a bot. In this section, you will learn about all the features provided by Desktop Studio using practical examples. You will be developing an automation solution for a business process with incremental learning of the features of Desktop Studio.

This section comprises the following chapters:

9
Desktop Studio Perspectives

Before starting any development, you must familiarize yourself with the development interface – that is, the **integrated development environment** (IDE). Once the business process for automation is finalized and the steps for automation are defined, IDEs are used to convert these agreed manual business steps into automation steps. **SAP Intelligent RPA** provides an IDE called the **Desktop Studio** to define the target application for automation and the steps to be performed on these target business applications.

Desktop Studio provides different *perspectives* that allow users to capture applications, capture screens/pages in the scope of the application, controls within application pages for automation, and define sequential actions to be performed on these controls. **Desktop Studio** also provides an interface that can be used to edit scripts generated by other perspectives.

Desktop Studio is structured in five perspectives. A *perspective* is an interface dedicated to a specific development task – for example, capturing applications, preparing a workflow or a sequence of execution instructions, or editing the scripts.

The five perspectives are as follows:

- The **Explorer** perspective
- The **Workflow** perspective
- The **UI Designer** perspective
- The **Editor** perspective
- The **Debug** perspective

By the end of this chapter, you will have a good understanding of the Desktop Studio perspectives and the role of these perspectives in automation solution development.

Let's start by looking at each of the perspectives provided by Desktop Studio.

Technical requirements

- Desktop Studio installed on your workstation
- **Microsoft .NET Framework 4.7**
- **Remote Tools** for **Visual Studio 2019** (for remote debugging)
- A source code comparison tool (for example, **KDiff3** or **Beyond Compare**)

KDiff3 can be downloaded from `http://kdiff3.sourceforge.net/`.

The Explorer perspective

The Explorer perspective provides an interface to declare applications, pages, and controls that are required to interact as part of a business process automation.

We can use this perspective for the following:

- Defining applications foremost that are involved in the scope for automation.
- Performing screen captures and the controls within the page and defining the criteria to uniquely identify them at runtime. The applications, pages, and controls captured and declared in this perspective will be used in the Workflow perspective to create a sequence of actions that completes a business process.

- Defining the criteria by highlighting any potential conflicts in the identification of a page or control. For example, more than one control may be of the same type, so we can make the criteria unique by adding a label or control ID as part of the criteria. Similarly, more than one page in an application may have the same title. Desktop Studio provides multiple options to uniquely identify a page based on a control within the page.

- Viewing the relationships between declared applications, pages, and controls in a hierarchical tree structure.

The **Explorer** perspective can be selected by clicking the ⬜ button on the left pane in the Desktop Studio. This perspective includes multiple panels, as shown in the following screenshot:

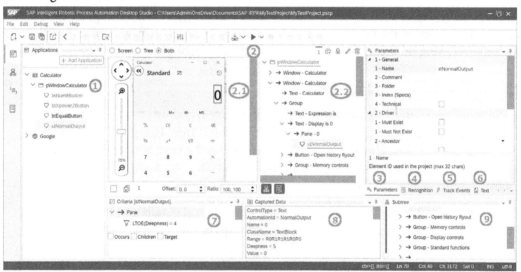

Figure 9.1 – The Explorer perspective and its panels

All of the panels in the Explorer perspective are explained in the following sections.

The Applications panel

The **Applications** panel (marked as *1* in *Figure 9.1*), also referred to as the *Project tree*, displays all the applications, pages, and UI elements that are declared. This panel can be used to declare new applications, pages, or controls for automation, or it can be used to edit the existing items.

Items are highlighted in different colors based on their unique recognition status. All items in green are properly recognized. Items displayed in red require criteria to be defined to make that element uniquely identifiable. We will look at defining the criteria for applications, pages, and controls in upcoming chapters.

The Display panel

The **Display** panel (marked as *2* in *Figure 9.1*) displays the screen and source captured by SAP Intelligent RPA. The panel display can be controlled by selecting **Screen**, **Tree**, or **Both**.

The Screen Display panel

The **Screen Display** panel (marked as *2.1* in *Figure 9.1*) shows the screen capture of the page that is selected in the Project tree. Visible elements within the page can be directly selected by clicking on them. The selected component is highlighted by a blue rectangle.

The Source Tree Display panel

The **Source Tree Display** panel (marked as *2.2* in *Figure 9.1*) shows the **DOM** tree, that is, the internal structure of the selected item in the Project tree. This panel is useful for identifying and selecting elements that are not visible on the page but are required to interact with the business process automation; for example, a menu item under a menu, or a list of items in a combo box.

This panel is also very useful for understanding the technical details and the organization of the controls, as well as the parent-child relationships of the controls within a page.

The Parameters panel

The **Parameters** panel (marked as *3* in *Figure 9.1*) allows us to edit the parameters for an application, page, or control. The editable parameters available in this panel are specific to the element type that is selected in the Project tree.

The Recognition panel

The **Recognition** panel (which can be accessed via the tab marked as *4* in *Figure 9.1*) shows the component associated with the selected element in the Project tree and the corresponding recognized components based on the component hierarchy in the application. Any issues with identifying the required elements can be investigated in this panel.

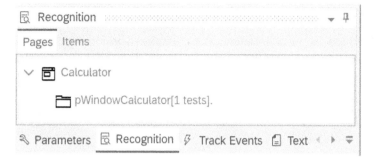

Figure 9.2 – The Recognition panel

The pages and controls under the page that are uniquely recognized will be displayed in green, as shown in *Figure 9.2*.

The Track Events panel

The **Track Events** panel (which can be accessed via the tab marked as *5* in *Figure 9.1*) lets you check/uncheck event tracking for an application, page, or element. Events listed in this panel are dependent on the type of element selected in the Project tree. The following figure shows what the Track Events panel looks like:

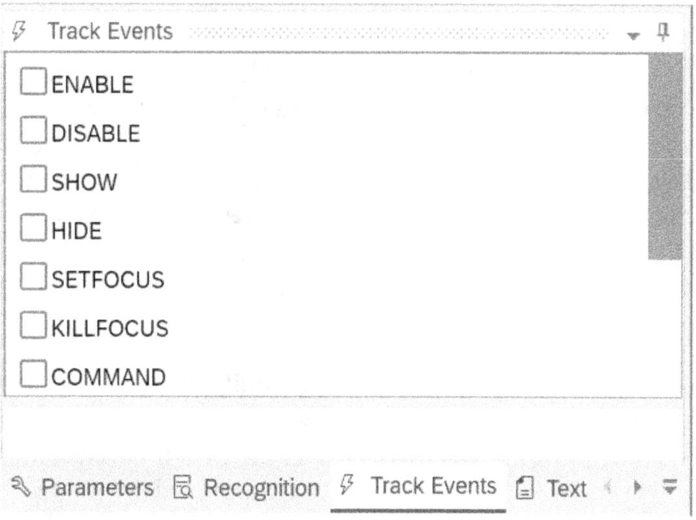

Figure 9.3 – The Track Events panel

The Text panel

The **Text** panel (which can be accessed via the tab marked as *6* in *Figure 9.1*) displays the text of the controls captured when declaring the pages. This will help us select the controls based on the displayed text. The text of all the controls is displayed in a list, as shown in the following screenshot:

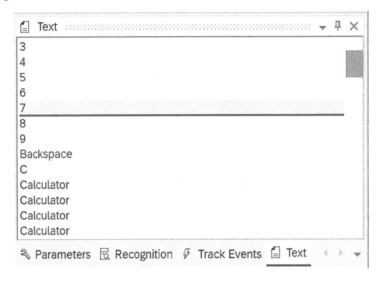

Figure 9.4 – The Text panel

While the visible controls on the page can be selected from the **Screen Display** panel, invisible controls on the page, such as items in a combo box or menu items and menus, can be selected either from the **Source Tree display** panel or from the text in the Text panel. The text selection in this panel highlights the corresponding control in the **Screen Display** panel.

The Criteria panel

Criteria are rules or properties used by the **Desktop Studio** connectors to recognize applications, pages, or controls that were declared and used in the workflow to execute the business steps. SAP Intelligent RPA recognizes an element if the element properties match the criteria defined for the element. If the criteria defined do not match the element properties, the execution will fail. So, it is important that the criteria for the element are selected, taking the properties of the elements at runtime.

This **Criteria** panel (marked as *7* in *Figure 9.1*) allows us to add or edit element criteria for unique identification. The element criteria must be unique so the automation solution can identify the controls/elements for the action. Elements with no or conflicting criteria are highlighted in red in the Project tree. The **Captured Data** panel can be used to identify the properties that can be used to uniquely identify an element.

The Captured Data panel

The **Captured Data** panel (marked as *8* in *Figure 9.1*) lists the properties that were captured by SAP Intelligent RPA for the selected element. This list can be used when defining the unique criteria for any item.

The Subtree panel

This **Subtree** panel display (marked as *8* in *Figure 9.1*) is the same as the **Source Tree Display** panel, except that it displays only the part of the tree that is the three parent levels of the item associated with the element selected in the Project tree.

We will learn more about this perspective and how its panels are used in upcoming chapters. Now, let's look at the Workflow perspective and gain a basic understanding of its features.

The Workflow perspective

The Workflow perspective provides an interface to design the automation workflows/scenarios using the applications, pages, and controls captured in the Explorer perspective. The screens and items that can be used in a workflow must first be declared in the Explorer perspective.

We can use this perspective for the following:

- Describing the automation sequences of the business process
- Defining the activities to be performed as steps in the automation sequences
- Defining the context structure also called as variables to store information for data management

The Workflow perspective can be selected by clicking the ⚬ button from the left pane in **Desktop Studio**. The panels included in this perspective are shown in the following screenshot:

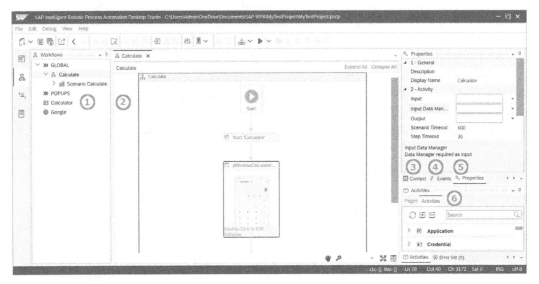

Figure 9.5 – The Workflow perspective and its panels

Let's discuss each panel in this perspective.

The Workflows panel

Automating a business process is often split into multiple scenarios or workflows. The Workflows panel (marked as *1* in *Figure 9.5*) shows the list of all of the workflows created, and it allows users to define new workflows. Right-clicking on this panel provides an option to create a new workflow. Workflows can be created under global or specific applications. All applications captured in the Explorer perspective are listed in this panel, so workflows can be created based on the declared applications.

The Workspace/Workflow Designer panel

A *workflow* is a sequence of steps. The Workflow Designer panel (marked as *2* in *Figure 9.5*) provides a canvas to create a sequence of steps using the already declared application pages and controls required to automate a business process.

This panel provides a canvas (that is, a graphical view) for the design of our scenarios that enables us to implement automation sequences in functional steps. In this panel, we can define the sequence of the screens involved so as to invoke them when the business process executes and the actions to perform on each screen, as well as the data to collect from the screen or elements, or we can set the data for the elements. Activities can be dragged and dropped into this panel from the **Activities** panel.

The Context panel

The **Context** panel (which can be accessed via the tab marked as *3* in *Figure 9.5*) contains the context/data structure of the project. In other words, this panel is used for creating the variables to store the information relevant to the automation solution. The data structure is composed of folders and items. Items can also be defined as an array by selecting the checkbox displayed next to the item. SAP Intelligent RPA uses **JavaScript** as the automation language and therefore, it does not require us to define the item type (for example, an integer or a string). A sample list of the variables created in the **Context** panel is displayed in the following screenshot:

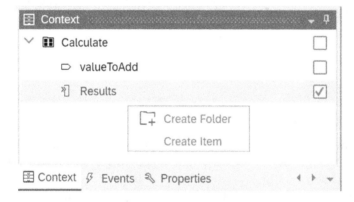

Figure 9.6 – The Context panel

The Events panel

The **Events** panel (which can be accessed via the tab marked as *4* in *Figure 9.5*) allows us to define functional events on the applications declared in the Explorer perspective. A functional event has a name and can transport data (such as a string or JavaScript object) to a receiver when a defined event occurs on a sender. The default view and the context menu of this panel are shown in the following screenshot:

Figure 9.7 – The Events panel

The Properties panel

The **Properties** panel (marked as *5* in *Figure 9.5*) will display properties specific to the activity selected in the Workflow Designer panel, and it allows us to modify activity properties.

The Activities panel

The **Activities** panel (marked as *6* in *Figure 9.5*) displays a list of pages or activities available to perform on pages or controls. Pages or activities available in this panel can be dragged and dropped into the Workflow Designer panel. Activities in this panel are logically grouped for the scope in which the activities are applicable.

Any errors identified during the design of the workflow are listed in the **Error List** panel within this panel. This helps users to view and correct any issues within the workflow.

Before we try to develop a deep understanding of this perspective and start using it to create workflows in upcoming chapters, we will have a look at the other perspectives. Next, we will learn about the UI Designer perspective.

The UI Designer perspective

The UI Designer perspective is used to design custom user interfaces and like input forms for capturing user input when running automation solutions.

The features of the UI Designer perspective are as follows:

- A graphical view of the custom UI
- The UI structure displayed in a tree view
- Editable JavaScript code for the custom UI

The UI Designer perspective can be selected by clicking the ⊟ button on the left pane in the Desktop Studio. The panels included in the UI Designer perspective are shown in the following screenshot:

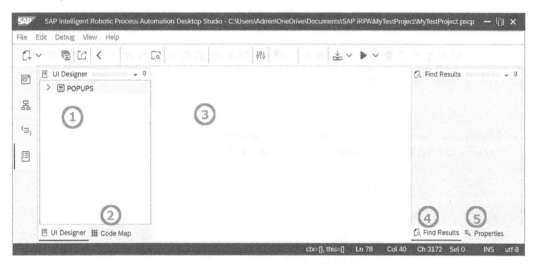

Figure 9.8 – The UI Designer perspective and its panels

A brief explanation of each panel is included in the following sections.

The UI Designer panel

The **UI Designer** panel (marked as *1* in *Figure 9.8*), also referred to as the *Resources tree*, displays the list of the popups created in the project. It allows you to do the following:

- Create and manage the custom popups required by automation solutions
- Manage the source files used by the custom popups
- Design and update the items to be displayed in the custom popups

Here, we can add a new popup that can be used in the current project by right-clicking the **POPUPS** node in the UI Designer panel and selecting **Add a New Popup...** from the context menu.

Figure 9.9 – The UI Designer panel

A dialog will be displayed that allows us to do the following:

- Enter a unique name for the new popup.
- Choose the template that best matches the automation solution needs. The available options are **An Empty Popup** or **An Empty AppBar**.

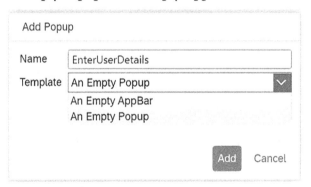

Figure 9.10 – The Add Popup dialog

When the required details are entered and the **Add** button is clicked, a new pop-up dialog will be created under the **POPUPS** node of the panel, and the Resource tree will include new files created that will allow users to design the new popup.

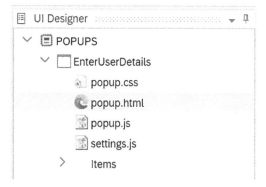

Figure 9.11 – The tree structure of the pop-up dialog in the UI Designer panel

Each popup created will include a list of source files created and displayed in this panel in a tree view. Each pop-up subtree displays a list of files used by the popup and can be edited in the **Designer View** panel. The pop-up source files include the following items:

- `popup.html`: This is the HTML page. A finalized popup can be viewed in the browser.

- `settings.js`: This is the pop-up JavaScript source file with the page design.

- `popup.js` and `popup.css`: These are the customizable page behavior and style sheet, respectively.

The Designer View panel

Once a new popup is created, it can be designed by adding the required controls in a specific layout design in the **Designer View** panel (marked as **3** in *Figure 9.8*). This panel is split into two views – the **Designer View** and the **Editor View** – as shown in the following screenshot:

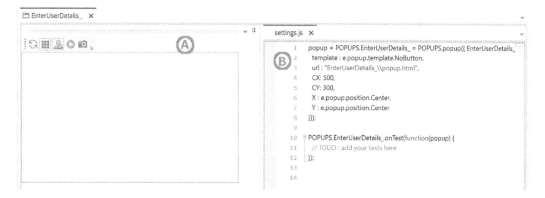

Figure 9.12 – The designer view panel

The Designer view

This view (marked as *A* in *Figure 9.12*) allows us to graphically design a new pop-up dialog. Right-clicking in the designer view will list all of the controls that can be added to the popup along with the available layout options.

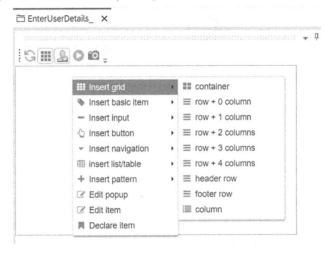

Figure 9.13 – The options available in the context menu of the designer view popup

A sample popup, capturing basic user information, is shown in the following screenshot:

Figure 9.14 – A sample pop-up design

The Code Editor view

The HTML, JavaScript, and CSS files generated for the popups can be edited in the **Code Editor view** (marked as **B** in *Figure 9.12*).

The **Code Editor view** provides various features, including syntax highlighting, **IntelliPrompt**, and more. These features are discussed in detail in *The Editor perspective* section.

The Code Map panel

The **Code Map** panel (marked as *2* in *Figure 9.8*) displays the code structure of the popup selected in the **Designer view**. Here, we can quickly navigate to the code by selecting the desired map entry in this panel. The **Code Editor view** automatically scrolls to the first line of the corresponding code block.

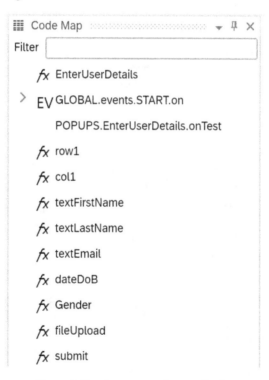

Figure 9.15 – A source code map display

The Find Results panel

You will see the **Find Results** panel included in multiple perspectives. This panel displays the user search results. Please refer to *The Find Results panel* subsection in *The Editor perspective* section for more details.

The Properties panel

The **Properties** panel (marked as *5* in *Figure 9.8*) allows us to change the properties of the popups and the items defined under the popups. The properties of an item can be viewed by clicking the **Edit** button in the context menu, double-clicking the item in the **UI Designer** panel, or selecting the item in the **Designer View** panel. The properties that are displayed are in context with the item selected. The **Properties** panel is shown in the following screenshot:

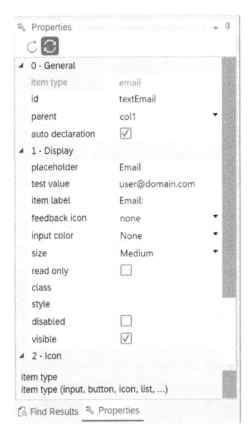

Figure 9.16 – The Properties panel for the selected popup

The editable properties displayed in this panel are specific to the item type.

As we can see, SAP Intelligent RPA allows us to create custom dialogs that can be integrated into a workflow like any application screen. Once all applications are captured and a workflow is created, we need to generate the code by building the project. We can then view, update, or add custom code to the source generated by Desktop Studio.

The Editor perspective allows users to perform actions on the source code, which we'll look at next.

The Editor perspective

After our workflows are created, the JavaScript code can be generated by clicking the ⬇ button or pressing the *Ctrl + B* shortcut. The generated code contains the JavaScript code for the following:

- The scenario declaration
- The automation steps implementation
- A function declared for each activity within the scenario
- The script file for the variables declaration

The generated code can be viewed and edited in the Editor perspective. SAP Intelligent RPA provides a powerful JavaScript code editor. The Editor perspective can be selected by clicking the ⬅ button in the left pane in Desktop Studio. The default display of the Editor perspective is shown in the following screenshot:

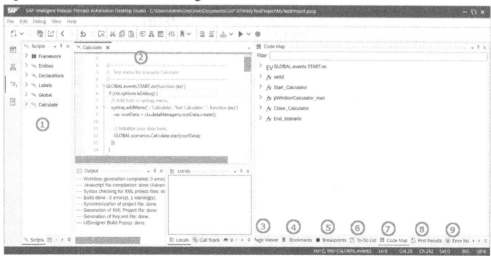

Figure 9.17 – The Editor perspective and its panels

We will explain each of the panels in the Editor perspective in the following subsections.

The Scripts panel

This **Scripts** panel (marked as *1* in *Figure 9.17*), also referred to as the *Script tree*, displays the complete source code of the project in a tree view. This panel allows us to view and select the scripts for editing. All scripts generated by building the project can be found in this tree view. Code can be opened in the Document Editor panel by double-clicking the item in the **Scripts** panel.

These scripts include the following:

- SAP Intelligent RPA Framework code
- Entities code generated for the context/data structure declared in the Workflow perspective
- The declarations of the applications and their details, as captured in the Explorer perspective
- Workflow code

Please note, rebuilding the code after changes are made to workflows will regenerate the code. But any changes to the code in this perspective are not reflected in workflows. SAP Intelligent RPA will try to merge the differences between the existing and regenerated code. If there are any conflicts, SAP Intelligent RPA will open the source code comparison tool, highlighting the code conflicts to allow us to merge and resolve conflicts manually before generating the final code.

The Document Editor/Code Editor panel

SAP Intelligent RPA provides a very powerful text editing panel that helps developers to accelerate their development. This panel (marked as *2* in *Figure 9.17*) provides all the features developers expect from an IDE to allow efficient code editing, including syntax highlighting, code outlining, IntelliPrompt, and many more. Think of any advanced development IDE, and all those features are available in this code editor.

This panel provides the most useful development features – namely, IntelliPrompt features and indicator features.

We will now look at the IntelliPrompt features provided by Desktop Studio.

The IntelliPrompt features in Desktop Studio

The following are the IntelliPrompt features provided by Desktop Studio:

- In-context completion lists to improve development productivity. For example, CTRL + SPACE will list the available options to auto-insert partially typed object names, or typing . will list the available methods for an object.

- Information on the parameters of any method or JavaScript function. This includes a display of the multiple signature overloads of the methods and highlighting the current parameter that is being edited.

- Desktop Studio allows predefined code snippets to be inserted into the editor. The code snippets can be inserted into the code by selecting one of the following options from the context menu:

Figure 9.18 – The options to insert code snippets from the context menu

Let's now look at the indicator features provided by Desktop Studio.

The indicator features in Desktop Studio

The following are the indicator features provided by Desktop Studio:

- **Bookmark indicator** ( ): A code line can be bookmarked for future reference. The options for bookmarks can be viewed by clicking the ∨ menu button in the menu bar:

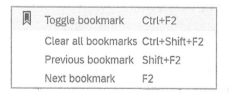

Figure 9.19 – The available bookmark options in the context menu

1. **Breakpoint indicator** (●): Breakpoints are used when debugging the application to indicate executions to pause at a selected step so that developers can monitor the state of the execution step. Breakpoints can be set to any execution step by clicking the gray margin area before the line or by clicking the ● button in the menu bar. The shortcut key to toggle the breakpoint is *F9*.

2. **TODO indicator** (◯): This feature will be useful for marking a line for incomplete implementations to get an indication of work that is pending in the code. This indicator will be displayed for all lines that start with `// TODO`. Please note that this TODO comment is case-sensitive and so is not the same as `// todo` or `// ToDo`.

3. **Current execution line indicator** (⇨): This is displayed when debugging the application. The current line being executed by SAP Intelligent RPA is highlighted with this indicator.

The Page Viewer panel

The **Page Viewer** panel (which can be accessed via the tab marked as *3* in the Editor perspective in *Figure 9.17*) displays the pages captured/declared in the Explorer perspective. An application, page, or control can be selected to view in this panel.

Figure 9.20 – The Page Viewer panel

The Bookmarks panel

The **Bookmarks** panel (which can be accessed via the tab marked as *4* in *Figure 9.17*) lists all of the bookmarks for quick navigation. The bookmarks are grouped under the script name, as shown in the following screenshot:

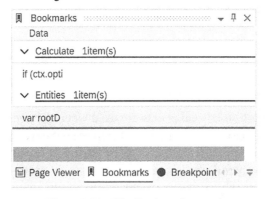

Figure 9.21 – The Bookmarks panel

The Breakpoints panel

The **Breakpoints** panel (which can be accessed via the tab marked as *5* in *Figure 9.17*) lists all breakpoints for quick navigation. The breakpoints are grouped under the script name, as shown in the following figure:

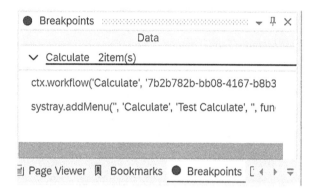

Figure 9.22 – The Breakpoints panel

The To-Do List panel

The **To-Do List** panel (which can be accessed via the tab marked as *6* in *Figure 9.17*) lists all lines marked as // TODO for quick navigation. The *to-do* items are grouped under the script name, as shown in the following screenshot:

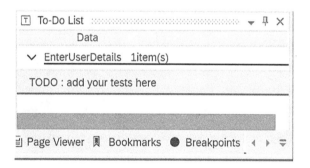

Figure 9.23 – The To-Do List panel

The Code Map panel

The **Code Map** panel (which can be accessed via the tab marked as *7* in *Figure 9.17*) displays the structure of the code, grouped by functions or execution code blocks. We can use this panel to quickly navigate to the code by selecting the desired function name or code block. The code block is then automatically selected in the code editor.

By selecting the **Show in code map** option from the context menu in the code editor, users can view the map entry in the code map tree. The **Code Map** panel displays all of the functions coded in the script.

The Find Results panel

SAP Intelligent RPA provides standard code search options. This option can be accessed from the **Edit | Find and Replace** menu item or from the context menu. All of the search options available in the context menu are shown in the following figure:

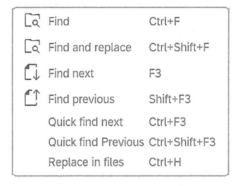

Figure 9.24 – The Find and Replace Menu options

The **Find and Replace** dialog provides many options to search for a specific word or use regular expressions in either the current file or all files in the project. The **Find and Replace** dialog is shown in the following screenshot:

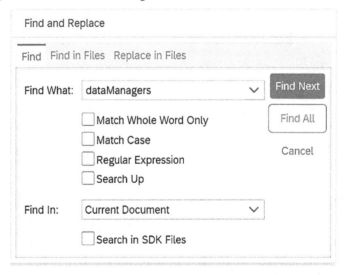

Figure 9.25 – The Find and Replace dialog

As you can see from the preceding screenshot, this dialog allows us to search for specific text in a file or in all files in the project. This also allows us to replace a specific piece of text with another in all files in the project.

The results of the search can be found in the **Find Results** panel (which can be accessed via the tab marked as *9* in *Figure 9.17*). This panel also displays the previous search keywords for quickly re-running searches.

The Error list panel

The **Error list** panel (which can be accessed via the tab marked as *9* in *Figure 9.17*) displays all the errors and warnings raised when building the solution. All errors and warnings are grouped by their script name to allow quick and easy navigation to error locations within a script, as shown in the following screenshot:

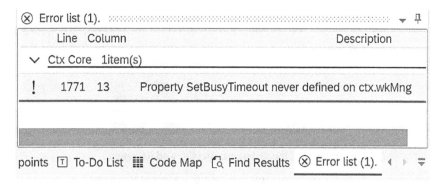

Figure 9.26 – The Error list panel

We have now looked at the Editor perspective and its panels. Desktop Studio provides most of the features that developers desire in any IDE. We will explore and use these panels and features in future chapters. Now, we will look at the Debug perspective.

The Debug perspective

Desktop Studio includes a debugger that lets you control the step-by-step execution of automation scenarios.

After the project build is successful, a project can be debugged step by step to understand the flow of the execution and the data flow between different steps, as well as the state of the context after each step. The Debug perspective helps us view and resolve any issues with the code, flow, or application states.

The Debug perspective can be launched by clicking the ▶ button on the menu bar or by pressing the *F5* key. Once the debugging is started, you will see the debug window open, as shown in the following screenshot:

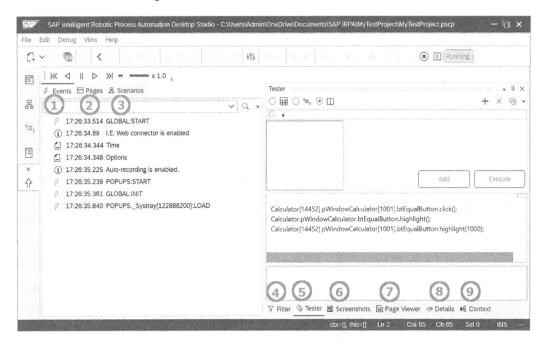

Figure 9.27 – The Debug perspective and its panels

We will now discuss each of the panels available in the Debug perspective.

The Events panel

The **Events** panel (marked as *1* in *Figure 9.27*) displays all the events received and the actions executed based on the received events. For example, an application declared in the **Explorer** perspective and used in the workflow will have a **START** event after the application is started and when executing. Similarly, a page captured under the application will have a **LOAD** event. This panel helps us understand the sequence of events and any failures to handle events. Based on the errors displayed, we can understand the exact step in the workflow or automation scenario where the error occurred and take corrective actions.

Details of each line item in this event can be viewed in the **Details** panel.

The Pages panel

The **Pages** panel (which can be accessed via the tab marked as *2* in *Figure 9.27*) displays all the applications and the pages under each application. This panel also highlights the loaded pages in green. Application pages highlighted in green can be used for testing in the **Tester** panel to execute specific commands.

If the application or page is not displayed in green, even after the application is loaded when executing the scenario, we need to reexamine the unique criteria defined for the application or page. Refer to the following screenshot:

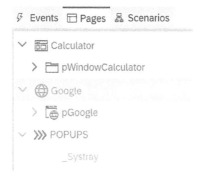

Figure 9.28 – The Pages panel

The Scenarios panel

The **Scenarios** panel (marked as *3* in *Figure 9.27*) displays the automation scenario currently being executed:

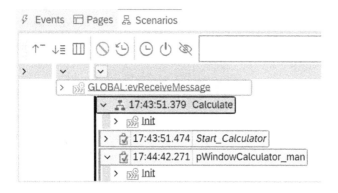

Figure 9.29 – The Scenarios panel

The Filter panel

The **Filter** panel (which can be accessed via the tab marked as *4* in *Figure 9.27*) can be used to filter the displayed events or applications to allow more focused information during debugging. For example, we can select a specific application start event to filter and then look at the details in the **Details** panel. This panel allows us to select the event to filter, as shown in the following screenshot:

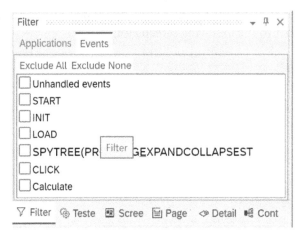

Figure 9.30 – The events available in the Filter panel

The Tester panel

The **Tester** panel (which can be accessed via the tab marked as *5* in *Figure 9.27*) helps us to execute the commands on captured applications, pages, and controls during debugging. This panel provides multiple subpanels to allow us to execute commands on a specific page or control. The available subpanels can be seen in the following figure:

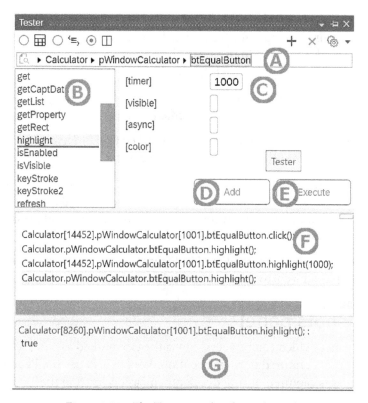

Figure 9.31 – The Tester panel and its subpanels

Let's describe each subpanel in the **Tester** panel:

- **The loaded elements list**: This is marked as *A* in *Figure 9.31*. The currently loaded application, page, or element can be selected here. Only elements that are already loaded will be available for selection.

- **The available methods list**: This is marked as *B* in *Figure 9.31*. This subpanel lists the actions available for the selected element or page. We can select any action available in this list to execute it.

- **Parameters**: This is marked as *C* in *Figure 9.31*. This subpanel displays the list of parameters required to input for the selected action/method. For example, if the highlight method is selected in the available methods list, this subpanel will display the parameters required by the highlight method.

- **The Add button**: The **Add** button is marked as *D* in *Figure 9.31*. Clicking this button will add the selected method with its specified parameters to the commands list.

- **The Execute button**: The **Execute** button is marked as *E* in *Figure 9.31*. Clicking this button will execute the selected method on the control.

- **The commands list**: This is marked as *F* in *Figure 9.31*. This lists the commands added that are available for execution. A user can select a single command or a sequence of commands to execute. Select the commands and press the **Execute** button, or press *F7* to see the results.

- **Results subpanel**: This is marked as *G* in *Figure 9.31*. Here, the result of the last command execution is displayed (whether that is a failure or success).

The Screenshots panel

The **Screenshots** panel (which can be accessed via the tab marked as *6* in *Figure 9.27*) displays the screenshots captured during execution. We can also use the **Page Viewer** panel to view the pages captured during development, as declared in the **Explorer** perspective.

The Page Viewer panel

The **Page Viewer** panel (which can be accessed via the tab marked as *7* in *Figure 9.27*) displays the pages captured in the **Explorer** perspective that are currently loaded during the execution of the scenario.

The Details panel

The **Details** panel (which can be accessed via the tab marked as *8* in *Figure 9.27*) is used to view the details of the selected event in the **Events** panel or the selected scenario step in the **Scenarios** panel.

Figure 9.32 – The Details panel is used to view the details of events or scenarios

The Context panel

The **Context** panel (which can be accessed via the tab marked as *9* in *Figure 9.27*) displays the context of the currently executing scenario, including the running application process details. This panel displays both user-defined and system-defined variables, along with the current values. This can be seen in the following screenshot:

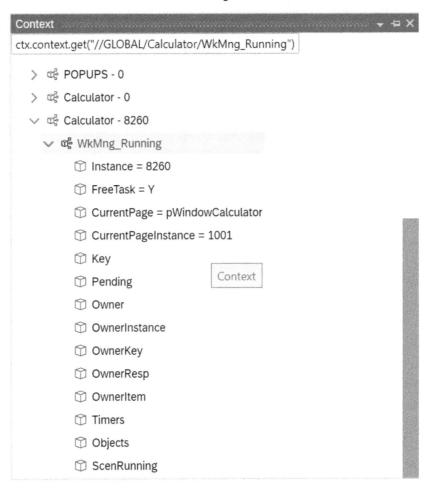

Figure 9.33 – The Context panel

The Debug perspective is very useful for viewing and correcting issues relating to capturing applications or issues with the workflow. By executing the code step by step and observing the application state changes after each step, we can understand and resolve any issues.

Summary

You should now be familiar with the development environment and the different perspectives provided by Desktop Studio. We can use the Explorer perspective to capture applications, pages, or controls that are required to automate a business process. Or, we can create a workflow or sequence of steps to be performed for a business process using the Workflow perspective. Once the workflow is created, the Editor perspective is used to generate, view, and update the code, and we can use the Debug perspective to debug our code. With the features provided by Desktop Studio, we can achieve accelerated productivity. Advanced debugging options enable us to quickly identify and resolve any issues relating to capturing and declaring applications, pages, and elements in scope for automating business scenarios. Desktop Studio also includes the UI Designer perspective, which allows us to create custom pages to accept user inputs, as required by the business process. Custom pages can be used in a similar way to any normal application in the process workflow.

You will learn more about working with most of these features in upcoming chapters. However, before starting any automation solution using the Desktop Studio features, first, a Desktop Studio project needs to be created. We will learn how to create and manage a project in our next chapter.

Questions

Here are some questions for you to test your knowledge. The answers to these questions can be found at the back of the book in the *Assessments* section:

1. How can the Debug perspective be launched?
2. Why are some pages or controls displayed or highlighted in red?
3. Does Desktop Studio provide an option to create custom dialogs? If so, which perspective is used to create custom dialogs?
4. Can you name a couple of panels that are displayed in more than one perspective?

10
Creating and Managing Projects

By now, you should be familiar with **Systems Applications and Products in Data Processing Intelligent Robotic Process Automation (SAP Intelligent RPA)** Desktop Studio. In *Chapter 9*, *Desktop Studio Perspectives*, we looked at the different views and panels provided by **SAP Intelligent RPA Desktop Studio**. You also got a glimpse of a few of the actions available to help develop an automation solution.

In this chapter, we will expand on this knowledge by starting with the first step of the development phase, which is to create a project.

After covering the topics in this chapter, you will have knowledge of the following:

- Creating a new project and updating projects
- Exploring the project structure and folder organization
- Editing project details
- Archiving a project
- Exporting a project for deployment into the SAP Intelligent RPA tenant

By the end of this chapter, you should be able to create a project and have an understanding of how projects are organized within a folder structure. You will also have learned about updating project details and including additional dependencies required by a project, as well as updating the version of the project.

Let's start by creating a new project in Desktop Studio.

Technical requirements

- Desktop Studio installed on your workstation
- Microsoft .NET Framework 4.7
- Remote Tools for Visual Studio 2019 for remote debugging

Creating a new project and updating projects

An automation solution for a business process in **Desktop Studio** is organized as a project. So, the first step for a developer to start with the automation solution development after understanding the business process use case is to create a project in Desktop Studio.

Let's execute the steps to create our own first automation project with SAP Intelligent RPA Desktop Studio, as follows:

1. In the menu bar, go to **File | New Project...** or press the *Ctrl + N* shortcut key to create a new project, as shown here:

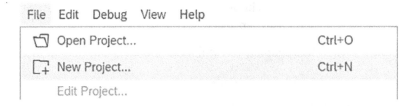

Figure 10.1 – Menu option to create a new project

2. Enter the project details in the **New project** dialog, as follows:

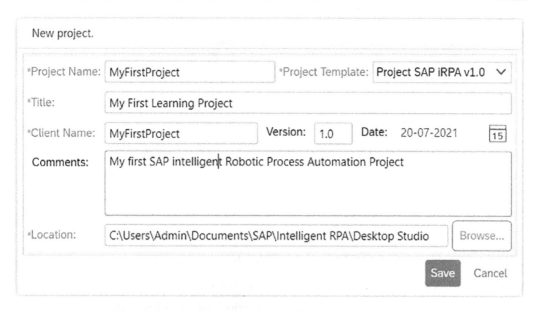

Figure 10.2 – Details to be entered while creating a new project

From *Figure 10.2*, you will note the following:

- We have entered MyFirstProject in the **Project Name** field. This is a mandatory field.

- We have entered My First Learning Project in the **Title** field. This is a mandatory field.

- We have kept the **Project Template** selection as it is. The default selected will be the latest template available.

- We have entered MyFirstProject in the **Client Name** field.

- We have kept the default **Version** value as 1.0. This can be updated later for upgrading the project version.

- The current date is displayed by default in the **Date** field. You can keep this date as-is or choose to change the date to any date by clicking the calendar button next to it.

- You can optionally enter comments about a project in the **Comments** field. Enter My first SAP intelligent Robotic Process Automation Project or anything else you wish.

- In the **Location** field, specify where the new project is to be created and click on **Save**.

You should now see a folder with our project name created under the location specified, as illustrated in the following screenshot:

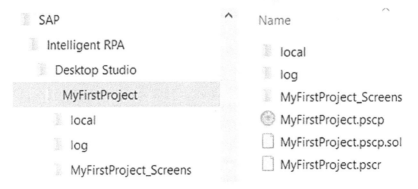

Figure 10.3 – A new project folder created in the system

Your first project now is created for further development.

Let's understand the different folders created under the project and how these folders are organized.

Exploring the project structure and folder organization

SAP Intelligent RPA stores complete information related to an automation solution in a folder structure that can be viewed in Windows Explorer. Let's briefly look at the key folders and types of files/information stored in those folders by SAP Intelligent RPA.

The following folder structure is created by Desktop Studio when creating a project:

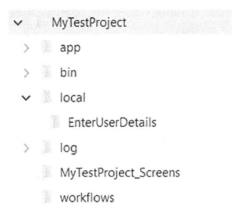

Figure 10.4 – Organization of folders under the project

You might have observed that Desktop Studio created a number of folders under the project name folder when creating a project. We will now look at the purpose of these folders and what information is stored in these folders, as follows:

- The `app` folder: This includes details about applications and screens captured in the Explorer perspective.
- The `bin` folder: This contains all project files required by Desktop Studio for executing a project. This folder includes subfolders containing language framework files, extensions, and libraries that are copied from the **software development kit (SDK)** while creating or updating a project.
- The `local` folder: This is used by SAP Intelligent RPA when deploying the automation solution in the local system.
- The `log` folder: This is used as a working directory to store the log files that are generated by **Desktop Agent** when the project is tested with Desktop Studio.

Other folders are also created when archiving or exporting a project.

`<project>.pscp`, created under the root project folder, is the main project file that stores project information in **Extensible Markup Language (XML)** format. Project files stored will be updated by Desktop Studio per developer changes; these can be viewed by any text editor or edited by a text editor in rare cases.

In this section, we created a new project and understood how a project is organized in folders. Let's next learn how a project can be edited to include additional dependencies and update the version of the project.

Editing project details

When creating a new project, a few libraries will be included as default dependencies. You might want to add more libraries as dependencies based on project requirements. Further, it is a good practice to update the project versions for every deployment of a project in the production environment so that you will be able to roll back to previous versions of the project when there is an issue with the current version of the project. Editing the project details after opening the required project in Desktop Studio will allow you to change the project details. Here's how it is done:

1. In the menu bar, go to **File| Open Project...** or press the *Ctrl + O* shortcut key to select an existing project to open in Desktop Studio.

2. In the **Open** dialog box, navigate to the location specified while creating the project and select `MyFirstProject.pscp`. Click on **Open**, as shown in the following screenshot:

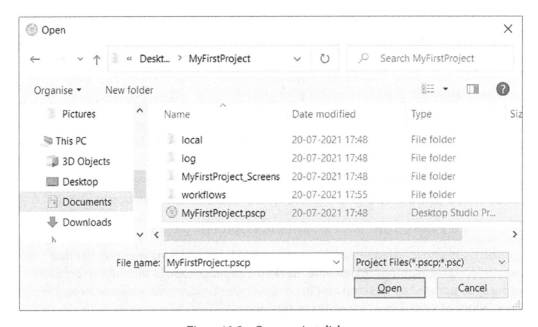

Figure 10.5 – Open project dialog

3. Only after the project is opened will the **Edit** project option be enabled in the **File** menu. Click on **File | Edit Project...** in the menu bar.

    The **Edit project** dialog will be opened. You will notice four tabs in this dialog. Let's understand each of them, as follows:

- **General**: This has the details entered while creating a project. You can edit these details or update the version of the project in this tab, as shown in the following screenshot:

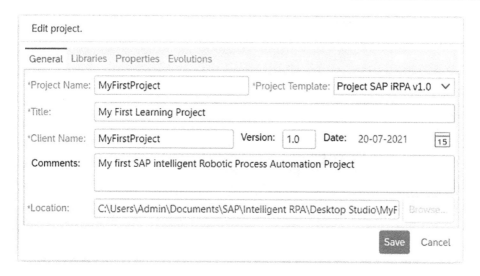

Figure 10.6 – General properties of the project

- **Libraries**: Here, additional libraries or dependencies required by the project can be included. For example, if the automation solution required integration with a **Microsoft Office** Excel application, keep the **Excel Integration** option checked in this tab:

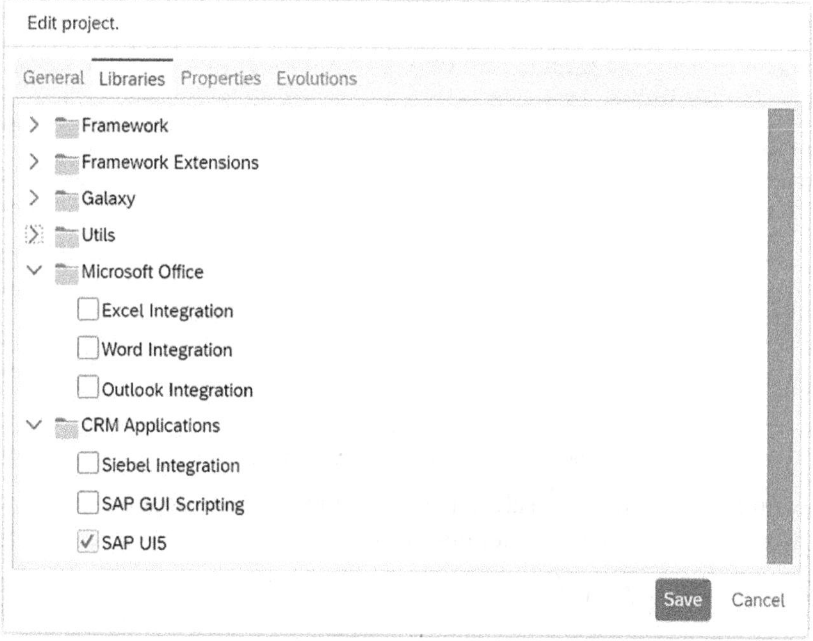

Figure 10.7 – Updating dependent libraries

- **Properties**: Update the project properties in this tab, as illustrated in the following screenshot:

Edit project.

General Libraries Properties Evolutions

```
<Properties>
    <Property Name="validity" />
    <Property Name="cyphering">0</Property>
    <Property Name="compression">1</Property>
</Properties>
```

Save Cancel

Figure 10.8 – Project properties

- **Evolutions**: Project evolutions—that is, version and release information—can be updated in this tab, as illustrated in the following screenshot:

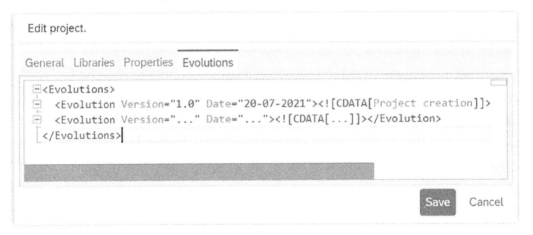

Edit project.

General Libraries Properties Evolutions

```
<Evolutions>
    <Evolution Version="1.0" Date="20-07-2021"><![CDATA[Project creation]]>
    <Evolution Version="..." Date="..."><![CDATA[...]]></Evolution>
</Evolutions>
```

Save Cancel

Figure 10.9 – Project version history

We have now understood how to create a new project and update dependencies or update a project version. Let's now look at other options provided by Desktop Studio for actions on a project.

Archiving a project

The best way to keep the source secure and share it with other developers involved in the development of the same business process is to use **source control** systems. However, SAP Intelligent RPA provides an option to archive a project for storing or to share with other developers.

A project can be archived by selecting the **File | Archive Project** menu, as illustrated in the following screenshot:

Figure 10.10 – Menu option to archive a project

Once this option is selected, a message such as this is displayed after the project is archived:

Figure 10.11 – Success message after archiving a project

A new folder called `archive` will be created under the project folder and the archived project source is stored in this folder. The archive file is a `.zip` file and the filename includes the timestamp at which the archive was created. The zipped archive can be shared with other developers who then can extract the source and continue with business process development with Desktop Studio in their system.

While archived project sources can be used to share the project source with other developers to store it as backup, deploying a project after completion of testing requires us to export the project. Let's now look at how to export a project for deployment.

Exporting a project for deployment into the SAP Intelligent RPA tenant

Exporting a project is similar to archiving a project. However, both have different purposes. A project is archived to store or to share with other developers, but to deploy a project in **SAP Intelligent RPA Cloud Factory** after testing and satisfactory automation results, the project needs to be exported. For doing this, Go to the **File | Export Project** option from the menu bar, as illustrated in the following screenshot:

Figure 10.12 – Menu option to export a project

Once the project is exported, a success message is displayed, as follows:

Figure 10.13 – Success message after exporting the project

You will then see a new folder called export created under the project folder and a .zip file is created under the export folder. The export filename includes the project version in the name. If an export file is already created with the current project version, you will see a message to allow you to overwrite the existing export file or to update the project to a new version, as illustrated in the following screenshot:

Figure 10.14 – Version confirmation message while exporting a project

This export file can then be imported to SAP Intelligent RPA Cloud Factory when needed for deployment. We will see more about project deployments in later chapters.

We have seen the actions that are possible at a project level. You will learn how and when these options can be used while automating a business process in upcoming chapters.

Summary

As a bot developer, you will use many of the different actions at the project level provided by Desktop Studio and available to you.

In this chapter, we have looked at creating a project as the first step to start with development, updating a project to include additional dependencies, and updating the project version. Although this chapter explains how to create a project, it doesn't really perform any automation tasks. As a best practice, ensure that the project details entered while creating a project are very relevant and unique to the process to understand the business process in scope for automation.

We also learned how a project can be archived to store or share the code with other developers and export the project for deployment. We will start with automation solution development by learning about declaring applications in the next chapter.

Questions

Here are some questions for you to test your knowledge of this chapter. The answers to these questions can be found at the back of this book, in the *Assessments* section:

1. Which options or actions are provided by SAP Intelligent RPA Desktop Studio at the project level?
2. How do you include additional library dependencies for a project?
3. When does a project version need an update?
4. What is the difference between exporting a project and archiving a project?

11

An Introduction to Technology Connectors

We created a project called `MyFirstProject` in the previous chapter. In this chapter, we will start learning about what **SAP Intelligent RPA** offers when it comes to capturing and declaring different types of applications that need to be automated. Any application that is used in a business process will be the target application while developing the automation solution. The automation target applications could contain many technologies, such as web applications that can be accessed using browsers or Windows applications. Similarly, many technologies can be used to develop Windows applications that will run as executables.

SAP Intelligent RPA provides a set of technology connectors to automate the automation target applications. We will discuss capturing and declaring applications and entities in the following chapters but first, we need to understand the technology connectors and how to use them for different types of applications.

In this chapter, we will cover the following topics:

- The **Win32** connector
- The **Web** connector
- The **UI Automation** connector
- The **SAP GUI** connector
- The **SAPUI5** and **S/4HANA** connector
- The **Java/SWG** connector
- The **HLLAPI** connector
- The **OCR** connector

By the end of this chapter, you will have a sound understanding of the five (Win32, Web, UI Automation, SAP GUI, and SAPUI5) technology connectors and where and how these connectors can be used. You will have also been introduced to the rest of the connectors. First, let's look at the various available technology connectors.

Technical requirements

- Desktop Studio installed on your workstation.
- Microsoft .NET framework 4.7
- Remote Tools Visual Studio 2019 for remote debugging
- Kdiff3 must be installed on your workstation. Kdiff3 is a source code comparison and merger tool that's used by SAP Intelligent RPA. Please refer to *Chapter 4*, *Setting Up SAP Intelligent RPA On-Premise Components*, for more details on the source code **compare** tool.
- An internet connection.
- A SAP Intelligent RPA supported browser and the SAP Intelligent RPA extension must be installed and enabled. Please refer to *Chapter 4*, *Setting Up SAP Intelligent RPA On-Premise Components*, for more details on browser extensions.
- SAP GUI version 7.5 or later must be installed.
- You must have access to SAP Server so that a connection can be made from SAP GUI. This is only required if you are automating any business processes; that is, you're using SAP as an automation target application.

Introduction to technology connectors

Before we start learning about the different technology connectors at our disposal, we will briefly look at the automation solution development sequence.

As with any automation solution development, we need to do the following:

1. Understand and document the business process and the target applications. All the applications that are involved in executing the business process are referred to as automation target applications.

2. Document the page transitions, along with each step and required interactions with elements on the page.

3. Prepare the sequence of steps to execute a business process.

4. Develop the solution using SAP Intelligent RPA.

5. Test and debug the automation solution for completeness and correctness.

6. Deploy the automation solution in the production environment.

As we can see, complete and clear documentation is the key to the success of the automation process. Once the documentation is complete, developers can use **SAP Intelligent RPA** to automate the business process.

Now, let's look at what **SAP Intelligent RPA** offers for automating a business process:

1. Create a project.

2. Capture and declare applications.

3. Capture and declare all the pages of an application that are involved in the business process.

4. Capture and declare the elements that are required to interact during the business process. These elements are captured from pages.

5. Prepare the workflow.

6. Generate the code. Edit or update the generated code for completeness.

7. Test and debug the project.

8. Deploy the project for the business team to use.

We created a project in *Chapter 10, Creating and Managing Projects*, so now, we need to start capturing the applications and pages. As you are aware, automation targets applications that need to interact during the business process's execution can be developed with any technology, such as the web, Windows, or SAP. Since capturing and executing the actions on the application or pages depends on the type of application, SAP Intelligent RPA provides eight (at the time of writing) different technology connectors to capture and define the applications for automating different types of applications.

These technology connectors are as follows:

- The **Win32** connector
- The **Web** connector
- The **UI Automation** connector
- The **SAP GUI** connector
- The **SAPUI5** and **S/4HANA** connector
- The **Java/SWG** connector
- The **HLLAPI** connector
- The **OCR** connector

Some of these technology connectors are available while capturing applications, but a few of them are only available for capturing the page within the application. The rest of this chapter covers the specific properties of these technology connectors and how to use a specific connector to capture and define various applications and pages using sample applications.

We will look at where and how these technology connectors are used to develop an automation solution. First, we will learn how to add a new application to our project.

Let's start by opening the `MyFirstProject` project, which we created in *Chapter 10, Creating and Managing Projects*, in **Desktop Studio**, and going to the **Explorer** perspective:

1. Click on the **+ Add Application** button in **The Project Tree** panel. The button is highlighted in the following screenshot. This will launch the **Capture Application** dialog. You can also launch the **Capture Application** dialog by selecting **Add a New Application...** from the **Context Menu** area:

Figure 11.1 – Adding a new application

You will see the following **Capture Application** dialog in **Desktop Studio**:

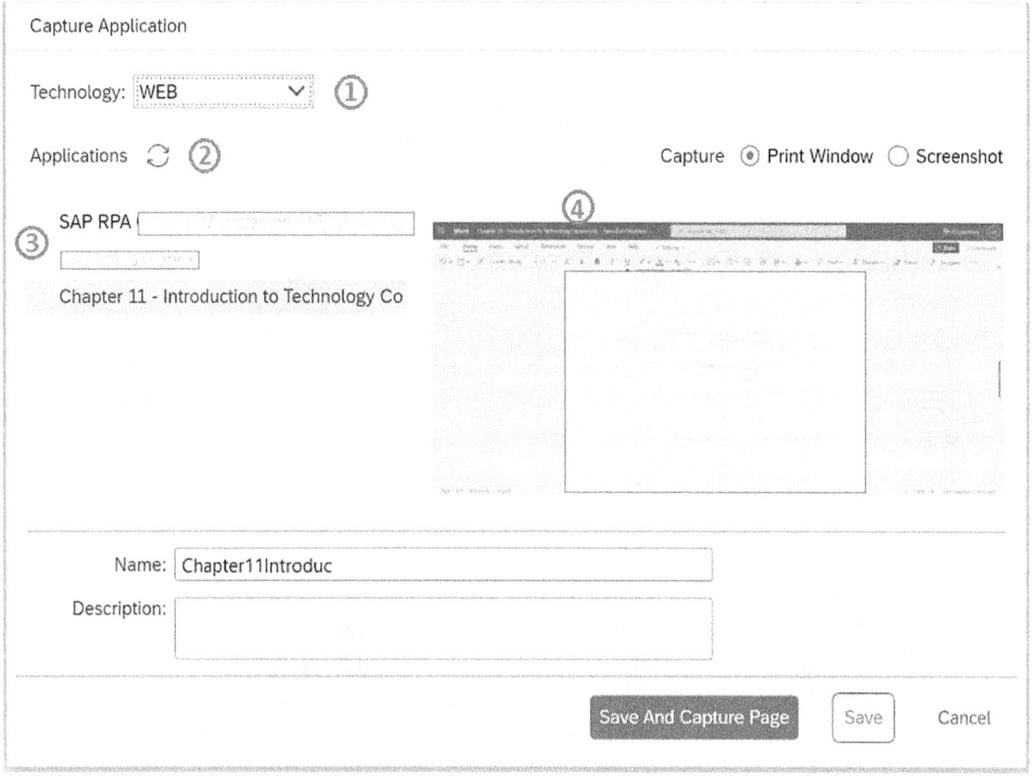

Capture Application

Technology: WEB ⌄ ①

Applications ↻ ②   Capture ⦿ Print Window ◯ Screenshot

③ SAP RPA

Chapter 11 - Introduction to Technology Co   ④

Name: Chapter11Introduc

Description:

Save And Capture Page   Save   Cancel

Figure 11.2 – The Capture Application dialog

2. Select the right options to capture the target application in the **Capture Application** dialog. Let's look at these options in more detail:

    - **Technology**: You will notice a combo box displaying a list of technologies. This list of technologies is shown in the following screenshot. You must select the correct technology for the application that needs to be captured:

Figure 11.3 – Technologies available while capturing applications

    - **Applications**: The **Capture Application** dialog displays all the applications that are already open in the system where **Desktop Studio** is running. If the application is not displayed for selection and capturing, click on the ↻ button to refresh the application list after opening the application. To capture a web application that's open in a browser, it should be in the active tab. It is always suggested to open the web application in a separate browser window before capturing the application.

    - **Application List**: This lists all the open applications in the system based on the technology that's selected for **Technology**. Choose different technologies to see the changes in the application list. An application can be listed with more than one technology. You need to select the right technology based on the activities to be performed on the application. If more than one web page is opened in the browser, the web application in the active tab alone will be listed in this panel. Ensure that the tab that the web application needs to be captured in is displayed as active and then refresh the application list to capture the required web application.

    - **Application Capture**: You will see the application screen captured by **Desktop Studio** in this area. Ensure that the captured screen is displaying the right application. If the screen capture is not correct, you will need to bring the application into the foreground and then select the application again so that the correct screen is captured.

3. Select either the **Save And Capture Page** button to save the application and proceed with the page capture or the **Save** button to save the application.

These steps are common for capturing any type of application, be it a Windows, web or SAP application. The only difference is that we will be selecting the technology based on the application that is being captured. Capturing the applications with the right technology connector is very important for identifying the controls to be used by the automation solution.

Now let's look at the various technology connectors that are available so that we can decide which to use for different types of applications.

The Win32 connector

This connector can be used to capture desktop applications. To capture a standard Windows application for automating, you need to select **WIN** from the **Technology** combo box while capturing the application.

We will try this connector by using the **Notepad** application, which is available in any Windows system. We will use the same MyFirstProject to capture the application.

Perform the following steps to start capturing the Notepad application:

1. Start the **Notepad** application.
2. Start **SAP Intelligent RPA Desktop Studio**.
3. Open the MyFirstProject project.
4. Go to the **Explorer** perspective.
5. Click the + **Add Application** button.
6. Select **Win** from the **Technology** combo box.
7. Select **Untitled-Notepad** from the application list. If the **Untitled-Notepad** application is not displayed in the application list for selection, then click on the refresh button after ensuring Notepad is open.

You will see the following **Capture Application** screen:

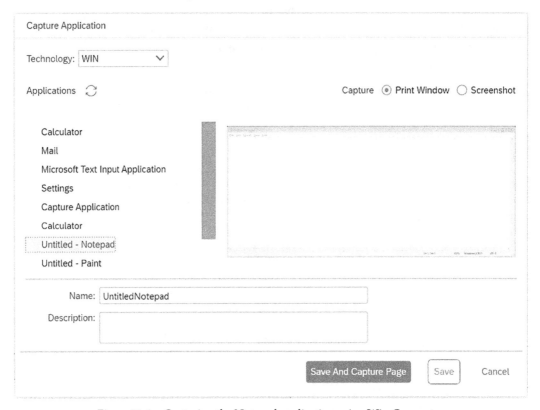

Figure 11.4 – Capturing the Notepad application using Win Connector

8. Click the **Save And Capture Page** button.

    You will see a new application named UntitledNotepad and that the **Capture Page** dialog is open:

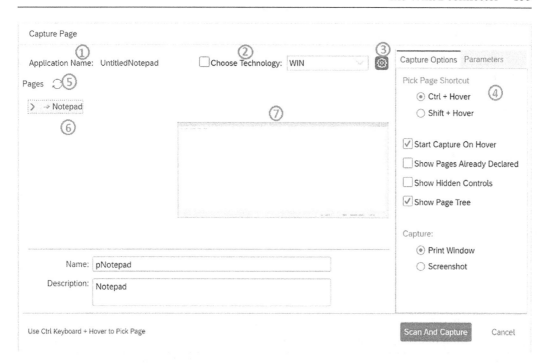

Figure 11.5 – The Capture Page dialog using Win Connector

9. Now, we must select some options in the **Capture Page** dialog. Let's look at the different components and the options that are available in the **Capture Page** dialog:

- **Application Name**: The name of the application from the **Explorer** perspective.

- **Choose Technology**: The list of technologies that be used at the page capture level. **Desktop Studio** provides options for capturing pages with either **WIN** or **WEB**. Selecting the **Choose Technology** checkbox allows us to change the technology for capturing the page. If a Windows application displays HTML data in the application, then that needs to be captured using **WEB**. We will use **WIN** for now.

- **Settings** ⚙ : This button can be used to display the page's **Capture Options**.

- **Capture Options**: Here, we can control how a page can be captured. We will look at these options and ways to capture multiple pages for applications later in this chapter.

- **Pages**: This dialog displays the pages of the application for which pages are being captured. If the page list is empty for selection and capturing, click on the ↻ button to refresh the page list after opening the application.

- **Page List**: Lists all the pages and elements of the application.

- **Page Capture**: Here, you will see the page screen that's been captured by **Desktop Studio**.

10. Once you've selected a page, click on the **Save And Capture** button to capture the page.

A new page will be added under the `UntitledNotepad` application in the **Explorer** perspective, as follows:

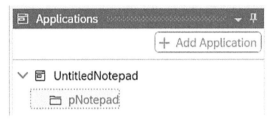

Figure 11.6 – The Notepad application and a page captured using Win connector

We will discuss applications, pages, and capturing the elements within pages in more detail in the next chapter. Now, let's explore how to use Web connector to capture an application and a page.

The Web connector

This connector is used for capturing and declaring HTML pages that are displayed in web browser tabs. Please note that a browser is a Windows application, so any dialog that's displayed by the browser can be captured as a desktop application using the Win32 connector. Web pages that are displayed by the browser are declared as `Web`.

We will use `https://www.packt.com` to capture and create a new web application in **MyFirstProject**.

SAP Intelligent RPA supports the following web browsers:

- Microsoft Edge
- Google Chrome
- Firefox
- Internet Explorer

Perform the following steps to capture the web application:

1. Start the browser application.

2. Navigate to `https://www.packt.com`.

3. Open the `MyFirstProject` project.

4. Go to the **Explorer** perspective.

5. Click the **+ Add Application** button.

6. Select **WEB** from the **Technology** combo box in the **Capture Application** dialog.

7. Select the application starting with **Packt** from the application list. If this is not displayed, click on the refresh button after ensuring `https://www.packt.com/` is open in your web browser.

8. Click the **Save And Capture Page** button.

9. In the **Capture Page** dialog, select the page name starting with **Packt**. Wait until the **Save And Capture** button is enabled. If this button is not enabled, try clicking the ❯ icon that's displayed next to the page.

10. Click the **Save And Capture** button. **SAP Intelligent RPA** will scan and read the complete **DOM** structure of the HTML page, so it might take a few seconds to capture the page. The total time it will take depends on the number of elements on the page. The **Capture Page** dialog will close after the page scan is complete.

You will now see an application and a page defined in the **Explorer** perspective, as follows:

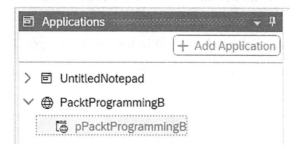

Figure 11.7 – The web application captured using Web connector

With that, we have captured a web application and a page using the **Web** connector. Ignore the fact that the new page we've captured is highlighted in red for now as we will discuss such page criteria in detail in the next chapter. For now, we will proceed with capturing more sample applications using the **UI Automation** connector.

The UI Automation connector

UI Automation is a standard protocol that was developed by Microsoft to automate applications that had been developed with the following technologies:

- Microsoft technologies such as **Win32**, **WinForm**, **WPF**, and **Silverlight**
- Any technology that supports **Microsoft Active Accessibility** (**MSAA**), such as **QT**

If a Windows application is captured with the **Win32** connector but does not allow you to select the elements that are required for automation, you can use this connector. We will learn more about element declaration in the next chapter.

Let's use Kdiff.exe to capture and create a new application in MyFirstProject using the **UI Automation** connector by performing the following steps:

1. Start Kdiff3.exe. Cancel the default dialog that is displayed in the **Kdiff3** application.
2. Open the MyFirstProject project, if it's not already open in **Desktop Studio**.
3. Go to the **Explorer** perspective.
4. Click the + **Add Application** button.
5. Select **UIAutomation** from the **Technology** combo box in the **Capture Application** dialog.
6. Select the **Kdiff3** application from the application list. If this is not displayed, click on the refresh button after ensuring that Kdiff3.exe is running in the system.
7. Click the **Save And Capture Page** button.
8. In the **Capture Page** dialog, select the **Window - KDiff3** page.

   You can look at the elements that have been captured on the page by clicking the ❯ icon next to this page:

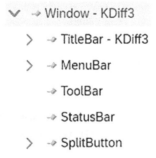

Figure 11.8 – Elements within the Kdiff3 page captured by the UI Automation connector

You can try capturing the same **Kdiff3** application using the **Win32** connector and see the difference between the elements that are captured by **SAP Intelligent RPA**:

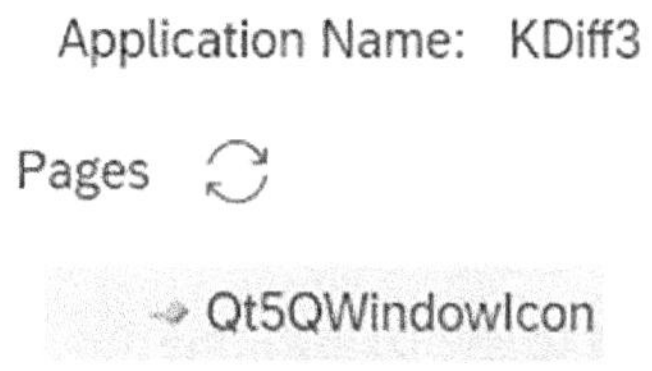

Application Name: KDiff3

Pages   ⟳

⇢ Qt5QWindowIcon

Figure 11.9 – Elements within the Kdiff3 page captured by Win Connector

You will notice that very few elements are captured when you capture the same **Kdiff3** application using the **Win32** connector. The reason for this is that the user interface for the **Kdiff3** application is developed with the Win32 (MS Windows), KDE, and QT technologies. So, to capture all the controls in this application, the right technology connector to use is the **UI Automation** connector.

You can try this on CALC.exe as another example to compare the differences between the **Win32** connector and the **UI Automation** connector.

9. Click the **Save And Capture** button. **SAP Intelligent RPA** will scan for and read the complete DOM structure of the **Kdiff3** application page. The **Capture Page** dialog will close after the page scan is complete and all the elements have been captured.

You will now see an application and a page defined in the **Explorer** perspective as follows:

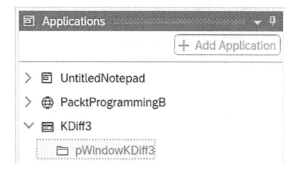

Figure 11.10 – The Kdiff3 application captured using the UI Automation connector

With that, we have captured the **Kdiff3** application using the **UI Automation** connector. Now, let's try using the **SAP GUI** connector to capture the SAP GUI application.

The SAP GUI connector

SAP GUI for Windows is an application that can be used to access SAP applications such as SAP ERP and SAP Business Suite. You can capture SAP applications using the **SAP GUI** connector. To automate a SAP GUI application as part of business process automation, **SAP Intelligent RPA** provides a specific connector called the **SAP GUI** connector.

SAP GUI connector is an extension to the **UI Automation** connector. In the previous section, you may have noticed that the **Capture Application** dialog does not list the **SAP GUI** connector. So, the SAP GUI application needs to be captured using the **UI Automation** connector and then you must select the **SAP GUI** connector from the **Capture Page** dialog. We will learn how to capture a page in SAP GUI in detail shortly.

Furthermore, note that scripting should be enabled in both SAP Client – that is, SAP GUI – and SAP Server before we can capture the SAP GUI applications to allow the automation solution to interact with the SAP application. By default, SAP disables scripting to help you make a conscious decision to enable scripting. In the following subsections, we will enable SAP scripting in the following two instances:

- Enabling SAP client-side scripting
- Enabling SAP server-side scripting

Let's discuss the steps that are required for each instance in detail.

Enabling SAP client-side scripting

By performing the following steps, you can enable client-side scripting in SAP GUI:

1. Launch the SAP GUI application; that is, SAPlogon.exe.
2. Go to the **Options…** menu.

   You can also select **SAP GUI Configuration (32-Bit)** from the control panel to open the SAP GUI options.
3. Expand **Accessibility & Scripting** in the left pane.
4. Select the **Scripting** option.
5. Check the **Enable scripting** checkbox in the right-hand pane. Please see the following screenshot for details of where to enable client-side scripting:

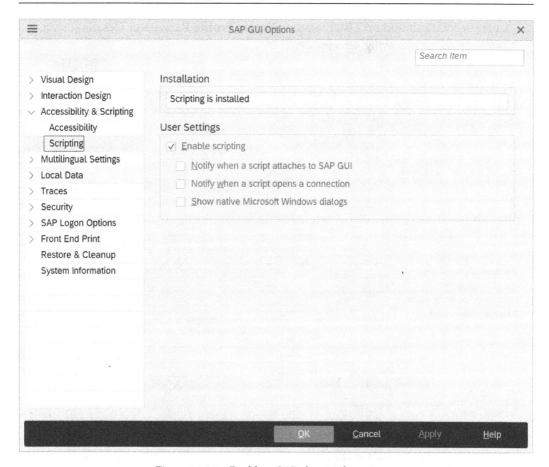

Figure 11.11 – Enabling SAP client-side scripting

6. Click the **Apply** button and then click the **OK** button to close this dialog.

That's it – scripting is now enabled on the client-side. Now, let's learn how to enable SAP server-side scripting.

Enabling SAP server-side scripting

By performing the following steps, you can enable server-side scripting in SAP GUI:

1. Launch the SAP GUI application and connect to SAP Server.

2. You will see the **SAP Easy Access** screen, where you need to enter a transaction code; that is, RZ11.

3. You will then see the **Maintain Profile Parameters** screen. Enter sapgui/user_ scripting as the parameter name and click the **Display** button.

4. **Current Value** should be **TRUE** on the **Display Profile Parameter Details** screen, as shown in the following screenshot:

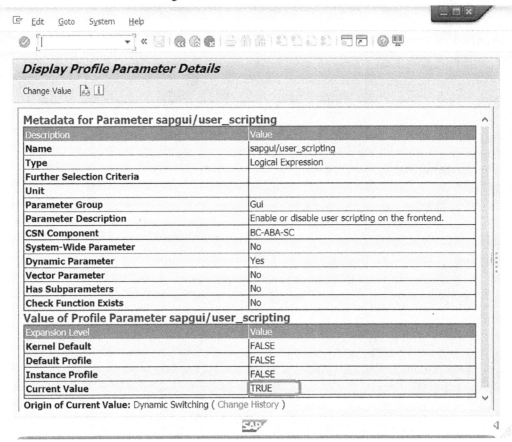

Figure 11.12 – The user_scripting parameter's status in the server

5. If this value is **FALSE**, then you will need to click on **Change Value**. If you do not have access to edit the value, then please connect to a SAP administrator who can change this value.

6. Set **New Value** to TRUE on the **Change Parameter Value** screen, as shown here:

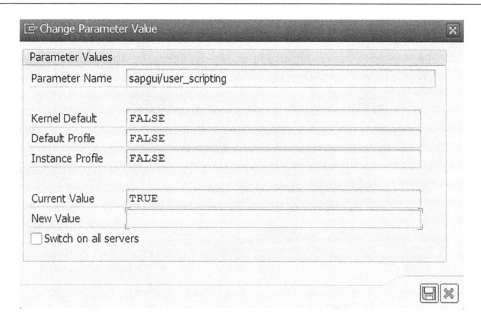

Figure 11.13 – Changing the value of the user_scripting parameter

7.   Click the **Save** 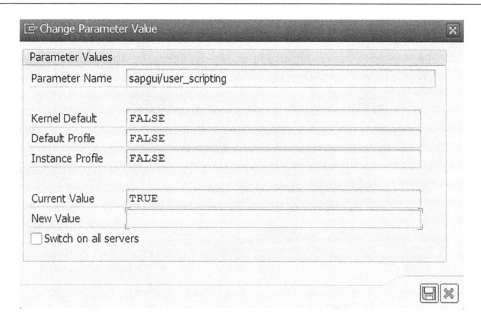 button to save the new value.

Server-side scripting is now enabled. Log back into SAP Server to confirm its status before starting following the next set of steps to capture the **SAP GUI** application using the **SAP GUI** connector in **Desktop Studio**.

Now, let's capture and declare the **SAP GUI** application in **Desktop Studio**:

1.   Start the `saplogin.exe` application.

2.   Open the `MyFirstProject` project, if it's not already open in **Desktop Studio**.

3.   Go to the **Explorer** perspective.

4.   Click the + **Add Application** button.

5.   Select **UIAutomation** under the **Technology** combo box in the **Capture Application** dialog. Notice that there is no **SAP GUI** connector available here to select. We need to capture the SAP GUI application using the **UI Automation** connector.

6.   Select the **SAP Logon** application from the application list. Please note that the application's name might also have a version, such as *760*. So, for example, the application name will be **SAPLogon760** if you are using this version. If this is not displayed, click on the refresh button after ensuring that `saplogon.exe` is running in the system.

7. Click the **Save** button.

    You will notice that a new application has been added in the **Applications** panel with no pages under it, as shown in the following screenshot:

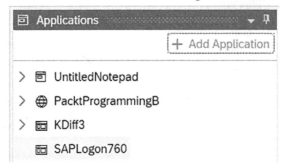

Figure 11.14 – The SAP Logon application captured with the UI Automation connector

Before we start capturing pages under the SAPlogon application, we will open multiple pages so that we can capture these pages with different connectors.

8. In the **SAP Logon** application, define a connection to **SAP Server** and open that connection. You will be presented with the following page, which allows you to enter credentials for the server:

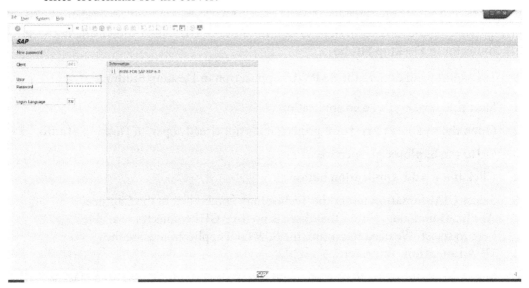

Figure 11.15 – SAP allowing you to log into SAP Server

You will also notice that two different applications are running in the system now:

Figure 11.16 – Two SAP applications running in the system

Now that two screens are open, let's proceed with capturing the pages for the **SAP Logon** application.

9. Go to the **Desktop Studio Explorer** perspective and right-click on the **SAPLogon760** project. Select **Capture a New Page...** from the context menu:

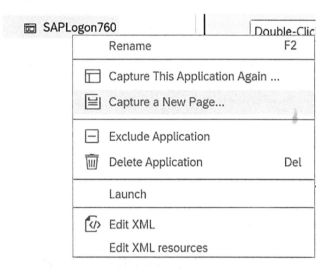

Figure 11.17 – Using the context menu to create a page under the application

10. The **Capture Page** dialog will be displayed. The default display will look as follows:

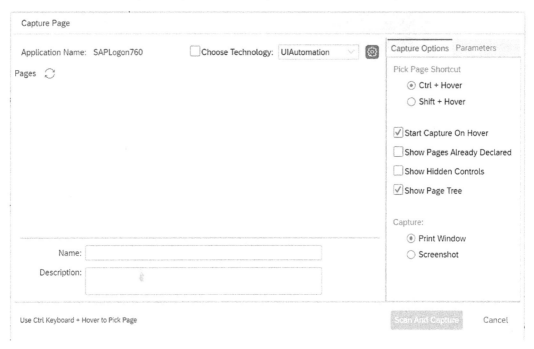

Figure 11.18 – The Capture Page's default display

11. Refresh the page list by clicking the ↻ button; keeping the **SAP Login** page in the foreground ensures the page capture is taken correctly.

12. You will notice only one entry in the page list that you can select; that is, **Window - SAP Logon 760**. Select **Choose Technology** from the **Capture Page** dialog and change the technology to **SAPGUI**:

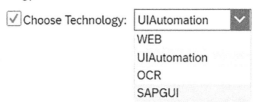

Figure 11.19 – Choosing a technology in the Capture Page dialog

13. Refresh the page list by clicking ↻. Keeping the **SAP Login** page in the foreground ensures the page is captured properly. The page list will change and show that the **GuiMainWindow - SAP** page can be captured.

> **Note**
>
> The page list in the **Capture Page** dialog depends on the technology that is selected. If there is a page in the application that can be captured with the selected technology, then you will be able to choose it in this dialog.

14. Click the **Save And Capture** button.

15. You need to capture both pages by selecting **Capture Dialog** from the context menu for the application.

    You will now see that two different pages are defined in the **Explorer** perspective under the **SAPLogon760** application, as shown here:

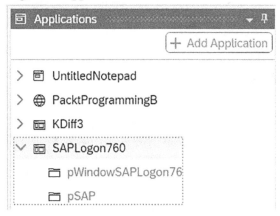

Figure 11.20 – The SAP GUI application and two pages captured using two different connectors

With that, we have learned how to capture the SAP GUI application and the SAP pages using the **SAP GUI** connector. You can practice capturing multiple pages by opening different pages in the **SAP Logon** application. Now, let's start understanding the SAPUI5 technology connector that's provided by **SAP Intelligent RPA**.

The SAPUI5 and S/4HANA connector

SAPUI5 connector is an extension of the Web connector. SAPUI5 is a framework that provides a list of libraries for building web applications. Any SAPUI5 application or web page can be captured as a standard web application. Even if the **Web** connector is used to capture SAPUI5, SAP Intelligent RPA identifies the SAP pages and SAP controls and provides methods that are specific for automating custom SAPUI5 controls. These additional methods will be available while you're developing the workflow and code. There will be no difference while capturing the page.

We will use the `https://sapui5.hana.ondemand.com/#/demoapps` application to capture a new web application in `MyFirstProject`. You can also try capturing any other application that's been developed with SAPUI5, such as **SAP SuccessFactors**, if you have access to the **SuccessFactors** instance.

Perform the following steps to capture an application that was developed using the SAPUI5 technology:

1. Start up your browser.

2. Navigate to `https://sapui5.hana.ondemand.com/#/demoapps`.

3. Open any one of the demo applications provided here, such as `Manage Products` or `Employee Directory`.

4. Open the `MyFirstProject` project.

5. Go to the **Explorer** perspective.

6. Click the **+ Add Application** button.

7. Select **WEB** from the **Technology** combo box in the **Capture Application** dialog.

8. Select the demo application that was launched from the application list. If this is not displayed, click on the refresh button after ensuring that the application you selected is open in your web browser.

9. Click the **Save And Capture Page** button.

10. In the **Capture Page** dialog, select the demo application. Wait until the **Save And Capture** button is enabled.

11. Click the **Save And Capture** button. **SAP Intelligent RPA** will scan and read the complete DOM structure of the HTML page, so it might take a few seconds to capture the page. The total time it will take depends on the number of elements on the page. The **Capture Page** dialog will close after the page scan is complete.

You will now see a new application and a page defined in the **Explorer** perspective as follows:

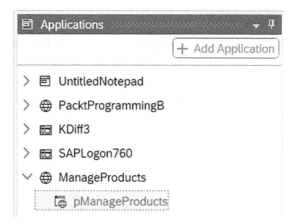

Figure 11.21 – The SAPUI5 application captured using Web connector

With that, we've learned how to capture an application that's been developed using SAPUI5. You can practice capturing multiple demo applications provided by SAP.

There are more technology connectors provided by **SAP Intelligent RPA** than the ones we covered here. We will provide a brief description of these connectors over the following three sections. You can try these connectors out based on the availability of different types of applications.

The Java/SWG connector

This connector is used for defining applications and entities for a desktop application that's been developed with Java and its related technologies. Please note that all Java applications will run as `Java.exe` or `javaw.exe` with a main execution `entry` class as a parameter. We need to identify the actual `.exe` that is running and the main entry class while defining the criteria for the application. We will discuss such criteria in more detail in *Chapter 12, Capturing and Declaring Applications, Pages, and Items*.

The HLLAPI connector

HLLAPI is an IBM API that's used to communicate with mainframe applications such as AS400 and terminal emulators. The mainframe applications that are running in a web terminal emulator must be captured using the **Web** connector. This connector can be used for the mainframe applications that are running in a desktop terminal emulator. Please note that this connector requires the HLLAPI protocol to be enabled in the terminal emulator so that you can control the application. Entities within the mainframe application are identified by the position of the element.

The OCR connector

Surface automation is a technique where image recognition and OCR are used to automate user interfaces whose underlying technologies aren't accessible by **SAP Intelligent RPA**. If an application is running in a virtual machine or Citrix environment, **SAP Intelligent RPA** will not be able to read the page elements. In this case, surface automation can be used to perform actions on the application by identifying the elements visually.

Now, let's summarize what we learned in this chapter.

Summary

In this chapter, we learned about capturing applications using a wide variety of connectors. We also learned that the steps we must follow to capture an application are almost the same for each controller, except that you will need to select the right technology connector while capturing the page. Using the wrong technology connector to capture the application might cause issues with capturing the required controls in the pages, so you must ensure that a proper technology connector is used to capture the application.

After capturing and defining the applications and pages, we need to identify the controls or elements in each of the pages that are participating in the business process; that is, the applications, pages, and elements that must be controlled so that we can execute the automated business process to be identified and declared before we design the process workflow.

In the next chapter, we will learn about how to identify elements.

Questions

Here are some questions for you to test your knowledge of this chapter. The answers to these questions can be found at the back of this book, in the *Assessments* section:

1. Why are some technology connectors not available for capturing the application?
2. I captured an application, but the captured screen does not display a proper screenshot. What should I do to get a proper screenshot of the application or page?
3. Why is the **Save And Capture** button on the **Capture Page** dialog taking a long time to become enabled?

12

Capturing and Declaring Applications, Pages, and Items

In the previous chapter, you saw how to capture applications and pages using the technology connectors provided by **SAP Intelligent RPA**. Once an application or page is captured and declared, we need to define the criteria for each application and page so the SAP Intelligent RPA can identify them uniquely. These criteria are used by **SAP Intelligent RPA Desktop Studio** at development time and by the **Desktop Agent** at runtime to recognize the application or page that is included in the workflow to perform actions.

In this chapter, we will expand on this knowledge by considering the vendor invoice-posting business process using the **FB60** SAP transaction code on the SAP server. We will gain knowledge on the following topics:

- Starting your first automation project
- Capturing applications and pages
- Defining the criteria for applications and pages
- Defining UI elements/controls
- Variable declaration

By the end of this chapter, you will have a project created with all the pages, subpages, and controls captured and declared. How these elements are used to create a workflow will be detailed in the forthcoming chapters.

Let's first create a project.

Technical requirements

- Desktop Studio installed on your workstation
- An internet connection
- The SAP GUI version 7.5 or later installed
- Access to the SAP server so that a connection can be made from the SAP GUI to the FB60 transaction code on the SAP server

Starting your first automation project

Before proceeding further, let's first understand the vendor invoice-posting business process.

In this process, the bot needs to perform the following steps:

1. Start the **SAP Logon** application.
2. Select an existing connection to the SAP server from the **SAP Logon** page. The **SAP** page to enter the credentials to the SAP server is displayed.
3. Enter the credentials on the **SAP** page and log in to the SAP server. This will take you to the **SAP Easy Access** page.
4. Enter the FB60 SAP transaction code on the **SAP Easy Access** page to navigate to the **Enter Vendor Invoice** page.

5. On the **Enter Vendor Invoice** page, we will fill in the details of the different controls by navigating to multiple tabs/subpages and then post the vendor invoice. The details we will enter for invoice posting are **Vendor**, **Invoice Date**, and **Amount** in the **Basic data** tab. Then, navigate to the **Tax** tab to enter the tax code. We will also fill in the **G/L acct** and **Amount in doc.curr.** fields on the **Enter Vendor Invoice** page.

6. Exit the **Enter Vendor invoice** page by clicking the **Exit** button.

7. Exit the **SAP Easy Access** page by clicking the **Log-off** button.

8. Close the **SAP Logon** application.

As you can see from the previous steps, this business process navigates to multiple pages and accesses different controls to action, such as entering data in a control or clicking a button. We will perform activities step by step, enabling you to have the application, pages, and controls captured and declared by navigating through each page as needed.

Now, we will start the development of the automation solution by creating a project named **Vendor Invoice Posting**.

The creation of the project is detailed in *Chapter 10, Creating and Managing Projects*:

1. In the menu bar, go to **File | New Project...** or press *Ctrl + N* to create a new project.

2. In the **New Project** dialog, enter the details as follows:

    1. Enter Vendor Invoice Posting in the **Project Name field**.

    2. Enter SAP - FB60 in the **Title field**.

    3. Keep the **Project Template** selection as it is to create the project using the latest project template.

    4. Enter Vendor Invoice Posting in the **Client Name field**.

    5. Keep the default **Version** value as **1.0**.

    6. We will keep **Date** as the current date.

    7. Enter SAP intelligent RPA Project for automating SAP FB60 transactions in the **Comments field**.

    8. Specify the location where the new project is to be created.

The filled **New Project** dialog will look as follows:

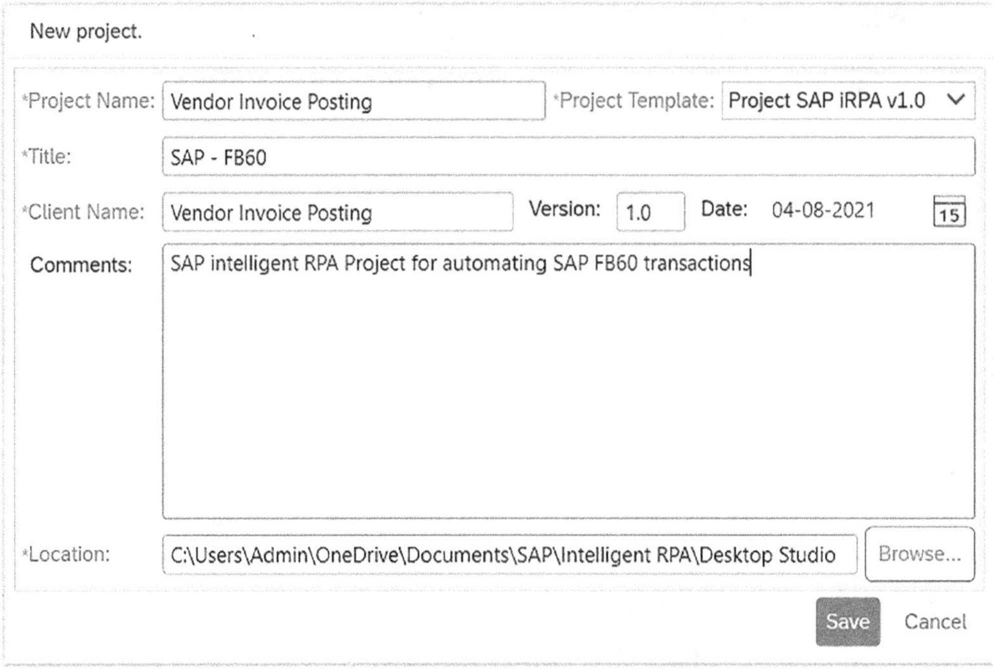

New project.

*Project Name:	Vendor Invoice Posting	*Project Template: Project SAP iRPA v1.0 ∨
*Title:	SAP - FB60	
*Client Name:	Vendor Invoice Posting	Version: 1.0 Date: 04-08-2021 [15]
Comments:	SAP intelligent RPA Project for automating SAP FB60 transactions	

*Location: C:\Users\Admin\OneDrive\Documents\SAP\Intelligent RPA\Desktop Studio   Browse...

Save   Cancel

Figure 12.1 – Details that are entered while creating the project

Click on the **Save** button.

Desktop Studio then will create a project in the folder location specified in the **New Project** dialog. We are now ready to start capturing the application from the **Explorer** perspective.

Capturing applications and pages

Our business process requires the SAP Logon application to be started and for us to execute a sequence of steps that includes navigating multiple pages. We will start with capturing the application. For this, we need to first start the SAP Logon application on the system/workstation where the automation solution is being developed.

Capturing SAP Logon application

Execute the following steps to capture the SAP GUI application:

1. Start the saplogin.exe application. Please refer to the *The SAP GUI connector* section in *Chapter 11, An Introduction to Technology Connectors*, to ensure that the scripting is enabled at both the SAP client and server.

2. Go to the **Explorer** perspective in Desktop Studio.

3. Click the **+ Add Application** button.

4. Select **UIAutomation** as the technology in the **Capture Application** dialog.

5. Select the **SAP Logon** application from the application list. If the SAP GUI application is not displayed in the list, click on the refresh button after ensuring that `saplogon.exe` is running on the system.

6. Click the **Save** button.

Your **Explorer** perspective will now have the **SAPLogon760** application declared. The version number in the application name is the same as the version of the SAP GUI on the machine where the application is being captured. Let's start with capturing the pages in the SAP GUI application that are required to execute our business process steps.

Capturing the SAP Logon application pages

Before we start capturing the pages, we will first explore the options that Desktop Studio provides to capture pages.

First, you need to be on the same page that is to be captured. So, you will be navigating to all the pages manually and capturing each page:

1. If you have clicked the **Save And Capture Page** button in **the Capture Application** dialog, the **Capture Page** dialog will be opened automatically. If you want to capture more pages, select the **Capture a New Page...** menu item from the context menu.

2. The **Capture Page** dialog allows you to choose technology connectors to capture a page, depending on the technology connector used for application capture.

3. You can select a page from the **Pages** list in the **Capture Page** dialog. You can also press the *Ctrl* key and hover the mouse over the page to be captured. The **Capture Page** dialog allows you to change this option to *Shift + Hover* instead of *Ctrl + Hover*.

4. When capturing the page, Desktop Studio highlights the pages that are being captured in red so that proper page capturing is ensured.

The following screenshot shows the initial display of the **Capture Page** dialog when selected:

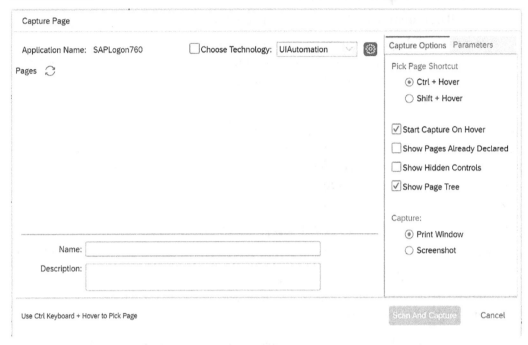

Figure 12.2 – The Capture Page default display

We will now start capturing all the pages required for each step in our business process, as discussed in the *Starting your first automation project* section in this chapter. Let's follow each business process step and capture the pages required to be transitioned.

The first page that needs to be captured for the **SAP Logon** application is the page that selects a connection. So, we will start by capturing the **SAP Logon** application page.

Capturing the SAP Logon page

Execute the following steps to capture the **SAP Logon** application page, which will be the first page under the **SAPLogon760** application:

1. Go to the **Explorer** perspective in Desktop Studio.
2. Start the `saplogin.exe` application if it's not already started.
3. Select **Capture a New Page...** from the context menu by right-clicking on the **SAPLogon760** application.
4. In the **Capture Page** dialog, click on the ⟳ (refresh) button to get the available page list for selection.

5. Select **Window - SAP Logon 760** from the page list. The **Capture Page** dialog will look like the following screenshot, with a page preview showing the SAP Logon window:

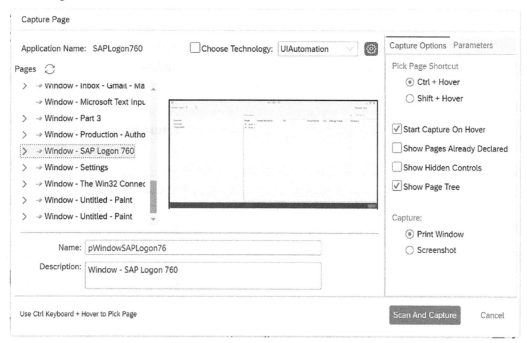

Figure 12.3 – The Capture Page dialog with SAP Logon page capture display

6. Click on the **Scan and Capture** button. You will now see that a page is added to the **Explorer** perspective, as shown in the following screenshot:

Figure 12.4 – The SAP Logon page captured under the SAP Logon application

We have now captured our first page, named pWindowSPLogon76. We will now move on to capturing the next page.

Capturing the SAP page

The next page to capture is the SAP Login screen where users can enter credentials on the SAP server:

1. To capture this page, open the page by selecting any available connection in the **SAP Logon** application and click on the **Log On** button to display the **SAP Login** page.

2. Select **Capture a New Page...** from the context menu by right-clicking the **SAPLogon760** application in the **Explorer** perspective to capture a new page.

   Note that all the pages to be captured from now on are SAP screens, so we need to ensure that the **SAPGUI** technology is selected in the **Capture Page** dialog while capturing the pages.

3. In the **Capture Page** dialog, check the **Choose Technology** checkbox, change the selection to **SAPGUI**, and click on the refresh button. The **Capture Page** dialog will display **GUIMainWindow - SAP** to capture the SAP Login page. The dialog display will look like the following screenshot:

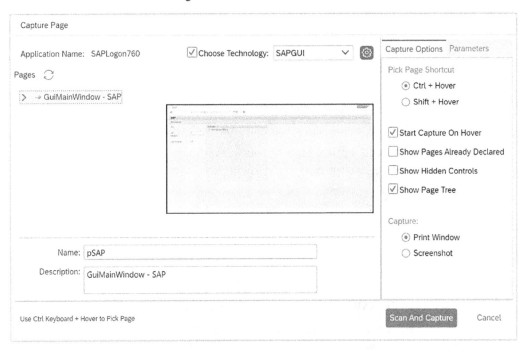

Figure 12.5 – The SAP Login page captured under the SAP Logon application

4. Click on the **Scan and Capture** button. You will now see that the SAP page is added to the **Explorer** perspective, as shown in the following screenshot:

Figure 12.6 – The SAP Login page captured under the SAP Logon application

We have captured the page required to enter the SAP credentials. Once we are logged in, we will be presented with the **SAP Easy Access** page where we need to enter the SAP transaction code. Let's now capture the **SAP Easy Access** page.

Capturing the SAP Easy Access page

Execute the following steps to capture the **SAP Easy Access** page:

1. Enter your SAP server credentials and log in to the server on the **SAP Login** page to get the **SAP Easy Access** page. This page is shown in the following screenshot:

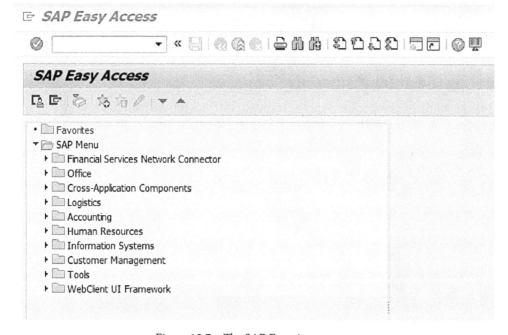

Figure 12.7 – The SAP Easy Access page

2. Select the **Capture a New Page...** menu item from the context menu by right-clicking on the **SAPLogon760** application in the **Explorer** perspective to capture a new page.

3. In the **Capture Page** dialog, check the **Choose Technology** checkbox, change the selection to **SAPGUI**, and then click on the refresh button. The **Capture Page** dialog will display **GuiMainWindow - SAP Easy Access** in the page list. Select this page to preview the page capture.

4. Click on the **Scan and Capture** button. You will now see that the **SAP Easy Access** page is added to the **Explorer** perspective, as shown in the following screenshot:

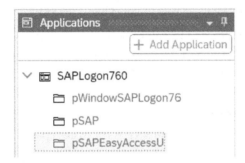

Figure 12.8 – The SAP Easy Access page captured under the SAP Logon application

The three pages that we have captured so far are standard in automating any business process that uses SAP as a target business application. Now, we will capture the pages that are needed to complete the business process for the FB60 transaction code.

Capturing the Enter Vendor Invoice page

We are now ready to capture the pages specific to the SAP transaction that we want to perform. Execute the following steps to capture the pages displayed for the FB60 transaction code:

1. On the **SAP Easy Access** page, enter the FB60 transaction code, as shown in the following screenshot, and press *Enter* or click the green tick button:

Figure 12.9 – The SAP Easy Access page captured under the SAP Logon application

2. You will be presented with the **Enter Vendor Invoice** screen, where you need to enter the invoice details for submission. If this is your first access to the SAP server, you will be asked to enter a company code before this page can be displayed:

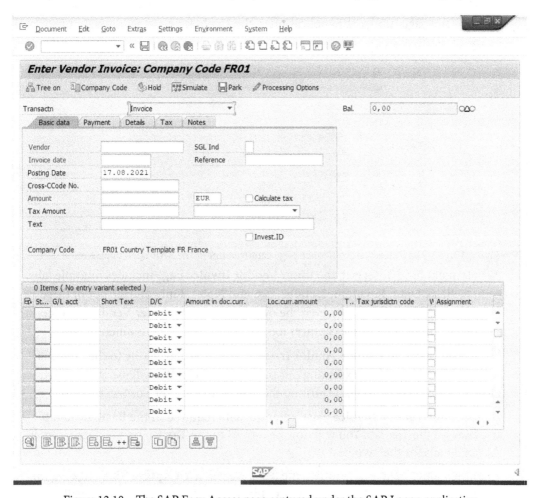

Figure 12.10 – The SAP Easy Access page captured under the SAP Logon application

3. We will follow the same steps as the **SAP Easy Access** page to capture this page. In the **Capture Page** dialog, change the technology to **SAPGUI**, select **GuiMainWindow - Enter Vendor Invoice** in the page list after refreshing it, and click on the **Scan and Capture** button. You will now see that a new page is added to the pages under the application in the **Explorer** view, as shown in the following screenshot:

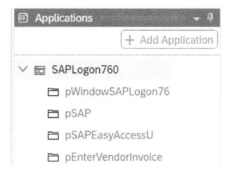

Figure 12.11 – The Enter Vendor Invoice page captured under the SAP Logon application

As you might have observed, the **Enter Vendor Invoice** page includes multiple tabs, namely, **Basic Data**, **Payment**, **Details**, **Tax**, and **Notes**. Only one tab out of these five is displayed at a time. However, the overall page is still **Enter Vendor Invoice**. So, we need to have multiple captures for this page navigating to different tabs.

We will re-capture the **Enter Vendor Invoice** page after navigating to the tabs that require user inputs while executing our business process. We will use the updated **Basic Data** and **Tax** tabs while posting the vendor invoice for our business process.

4. On the **Enter Vendor Invoice** page, enter the data required in the **Basic Data** tab and click on the **Tax** tab. You will now be moved to the **Tax** tab on the page to enter the tax details for the invoice.

5. To capture another screen for the same page, we will use **Capture This Page Again** on the context menu of the page in the **Explorer** perspective. This option will be available for pages that are already captured:

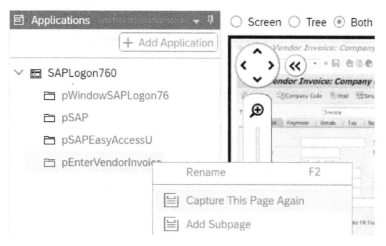

Figure 12.12 – The context menu option to capture multiple screens for the same page

6. In the **Capture Page** dialog, ensure that the technology is still **SAPGUI** and click on the **Scan and Capture** button after selecting **GuiMainWindow - Enter Vendor Invoice** from the page list.

7. As we want to keep both the screen captures for this page, ensure that you select **No** in the confirmation dialog to replace the existing capture:

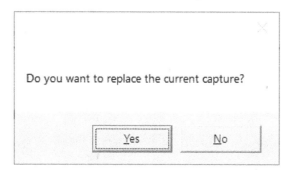

Figure 12.13 – Confirmation to replace the existing capture

8. You will now see two page captures available for the same page in the **Explorer** perspective. You can select the page capture by clicking the numbers displayed in the **Explorer** perspective when this page is selected.

Figure 12.14 – The display for multiple captures for the same page

Observe the difference between the two captures of the pages. You will see only the difference in the **Tab** area as the rest of the controls are the same for both screens. To handle the same page, which has multiple displays, SAP Intelligent RPA provides an option to define subpages. In this type of scenario, where a part page is changed based on a user selection, the area within the page that is being changed can be defined as a subpage. Let's learn how to define a subpage for a page in the following steps. We will define two subpages for the **Basic data** and **Tax** tabs that update as part of our vendor invoice-posting business process.

There are multiple ways to add a subpage to an existing page in the **Explorer** view – one option is to select **Add Subpage** from the context menu of the page in the **Explorer** perspective and follow the same steps as defining a page. Another option is to use the source tree for the page capture. We will use the latter option to define our two subpages.

Capturing the Basic data subpage

Let's start with capturing the first subpage displayed as the **Basic data** tab:

1. In the **Explorer** perspective, select the **Both** radio button in the screen capture area to display both the screen capture and the source associated with the screen capture. The source tree displays the complete DOM structure of the page and allows you to navigate to the required control for selection.

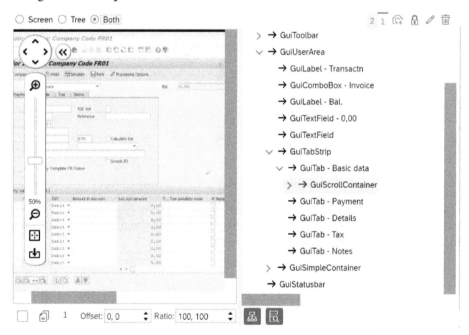

Figure 12.15 – The screen capture area with Both selected

2. Ensure that you have selected the first screen capture and then navigate to **GUITab – Basic data**, as shown in the preceding screenshot.

3. Right-click on **GUIScrollContainer** under **GUITab - Basic data** and select the new **Create New Page** option.

Figure 12.16 – The context menu to add a Basic data subpage

4. A subpage called **pGuiScrollContainer** has been added under the **pEnterVendorInvoice** page, as shown in the following screenshot:

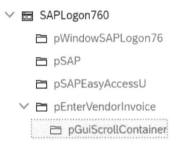

Figure 12.17 – A new subpage was added under the page

5. We will rename the **pGuiScrollContainer** page to **pGuiBasicData** by selecting the page and pressing the *F2* shortcut key.

We have captured one subpage called **pGuiBasicData**. We will now proceed to capture the **Tax** tab as a subpage.

Capturing the Tax subpage

We will now capture our second subpage from the **Tax** tab. Note that the steps are the same as those used to capture the **pGuiBasicData** subpage, except that the node we select to capture this subpage in the **Source Tree Display** panel is different. Execute the following steps to capture this page:

1. Select **pEnterVendorInvoice** in the resource tree of the **Explorer** perspective and select the second screen capture in the screen capture area to capture the **Tax** tab as a subpage.

Figure 12.18 – The second screen capture is selected in the screen capture area

2. Navigate to **GUITab - Tax** in the source tree. Right-click on **GUIScrollContainer** under **GUITab - Tax** and select the new **Create New Page** option, as shown in the following screenshot:

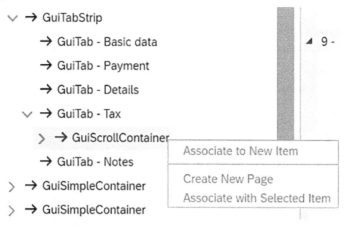

Figure 12.19 – The context menu to add a Tax subpage

3. A subpage called **pGuiScrollContainer** has been added under the **pEnterVendorInvoice** page.

4. We will rename the **pGuiScrollContainer** page to **pGuiTax** by selecting the page and pressing the *F2* shortcut key. By the end of this step, the **Applications** panel in the **Explorer** perspective should look like the following screenshot:

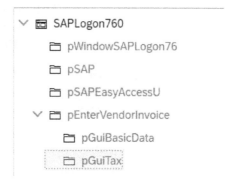

Figure 12.20 – The Applications panel with the subpage added under a page

We have captured all the pages required to execute the business process. Once the details have been entered and the invoice has been successfully posted, exit the **Enter Vendor Invoice** page. Let's now capture the screen to confirm we have exited the editing of the **Enter Vendor Invoice** page.

Capturing the Exit confirmation page

We need to confirm the exit of the **Enter Vendor Invoice** page after we have posted the vendor invoice. Execute the following steps to capture the **Exit confirmation** page:

1. Press the *Shift + F3* shortcut on the **Enter Vendor Invoice** screen to exit the invoice editing. SAP displays a confirmation dialog when exiting editing, as shown in the following screenshot:

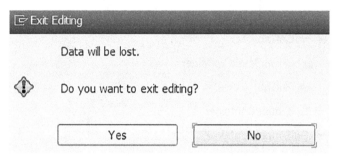

Figure 12.21 – The Exit Editing confirmation dialog of the vendor invoice

2. We will follow the same steps that are used to capture other SAP pages. Go to the **Explorer** perspective in Desktop Studio and select **Capture a New Page...** from the context menu by right-clicking the **SAPLogon760** application.

3. In the **Capture Page** dialog, check the **Choose Technology** checkbox, change the selection to **SAPGUI**, and then click on the refresh button. The **Capture Page** dialog will display **GuiModalWindow - Exit Editing** in the page list. Select this page and click on the **Scan and Capture** button. A new page with the name **pExitEditing** will appear under the **SAPLogon760** application.

After exiting the **Enter Vendor Invoice** page, we will be logging off from the SAP server by clicking the logoff button on the **SAP Easy Access** page and confirming we have logged off by clicking the **Yes** button in the **Log Off** confirmation dialog.

Capturing the Log Off confirmation page

We need to confirm logging off from the SAP server. Execute the following steps to capture the **Log Off** confirmation page:

1. Click on **Yes** in the **Exit Editing** dialog to close the screen. We will then be redirected to the **SAP Easy Access** page. We will then capture the **Log Off** confirmation dialog to log off from the SAP server.

2. Press the *Shift + F3* shortcut on the **SAP Easy Access** screen to log off from the SAP server. SAP displays a confirmation dialog to log off, as shown in the following screenshot:

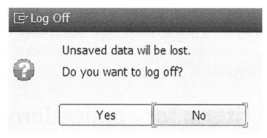

Figure 12.22 – The Log Off confirmation dialog from the SAP Easy Access page

3. Go to the **Explorer** perspective in Desktop Studio, and then select **Capture a New Page...** from the context menu by the **SAPLogon760** application.

4. In the **Capture Page** dialog, check the **Choose Technology** checkbox and change the selection to **SAPGUI**, and then click on the refresh button. The **Capture Page** dialog will display **GuiModalWindow - Log Off** in the page list. Select this page and click on the **Scan and Capture** button. A new page with the name **pLogOff** will appear under the **SAPLogon760** application.

After executing all the steps, you will have six pages captured in the **Explorer** perspective and two subpages under the **pEnterVendorInvoice** page in the **Explorer** perspective, as shown in the following screenshot:

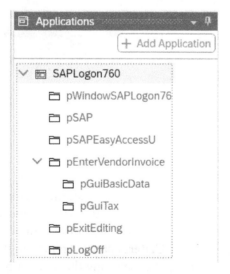

Figure 12.23 – The list of pages captured for executing the Vendor Invoice Posting process

By now, we have captured all the pages that are required to automate our business process. Note that all pages in the **Explorer** perspective are currently displayed in red, which means there are no criteria defined for these pages yet, so SAP Intelligent RPA can uniquely identify them.

The criteria should be unique to each application, page, and control, so SAP Intelligent RPA can recognize the items while running the automation solution. We will discuss defining the criteria for pages next.

Defining the criteria for applications and pages

We have captured one application and multiple pages; we will now start with defining the criteria for the application and the pages. As discussed in *Chapter 9, Desktop Studio Perspectives*, Desktop Studio provides the **Criteria** panel in the **Explorer** perspective, which we need to use to define the criteria for each item. The data captured by Desktop Studio for each item is available in the **Captured Data** panel, which we can use to define the criteria. Let's first look at the **Criteria** panel and the different actions available in this panel. Data displayed in these panels is specific to the item that is selected in the **Applications** panel, so the criteria are specific to the item.

Defining the criteria for the SAPLogon760 application

The following screenshot shows the **Criteria** and **Captured Data** panels for the **SAP Logon** application when the **SAPLogon760** application is selected in the **Applications** panel:

Figure 12.24 – The Criteria and Captured Data panels for the SAP Logon application

The criteria can be updated by double-clicking any parameter from the **Captured Data** panel. For example, to add the application title to the criteria, double-click on the **TITLE** item in the **Captured Data** panel. Alternatively, select the item in the **Captured Data** panel and click on the + button in the **Criteria** panel. An item in the criteria can be deleted by simply clicking the *Del* key after selecting the item, or by clicking the – button in the **Criteria** panel.

> **Important Note**
> The items in the **Criteria** panel can be repeated, which means we can add **TITLE** multiple times to the **Criteria** panel.

The rule that SAP Intelligent RPA follows to identify an item is to match all the criteria defined. If both **EXE** and **TITLE** are added to criteria, SAP Intelligent RPA identifies the applications that match both the conditions. However, if the same criteria are used multiple times, then SAP Intelligent RPA checks for matching with at least one criterion. So, if **TITLE** is added multiple times with different values, SAP Intelligent RPA matches the application title with one of the **TITLE** criteria. Consider the following criteria defined for the SAP Logon application:

Figure 12.25 – Multiple criteria defined for the SAP Logon application

In this case, SAP Intelligent RPA identifies any **SAPLOGON.exe** application that has a title of either SAP Logon 750 or SAP Logon 760. This way, we can handle applications that include a specific application version in the title. There are advanced options to define the unique criteria for the items that are discussed in upcoming chapters.

After defining the criteria for the application, we will proceed with defining the criteria for the pages that we captured.

Defining the criteria for the pages

We will start with defining the criteria for all the pages that we captured under the SAPLogon760 application. Note that the criteria can be defined the same way for all types of items in the **Applications** panel. The data displayed in the **Captured Data** panel is specific to the item for which the criteria are currently being defined. We will now define the criteria for our first page – the **pWindowSAPLogon76** page:

Defining criteria for the pWindowSAPLogon76 page

Let's start with defining the criteria for the **pWindowSAPLogon76** page:

1. Select the **pWindowSAPLogon76** page in the **Applications** panel and define **Name** and **Deepness** in the criteria, shown as follows:

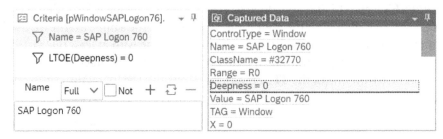

Figure 12.26 – Criteria for the pWindowSAPLogon76 page

> **Important Note**
>
> Deepness defined in the criteria will help SAP Intelligent RPA identify the page faster, considering that SAP Intelligent RPA scans through the complete DOM structure of the page and this helps the deepness criteria to restrict up to a level deep in the DOM structure of the page, to that which needs to be scanned.

Once the unique criteria are defined on this page, the page will turn green in the **Applications** panel. We will define the criteria for the next page now.

Defining criteria for the pSAP page

We will now define criteria for the **pSAP** page by executing the following step:

1. Select the **pSAP** page in the **Applications** panel and define **Type, Name,** and **Deepness** in the criteria, as follows:

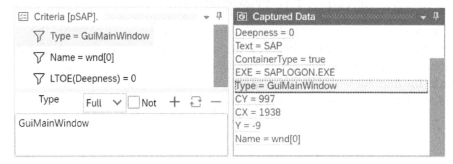

Figure 12.27 – Criteria for the pSAP page

Other than **Name** and **Deepness**, we have also included **Type** in the criteria for this page. Remember that this page is captured with the SAPGUI technology connector, and **Type** is specific to SAP technology. You will see **Type** starting with the word Gui for all the items that are captured with SAP technology. Once the unique criteria are defined on this page, the page will turn green in the **Applications** panel. Let's define the criteria for the next page.

Defining criteria for the pSAPEasyAccessU page

Let's proceed and define the criteria for the **pSAPEasyAccessU** page:

1. Select the **pSAPEasyAccessU** page in the **Applications** panel and define **Type**, **Name**, and **Deepness** added to criteria. Note that these details are the same as the **pSAP** page. So, this still will be in red in the **Applications** panel, as there is a criteria conflict within the **pSAP** page. We need to add additional criteria for this page to identify this page uniquely. Let's add **Text** from the **Captured Data** panel to the criteria for both the **pSAP** page and the **pSAPEasyAccessU** page. The updated criteria for **pSAP** can be seen in the following screenshot:

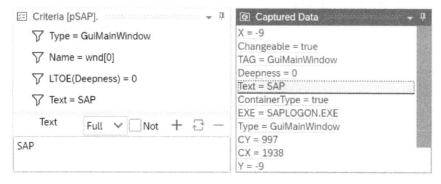

Figure 12.28 – The updated criteria for the pSAP page

2. The criteria for the **pSAPEasyAccessU** page can be seen in the following screenshot. This should now turn green in the **Applications** panel:

Figure 12.29 – The updated criteria for the pSAPEasyAccessU page

> **Important note**
>
> Based on the version of the SAP GUI in the machine where screens are captured, **Text** on this page might include the user ID that is used to log in to the SAP server. As seen in the preceding screenshot, the value for **Text** ends with **User Menu for <user id>** What if a different SAP login ID is used? The automation solution will fail to recognize the page, as **Text** does not match what is defined.

SAP Intelligent RPA provides an option to use part of **Text** in the criteria, which we will explore in the upcoming chapter. We will now define the criteria for the next page.

Defining criteria for the pEnterVendorInvoice page

We will proceed and define the criteria for the **pEnterVendorInvoice** page and two subpages captured under it:

1. Select the **pEnterVendorInvoice** page in the **Applications** panel and define **Type**, **Text**, and **Deepness** in **criteria**. The updated criteria for the **pEnterVendorInvoice** page looks like the following:

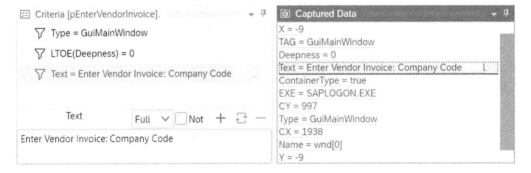

Figure 12.30 – Criteria for the pEnterVendorInvoice page

As **Text** for **pSAPEasyAccessU** ends with an SAP Login ID, so the **Text** value for the **pEnterVendorInvoice** page ends with a company code. So, if we use these criteria, SAP Intelligent RPA will be able to identify this page only if a company code is selected. To avoid this situation, we need to use part of the value, which will be explained in the upcoming chapter. Let's proceed and define the criteria for the subpages under the **pEnterVendorInvoice** page.

Defining criteria for the pGuiBasicData subpage

Let's now define the criteria for the **pGuiBasicData** subpage. Execute the following step to set the criteria:

1. Select the **pGuiBasicData** subpage under the **pEnterVendorInvoice** page in the **Applications** panel and define **Id** and **Deepness** in criteria, as follows:

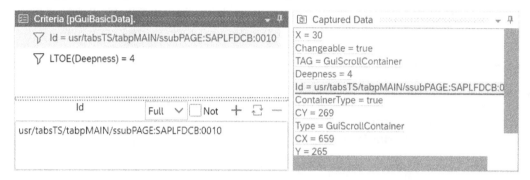

Figure 12.31 – Criteria for the pGuiBasicData subpage

We have now defined the criteria for the **pGuiBasicData** subpage, so we will move on to defining the criteria for the **pGuiTax** subpage.

Defining criteria for the pGuiTax subpage

The items in the criteria for the **pGuiTax** subpage are the same as the criteria for the **pGuiBasicData** subpage. Select the criteria for this page as follows:

1. Select the **pGuiTax** subpage under the **pEnterVendorInvoice** page in the **Applications** panel and define **Id** and **Deepness** in the criteria, as follows:

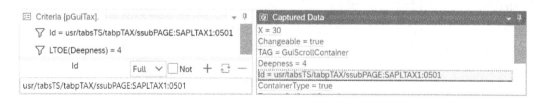

Figure 12.32 – Criteria for the pGuiTax subpage

> **Important note**
>
> Observe the value for the **Id** item in criteria for both the **pGuiBasicData** and **pGuiTax** subpages. This ID will be unique for the SAP screens though, so careful consideration is required when selecting the ID as criteria for pages and controls where these IDs are dynamically generated at runtime.

We have defined the criteria for the subpages. We will now proceed and define the criteria for the rest of the pages.

Defining the criteria for the pExitEditing page

We will now define the criteria for the **pExitEditing** page by executing the following steps:

1. Select the **pExitEditing** page in the **Applications** panel and define **Type**, **Text**, and **Deepness** in **criteria**, as follows:

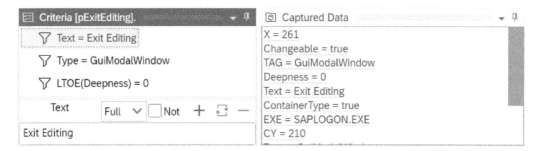

Figure 12.33 – Criteria for the pExitEditing page

We will now proceed and define the criteria for the next page – the **pLogOff** page.

Defining criteria for the pLogOff page

The final page for which we define the criteria is the **pLogOff** page. Execute the following step to define the criteria for this page:

1. Select the **pLogOff** page in the **Applications** panel and define **Type**, **Text**, and **Deepness** in **criteria**, as follows:

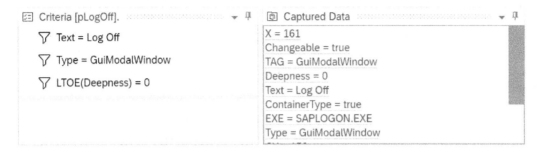

Figure 12.34 – Criteria for the pLogOff page

Now we have defined the criteria for all the pages that were captured in the **Explorer** perspective. You are now familiar with capturing the application, capturing the pages based on the process selected for automation, and defining the criteria for each page. You also now know that pages with unique criteria defined will be displayed green in the **Applications** panel. Any page that still shows in red requires the criteria to be updated.

Once the pages are defined, we need to capture the controls/UI elements for each page that is to be used while executing the business process. We will now look at capturing the required UI elements for each page.

Defining UI elements/controls

SAP Intelligent RPA provides multiple options to select and define a control. Please remember that the complete page is scanned, and the DOM structure is read by SAP Intelligent RPA while capturing the page. This includes any hidden controls, such as an item in a combobox where only the selected item is visible but there are more items within for selection at runtime. SAP Intelligent RPA allows developers to define the controls by selecting from the **Screen Display** panel or the **Source Tree Display** panel.

To select a control from the **Screen Display** panel, simply double-click on the visible control; SAP Intelligent RPA then will add the control to the **Applications** panel with the default criteria defined. Alternatively, navigate to the control in the DOM structure of the page in the **Source Tree Display** panel, and select **Associate to New Item** from the context menu.

Let's go through each page and define the controls that are required for our business process.

Defining controls under the pWindowSAPLogon76 page

The first page used in our business process is the **SAP Logon** page, where we will select an existing connection to SAP. On this page, we need to select an existing connection from the right pane of the page and then click on the **Log On** button to get to the **SAP login** page. So, we will capture these two items on this page:

1. Select the **pWindowSAPLogon76** page in the **Applications** panel.

2. In the **Screen Display** panel, click on the **Log On** button. This button now should be highlighted with a blue border, as shown in the following screenshot. If the control is not highlighted in blue, that means the page is not captured properly and you need to recapture it.

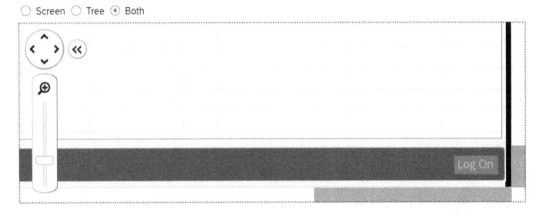

Figure 12.35 – Selecting the Log On button in the pWindowSAPLogon76 page

3. Double-click on the **Log On** button; you should now see **btLogOn** defined in the **Applications** panel under the **pWindowSAPLogon76** page, as shown in the following screenshot:

Figure 12.36 – The Log On button declared under the pWindowSAPLogon76 page

4. The default criteria selected by SAP Intelligent RPA will include only **Automation ID**. Let's update the criteria for the **btLogOn** criteria with **Name** and **Deepness**, as shown in the following screenshot:

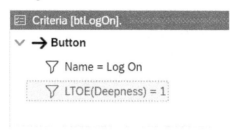

Figure 12.37 – Criteria for the btLogOn button

Now, we will define the connection item that needs to be used for logging in to the SAP server from the **Source Tree Display** panel.

5. The exiting connections are displayed as a list in the UI. We will be selecting and defining the complete row item in the available connection list. In the **Source Tree Display** panel, navigate to the data item with the name of your connection, as shown in the following screenshot:

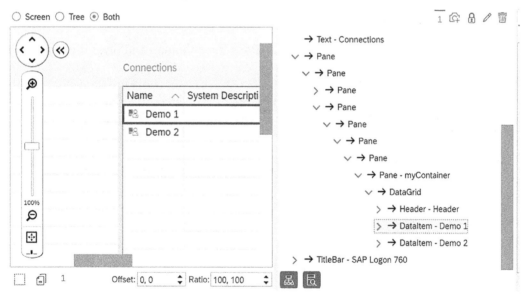

Figure 12.38 – Navigating to the required item in the Source Tree Display panel

6. Right-click on the data item that will be used for connecting while executing the business process and select **Associate to New Item** from the context menu. SAP Intelligent RPA will create a control under the page with the name defined in the criteria for the new control, as shown in the following screenshot:

Figure 12.39 – The connection data time declared under the pWindowSAPLogon76 page

7. The default criteria for this data item include **Name**. We can additionally add **Deepness** to the criteria.

We have now captured two controls, **btLogon** and **oDemo1**, on this page. You can also capture the close button from the title bar of the page so that the application can be closed by clicking this button at the end of our business process execution. Let's move on to the **pSAP** page to capture the controls.

Defining controls under the pSAP page

On the **pSAP** page, we will need to enter the SAP server credentials and press the login button. We will capture three controls on this page:

1. Double-click on the textboxes for the **User** and **Password** controls and the button with the tick/check mark in the **Screen Display** panel. These three controls are highlighted in the green border in the following screenshot:

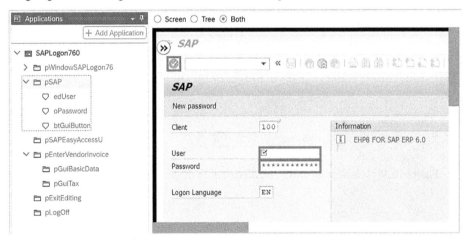

Figure 12.40 – The controls captured in the pSAP page

2. You will now see the three controls defined under the **pSAP** page. The default criteria for these controls include **Name** only. The **User** control is defined as edUser and the **Password** control is defined as oPassword. These two controls are of the **Text** field type, labeled with **User** and **Password,** respectively. You can add **Deepness** and the **LeftLable** item from the **Captured Data** panel for these items.

The third control will be defined as **btGuiButton**, which is of the **Button** type with no label; we can add **ID** and **Deepness** to the criteria for this control. We have now captured the required controls on this page, so let's move to the next page.

Defining controls under the pSAPEasyAccessU page

On this page, we need to enter the SAP transaction code and enter the next page by clicking the *Enter* button. Let's now capture the textbox to enter the transaction code and the *Enter* button on this page:

1. Select the **pSAPEasyAccessU** page in the **Applications** panel; we only need to enter the transaction code and press the button to move to the next page. We will declare these two controls from the **Screen Display** panel and update the criteria to include **Deepness** and **ID**. The **Screen Display** panel will have the captured controls highlighted in green, as shown in the following screenshot:

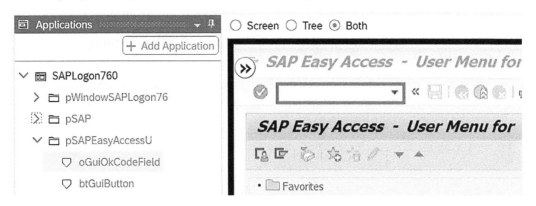

Figure 12.41 – The controls captured on the pSAPEasyAccessU page

Now, we will move on to the pages specific to the FB60 transaction code.

Defining controls under the pEnterVendorInvoice page

In the **pEnterVendorInvoice** page, we will capture the following controls by double-clicking on each of the items:

- The **Basic data** tab header: This button is used to move to the **Basic data** tab from the **Tax** tab. Include **Name** and **Deepness** in the criteria. The name of this control is defined as **oBasicData**.

- The **Tax** tab header: This button is used to move to the **Tax** tab from the **Basic data** tab. Include **Name** and **Deepness** in the criteria. The name of this control is defined as **oTax**.

- **G/L acct** in the first row: The edit box is used to enter the **G/L** account for the invoice being posted. Include **Name** and **Deepness** in the criteria. The default name of the control will be **edGuiCTextField**. You can rename it to `edGLAccount`.

- **Amount in doc.curr.** in the first row: The edit box is used to enter the amount in the **G/L** account for the invoice being posted. Include **Name** and **Deepness** in the criteria. Rename the defined control from **edGuiTextField** to `edGLAmount`.

- The **Park** button: This button, defined as **btPark**, is used for posting the vendor invoice after entering the details in both the **Basic data** and **Tax** tabs. Include **Name**, **Text**, and **Deepness** in the criteria.

- The **Status** bar: The result of the invoice posting is displayed in this area. Include **Name** and **Deepness** in the criteria. This will be defined with the name of **oGuiStatusbar**.

- The **Cancel** button: This button is used to exit the invoice editing screen after posting the invoice. Include **Name** and **Deepness** in the criteria. Rename the control from the default **btGuiButton** to `btCancel`.

All the controls captured in the **pEnterVendorInvoice** page are highlighted in green in the following screenshot:

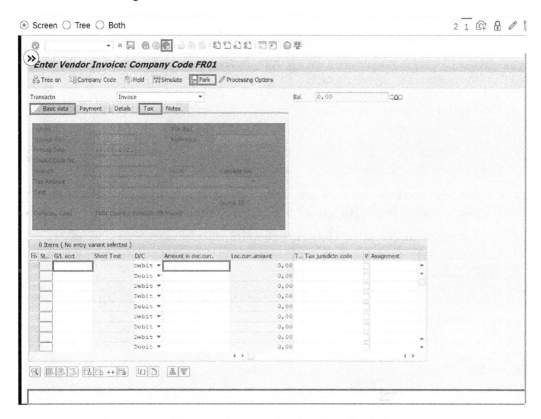

Figure 12.42 – The controls captured in the pEnterVendorInvoice page

We are ready to define the controls in the two subpages.

Defining the controls under the pGuiBasicData subpage

Move on to the **pGuiBasicData** subpage under the **pEnterVendorInvoice** page in the **Applications** panel to capture the controls that need filling in while executing the vendor invoice-posting business process. We will capture the following mandatory controls that need filling in before posting the invoice:

- The **Vendor** text field: We will enter the vendor ID here. Include **Name** and **Deepness** in the criteria. The name of the defined control is **edVendor**.

- The **Invoice date** text field: We will enter the date here. Include **Name** and **Deepness** in the criteria. The name of this control is **edInvoiceDate**.

- The **Amount** text field: We will enter the invoice amount here. Include **Name** and **Deepness** in the criteria. The name of this control is **edAmount**.

- The **Calculate tax** checkbox: Clicking here will enable us to enter the tax code in the **Tax** tab. Include **Name, Text**, and **Deepness** in the criteria. Rename this control from **oAmount** to `oCalculateTax`.

  Please refer to the following screenshot for the four controls that are captured on the **pGuiBasicData** subpage:

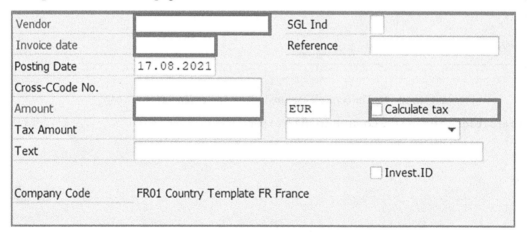

Figure 12.43 – The controls captured on the pGuiBasicData subpage

As with the **pGuiBasicData** subpage, we will need to capture the controls required on the **pGuiTax** subpage.

Defining the controls under the pGuiTax subpage

On the **pGuiTax** subpage under the **pEnterVendorInvoice** page, we only need to capture the first **Tax code** combobox, where we will enter the tax code for the invoice being posted:

1. The Tax code combo field in the first row: We will enter the tax code here. Include Name and **Deepness** in the criteria.

    Please refer to the following screenshot for the one control that is captured on the pGuiTax subpage:

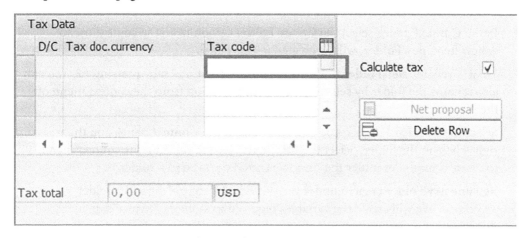

Figure 12.44 – The control captured on the pGuiTax subpage

On the following two pages, the **pExitEditing** page and the **pLogOff** page, we need to capture the **Yes** button so that we can click on this button while exiting the editing and then log off from the SAP server.

We have now captured all the controls that require action during the vendor invoice-posting business process on all pages. We have seen how to define the controls of the page directly from the **Screen Display** panel or the **Source Tree Display** panel. We also updated the default criteria suggested by SAP Intelligent RPA with additional criteria for each of the controls. With the definition of the controls in place, we need context or storage variables to store the information read from the controls or to set the values to the controls. We will now learn about creating the context relevant to our business process.

Variable declaration

Desktop Studio provides the **Context** panel in the **Workflow** perspective where we can create the context or storage variables that we will use to store information.

Follow these steps to create the variables that we will use while executing the vendor-invoice posting business process:

1. In Desktop Studio, go to the **Workflow** perspective. Please refer to *Chapter 9, Desktop Studio Perspectives*, for information on the panels available in this perspective.

2. In the **Context** panel, select the **Create Folder** option from the context menu. A new item, **newFolder**, will be created in this panel.

3. We will rename **newFolder** to VendorInvoiceDetails by pressing *F2*. You can also rename the folder by selecting the **Rename** option from the context menu of the item.

4. Select the VendorInvoiceDetails folder in the **Context** panel, and then right-click on the folder. Select the **Create Folder** option from the context menu to create a subfolder under the VendorInvoiceDetails folder.

5. Rename **newFolder** created under the VendorInvoiceDetails folder to Invoice. We will create the variables required to store the invoice data in this folder.

6. Right-click on the Invoice folder and select the **Create Item** menu item from the context menu. This will create **newItem** under the Invoice folder. We can rename this item to VendorNo. The steps to rename the item are the same as how we renamed a folder. You can either use *F2* or the **Rename** menu item from the context menu after selecting the item.

7. Repeat the process to create additional items, including the InvoiceDate, Amount, GLAccount, GLAmount, TaxCode, and Status variables.

After all the variables have been created, the **Context** panel should look like the following screenshot:

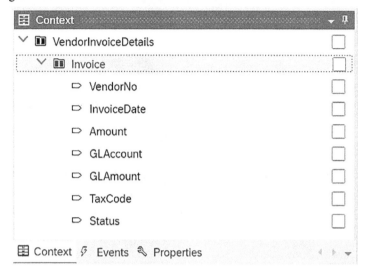

Figure 12.45 – A list of the folders and variables created in the Context panel

Okay, we are now ready with the pages and the controls are declared. The storage variables are defined to store the information from the controls or to set information to controls while executing the vendor invoice-posting business process. We are now ready to create the workflow for the business process in our next chapter.

Summary

In this chapter, we discussed automating a business process using the SAP as a target application and the FB60 transaction code. We learned about capturing the applications, pages, subpages, and controls required for automating the vendor invoice-posting business process. We also created the storage variable or context required to store the information relevant to our business process.

What we have learned is very important for anyone who wants to automate any business process. You need to first identify the target applications and page transitions after each step and define the controls that require interaction to complete the business process. It is also important to ensure that each page and control has the unique criteria defined so that SAP Intelligent RPA can recognize the pages and controls while running the process. The **Explorer** perspective highlights the pages and controls with no unique criteria or conflicting criteria with other pages or controls. Developers must ensure that they use the right criteria for each page and control to automatically execute the business process successfully.

We will learn about creating a workflow using the captured applications, pages, and controls in the next chapter, where we will start with creating a workflow that executes each step of the business process.

Questions

Here are some questions for you to test your knowledge of this chapter. The answers to these questions can be found at the back of this book, in the *Assessments* section:

1. Why are certain controls or pages still highlighted in red even after defining the criteria?

2. What option does SAP Intelligent RPA provide to define controls that are not directly visible on the screen?

3. Why does the capturing of some pages take longer than others?

13
Designing Scenarios

In *Chapter 12, Capturing and Declaring Applications, Pages, and Items*, we discussed the **Vendor Invoice Posting** business process. We have also captured the **Systems Applications Products (SAP) Logon** application, all pages needed to interact for the business process, and the controls that are needed to be actioned. The captured controls will be used to transition between pages, set the values, and get the values.

Once we have captured and defined the applications, pages, and controls, the next step is to create a workflow that visually describes the actions to be performed on the captured information by **SAP Intelligent Robotic Process Automation (SAP Intelligent RPA)** in sequence to complete a business process.

In this chapter, we will discuss how the captured information is used to create a workflow and gain knowledge on the following:

- Creating your first workflow
- Activities to handle applications
- Activities to handle pages and page transitions
- Activities to interact with **user interface (UI)** controls

By the end of this chapter, you should be able to create a workflow, define the steps to be performed on the application and each page that was captured, and define activities to be performed on the controls.

Let's start with creating a workflow in **Desktop Studio**.

Technical requirements

- Desktop Studio installed on your workstation.

- Ensure the **SAP Logon** application, pages, and controls are captured already, as discussed in *Chapter 12, Capturing and Declaring Applications, Pages, and Items.*

Creating your first workflow

Desktop Studio provides the **Workflow** perspective, which was discussed in *Chapter 9, Desktop Studio Perspectives.* We will be using this perspective to create the workflows. The application, pages, and controls captured in *Chapter 12, Capturing and Declaring Applications, Pages, and Items,* will be used to create a workflow that includes all the activities required to post a vendor invoice.

The steps to create the workflow are set out here:

1. Start **SAP Intelligent RPA Desktop Studio.**

2. Open the **Vendor Invoice Posting** project that was created in *Chapter 12, Capturing and Declaring Applications, Pages, and Items.*

3. Go to the **Workflow** perspective.

4. Right-click on the **GLOBAL** node in the **Workflow** perspective and select the **New Workflow…** option from the context menu. The context menu option is shown in the following screenshot:

Figure 13.1 – Context menu option to create a workflow

5. In the **New Workflow** dialog, change the **Workflow Name** field to
    SAPInvoicePosting. You can include comments optionally in this dialog,
    as illustrated in the following screenshot:

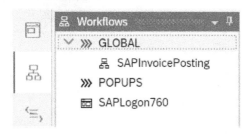

Figure 13.2 – New Workflow dialog

6. Click on the **Save** button in the **New Workflow** dialog. This will create
    a workflow under the **GLOBAL** node in the **Workflows** panel, as shown in the
    following screenshot:

Figure 13.3 – The SAPInvoicePosting workflow created under the GLOBAL node

You will notice that the newly created workflow, that is, the **SAPInvoicePosting** workflow,
is opened in the **Designer** panel immediately after creation. This workflow includes an
activity called **Start** as the first activity. We are now ready with our canvas to create the
workflow with the steps to post the vendor invoice.

We will now look at the activities to be performed on the **SAP Logon** application that
we already defined in the **Explorer** perspective.

Activities to handle applications

Before starting with including the activities in our workflow, it is suggested that you get familiarized with different activities that are available in the **Activities** panel of the **Workflow** perspective. The display of the activities in the **Activities** panel is in context to the selection in the **Designer** panel—that is, you will see the activities will change as per selection in the **Designer** panel. When you open the workflow, the **Activities** includes all the activities that you can use or drag and drop to the workflow canvas.

To execute the **Vendor Invoice Posting** business process, we need to start the **SAP Logon** application first, execute the steps on all pages that we captured, and then close the **SAP Logon** application at the end of the business process execution. We will be using the **Start** and **Close** activities that are grouped under the **Application** node in the **Activities** panel on the **SAP Logon** application to automate our **Vendor Invoice Posting** business process. Please refer to the following screenshot to locate the **Start** and **Close** activities that are grouped under the **Application** node:

Figure 13.4 – Activities available for application

All you need to do is to drag the **Start** activity from the **Activities** panel and drop it onto the workflow canvas under the **Start** activity that is already included in our workflow. Ensure that you drop the new activity onto the down arrow that is displayed under the existing activity so that a link is created between the two activities. You can observe that the down arrow is displayed under the existing activity while dropping the new activity onto the canvas, as shown in the following screenshot:

Figure 13.5 – Dropping the application Start activity under an existing activity

Alternatively, you can also drop the new activity in the canvas and draw a line from the previous activity to indicate the step execution flow. Notice the arrow direction of the link. This arrow direction indicates the execution flow.

OK—we captured the **SAP Logon** application and named it **SAPLogon760** in the *Capturing the SAP Logon application* section of *Chapter 12, Capturing and Declaring Applications, Pages, and Items*. We have an activity available now to start the application, so now we need to specify which application is required to start in the **Properties** panel. For this, we need to select the newly added application **Start** activity, then in the **Properties** panel, select the **SAPLogon760** application for the **Application** property, as shown in the following screenshot:

Figure 13.6 – Selecting the application in the Properties panel

You will notice that once the application is selected, the **Display name** property is changed to **Start 'SAPLogon760'** to include the application name. That's it—we've now instructed **SAP Intelligent RPA** that the **SAP Logon** application be started as the first step while executing the **Vendor Invoice Posting** business process.

You can repeat the same steps to include the **Close** activity as the last step of our business process execution, but before that, we need to include the pages that are required to be interacted with during the business process execution. Let's now look at adding pages to our workflow canvas.

Activities to handle pages and page transitions

We captured all the pages required to automate the **Vendor Invoice Posting** business process in the *Capturing SAP Logon application pages* section of *Chapter 12, Capturing and Declaring Applications, Pages, and Items*. To add these pages to the workflow canvas, you need to go to the **Pages** tab in the **Activities** panel. This tab includes all the pages that were captured in the **Explorer** perspective grouped under the application name, as shown in the following screenshot:

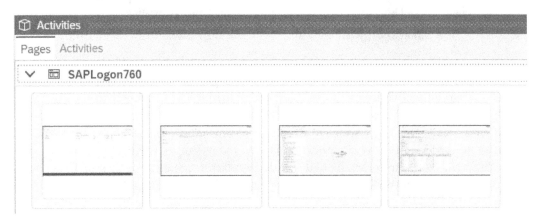

Figure 13.7 – Pages displayed under the Pages tab of the Activities panel

We need to drag each page from the **Pages** tab in the same order as they will transition during the execution of the **Vendor Invoice Posting** business process and link them in the same order.

Let's first drag the **pWindowSAPLogon76** page under the **Start 'SAPLogon760'** activity. This is the first page that will be displayed after the application is started. Create a link from the **Start 'SAPLogon760'** activity to the **pWindowSAPLogon76** page. Your workflow canvas should look like this:

Figure 13.8 – Workflow display after adding the first page

You can continue to add all pages that will be used by the business process in the same order of their transition during the execution.

First, we will understand the display order of the pages that will be used by the **Vendor Invoice Posting** business process based on actions on each page. These activities are grouped into three, as outlined next. We will include all pages in the same workflow in the order explained for each group for now:

- **Logging in to the SAP server**: For activities to log in to the SAP server, access the **Vendor Invoice Posting** screen.

- **Posting a vendor invoice**: Post an invoice by entering the required details and reading the status.

- **Logging off from the SAP server**: Log off from the SAP server and close the application.

Let's look at the page transition under each group.

Logging in to the SAP server

We will start with the activities required to log into the SAP server immediately after starting the application. The pages that we require to use in the workflow are in the order given in the following steps:

1. The **pWindowSAPLogon76** page: Select the connection to the SAP server. We already included this in our workflow. The **pSAP** page is displayed.

2. The **pSAP** page: Enter the SAP server credentials and log in. The **pSAPEasyAccessU** page is displayed next.

After executing this subprocess, we will be on the **pSAPEasyAccessU** page from where our next subprocess will start. Let's now look at the steps for the *Posting a vendor invoice* subprocess.

Posting a vendor invoice

Once logged in to the SAP server, we will be entering the FB60 transaction code and executing the activities required to post the vendor and then read the status. This is the page order for completing this action:

1. The **pSAPEasyAccessU** page: You will be entering the transaction code **FB60** on this page to move to the **pEnterVendorInvoice** page, with the **pGuiBasicData** subpage as the default display where we will enter vendor invoice basic data details. After execution of this, you can directly go to the **pGuiBasicData** subpage.

2. The **pGuiBasicData** subpage: Enter the vendor invoice basic data details and then move to the parent page, which is the **pEnterVendorInvoice** page.

3. The **pEnterVendorInvoice** page: Select the **Tax** tab to move to the **pGuiTax** subpage.

4. The **pGuiTax** subpage: Enter the vendor invoice tax details then move to the parent page.

5. The **pEnterVendorInvoice** page: Enter the **General Ledger** (**G/L**) account details, then click on the **Post** button to post the vendor invoice. After the post action is complete, we will read the status of the vendor invoice posting.

Let's now look at the next subprocess to log off from the SAP server.

Logging off from the SAP server

After the vendor invoice posting is complete, we will log off from the SAP server and close the application. This is a sort of cleanup activity, and the page order is explained in the following steps:

1. The **pEnterVendorInvoice** page: After successful completion of posting, read the status. A **pExitEditing** page is displayed to confirm the exiting of the page.

2. The **pExitEditing** page: Confirm the exit editing to move to the **pSAPEasyAccessU** page.

3. The **pSAPEasyAccessU** page: Log off from the SAP server. The **pLogOff** page is displayed to confirm you have been logged off.

4. The **pLogOff** page: Confirm logoff to close the window.

> **Note**
>
> You will notice that a page might appear multiple times in the flow. We need to include the page at all transitions to perform actions in the same order as required by the business process.

Add the pages to the workflow canvas in the same order based on the preceding explanation. Ensure that the arrows of the link are in the direction of the page that is being transitioned are after the actions in the current page.

You can include the application **Close** activity after the last page in the workflow so that the application is closed after all steps of the business process are performed.

By now, we have created our basic workflow that includes activities for the application and flow of pages as they will be transitioned while executing the business process. We need to include actions to be performed on each control under the pages for the business process workflow to be complete. We will learn how to add activities for the controls on the pages.

Activities to interact with UI controls

We captured the controls that need to be interacted with when executing the business process in the *Defining UI elements/controls* section of *Chapter 12, Capturing and Declaring Applications, Pages, and Items*. To add activities to be performed on these controls, we need to double-click on the parent page of the control in the workflow canvas. We already added pages to our **SAPInvoicePosting** workflow, so we will go to each page and add activities to be performed on the captured controls within each page.

We will start with adding activities to the **pWindowSAPLogon76** page by mouse double-clicking on the page in the workflow canvas. The **Designer** panel will then open the canvas to add activities to the page. The **Designer** panel for the page includes the **Screen** tab in which the captured screen of the page is displayed with all the controls defined. These are highlighted for easy recognition, as shown in the following screenshot:

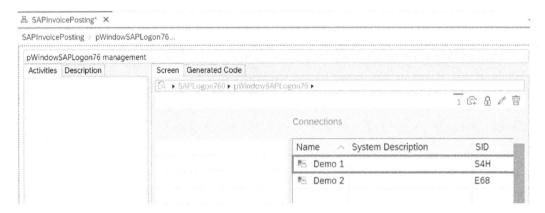

Figure 13.9 – Workflow Designer panel display for a page

Notice that for the activities that are available in the **Activities** panel, there will be more activity groups available in this panel that can be used to perform actions on controls on the page.

Have a look at the activities grouped under the nodes with a name starting with **Item** in the **Activities** panel, as shown in the following screenshot:

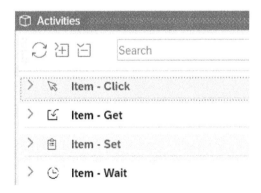

Figure 13.10 – Item activities grouped in the Activities panel

The item activities are grouped by **Item - Click**, **Item - Get**, **Item - Set**, and **Item - Wait** type actions. Expand each group to get a view of the activities. We can add activities simply by dragging the right activity that needs to be performed from the **Activities** panel and dropping it on the control on which we want to perform that activity. We will add the **Click** activity to the **pWindowSAPLogon76** page.

Adding a Click activity to a control

In the **pWindowSAPLogon76** page, we need to first select the Demo1 connection item that was declared on the **pWindowSAPLogon76** page in the **Explorer** perspective by clicking on it. So, we will drag the **Click** activity under the **Item - Click** activity group and drop it on the Demo1 item, as shown in the following screenshot:

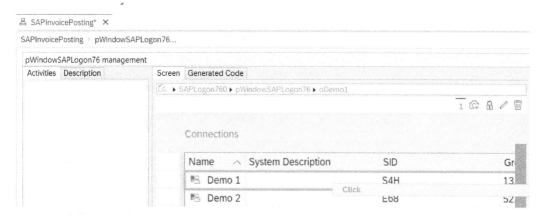

Figure 13.11 – Adding Click activity to connection item in the page

There will be an activity added to the page activity list with the name **Click on 'oDemo1 (1)'**, as shown in the following screenshot:

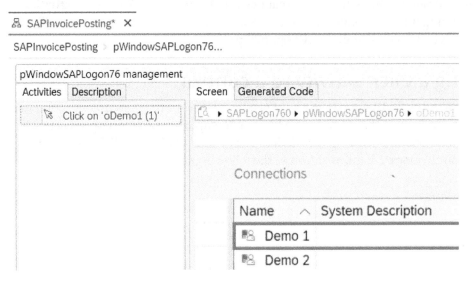

Figure 13.12 – Click activity added to the item

Observe the properties of this activity in the **Properties** panel. You will see that the **Item** property value resembles the hierarchy defined for the item in the **Explorer** perspective, as shown in the following screenshot:

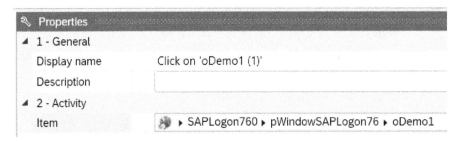

Figure 13.13 – Click on oDemo1 activity properties

Important Note

Activities can be added to the controls that were already captured, defined under the page in the **Explorer** perspective. If an item is not highlighted in the **Designer** panel to add an activity, you need to go to the **Explorer** perspective and define the item first.

We have added our first item activity to click on the connection name, so the next activity is to click on the **Log On** button on this page to get to the next page, which is the **pSAP** page. The **Log On** button on the **pWindowSAPLogon76** page is captured and defined as **btLogOn** in the **Explorer** perspective.

We will use another way that Desktop Studio provides to define an activity for an item or control. Drag the **Click** activity under the **Item - Click** activity group and drop it in the page's **Activities**. This will create a blank **Click** activity, as shown in the following screenshot:

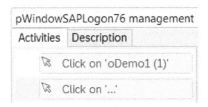

Figure 13.14 – A new Click activity added to the page

We then can update the **Item** property in the **Properties** panel to specify the control on which the activity is to be performed. You need to select the **SAPLogon760** application, then the **pWindowSAPLogon76** page, and then the **btLogOn** control for the **Item** property value. The final selection for the click item activity for the **btLogon** button will look like this:

Figure 13.15 – Click on the btLogon button activity properties

You will notice that the **Display name** property is still **Click on '…'**. When you directly drop the activity on the control, the text will include the item name in the **Display name** property. Because we created a blank activity and then updated the **Item** property, we need to change the **Display name** property manually and enter a value that describes the activity. Let's change the **Display name** property value to **Click on 'btLogOn (2)'**. The number at the end of the **Display name** property that is surrounded by brackets, (), denotes the sequence or index of the activity on the page. You will see the activity index **Screen** tab in the **Designer** panel. The activity index is now displayed in this tab, as shown in the following screenshot:

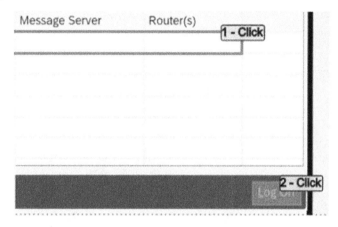

Figure 13.16 – Display of indexed Item activities in the Designer panel

These are the only two activities we require on this page. Save the workflow by using the *Ctrl + S* shortcut keys or clicking on the **Save** button in the menu bar. We can move to the main workflow by selecting **SAPInvoicePosting** in the navigation bar, just under the title of the workflow, highlighted in red in the following screenshot:

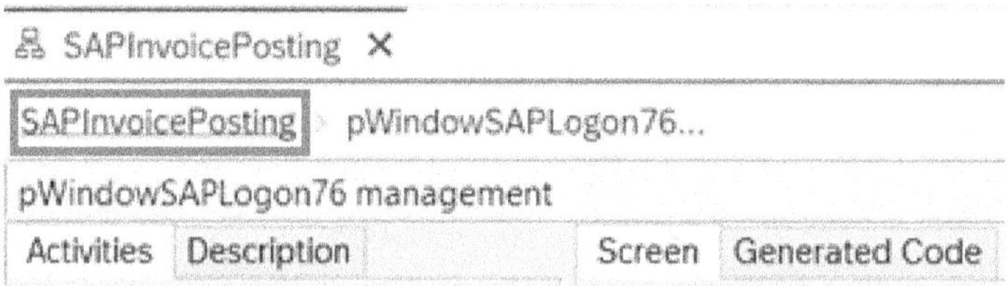

Figure 13.17 – Navigation to the Designer panel

We will now proceed with activities to be performed on the **pSAP** page that will be displayed when we press the **Log On** button on the **pWindowSAPLogon76** page. On the **pSAP** page, we need to enter the username and password for the SAP server and then either click on the **Enter** button or press the *Enter* key on the page to log in to the SAP server. We will now learn about setting values to a control.

Setting text values to a control

On the workflow canvas, mouse double-click on the **pSAP** page to enter the page **Designer** panel. We already captured the **edUser** and **oPassword** controls for this page where we need to set the values. If these controls are not already captured, please refer to *Figure 12.38* in *Chapter 12, Capturing and Declaring Applications, Pages, and Items*. We will set the values to these two controls by dragging the **Set** activity under the **Item - Set** activity group in the **Activities** panel and drop on the controls. The **Set** activity that is used to set values to controls is highlighted in red in the following screenshot:

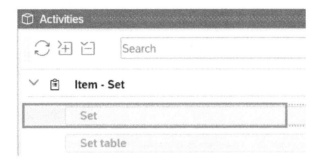

Figure 13.18 – The Set activity to set the text values on UI elements

We will drop the **Set** activity on **edUser** first and then on **oPassword** as the second activity. That will create two activities for us to edit the properties in the activities, as shown in the following screenshot:

Figure 13.19 – Two Set activities for username and password

Go to the **Properties** panel of the **SAPLogon760Data.pSAPData.edUser in 'edUser (1)'** activity. You will notice the **Source data** property includes $data$ and the data entered as **SAPLogon760Data.pSAPData.edUser** by default, as shown in the following screenshot:

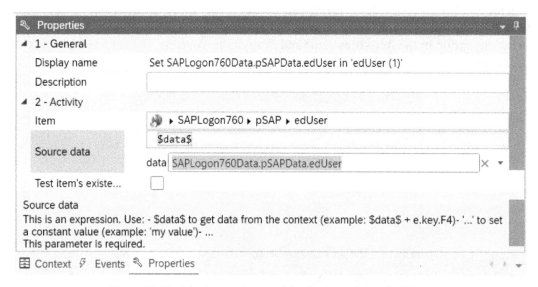

Figure 13.20 – The Properties panel for the Set activity of edUser

The $data$ expression means that the value is to be set from the context that is created in the **Context** panel. You will also observe that **SAP Intelligent RPA** created a new folder structure named SAPLogon760Data created in the **Context** panel with two variables, as shown in the following screenshot:

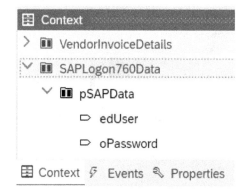

Figure 13.21 – Context created for the Set activity

We will learn about setting values from contexts later in this chapter when we will be setting the username and password values directly to the controls. So, you can delete the newly created **SAPLogon760Data** folder in the **Context** panel. Press **Yes** to confirm deletion of the folder and **No** to confirm deletion of the complete folder structure. Go to the **Properties** panel and enter your username to log in to the SAP server in place of $data$, as shown in the following screenshot:

Figure 13.22 – Setting username to edUser control

You need to replace the <<Username>> value with your username to the SAP server. Similarly, change the **Source data** property value for the **Set** activity for the **oPassword** control to your password to the SAP server. You will see the following two activities in the **Activities** tab for the **pSAP** page:

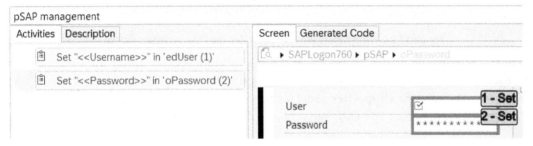

Figure 13.23 – Activities to enter SAP server credentials

> **Note**
>
> SAP Intelligent RPA provides a secure way to store the credentials in the SAP Intelligent RPA tenant and read them when required. We will be looking at that option in the upcoming chapters, but for now, the values are visible to everyone who had access to the source.

Once the username and password are entered onto the page, we need to either click on the **btGuiButton** that we captured from the page or press the *Enter* key on the page. We have already learned about adding an activity to click on the button, so we will use a keyboard activity to press *Enter* on the page.

Sending a Keystroke activity to a page

We will be sending the *Enter* key to the **pSAP** page as an alternative to clicking on the button control. You will see a **Keystroke** activity under the **Item - Set** activity group, which can be used to press the entered keystrokes to a specific control, but we will be using the **Keystroke** activity available under the **Page** activity group, which is highlighted in the following screenshot:

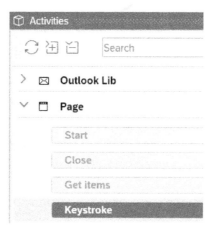

Figure 13.24 – The Keystroke activity under the Page activities group

Drag this activity and drop it anywhere on the page displayed in the **Designer** view. We then need to specify which key is to be pressed on the page in the **Properties** panel of the activity. Go to the **Properties** panel for the activity and replace the **Key sequence** property with e.SAPScripting.key._Enter_, as shown in the following screenshot:

Figure 13.25 – Setting the Key sequence property for Keystroke activity

Let's get a brief overview of the properties in the **Properties** panel of the **Keystroke** activity, as follows:

- The **Page** property: Here, we will select the current page where the keystroke is to be sent while executing the business process. The page is by default selected by **SAP Intelligent RPA** because we dropped the activity onto the page.

- The **Key sequence** property: Here, we will be entering the actual key that needs to be sent to the page. Note the value we entered is `e.SAPScripting.key._Enter_`. **SAP Intelligent RPA** provides a **software development kit (SDK)** and framework, including many libraries and constants that will be used in the code.

  We will understand these libraries in upcoming chapters, but for now, we will use the `e.SAPScripting.key._Enter_` constant defined by **SAP Intelligent RPA**. Since this is an SAP page, we will be using the keys defined under `SAPScripting` and not `e.key.Enter`, which can be used for non-SAP pages.

Don't forget to save the workflow by pressing the *Ctrl + S* shortcut keys. We have added all three activities required on the **pSAP** page. After the **Keystroke** activity on this page, the **pSAPEasyAccessU** page will be displayed where we need to add two activities, as follows:

1. Set the `FB60` SAP transaction code in the **oGuiOkCodeField** text field. Use the **Set** activity under the **Item - Set** activity group to set `FB60` to **oGuiOkCodeField**, in the same way we set the username on the **pSAP** page.

2. Press the **btGuiButton** button. You can use the **Click** activity under the **Item - Click** activity group to click on the **btGuiButton** button. Upon clicking this button, the **pEnterVendorInvoice** page will be displayed with the **pGuiBasicData** subpage on it.

The next page that will be displayed is the **pGuiBasicData** subpage. Let's look at the activities required on the **pGuiBasicData** subpage to set the values.

Setting a value from a variable to a control

In the **pGuiBasicData** subpage, we will use the context created in the **Context** panel, as explained in the *Variable declaration* section of *Chapter 12*, *Capturing and Declaring Applications, Pages, and Items,* to set the values to controls. Mouse double-click on the **pGuiBasicData** subpage in the workflow **Designer** panel to go to the page **Designer** panel. To set the values from the variables to controls, all you need to do is to drag the variable from the **Context** panel and drop it on the control. For example, drag the VendorNo variable from the **Context** panel and drop it on the **edVendor** control in the **Screen** panel, as shown in the following screenshot:

Figure 13.26 – Dropping the VendorNo variable on the edVendor control

A new activity is created by Desktop Studio to set the value from the VendorNo variable to the edVendor control that can be seen in **Activities**. Go to the **Properties** panel of the new activity, where the values for the **Item** and **Source data** properties are set by Desktop Studio, as shown in the following screenshot:

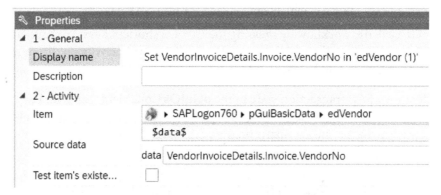

Figure 13.27 – Properties of the Set value to a control activity

Proceed and set the value for **edInvoiceDate** from the `InvoiceDate` variable and the **edAmount** value from the `Amount` variable. You also need to add a **Click** activity from the **Item - Click** activity group to click on the **Calculate Tax** checkbox. The **Calculate Tax** is **GuiCheckBox** type, so you can also use the **Set** activity from the **Item - Set** activity group with true as the parameter. The list of activities on this page are listed in the following screenshot:

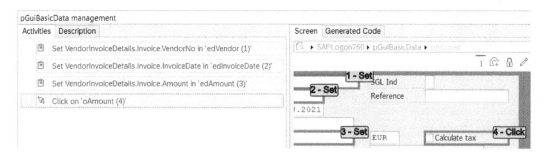

Figure 13.28 – Activities added to the pGuiBasicData subpage

After the activities are added to the **pGuiBasicData** subpage, the business process requires us to move to the **pEnterVendorInvoice** page to enter the values to the **G/L Account** and **Amount in doc.curr.** controls from the `GLAccount` and `GLAmount` variables respectively, then click on the **Tax** tab that was declared as the **oTax** control. That will be three activities added to the **pEnterVendorInvoice** page—two activities to set the values to the **G/L Account** and **Amount in doc.curr.** controls and a third activity to click on the **Tax** tab. The display will be moved to the **pGuiTax** subpage.

The only activity required in the **pGuiTax** subpage is to set the value for the **Tax code** control from the `TaxCode` variable. Add this activity to the page by dragging the `TaxCode` variable from the **Context** panel to the control in the **Screen** panel.

We have now added all activities, from starting the **SAP Logon** application, making a connection to the SAP server, invoking the **Vendor Invoice Posting** transaction, to entering the required values on pages and subpages. We need to click on the **Park** button, captured and declared as **btPark**, to complete the posting of a vendor invoice.

Once the vendor invoice posting is complete, SAP displays the status of the invoice posting on the status bar. Let's now learn how to get the text from the **Status** bar and store it in a variable.

Getting a value from a control to store in a variable

A simple way to get a value from a control to a variable is to drag the control and drop it on the variable where we want to store the value. So, we will be dragging the **oGuiStatusbar** control from the **Screen** panel and dropping it on the Status variable to get the status text value and store it in the Status variable. This is like how we set the variable value to a control but only in the reverse direction, as shown in the following screenshot:

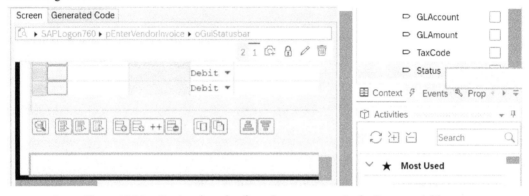

Figure 13.29 – Getting the value from Status to store in the Status variable

The control that is being used is highlighted in red by Desktop Studio. Once dropped on the variable, you will see a new activity created in the **Activities** tab for the page, as shown in the following screenshot:

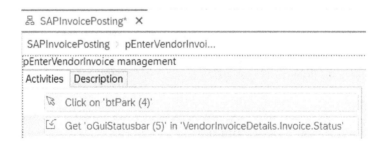

Figure 13.30 – Activities to complete the invoice posting

Save the workflow before moving on to create the next activities, which are exiting the invoice editing page and then logging off from the SAP server.

Add the activities required for each of the remaining pages, as follows:

- The **pEnterVendorInvoice** page: Add an activity to send an **e.SAPScripting. key._Shift__F3_** keystroke activity under the **Page** activity group to get the exit confirmation screen—that is, the **pExitEditing** page. You can alternatively add an activity to click on the **Exit** button.

- The **pExitEditing** page: On this page, you can add an activity to click on the **Yes** button captured as **btYes** to confirm the exit. The screen will then move to the **pSAPEasyAccessU** page.

- The **pSAPEasyAccessU** page: Add either activity to send an **e.SAPScripting.key._ Shift__F3_** keystroke activity available under the **Page** activity group or capture the **Log off** button and then add an activity to click on the **Logoff** button to get the **pLogOff** page to confirm logging off from the SAP server.

- The **pLogOff** page: Again, we need to confirm the logoff by adding an activity to click on the **Yes** button captured as **btYes** to confirm the logoff.

Save your workflow. We have added all activities required to execute the **Vendor Invoice Posting** business process. We are now ready to build our project to generate the code. Before that, we will learn about more declarations, where we will define the criteria control in relationships with other controls and learn about capturing and defining repeated entries such as rows or columns in a table. Another example of repeated controls is to capture search results from a web page.

Summary

In this chapter, we created a workflow and learned about the sequencing of the pages after starting an application in the workflow. We also learned three types of activities—to click on the control of type **button**, set the static text from a variable to controls on a page, and get values from the controls to store in a variable.

The key to enabling faster automation is to split the business process into multiple but simple workflows, keeping the reusability in mind as we split the process into three different subprocesses in this chapter. **SAP Logon** and **SAP Logoff** subprocesses designed in this chapter can be used in any SAP process automation.

While creating a workflow, we must ensure that the order of the page transition activities to be performed are the same as how a user performs a business process manually. There may be multiple activities that are possible—for example, a button can be clicked, or you can send a keyboard shortcut key. In general, keyboard shortcut keys are faster when compared to performing actions on the control. So, explore alternative activities for each action that the user performs while executing the business process manually.

We will learn about the advanced declaration options provided by SAP Intelligent RPA in the next chapter.

Questions

Here are some questions for you to test your knowledge of this chapter. The answers to these questions can be found at the back of this book, in the *Assessments* section:

1. Why are the activities to perform actions on controls visible when the workflow canvas is opened?

2. What is the difference between the **Keystroke** activity under the **Item - Set** activity group and the **Keystroke** activity under the **Page** activity group in the **Activities** panel?

14
Advanced Criteria Definition

In *Chapter 12*, *Capturing and Declaring Applications, Pages, and Items*, we learned about declaring the applications, pages, and **user interface** (**UI**) controls that are required for the **Vendor Invoice Posting** business process. In that chapter, we learned about defining criteria for captured elements using data from the **Captured Data** panel. The criteria definitions used are sufficient to automate the business process that was discussed in the *Starting with your first automation project* section of *Chapter 12*, *Capturing and Declaring Applications, Pages, and Items*. So, the declarations were used to create the SAPInvoicePosting workflow in *Chapter 13*, *Designing Scenarios*. More advanced definitions need to be used in situations when more than one control in the page has the same properties in the **Captured Data** panel or the properties of the control in the **Captured Data** panel change dynamically for each run of the application. **SAP Intelligent Robotic Process Automation** (**SAP Intelligent RPA**) provides advanced recognition methods to define criteria based on parent-child relationships or capture repeated values such as rows in a table.

In this chapter, we will learn about the advanced recognition methods provided by SAP Intelligent RPA, covered in the following topics:

- Setting parameters for advanced recognition
- Refining criteria in the **Criteria** panel
- Capturing repeated elements

By the end of this chapter, you will understand advanced criteria defined for pages or UI controls based on relationships with other controls and capturing data from tables.

We will first look at the properties for the pages and UI controls that can be used to define advanced criteria.

Technical requirements

- Desktop Studio installed on your workstation.
- An internet connection.
- A browser and the **SAP Intelligent RPA Extension** for the browser are to be installed, as discussed in *Chapter 4, Setting up SAP Intelligent RPA On-Premise Components.*

Setting parameters for advanced recognition

We used data captured by SAP Intelligent RPA from the **Captured Data** panel to define criteria for multiple SAP pages and UI controls under each page in *Chapter 12, Capturing and Declaring Applications, Pages, and Items.* While transitioning to the next page based on the activity executed on the current page, loading the next page might take a long time, considering various factors such as network speed and the SAP server performance. For example, by clicking on the btLogOn button on the pWindowSAPLogon76 page, the pSAP page will load, but executing activities on pSAP cannot occur till the page load completes and controls are accessible. SAP Intelligent RPA provides options in the **Parameters** panel to specify which controls must and must not be present before recognizing the page load and being ready to perform activities.

Look at the parameters under the **Driver** parameter group in the **Parameters** panel for the btLogOn button in the **Explorer** perspective, which is displayed in the following screenshot:

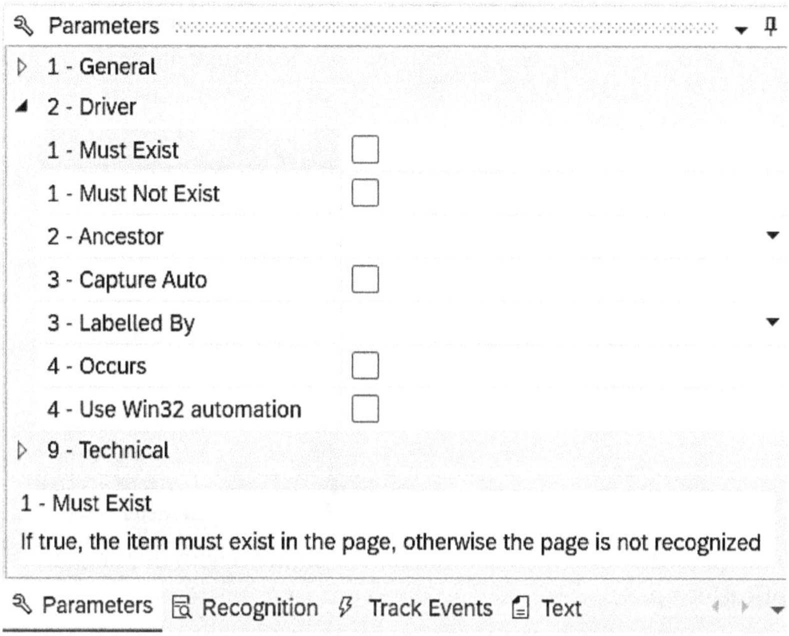

Figure 14.1 – Parameters under the Driver group

These parameters are in the context of the technical connector used to capture the page, so you might see a change in the list of parameters for different controls. The btLogOn button is on the pWindowSAPLogon76 page, which is captured using the **UI Automation** connector. So, it has a **Use Win32 automation** parameter that will not be available for other controls captured using the **SAP GUI** connector. You can check the explanation for the **Use Win32 automation** parameter in the **Parameters** panel, but we will now learn about the most used parameters in this panel to declare criteria for pages and controls.

We will now learn about the **Must Exist** parameter.

The Must Exist parameter

The **Must Exist** parameter can be selected for controls that must exist on the page before SAP Intelligent RPA recognizes that the page is loaded. SAP Intelligent RPA recognizes a page only if all controls with the **Must Exist** parameter set in the page exist on the page while running the automation solution. This parameter is useful for ensuring that the automation solution is not executed till all controls under the page are available. The best practice is to set this property to the last control that is loaded during the execution of the page; you can also set this parameter for all controls under pages.

You can select the **Must Exist** parameter for all the button-type controls under each page in the `Vendor Invoice Posting` project. Notice the change in the icon for control in the **Applications** panel for the **Must Exist** controls. The icon will now be filled, as shown in the following screenshot:

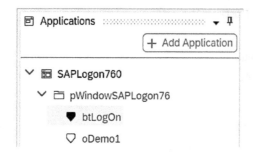

Figure 14.2 – Icon for the controls with the Must Exist parameter is set

The change in icon for the controls will help identify controls with different parameters from the **Applications** panel.

Similar to the **Must Exist** parameter, SAP Intelligent RPA provides the **Must Not Exist** parameter for UI controls. We will now look at the usage of this parameter.

The Must Not Exist parameter

While the **Must Exist** parameter is used to check the existence of a UI control on a page, the **Must Not Exist** parameter is used to check the non-existence of a UI control on a page.

This parameter is useful while automating pages with the same captured data but when the controls under the pages are different. This parameter can be used if the UI controls on the page are changed dynamically through activities performed on the page.

Consider a scenario where the `pWindowSAPLogon76` page in the `Vendor Invoice Posting` project is to be recognized only if the `oDemo1` connection is present, with the `oDemo2` connection not being present. You can declare both `oDemo1` and `oDemo2` connections, as discussed in the *Defining UI elements* section of *Chapter 12, Capturing and Declaring Applications, Pages, and Items*. Set the **Must Exist** property for the `oDemo1` connection and the **Must Not Exist** property for the `oDemo2` connection.

The **Application** panel display for the pWindowSAPLogon76 page looks like this:

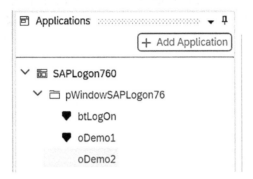

Figure 14.3 – The pWindowSAPLogon76 page with two connections

You will notice that the icons are different for the connections based on the parameter being set. If this change is saved, the pWindowSAPLogon76 page will not be recognized if there is an oDemo2 connection present on the page while executing the Vendor Invoice Posting project. You need to either unset the **Must Not Exist** property for the oDemo2 connection or delete this connection from the **SAP Logon** page for successful page recognition while executing the project.

While the **Must Exist** and **Must Not Exist** properties are used to control recognition of pages on which UI controls are present, SAP Intelligent RPA also provides two more parameters to define criteria for UI controls relating to other controls. So, first, we will look at defining the **Ancestor** parameter.

The Ancestor parameter

The **Ancestor** parameter is used to define controls based on the parent hierarchy of the control in the **Document Object Model (DOM)** structure of the page. You must first capture and declare the parent control so that it is available for selection for the child controls in the **Ancestor** parameter.

Let's look at the **Ancestor** parameter in the **Parameters** panel for the `edGLAccount` and the `edGLAmount` controls captured under the `pEnterVendorInvoice` page in the *Defining UI elements* section of *Chapter 12, Capturing and Declaring Applications, Pages, and Items*. Click on the down arrow next to the value for the **Ancestor** parameter for these controls. It currently displays an empty list, as shown in the following screenshot:

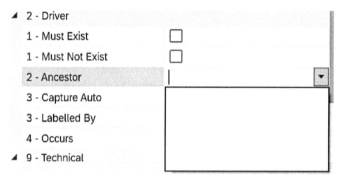

Figure 14.4 – Empty list of ancestors for a control

There are no ancestors that can be selected for these two controls as there are no controls in the hierarchy that are captured yet. We will declare the parent control under which the `edGLAccount` and `edGLAmount` controls are available by double-clicking on the table control. You can also declare the table control by navigating to `GuiTableControl` in the **Source Tree Display** panel and then selecting **Associate to New Item** from the context menu, as shown in the following screenshot:

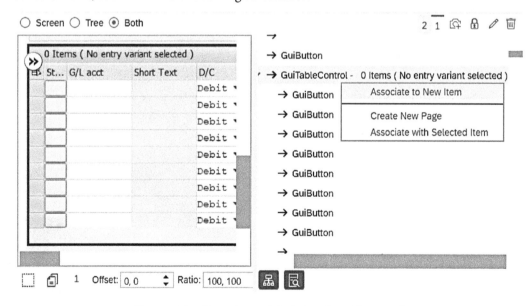

Figure 14.5 – Capturing and declaring the table control

The `tcItemsNoEntry` control with **Name** as the criteria will be declared under the `pEnterVendorInvoice` page. As this control is in the hierarchy of the `edGLAccount` and `edGLAmount` controls, this control should now be available for selection as **Ancestor** in the **Parameters** panel, as shown in the following screenshot:

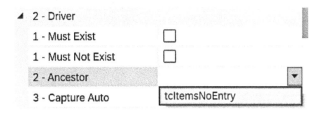

Figure 14.6 – Ancestor available for selection of a control

You can select **Ancestor** for both the `edGLAccount` and `edGLAmount` controls. The **Ancestor** parameter defined for the control need not be an immediate parent control in the DOM structure of the page, but it should be in the hierarchy of the control from the root element to the control. This property is most useful to automate pages containing controls with the same captured data, and so unique criteria cannot be defined using only captured data.

We have now seen how to define an ancestor for a control to make it uniquely identifiable while executing the automation solution. There is another parameter called **Labelled By** that is used to identify controls based on labels displayed on the screen. We will check that next.

The Labelled By parameter

Consider an automation scenario that requires capturing pages using the **OCR** connector that was briefly introduced in *The OCR connector* section of *Chapter 11, An Introduction to Technology Connectors*. The **OCR** connector is used for surface automation when the technology of the automation target application and pages is not accessible by SAP Intelligent RPA, and so the DOM structure of the page cannot be read while capturing the page. We can try this parameter for the `pSAP` page that we captured in the *Capturing SAP Logon application pages* section of *Chapter 12, Capturing and Declaring Applications, Pages, and Items*.

To recognize a control based on a label, you need to capture the label control and then set the label control in the **Labelled By** parameter in the **Parameter** panel. Let's now capture labels for the edUser and oPassword controls declared under the pSAP page by double-clicking on the **User** and **Password** labels in the **Screen Display** panel of the **Explorer** perspective. This will add the oUser and oPassword1 UI controls under the pSAP page in the **Applications** panel, as shown in the following screenshot:

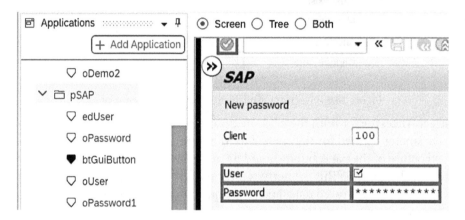

Figure 14.7 – Two labels captured under pSAP page

You can then select the oUser control for the **Labelled By** parameter for edUser and the oPassword1 control for the **Labelled By** parameter for oPassword.

We used the **Labelled By** parameter for the page captured by the **SAP GUI** connector, but this is mostly used for surface automation. When this parameter is used, the control will be recognized based on its distance from the label control while running the automation solution.

We have seen the parameters available for a UI control in the **Parameters** panel to define recognition criteria of the pages and the controls. There is also one parameter called **Root Item** available for pages captured using the **UI Automation** connector or the **SAP GUI** connector. This parameter is mostly useful for subpages where the root item can be set to a control captured in the page for the subpage.

In this section, we learned about the parameters that can be used to define additional criteria for pages or controls. There are also options in the **Criteria** panel to fine-tune the criteria based on data in the **Captured Data** panel or from the **Subtree** panel. We will learn about these options now.

Refining criteria in the Criteria panel

We learned about defining criteria for applications and pages in the *Defining criteria for applications and pages* section of *Chapter 12, Capturing and Declaring Applications, Pages, and Items*, using data in the **Captured Data** panel. We also learned to add the same criteria multiple times for an application, such as the `TITLE` criteria for the application to handle multiple versions of the application, as in *Figure 12.25* of that chapter. There are more options provided by SAP Intelligent RPA in the **Criteria** panel to support partial values for text values in the criteria or based on conditions for numbers in the criteria. We will now look at including conditions using operators in the **Criteria** panel.

Defining criteria using operators

The current criteria defined for the `SAPLogon760` application include supporting two versions of the SAP Logon application. The criteria for the `SAPLogon760` application look like this:

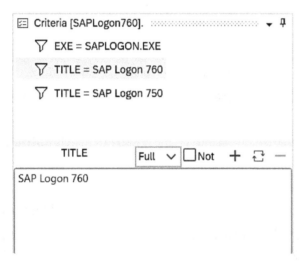

Figure 14.8 – Multiple TITLE criteria defined for SAP Logon application

Adding the same criteria will be considered by SAP Intelligent RPA to identify the application—that is, the application will be recognized with any one of the values added to `TITLE` defined for the application. Consider that a new SAP Logon application version is installed on the machine where the automation solution is to run. The title of the application will change according to the version of the application, and so the criteria for the application need to be updated every time a new version is deployed. SAP Intelligent RPA provides an option to check for partial text in the criteria. You can see the available operators include partial text in the criteria by clicking the down arrow of the combo box, which displays **Full** by default.

The available options depend on the type of value for the selected criteria—that is, either text or a number. Different operators available for TITLE as text are shown in the following screenshot:

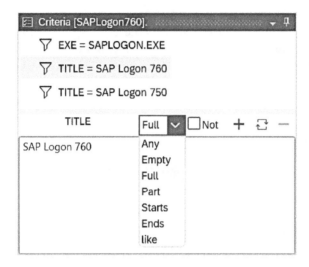

Figure 14.9 – Operators available for text criteria

We will first explain each of the operators before using the right operator in the criteria for the SAPLogon760 application, as follows:

- **Any**: This operator can be used to define criteria to match with any text value.
- **Empty**: This operator is used when the specified criteria should have an empty value.
- **Full**: This operator is used to match the exact text specified for the criteria.
- **Part**: This operator will match the text if that is contained in the criteria. The application, page, or UI control can have any text, but that should contain the value set in the criteria.
- **Starts**: The text of the property must start with the text defined in the criteria.
- **Ends**: The text of the property must end with the text defined in the criteria.
- **like**: This is like **Part** but is considered a **regular expression** (**regex**) to match the text value.

We can update the criteria for the SAPLogon760 application to use the **Starts** operator for the TITLE criteria with text SAP Logon using the following steps:

1. Select the TITLE criteria for the SAPLogon760 application in the **Criteria** panel.

2. Select the **Starts** operator for the text.

3. Remove the application version text (that is, 760) from the text.

4. Click on the **Update Criteria** button displayed with the refresh icon to update the criteria.

5. Remove the second TITLE criteria by selecting and then pressing the *Delete* button.

The updated criteria for the SAPLogon760 application should look like this:

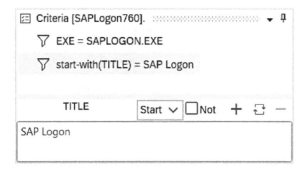

Figure 14.10 – Updated criteria for SAPLogon760 application

You can now see that the value for the TITLE criteria is updated to specify the operator being used. The updated criteria will now recognize any version of the SAP Logon application, ignoring the version of the application included in the title of the application.

You can also update the criteria for the pWindowSAPLogon76 page to use the **Part** text operator, as shown in the following screenshot:

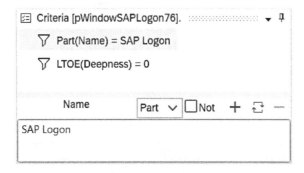

Figure 14.11 – Updated criteria for pWindowSAPLogon76 page

The pWindowSAPLogon76 page should now be recognized irrespective of the version of the application included in the name of the page.

As with the different operators available for the text properties of the application, page, or UI controls, there are operators available to define conditions for numeric values.

The available numeric operators can be seen by selecting a property with a numeric value in the **Captured Data** panel for an application, page, or UI control. The following screenshot shows the available CX property selected in the **Captured Data** panel for the pWindowSAPLogon76 page:

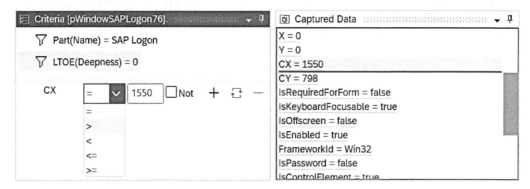

Figure 14.12 – Operators available for numeric criteria

Defining criteria with partial text must be used with caution as it might result in matching more than one application, page, or UI control that has the properties matching the defined criteria. SAP Intelligent RPA will recognize the first element with matching criteria to perform the activities defined on the control.

While using the text or numeric operators in the **Criteria** panel can cover most automation scenarios, there could be applications that pose challenges in defining criteria. SAP Intelligent RPA provides one more option to include the hierarchy while defining criteria for UI controls. We will learn how to define hierarchical criteria next.

Adding the parent hierarchy to criteria

We learned about defining criteria for pages and UI controls in *Chapter 12, Capturing and Declaring Applications, Pages, and Items,* using data in the **Captured Data** panel. We also learned how to use the **Parameters** panel or text and numeric operators in the **Criteria** panel to define additional criteria in this chapter. These methods cover most scenarios, though to automate a web page such as http://www.rpachallenge.com/, where the captured data for controls on the page will change after every loading of the page, you will notice that the order of controls and the properties of controls such as the **identifier** (**ID**) or the name of the control will change every time the page loads.

We need more options to define criteria to handle these types of pages. We will look at options provided by SAP Intelligent RPA to automate such pages with dynamic controls with no fixed data that can be directly used to define criteria for pages or UI controls. One option that SAP Intelligent RPA provides is to include the hierarchy in the criteria so that the target control is identified based on the parent hierarchy. We will look at this option now.

We will learn how to define hierarchical criteria using the `MyFirstProject` project that was created in *Chapter 10*, *Creating and Managing Projects*. Before we learn about the hierarchical criteria, let's move to the stage where we have the `Rpa Challenge` page captured by executing the following steps:

1. Open the `MyFirstProject` project in **Desktop Studio** and go to the **Explorer** perspective.
2. Click on the **+ Add Application** button in the **Project Tree** panel.
3. Launch `http://www.rpachallenge.com/` in the browser.
4. Select **Web** in the **Technology** field and refresh **Application List** in the **Capture Application** dialog.
5. Select the `Rpa Challenge` application from **Application List** and click on the **Save And Capture Page** button.
6. Select the `Rpa Challenge` page from **Page List** in the **Capture Page** dialog and then click on the **Scan And Capture** button.

    By the end of this step, you will have the `RpaChallenge` application declared in the **Applications** panel and the `pRpaChallenge` page captured under the application.

7. Add `DOMAIN` and `TITLE` values to the **Criteria** panel by double-clicking on them in the **Captured Data** panel for the `pRpaChallenge` page.

We now have the application and page ready to learn about defining criteria for the UI controls under the page. We will try capturing text fields where we need to enter data relevant to the label of the field—for example, we need to enter a valid phone number in the text field next to the **Phone Number** label on the page.

You can execute the following steps to capture fields:

1. In the **Screen Display** panel for the `pRpaChallenge` page, double-click on the input text field under the **Phone Number** label. Rename the newly captured control under the page `oPhone` from the default.

This will declare the text control under the `pRpaChallenge` page in the **Applications** panel, as shown in the following screenshot:

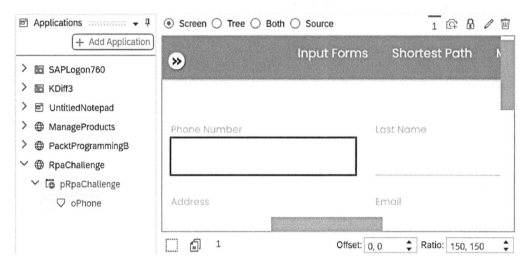

Figure 14.13 – The Phone Number input text field declared

The default criteria for this control will include the name of the control. As the name and ID of the controls on this page are dynamic and change for each page load, we cannot use these details in the criteria. So, remove the name from the criteria.

2.   In the **Subtree** panel for the `oPhone` control, select the parent **DIV** element. This element will have **LABEL – Phone Number** as the first child, as shown in the following screenshot:

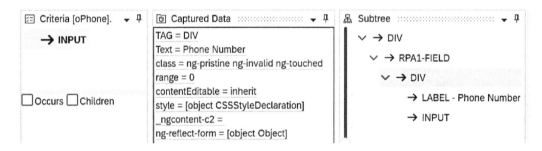

Figure 14.14 – Selecting the parent DIV element for the oPhone control

3.   Right-click on the selected **DIV** element and then click on the **Add as New Component in the Pattern** option from the context menu, as shown in the following screenshot:

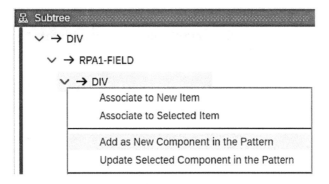

Figure 14.15 – Option to add the parent to criteria

4. The **Criteria** panel for the oPhone control will include the **DIV** element as a parent. You need to add **Text** as criteria for the **DIV** element with Phone Number as the value.

5. You will notice that the **Children** and **Target** checkboxes for INPUT in the **Criteria** panel are selected. The **Criteria** panel for the oPhone control will look like this:

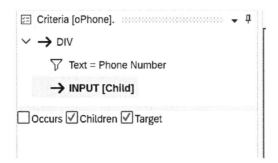

Figure 14.16 – The updated Criteria panel for oPhone

6. The updated criteria will instruct SAP Intelligent RPA to recognize any input text control under the **DIV** element with the **Text** property as Phone Number during runtime.

7. You can follow the same steps to capture all text fields on the page and add a parent **DIV** element with **Text** in the criteria.

Here, we have seen how to add one parent to the criteria; you can add the hierarchy from the root element in the criteria for the control. One example with three levels of hierarchy added to the input text for **Email** is shown in the following screenshot:

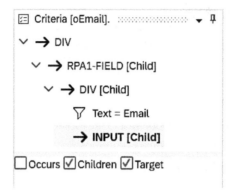

Figure 14.17 – The hierarchy of the parents added to the criteria

We learned how to use the parent hierarchy to recognize UI controls on the page. SAP Intelligent RPA will identify the control by recognizing the parent control first and then the children in the hierarchy. This feature will help you recognize controls with unique criteria available for parent controls if the target control does not have captured data that can be used to recognize the control.

We now know about the options provided in the **Criteria** panel to make the criteria as unique as possible for controls, but these options are not enough for capturing repeated elements such as rows or columns in a table or a list of search results on a web page. We will learn how to capture list data now.

We will learn about how the **Criteria** panel in **Desktop Studio** includes the **Occurs** option, which can be used to declare controls as an array.

Capturing repeated elements

We discussed posting a vendor invoice business process in the *Starting with your first automation project* section of *Chapter 12, Capturing and Declaring Applications, Pages, and Items*. Our target was to make only one entry for **G/L acct** and **Amount in doc.curr** in that business process, so we captured edGLAccount and edGLAmount controls from the first row of the table. SAP Intelligent RPA will identify the first control matching the criteria defined for UI controls, so the controls in the first row are recognized.

The FB60 transaction code that we aimed to automate as the business process allows business users to enter multiple **G/L acct** and **Amount in doc.curr** values for a single invoice. So, if we need to support multiple values to enter for these two, we need to capture all the **G/L acct** and **Amount in doc.curr** controls available under the tcItemsNoEntry table that we defined as **Ancestor** in the *The Ancestor parameter* section of this chapter.

SAP Intelligent RPA provides the **Occurs** option in the **Criteria** panel, which can be used to define control matching. Control matching defined criteria should be recognized as an array of controls instead of recognizing only the first control matching the criteria. This **Occurs** option is also available in the **Parameters** panel. You can use this option from either of the panels to specify a control is repeated. We can define **G/L acct** and **Amount in doc.curr** controls as an array by executing the following steps:

1. Open the Vendor Invoice Posting project and go to the **Explorer** perspective.

2. Select the edGLAccount control under the pEnterVendorInvoice page in the **Applications** panel.

3. Go to the **Criteria** panel and select the **Occurs** checkbox.

4. You will notice that all **G/L acct** controls matching the criteria are highlighted in the **Screen Display** panel, as shown in the following screenshot:

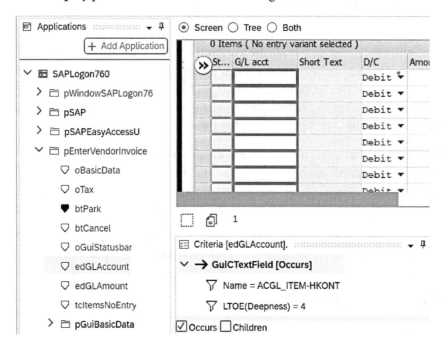

Figure 14.18 – Capturing an array of controls matching the criteria

5. You need to select the **Occurs** option in the **Criteria** panel for the edGLAmount control to recognize it as an array of controls.

After updating the criteria for both edGLAccount and edGLAmount controls to declare these controls as an array, the **G/L acct** and **Amount in doc.curr** controls in all rows are highlighted in the **Screen Display** panel. If you want to set values for these controls, you need to access them using an index such as edGLAccount[0] for the first control in the array in a loop.

We have now learned how to recognize an array of controls; the same option can be used to capture a web page for a business process that requires reading repeated data, such as search results. Let's try capturing the books available on the https://www.packtpub.com/ web page by searching for automation.

First, we will prepare the page to capture in **Desktop Studio** by executing the following steps:

1. Open the https://www.packtpub.com/ page in the web browser.

2. Enter Automation in the **Search** box of the page and press *Enter*.

3. The page will navigate to https://www.packtpub.com/eu/ catalogsearch/result?q=Automation to display a list of books available on automation. The page display might change based on the country you choose on the site.

We have a page with a list of search results to capture in **Desktop Studio**. We already added the PacktProgrammingB web application to the MyFirstProject project for the https://www.packtpub.com/ web page in the *The Web connector* section of *Chapter 11, An Introduction to Technology Connectors*. We will use the same application to capture the search results page by executing the following steps:

1. Open the MyFirstProject project in **Desktop Studio** and go to the **Explorer** perspective.

2. Select the PacktProgrammingB application and select the **Capture a new Page...** menu option from the context menu.

3. Select the Search results for: Automation page from the **Page List** in the **Capture Page** dialog, and then click on the **Scan And Capture** button.

4. The pSearchResultsForA page will be added to the PacktProgrammingB application after the page scan is complete.

5. Add DOMAIN and TITLE values to the **Criteria** panel by double-clicking on them in the **Captured Data** panel for both the PacktProgrammingB application and the pSearchResultsForA page.

    We have the search results page declared in the **Applications** panel. We will aim to capture the titles of all the books, the number of pages in each book, and their prices.

6. Capture one book title. Titles are defined with a **B** tag in the source. Rename the title control oTitle.

7. Select the **Occurs** option in the **Criteria** panel for the oTitle control. We cannot use the title text in the criteria as the text will change for each book in the search results, so we will add three levels of the parent **DIV** element to the criteria. The **Criteria** panel for oTitle, after adding three levels of parent **DIV** tags, will look like this:

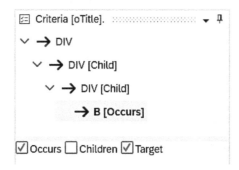

Figure 14.19 – Criteria defined for the oTitle control

The first level of the criteria for the oTitle control will be the **DIV** element where all the book search results are displayed. This will ensure only the title from the search results is captured, even if there is any other text on the whole page that is included in the **B** tag.

8. Capture a single text with pages of the book. Pages are defined with a **P** tag in the source. Rename this control oPages.

9. Select the **Occurs** option in the **Criteria** panel for the oPages control. Add only the **DIV** element where all the book search results are displayed, as with the criteria for the oTitle control. Further, the **Text** property in the **Captured Data** panel for this control will end with the text pages, so we can update the criteria as follows:

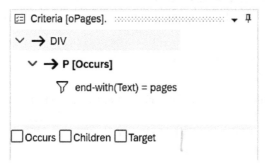

Figure 14.20 – Criteria defined for the oPages control

10. You can now capture the price for one book and then update criteria such as the oPages control to include the hierarchy. Prices are defined with a **SPAN** tag in the source. Rename the prices control as oPrice. You need to change the **Text** property to start with the currency symbol displayed on the page. The **Criteria** panel for oPrice looks like this:

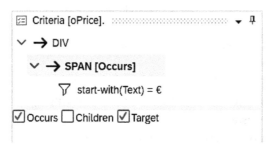

Figure 14.21 – Criteria defined for the oPrice control

After all three controls are defined under the pSearchResultsForA page, you should see that all the titles, pages, and prices for each book should be highlighted in the **Screen Display** panel for the page.

We have now learned how to capture a list of values from a web page in the **Explorer** perspective. These controls can be used to get values and store them in context variables that can be created, as discussed in the *Variable declaration* section of *Chapter 12, Capturing and Declaring Applications, Pages, and Items*. To store the values of controls with **Occurs** criteria set, you need to define a context variable with the **Is Array** option set to true.

We now have learned how to capture a list of values such as search results from a web page. Once context variables are created, you can try creating a workflow to read the search results from the web page. To process a list of results in the workflow, you need to know how loops can be implemented in a workflow.

Summary

In this chapter, we learned about different techniques or options that **SPA Intelligent RPA** provides to capture controls that allow us to automate any page. We learned about using the **Must Exist** and **Must Not Exist** parameters in the **Parameters** panel to recognize a page based on the controls on the page. We also learned how to use the **Ancestor** and **Labelled By** parameters to recognize controls relating to other controls on the page. We also learned how to use text and numeric operators and how to declare a list of elements in the **Criteria** panel.

These options will help developers to capture and uniquely recognize any page or control irrespective of the technology used to develop automation target applications.

We will learn about options provided by **Desktop Studio** to implement conditional flows and repeated execution of the same steps in a loop in the next chapter.

Questions

Here are some questions for you to test your knowledge. The answers to these questions can be found at the back of the book, in the section named *Assessments*:

1. There are two options to define a hierarchy for a control. One is to use the **Ancestor** parameter and the other is to add the parent hierarchy in the **Criteria** panel. When should you use each of these options?

2. Why are some parameters such as **Labelled By** not available for a few controls?

3. How do you read data from a control when **Occurs** is set in the **Criteria** panel?

4. How are controls recognized by SAP Intelligent RPA if there is more than one control with matching criteria?

15
Controlling Workflows and Scenarios

We already created a workflow called SAPInvoicePosting in *Chapter 13*, *Designing Scenarios*, with a single sequence of activities to complete the posting of a vendor invoice. In a real-time scenario, there might be conditions that mean we need to execute the same steps multiple times – for example, we need to post multiple vendor invoices. Another condition could be to skip or include a few steps based on a condition – for example, we need to skip the step to go to the tax tab for vendor invoices if tax is not applicable. Similarly, we might want to reuse certain steps, such as activities to log in to or log out of the SAP server.

Let's explore the options that **SAP Intelligent RPA** provides to cover the following topics:

- Creating reusable scenarios
- Creating a workflow with loops and conditional flows
- Adding loops in the workflow
- Adding conditional flows to the workflow
- Reusing the scenarios and passing data

By end of this chapter, you will have a sound understanding of creating scenarios that can be reused in multiple business processes, executing activities in a loop, and adding conditions to a scenario to execute additional activities or skip some activities.

Let's first work on creating scenarios to reuse.

Technical requirements

- Desktop Studio installed on your workstation.

- The SAP Logon application, pages, and controls have been captured, as discussed in *Chapter 12, Capturing and Declaring Applications, Pages, and Items.*

- The SAPInvoicePosting workflow that was discussed in *Chapter 13, Designing Scenarios*, has been created, and you are now familiar with adding activities to a workflow or page.

Creating reusable scenarios

Before proceeding with creating multiple scenarios to reuse certain scenarios, let's first look at the business process that we discussed in the *Starting with your first automation project* section of *Chapter 12, Capturing and Declaring Applications, Pages, and Items*, to automate. We will enhance the same business process, aiming to cover reusability, looping, and conditional flows.

The vendor invoice posting business process will be split into three subprocesses, and each subprocess will be automated as a separate workflow to perform certain steps, as explained in the following sections.

SAP Login subprocess

This subprocess is used to log in to the SAP server after starting the application. We will be creating the SAPLogin workflow that will perform the following steps:

1. Start the **SAP Logon** application.

2. Select an existing connection to the SAP server from the **SAP Logon** page. The **SAP** page to enter the credentials to the SAP server will be displayed.

3. Enter the credentials on the **SAP** page and log in to the SAP server. The page will transition to the **SAP Easy Access** page.

The steps that are required to log in to the SAP server are common for any business process or SAP transaction. Once this scenario is created, we will be able to include the same steps in all the business processes before entering the SAP transaction code specific to a business process.

The SAPPostVendorInvoice subprocess

For this subprocess, a SAPPostVendorInvoice workflow will be created with steps very specific to the FB60 transaction code. We can create specific scenarios for any SAP transaction code. This will be invoked after the SAPLogin workflow execution is complete:

1. Enter the FB60 SAP transaction code on the **SAP Easy Access** page to navigate to the **Enter Vendor Invoice** page.

2. Start the loop to post multiple vendor invoices.

3. In the **Basic data** tab of **Enter Vendor Invoice**, fill in the **Vendor, Invoice Date**, and **Amount** details.

4. Check the condition to include tax. If the tax code is available, then navigate to the **Tax** tab to enter the tax code. Skip this step if there is no tax to be included in the vendor invoice.

5. Fill in the **G/L acct** and **Amount in doc.curr.** fields in the **Enter Vendor Invoice** page and post the invoice.

6. Read the status of the invoice posting and store it in a variable.

7. Repeat steps *3 to 6* for all the invoices.

8. Exit the **Enter Vendor invoice** page by clicking the **Exit** button after all the invoices are posted.

As this workflow is specific to the SAP transaction code, we will not be able to reuse this workflow in other business processes. Let's now explore the SAPLogoff workflow.

The SAPLogoff subprocess

This process is used to log off from the SAP server after completing the process execution. This can be considered a cleanup scenario. We will be creating the SAPLogoff workflow that will perform the following steps:

1. Exit the **SAP Easy Access** page by clicking the **Log-off** button.

2. Close the **SAP Logon** application.

Once these three workflows are created, we will be creating a single workflow called `SAPInvoicePosting` that invokes these three scenarios in a sequence.

Let's first create the reusable scenarios.

Creating the SAPLogin workflow

We will follow the same steps that are used in the *Creating your first workflow* section of *Chapter 13*, *Designing Scenarios*, to create a new workflow with the name `SAPLogin`. Execute the following steps to create the workflow:

1. Open the `Vendor Invoice Posting` project in **Desktop Studio**.
2. Create a new workflow with the name `SAPLogin` under the **GLOBAL** node in the **Workflow** perspective.
3. Open the **SAPLogin** workflow by double-clicking on it, and include the following activities after the **Start** node.
4. Add the **Start** application activity to start the **SAP Logon** application.
5. On the **pWindowSAPLogon76** page, select the connection to the SAP server. We already included this in our workflow. The **pSAP** page will be displayed.
6. On the **pSAP** page, enter the credentials and log in to the SAP server.
7. Save the **SAPLogin** workflow.

The final list of activities for this workflow will be displayed, as shown in the following screenshot:

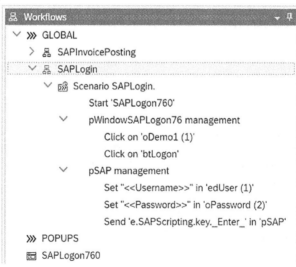

Figure 15.1 – The SAPLogin workflow activities

> **Important Note**
>
> You need to replace <<Username>> and <<Password>> with your
> SAP server credentials while adding the activities. Similarly, oDemo1 is the
> connection name you want to use to connect with SAP server.

We have now a workflow that can be used to connect and log into the SAP server.
Let's now create another workflow named SAPLogoff.

Creating the SAPLogoff workflow

We need to follow similar steps to what we used to create the SAPLogin workflow, but
the pages and activities in this workflow are for logging off from the SAP server. This
process starts after the business process execution is completed and we have exited the
vendor invoice process screens, so the steps for this process will start as follows:

1. Create a new workflow with the name SAPLogoff under the **GLOBAL** node in the
    Workflow perspective.

2. Open the SAPLogoff workflow by double-clicking on it, and include the following
    activities after the Start node.

3. On the **pSAPEasyAccessU** page, add an activity to send
    e.SAPScripting.key._Shift__F3_keystroke to log off from the SAP
    server. The **pLogOff** page will be displayed.

4. On the **pLogOff** page, click on btYes to confirm logout.

5. Add the **End** application activity to close the **SAP Logon** application.

6. Save the SAPLogoff workflow.

The final list of activities for this workflow will be displayed, as shown in the following screenshot:

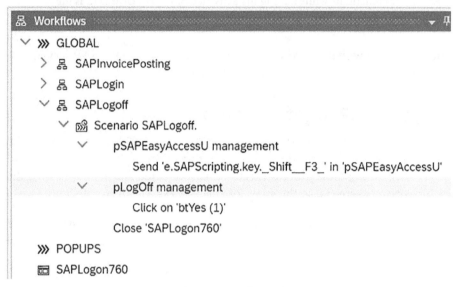

Figure 15.2 – The SAPLogoff workflow activities

Okay, we now have our two workflows that can be reused for any business process that requires login to the SAP server and logout at the end. We will now move on to the SAP post vendor invoice subprocess and create the SAPPostVendorInvoice workflow, which requires us to include loops and conditional flows.

We will start with creating the flow and look at the loops and conditional flows when required.

Creating a workflow with loops and conditional flows

We will create the workflow called SAPPostVendorInvoice, in which we will include all the steps required for the **SAP post vendor invoice** subprocess. We will use the same pages and activities that we used in *Chapter 13*, *Designing Scenarios*, to post the vendor invoice. We will additionally include activities required to loop through multiple invoices and post, and make the tax data optional in the workflow based on the availability of data.

Before we start with the workflow, as we want to post multiple invoices, we need to update the context to include an array of the invoices. We can do this by checking the box that is next to the Invoice variable folder in the **Context** panel to indicate it as an array, as shown in the following screenshot:

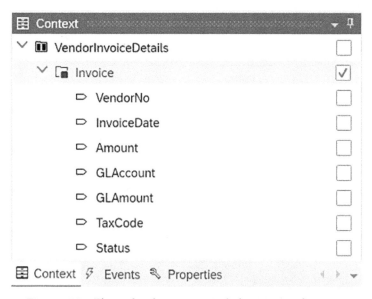

Figure 15.3 – The updated context to include an array of invoices

Our context to hold multiple invoices to post and fetch statuses is now ready. We will create the SAPPostVendorInvoice workflow by following these steps:

1. Add the **pSAPEasyAccessU** page next to the **Start** node.

2. Open the page **Designer** view by double-clicking on the **pSAPEasyAccessU** page and add the following two activities to the page:

   1. Add the **Set** activity from the **Item - Set** activity group to set **FB60** to **oGuiOkCodeField**.

   2. Add the **Click** activity from the **Item - Click** activity group to click on the **btGuiButton** button.

The next page to add is **pGuiBasicData**, but remember that we need to post multiple invoices with each invoice including its data, which needs to be set before posting the invoice. So, we need to start the loop here. We will now look at the activities that **SAP Intelligent RPA** provides to execute the same steps multiple times or in a loop.

Adding loops to the workflow

To execute the activities on pages or steps in a workflow, SAP Intelligent RPA provides activities under the **Flow – Loop** activity group in the **Activities** panel. As with the vendor invoice posting business process, we will be posting multiple vendor invoices with the same workflow by using these activities.

The loop activities are shown in the following screenshot:

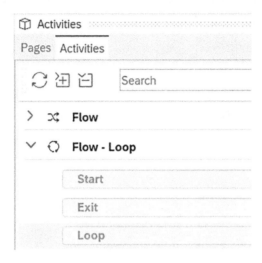

Figure 15.4 – The activities available to support the loop

Let's understand each of these activities and when to use them:

- The **Start** activity: This activity denotes when the loop starts in the workflow. We will include this activity at the start of the steps that require looping. In our business process, we will start the loop after entering the **Enter Vendor Invoice** page.

- The **Exit** activity: This activity follows the **Start** activity. Here, we will be specifying the condition to exit the loop. If we are looping through an array variable, we can specify the variable name for the exit condition.

- The **Loop** activity: This activity is to be included at the end of the steps within the loop. Execution will go back to the **Start** activity, check the condition, and either exit the loop based on the exit condition or continue with execution if more data is to be processed.

We will be using these activities to post multiple invoices by including these activities in our SAPPostVendorInvoice workflow.

Updating the SAPPostVendorInvoice workflow with a loop

Now that we understand the available activities, let's now use them in our workflow to define multiple invoice posting:

1. Add the **Start** activity from the **Flow – Loop** activity group after the **pSAPEasyAccessU** page in the SAPPostVendorInvoice workflow. This indicates the start of the steps that need to be executed in a loop.

2. Add the **pGuiBasicData** page next to the Start loop node.

3. Open the page **Designer** view by double-clicking on **pGuiBasicData**.

   The first activity we need to add to this page is the exit condition to the loop. Let's add the **Exit** activity from the **Flow – Loop** activity group to the page. We need to set the condition in the **Properties** panel for this activity, as shown in the following screenshot:

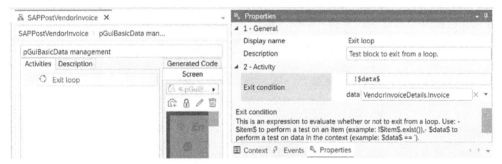

Figure 15.5 – Properties for the Exit loop activity

> **Important Note**
>
> The **Exit condition** value is added. We specified $data$ and the **data** value as the VendorInvoiceDetails.Invoice array variable from the context. This indicates that the loop must execute till there are no more elements in the array.

We have added the start loop and exit loop activity to our workflow. We need to add the loop activity that denotes the end of the steps to be executed in the loop. We will add this activity after adding the remaining activities to be executed in the loop:

4. Add the following three activities for the **pGuiBasicData** page after the Exit loop activity:

   1. Set the **VendorInvoiceDetails.Invoice.VendorNo** variable value to the **edVendor** control.

2. Set the **VendorInvoiceDetails.Invoice.InvoiceDate** variable value to the **edInvoiceDate** control.

3. Set the **VendorInvoiceDetails.Invoice.Amount** variable value to the **edAmount** control.

5. The next step is to click on the `oCalculateTax` control. However, we want to click `oCalculateTax` and go to the **pGuiTax** subpage only if there is a tax code available.

We will now look at the activities that are available to control the flow based on conditions.

Adding a conditional flows to the workflow

Let's now learn about the activities provided by SAP Intelligent RPA that we can use to execute the steps based on a certain condition.

SAP Intelligent RPA provides an activity called **Switches output** under the **Flow** activity group, highlighted in the following screenshot, that is used to include a conditional flow:

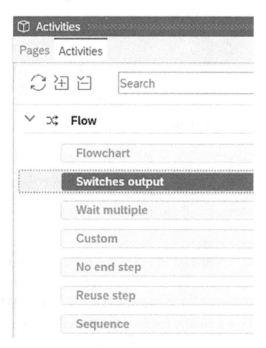

Figure 15.6 – Activities available to control the flow in a workflow

The **Switches output** activity is used to include a conditional flow based on the output returned by the previous step. That means we will need to return the output in the previous step based on the condition. Let's look at the activities that are available to set the output of the step and ways to check the conditions.

There are two activity groups, namely the **Flow – If** activity group and the **Flow** activity group. These two activity groups are available when adding activities to a page. Both activity groups are shown in the following screenshot:

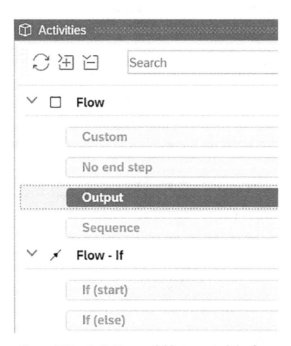

Figure 15.7 – Activities available to control the flow

Let's understand these activities and when to use them:

- The **Output** activity: This activity is used to return a value from the step.
- The **If (start)** activity: This activity is used to execute certain steps only if a condition is true.
- The **If (else)** activity: This activity is used to execute certain steps only if a condition is false. This activity must be included only if there is an **If (start)** activity.

We have seen the activities to control the flows; now, we need to use them in our business process.

Updating the SAPPostVendorInvoice workflow with conditions

As with the vendor invoice posting business process, we will include the following steps only if there is a tax code available in the vendor invoice. If there is no tax code, then we need to exclude these steps:

1. Click on the `oCalculateTax` control in the **pGuiBasicData** sub-page.

2. Click on the **oTax** control to move to the **pGuiTax** sub-page.

3. Set the tax code to **cbGuiComboBox**.

We need to use the **If (start)** and **If (else)** activities to check the tax value availability and define the control flow. We will also set the output for this step to include the conditional workflow. Execute the following steps on the **pGuiBasicData** page:

1. Add the **If (start)** activity from the **Flow - If** activity group to the **pGuiBasicData** page. Update the properties for this activity, as shown in the following screenshot:

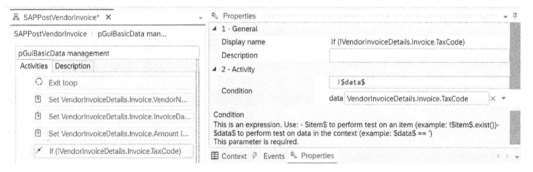

Figure 15.8 – The properties for the If (start) activity

> **Important Note**
>
> Observe the values added to the **Condition** property. We specified `!$data$` and the **data** value as the `VendorInvoiceDetails.Invoice.TaxCode` variable from the context. This indicates that the steps under this condition will execute only if there is no value for the tax code.

2.   Drag the **Output** activity from the **Flow** activity group and drop it on the **if (start)** activity added in the previous step. It should be dropped on the **If (start)** activity so that it is defined under the condition hierarchy, rather than at the same level of this activity. Update the **Output value** property to SkipTax. Look at the following screenshot to check how the **Output** activity is now aligned under the **If (start)** activity:

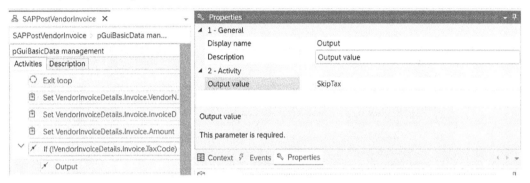

Figure 15.9 – The properties for the If (start) activity

The **Output value** property set as SkipTax will be used to control the next steps executed in the workflow.

3.   Add the **IF (else)** activity from the **Flow - If** activity group at the same level as the **Output** activity that was added in the previous step.

> **Important Note**
> The activities in the **Activities** panel can be rearranged by dragging them with the mouse and dropping them at the right position.

4.   Add the following activities under the **if (else)** activity.

1.   Set the oCalculateTax control as true.

2.   Add the **Output** activity from the **Flow** activity group and set the **Output value** property as ProcessTax.

The complete list of activities and the activity hierarchy for the **pGuiBasicData** sub-page can be viewed in the following screenshot:

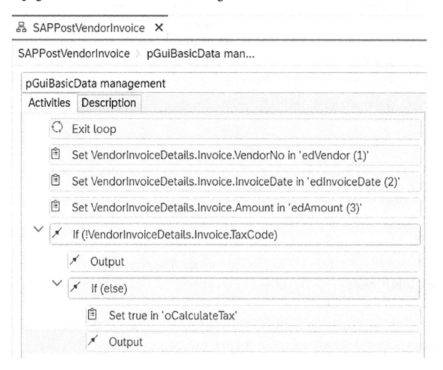

Figure 15.10 – Activities added to the pGuiBasicData subpage

We have added all the activities required for the **pGuiBasicData** page; we have also set the page output as required by the conditions. We need to use the output from this page to control the next steps in the workflow.

Go to the SAPPostVendorInvoice workflow, where we will continue updating the workflow by including the pages and activities.

5. Add the **Switches output** activity from the **Flow** activity group after the **pGuiBasicData** page. This activity allows us to add multiple flows based on the output value returned from the **pGuiBasicData** page. Remember that we have set two outputs, SkipTax and the ProcessTax, based on the conditions in the **pGuiBasicData** page.

6. Add the **pEnterVendorInvoice** page next to the **Switches output** activity. Remove the line with `Default` if that is added and add a new line from the **Switches output** activity to the **pEnterVendorInvoice** page. We need to change the label for the new line to `ProcessTax` for the **DefaultCaseDisplayName** property in the **Properties** panel for this line, as we need to enter this page and click the **Tax** tab only if there is a tax code available. Add the following activity to the page:

    - Add the **Click** activity from the **Item – Click** activity group to the `oTax` control.

7. Add the **pGuiTax** sub-page after the **pEnterVendorInvoice** page. We will add one activity in this page to set the tax code as follows:

    - Set the `VendorInvoiceDetails.Invoice.TaxCode` variable value to the `edGuiComboBox` control.

    The preceding two steps are required only if we need to process the tax, but the next step is required even if there is no tax.

8. Add the **pEnterVendorInvoice** page again after the **pGuiTax** sub-page. We will set the rest of the values on the page and post the invoice. Add the following activity to the page:

    1. Set the `VendorInvoiceDetails.Invoice.GLAmount` variable value to the `edGLAmount` control.
    2. Click on the `oBasicData` tab control.
    3. Send `e.SAPScripting.key._F8_` key to the page.
    4. Get the `oGuiStatusbar` value to store in the `VendorInvoiceDetails.Invoice.Status` variable.
    5. Set the `VendorInvoiceDetails.Invoice.GLAccount` variable value to the `edGLAccount` control.

9. We need to now draw another line from the **Switches output** activity to the **pEnterVendorInvoice** page added in the preceding step. The label name will be `SkipTax`, which is the same as one of the outputs from the **pGuiBasicData** page for this line.

10. Add the **Loop** activity from the **Flow – Loop** activity group after the **pEnterVendorInvoice** page.

We have now added all the activities required to post multiple invoices. The complete flow should look like the following screenshot:

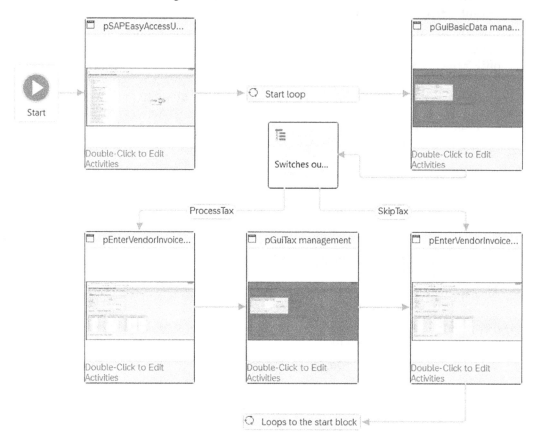

Figure 15.11 – The SAPPostVendorInvoice workflow

Furthermore, refer to the following screenshot for the complete list of activities added to the SAPPostVendorInvoice workflow:

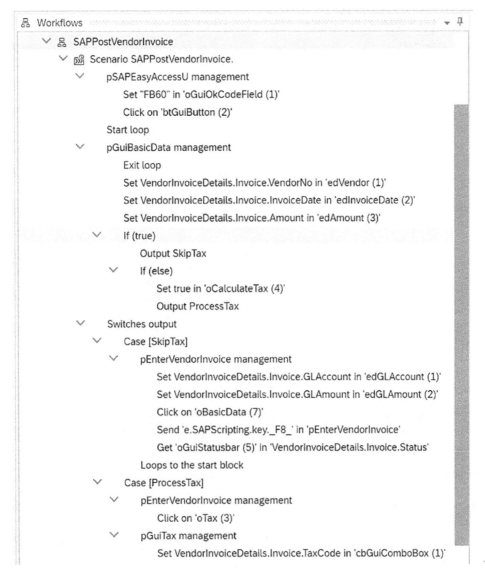

Figure 15.12 – Activities added to the SAPPostVendorInvoice workflow

We have now created workflows for all three scenarios. Let's learn how to use them to create a single workflow.

Reusing scenarios and passing data

SAP Intelligent RPA provides activities to start one scenario from another scenario. To do this, we can use the **Start** activity available under the **Scenario** activity group in the **Activities** panel, as shown in the following screenshot:

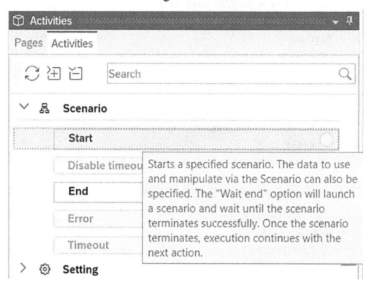

Figure 15.13 – The Start activity under the Scenario activity group

We will be using this activity to start the workflows created for each of the subprocesses. Let's first create a new workflow called `SAPInvoicePosting` using the same method to create previous workflows.

Execute the following steps to include existing workflows in this workflow:

1. Create a new workflow with the name `SAPInvoicePosting` under the `GLOBAL` node in the **Workflow** perspective.

    > **Important Note**
    > The workflow name should be unique within the hierarchy. If you already have a workflow with the same name, rename the existing `SAPInvoicePosting` workflow to `SAPSingleInvoicePosting` and then create a new workflow with the name `SAPInvoicePosting`.

2. Open the `SAPInvoicePosting` workflow by double-clicking on it.

3. Add the **Start** activity from the **Scenario** activity group after the `Start` node of the workflow and update the properties of the new activity, as shown in the following screenshot:

Figure 15.14 – The Scenario Start activity properties

Let's look at the properties of the **Scenario Start** activity:

- The **Scenario** property: This is the name of the workflow/scenario that we want to start. We want to start the SAPLogin workflow first in this workflow, so select this workflow name for this property.

- The **Data used with the scenario** property: Here, we are passing the VendorInvoiceDetails folder variable created in the **Context** panel to this scenario.

> **Important Note**
> We have not yet updated the values to the variables. We will look at setting the values of the variables in the upcoming chapters.

We included the SAPLogin workflow in the SAPInvoicePosting workflow. The same workflow can be included in multiple workflows with different data:

1. Add another **Start** activity from the **Scenario** activity group after the previously added node and select the SAPPostVendorInvoice workflow in the **Scenario** property. We need to set the VendorInvoiceDetails value for the Data used with the scenario property, as we will be processing the invoices in this context.

2. Add one more **Start** activity from the **Scenario** activity group after the previously added node and select the SAPLogoff workflow in the **Scenario** property. We do not need to set any value for the **Data used with the scenario** property, as no data is needed by this scenario.

3. Save the SAPInvoicePosting workflow.

We have added three workflows in the `SAPInvoicePosting` workflow to execute them sequentially. When executing this scenario, the bot logs into a selected SAP server connection, then processes all the invoices available in the context pass to the workflow, and then logs off the SAP server.

Our workflow is now ready to build, but before building the project and generating the code, we will look at the custom dialog creation feature provided by SAP Intelligent RPA.

Summary

In this chapter, we learned about creating reusable workflows and using them in another workflow. We also learned about creating conditional flows based on the output set by the previous step, and adding conditions to execute or skip some activities. Most real-life automation scenarios include conditions and looping through multiple data sets. SAP Intelligent RPA provides activities to support these scenarios. It is also important to look at a business's process steps and define workflows that can be reused to increase development productivity.

We created workflows that cover the conditions discussed in the business process and are ready to proceed with the next step, which is to build a project to generate code. We will learn about generating code in the upcoming chapters.

In the next chapter, we will learn about creating custom dialogs.

Questions

Here are some questions for you to test your knowledge. The answers to these questions can be found at the back of the book in the section named *Assessments*:

1. What is the mandatory condition to include an **if (else)** activity on a page?
2. Is it possible to include more than two conditional flows in a workflow?
3. What are `$data$` and `$item$`? Where can they be used?

16
Designing Custom Pages with UI Designer

We captured the pages and UI controls from the **SAP Logon** application and created a context in *Chapter 12*, *Capturing and Declaring Applications, Pages, and Items*. We used the captured information to create multiple workflows in *Chapter 15*, *Controlling Workflows and Scenarios*. Remember, the context was only declared and never initialized with values required to post an invoice. The information required for the business process can be captured in multiple ways, such as reading emails or processing Excel files. We will be exploring integration with Outlook or Excel in the upcoming chapters. One way to populate values to a context is to provide a custom page for users to enter the details.

SAP Intelligent RPA provides the **UI Designer** perspective to develop custom pages/dialogs. These custom pages can then be integrated with the workflow as any page that was captured from an application. In this chapter, we'll extend our knowledge about the **UI Designer** perspective that we learned in *Chapter 9*, *Desktop Studio Perspectives*, to create and design a custom page called VendorInvoice that enables the user to enter invoice details and store them in the context.

In this chapter, we will learn about the following topics:

- Creating custom pages
- Designing custom pages
- Using the custom pages in a workflow

By the end of this chapter, you should be comfortable with creating a custom page/dialog using **Desktop Studio**.

Let's now look at creating custom pages.

Technical requirements

- Have Desktop Studio installed on your workstation.
- Ensure the SAPInvoicePosting workflow that was discussed in *Chapter 15, Controlling Workflows and Scenarios*, is created.

Creating custom pages

To create custom pages, we will use the **UI Designer** perspective in **Desktop Studio**. The aim of the custom page that we are creating is to allow users to enter the invoice details that we need to post. So, we will be creating a custom page named VendorInvoice to allow users to enter the invoice details to post in the Vendor Invoice Posting project. Execute the following steps to create a custom page:

1. Start the Desktop Studio application and open the Vendor Invoice Posting project.
2. Go to the **UI Designer** perspective.
3. Right-click on the **POPUPS** node of the **UI Designer** panel and select **Add a new Popup...** from the context menu. The **Add Popup** dialog box is displayed.

4. Enter `VendorInvoice` for **Name** and select the **An Empty Popup** option for **Template**, as shown in the following screenshot:

Figure 16.1 – Add Popup dialog

5. Click on the **Add** button. This will create the `VendorInvoice` dialog under the **POPUPS** node. The page will be opened in the **Designer View** panel to add the controls.

Our page/dialog is ready to design now. We will be adding controls to the page where users can enter the invoice details. Let's proceed and design our page.

Designing custom pages

The `VendorInvoice` custom page requires UI controls to be added allowing users to enter the values to store in the context variables. Note that the `Status` variable is used to get the status of the invoice posting and so is not to be captured from the process user. We will add controls to this page to allow users to enter the values for other invoice details in the context.

Let's now add the controls to the `VendorInvoice` page in the **Designer View** panel to capture and store the information to six variables, which are `VendorNo`, `InvoiceDate`, `Amount`, `GLAccount`, `GLAmount`, and `TaxCode`. These values can then be used to set on the pages while executing the business process.

The **UI Designer** perspective provides many options for designing the popup and arranging the controls in a grid or table format. Control can then be added to a cell in the table or grid. The options available for designing the popup can be viewed from the context menu in the **Designer View** panel. Ensure that you are in **Design Mode** in the **Designer View** panel by clicking the **Grid** icon that is highlighted in the following screenshot. You can also see the context menu here:

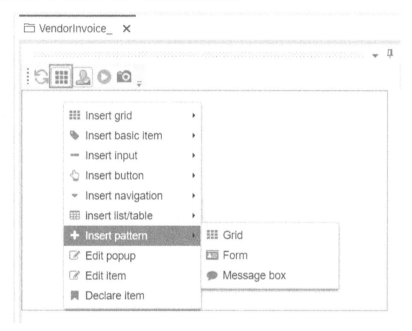

Figure 16.2 – Context menu of the Designer View panel

You can add as many rows and columns as required to the canvas, to place those required UI controls. You can directly add the UI controls to the canvas as well.

We will be adding the controls directly to the canvas from the context menu now by executing the following steps:

1. The first control to add to this popup is to capture the vendor number. Select the **Insert Input | Text** context menu option. A text control will be added to the canvas with default properties. We will then update the properties of the newly added control in the **Properties** panel as follows:

   1. Change the **id** property value to `VendorNo`.

   2. Change the **test** value property to `Enter Vendor Number`.

   3. Change the **item label** property to `Vendor Number:`.

   4. Change the **icon** property to **none**.

You can refer to the following screenshot for the updated properties list:

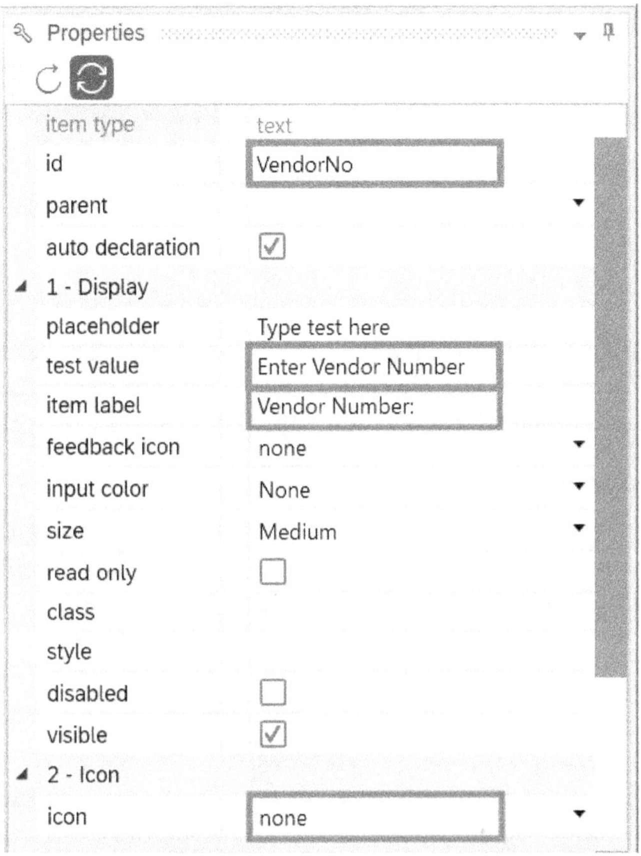

Figure 16.3 – Updated properties for VendorNo control

With one control added to the `VendorInvoice` custom page, we move to the next step of adding more UI controls to the page.

2. We will add a control now to allow the user to enter the invoice date. Select the **Insert Input | date** context menu option. Update the properties of the newly added date control in the **Properties** panel as follows:

    1. Change the **id** property value to `InvoiceDate`.

    2. Change the **item label** property to `Invoice Date:`.

3. The next control to add to this popup is to capture the invoice amount. The value entered here is stored in both the `Amount` and `GLAmount` variables. Select the **Insert Input | number** context menu option. Update the properties of this control in the **Properties** panel as follows:

    1. Change the **id** property value to `Amount`.

    2. Change the **item label** property to `Amount:`.

    3. Change the **icon** property to `usd`.

4. Now, we will add a checkbox control to allow users to specify whether tax is applicable for the invoice. We will be storing the tax code only if this checkbox is checked while submitting the data. We can add the checkbox by selecting the **Insert Input | checkbox** option from the context menu. Three checkbox items will be added by default. Update the properties of the checkbox control as follows:

    1. Change the **id** property value to `IncludeTax`.

    2. Remove the **item label** property value. We do not want to have a separate label for this control. We will be changing the checkbox label instead.

    3. Expand the **Items** property to display the list of default items.

    4. Change the **id** property value of the **[0]** item to `TaxCheck`.

    5. **[1]** and **[2]** under the **Items** property can be deleted by clicking on the – sign displayed next to the item.

5. We will now add a control to capture the tax code by selecting the **Insert Input | text** menu option from the context menu. Update the properties of this control as follows:

    1. Change the **id** property value to `TaxCode`.

    2. Change the **test value** property to `Enter Tax Code`.

    3. Change the **item label** property to `Tax Code:`.

    4. Change the **icon** property to **none**.

6. Add a new control to capture the G/L account by selecting the **Insert Input | number** menu option from the context menu. Update the properties of this control as follows:

    1. Change the **id** property value to `GLAccount`.

    2. Change the **item label** property to `G/L Account:`.

    3. Change the **icon** property to **none**.

We have now added all the controls required to input the invoice information.

We need to add a submit button so the information entered by the user in this dialog is stored in the context, as well as an option to cancel this dialog. We will add the submit and cancel buttons at the end of the page and align them to the right. To make the button aligned to the right, we will first add a row with four columns. Add the submit button to the third column and the cancel button to the fourth column. We will first add a row with four columns by executing the following steps:

1. Select the **Insert grid | row + 4 columns** context menu option to add a row with four columns to the page. Update the properties of the row as follows:

    1. Change the **id** property value to buttonRow.

    2. Change the **parent** property value of all four columns to buttonRow.

    3. Change the **id** property value of col3 to colSubmit.

    4. Change the **id** property value of col4 to colCancel.

2. Add a button to the page by selecting the **Insert button | button (label)** context menu option and update the properties as follows:

    1. Change the **id** property value to submit.

    2. Change the **parent** property to colSubmit.

    3. Change the **value** property to Submit.

    4. Keep the **submit** button property checked.

    5. Change the **icon** property to **plus**.

3. Add a button to the page by selecting the **Insert button | button (label)** context menu option and update the properties as follows:

    1. Change the **id** property value to cancel.

    2. Change the **parent** property to colCancel.

    3. Change the **value** property to Cancel.

    4. Keep the **close** button and escape key properties checked.

    5. Change the **icon** property to minus.

Note

The designer canvas size can be increased by updating the **CY** property of the page or in the settings.js file. Select the VendorInvoice page in the **UI Designer** panel to display the page properties and update the **CY** value to 500 to increase the page height.

Our page design is now complete. We have added all the controls required to capture invoice information and buttons to submit or cancel have been added. The completed page will look as in the following screenshot:

Figure 16.4 – Custom page designed to capture the invoice details

The VendorInvoice custom page is now ready. Use the *Ctrl + Shift + S* shortcut to save all files in the project.

We will now look at how to make the new popup available to include in a workflow.

Using the custom pages in a workflow

Before a custom page or popup can be used in the workflow, the page needs to be captured by clicking on the **Capture** (displayed as a camera) icon in the **Designer View** panel that is highlighted in the following screenshot:

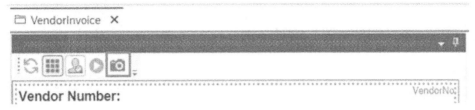

Figure 16.5 – Option to capture a custom page

You can ignore any warning that is displayed about the zoom size of the page by clicking the **Ok** button.

The **Capture Page** dialog is displayed. Click on the **Start Capture** button in the **Capture Page** dialog. Once the capturing of the page is completed, you will have the popup available in the **Pages** tab of the **Activities** panel in the **Workflow** perspective, as shown in the following screenshot:

Figure 16.6 – Pop-up page displayed in the Pages tab

You can then include this pop-up page in any workflow as required. Note that we haven't defined any criteria for the page or controls like we do for the pages captured from the application. We need to keep the combination of the **id** property and the **parent** property for the controls unique to identify the controls in the custom pages. All the controls that are added to the page are highlighted while adding the activities to the page.

You can try including this page as a first step in the SAPPostVendorInvoice workflow to capture the information from the user. You also want to learn about the **Wait click** activity under the **Item – Wait** activity group, which can be used to delay the execution of the workflow until the user clicks on an item on the page.

> **Note**
>
> There are more ways to make the workflow wait for certain conditions to be true. These activities are available under the **Flow – Wait** activity group. This activity group includes delaying the execution by specified milliseconds or waiting until a certain condition is true.

The example list of activities and the hierarchy of the activities are shown in the following screenshot:

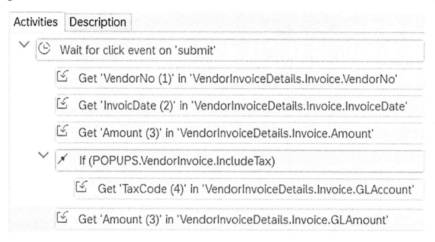

Figure 16.7 – Example activities added to pop-up page

The activities listed under the **Wait click** activity will be executed only after the user clicks on the item for which the activity is added. Similarly, the activity to get the tax code is added under the condition that the **IncludeTax** checkbox is checked before clicking the **Submit** button.

We used the VendorInvoice custom page in the workflow and added activities to it to wait until the user enters the information and clicks on the **Submit** button on the page to proceed with the execution of the next steps.

Our workflow is ready, and we can now proceed with building the project and generating the code.

Summary

In this chapter, we learned about creating a custom page and adding UI controls to the page, to allow the user to enter the invoice information that is required by a business process. We also learned about capturing a custom page by clicking on the **Capture** button, so it is available to use in the workflow. We have also used the **Wait Click** activity for workflow execution to wait for an action from the user, such as the click of a button. Custom pages are very helpful when automating a business process where user interaction is required.

We will learn about generating the code for a workflow in the next chapter.

Questions

Here are some questions for you to test your knowledge. The answers to these questions can be found at the back of the book in the section named *Assessments*:

1. How do you make the workflow wait for user inputs while executing?
2. A custom page is created but is not available in the **Pages** tab of the **Activities** panel. What could be the reason?

Part 4: Generating and Updating the JavaScript Code

After the applications, screens, and controls are captured and a workflow is created, the next step is to build the project to generate the code. This section includes an explanation of the options provided in SAP Intelligent RPA to generate, build, and edit the JavaScript code with the Desktop Studio Editor Perspective. This section also covers the Desktop SDK and its extensions that are used for managing Excel files or Outlook emails.

This section comprises the following chapters:

- *Chapter 17, Generating Code*
- *Chapter 18, An Introduction to the SDK Reference Guide*
- *Chapter 19, SDK Extension Libraries*
- *Chapter 20, Managing Environment Variables*

17
Generating Code

So far, we have learned about capturing and declaring applications, pages, and UI elements. We have also learned how to use these captured elements to create a workflow that includes a sequence of steps/activities to be performed to complete a business process. We also learned about creating custom pages as required by a business process and including them in a workflow. By now, the workflow that was discussed in *Chapter 16, Designing Custom Pages with UI Designer*, should be ready, allowing us to proceed with the next activity in the development process, which is to build the project to generate the code.

In this chapter, we will learn about generating code for the vendor invoice posting business process defined as the `SAPInvoicePosting` workflow, gaining knowledge on the following:

- Building a project to generate source files
- Introducing the SDK
- Exploring source code structure and source files

By end of this chapter, you will understand how a project can be built to generate code and the core **Software Development Kit (SDK)** classes provided by **SAP Intelligent RPA** that can be used to update the code.

Let's start with building the `Vendor Invoice Posting` project in **Desktop Studio**.

Technical requirements

- Desktop Studio installed on your workstation

- Microsoft .NET Framework 4.7

- Source code comparison tool (KDiff3 or Beyond Compare)

- The SAPInvoicePosting workflow that was discussed in *Chapter 15, Controlling Workflows and Scenarios*

Building the project to generate the source files

Once the workflow is created, we need to build the project to generate the source code that will convert the elements defined in the **Editor** panel and the workflows defined in the **Workflow** panel to the **JavaScript** code. The generated source code can then be updated for any manual addition as required by the business process that is being automated. This is where **Desktop Studio** provides **Build** and **Rebuild** options in all perspectives that can be used to build and generate the project. The **Build** and **Rebuild** options will convert the applications, pages, UI elements, context/variables, and workflow declarations to the JavaScript code. These options can be selected from either the **Debug** menu, the menu bar button, or simply by entering the keyboard shortcut keys. The shortcut key to building the project is *Ctrl + B*, and to rebuild the project, the shortcut key is *Ctrl + Shift + B*. The **Build** option is used to build the code incrementally, whereas the **Rebuild** option is used to clean the previously generated files and then regenerate the source code.

> **Important Note**
>
> When building the project that was already built, if any changes could not be merged automatically – that is, if there are conflicts between the generated code and the new code – then Desktop Studio will open the source comparison tool window for manually merging the changes to the file.

The steps to generate the code are as follows:

1. Start SAP Intelligent RPA Desktop Studio.

2. Open the Vendor Invoice Posting project in which we created the SAPInvoicePosting workflow in *Chapter 15, Controlling Workflows and Scenarios*.

> **Important Note**
> The project can be built at any stage of the project development – that is, after declaring the items in the **Explorer** perspective or after creating the workflow in the **Workflow** perspective.

3. Press the *Ctrl + B* shortcut key to generate the code.

Desktop Studio will start generating the code, and you will see command windows opened while the code generates. Once the code generation is completed, Desktop Studio will move to the **Editor** perspective. The status of the code generation is displayed in the **Output** panel. The errors and warnings are listed in the **Error List** panel. You can ignore any warnings that are listed in the **Error List** panel, but if there are any errors, then those need to be corrected, and you need to rebuild the project.

After the build is successful, you should see a message in the **Output** panel, stating that there are zero errors, as shown in the following screenshot:

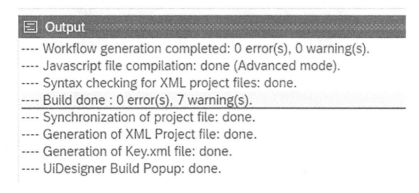

Figure 17.1 – The build status displayed in the Output panel

The generated files will then be available in the **Scripts** panel. As explained in this section, building the project and generating code can simply be done by pressing one of the *Ctrl + B* or *Ctrl + Shift + B* shortcut keys. It is a good practice to keep the source code generated after each development step that is after the declarations being completed, the variables being defined, and after the creation of each workflow. These incremental builds will help us understand the issues better, as they will be mostly on the newly generated code.

We will explore the generated code and its structure in this chapter, but before that, let's first understand the core SDK classes/libraries included in the project by SAP Intelligent RPA.

Introducing the SDK

The project source includes a list of core classes that are part of the SDK and required to execute the automation project. These classes are included under **Framework** in the **Scripts** panel of the **Editor** perspective. Most of these class names will start with Ctx, which refers to **Contextor**, the former name of SAP Intelligent RPA.

The source code and the methods provided by each of these classes can be explored by double-clicking the file to open it in the **Code editor** panel. It is not recommended to edit these files, as they are part of the framework.

Furthermore, you will also see additional framework libraries such as **CRM Applications** after **Framework**. The list of libraries included in the source is dependent on the libraries included in the project while editing the project. You can refer to the *Editing project details* section in *Chapter 10*, *Creating and Managing Projects*, on including additional libraries to the project. The list of files generated for the Vendor Invoice Posting project are shown in the following screenshot:

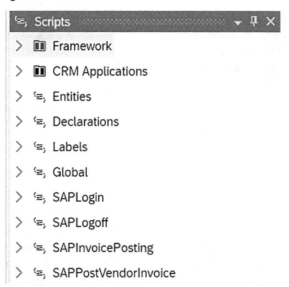

Figure 17.2 – Files generated after building the project

It is important to understand that there are core SDK classes included in the generated code. We will explore more about these SDK libraries and core classes the SDK provides in *Chapter 18*, *An Introduction to Desktop SDK*.

We will now explore the project files and the structure of the files that are generated for our SAPInvoicePosting business process.

Exploring source code structure and source files

We now understand from the previous section that generated source code includes a list of core SDK classes. The generated code also includes the source code for each of the declarations in the **Explorer** perspective and the **Workflow** perspective. Let's explore the generated source code and how the elements defined in the **Explorer** perspective and the workflows created in the **Workflow** perspective are converted to JavaScript code.

The SAP Intelligent RPA uses JavaScript as the language for generated files, and so you will see the files with the .js extension. You can refer to the *Exploring the project structure and organization* section of *Chapter 10*, *Creating and Managing Projects*, for project folder structure and where the files are stored in the filesystem. We will now relate the generated source files to the declarations in other perspectives.

Relating the generated source code with declarations

We will first look at the source files, also referred to as scripts, that are generated. Referring to *Figure 17.2*, which lists the source files that are generated, we will relate the generated source files with the elements defined in the **Explorer** perspective and the **Workflow** perspective:

- The Entities script: This includes the variables declared in the **Context** panel. All the variables will be defined under ctx.dataManager so that they can be accessed in the code referring to this instance.

- The Declarations script: Here, you will see the declaration of all the elements captured and defined in the **Explorer** perspective. The parent-child relationship defined in the **Explorer** perspective is retained – that is, the pages will be defined under the application and the UI elements are defined under a page. For example, to access the **pWindowSAPLogon76** page defined under the **SAPLogon760** application, you will use SAPLogon760.pWindowSAPLogon76 in the code.

- The scripts specific to each workflow: There will be one script generated for each of the workflows created. Here, you can see that there are four scripts generated, one for each SAPLogin, SAPLogoff, SAPPostVendorInvoice, and SAPInvoicePosting workflow.

As you can see, every declaration in the **Explorer** perspective and the **Workflow** perspective are included in the source code. The generated code will then be used for process execution, which we will learn about in the upcoming chapters.

Next, we will explore the structure of the generated source code for a workflow.

Structure of the source code generated for a workflow

The generated source code of any workflow will include the following defined methods:

- `GLOBAL.events.START.on`: This method includes the code that is executed when the execution is starting. By default, it adds a menu option to run the project from the **Desktop Agent**.

- `GLOBAL.scenario`: In this method, the sequence of the execution steps is defined. This method also includes the option to define the timeout value and the methods to be invoked in error or scenario timeout conditions. While the code in this method can be altered manually to change the execution sequence, the changes in the code will not be reflected in the **Workflow** perspective. So, it is recommended to make any change in the execution sequence in the **Workflow** perspective only and then build the code.

- `GLOBAL.step`: There will be one `GLOBAL.step` method in the generated source code for each of the steps defined in the workflow. The generation of code for each workflow can be controlled by selecting the **Is step** property of the activity in the **Properties** panel of the **Workflow** perspective. If the **Is step** property is checked, then this method will be generated for that step. You can see this **Is step** property in the following screenshot:

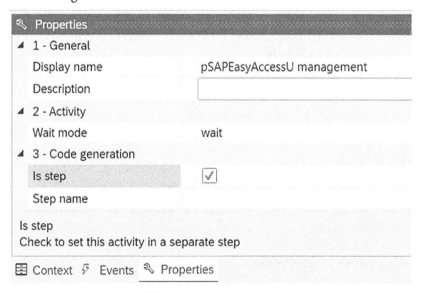

Figure 17.3 – The Is step property used to generate the separate step code

You can also update the **Step name** property in the activity's properties to bring clarity to the generated code. If the **Step name** property is not specified, Desktop Studio generates a default and unique step name while building the project.

In this section, we have looked at the basic structure and methods included in the generated source code.

Summary

In this chapter, we generated the source code and learned about the source code structure. We also learned that every declaration in the **Explorer** perspective is included in the Declarations source file. All the variables defined in the **Context** panel are declared in the Entities script file. A source file will be generated for each of the workflows created in the **Workflow** perspective. We also learned about the methods included in the generated source files for a workflow.

We will learn more about the SDK libraries provided by SAP Intelligent RPA and how they are used in the source code in the next chapter.

Questions

Here are some questions for you to test your knowledge. The answers to these questions can be found at the back of the book in the section named *Assessments*:

1. What is the difference between the **Build** and **Rebuild** options?
2. Why are the changes made to code missing after building it?
3. How do you include SDK extension libraries in a project?

18
An Introduction to Desktop SDK

We built the `Vendor Invoice Posting` project to generate the code in the previous chapter. We also got a brief introduction to the **Software Development Kit (SDK)** core classes included in the project in the same chapter. **SAP Intelligent RPA** provides libraries as part of the SDK included in **Desktop Studio**. The **SAP Intelligent RPA** refers to these classes collectively as Desktop SDK, or simply SDK. Here in this chapter, we will explore the libraries/classes and the methods they provide in more detail.

We will explore the core SDK and **Single Sign-On (SSO)** functional extension library in greater depth through the following topics:

- Exploring the Desktop SDK core classes
- Understanding the SSO class

By end of this chapter, you will have acquired knowledge of the core **SDK** classes provided by **SAP Intelligent RPA** and how they are used in the source code.

Let's start by exploring the **SDK** core classes and using these libraries in the source code.

Technical requirements

- Desktop Studio installed on your workstation

- Microsoft .NET Framework 4.7

- Source codes compare tool (Kdiff3 or Beyond Compare).

- The `Vendor Invoice Posting` project was built and the code was generated as discussed in *Chapter 17, Generating Code*.

Exploring the Desktop SDK core classes

The SAP Intelligent RPA provides a lot of libraries/classes as part of **SDK** for handling entities that are defined in the **Explorer** perspective or the scenarios/workflows that are created in the **Workflow** perspective. It provides many libraries for handling the context/managing the variables or the libraries for handling different technologies. The source code for the libraries included in the project will be available in the `<<project folder>>\bin\lib` folder.

The following screenshot shows the complete list of SDK core classes included in the project source:

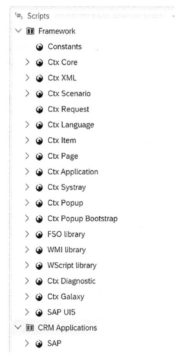

Figure 18.1 – SDK classes included in the project source

This list may vary depending on the libraries included in the project. The libraries/classes included under the **Framework** node are core SDK classes, whereas the libraries included under **CRM Applications** are extensions to the SDK. We will explore these libraries in the following sections.

> **Note**
>
> As the list of Desktop SDK classes is huge, we will be exploring only the core SDK classes that are used in the generated code. To read the complete list of classes, please refer to the link provided in the *Further reading* section.

Let's first look at the constants that are defined in the SDK and how they are used in the code.

Using the constants defined in SDK

The SDK includes many constants that can be used throughout the source code in the SDK in the `ctx.enum.js` file. The code for this file is displayed as **Constants** under **Framework** in the **Scripts** panel. This file can also be accessed from the `<<project folder>>\bin\lib\common` folder in the system. Refer to the *Exploring the project structure and folder organization* section of *Chapter 10, Creating and Managing Projects*, to know more about the project folder and where the project files are stored.

Desktop Studio provides an object called e to access the constants defined in this class. For example, you will see that all the keyboard function keys are defined as `e.key`.

Furthermore, there are extensions to the constants defined in `ctx.enum.js` specific to the technology. They will be defined in the libraries specific to the technology. For example, the keyboard shortcuts to be used for SAP screens are defined as constants in `sapscripting.js`, available under the `<<project folder>>\bin\lib\sap` folder. This file is available with the name **SAP** under **CRM Applications** in the **Scripts** panel.

Let's look at an example usage of the `e.logIconType` constant. The following line of code can be included in any method in the project source file to log a message:

```
ctx.log("Message to log…", e.logIconType.Error)
```

The `ctx.log` method requires two mandatory parameters; the first is the actual message for logging and the next is the message type. We used the `e.logIconType.Error` constant to log an error message. Search the constants to understand the options available for logging in to the `ctx.enum.js` file.

We have now learned that SDK defines many constants that can be used as needed in the source code using the object e. Have a look at the `ctx.enum.js` file to know the list of all constants provided by SDK. Let's now explore the `Ctx Core` library and how it is used in the source code.

Accessing the SDK libraries from the source code

You can find that the source code includes `Ctx Core` under **Framework** in which the core functions and the object for the libraries are defined. The source code for this library can be accessed from the `ctx.core.js` file in the `<<project folder>>\bin\lib\ctx` folder. An object called `ctx` will be provided in the generated workflow source code that will allow the methods and libraries defined in this library to be accessed. The `ctx` object will be the root that provides access to the **SDK** libraries.

These libraries are grouped based on their purpose and are explained in the following sections.

We will first look at the libraries/classes that are used to control the entities/elements defined in the **Explorer** perspective.

Defining the entities captured in the Explorer perspective

Referring to *Figure 18.1*, there are many SDK libraries included in the project source code. We will look at the following libraries that define and perform actions on the entities captured in the **Explorer** perspective:

- The `Ctx Application` class: This class provides the methods required to access and control the applications defined in the **Explorer** perspective. The source code for this library can be accessed from `ctx.application.js`. Refer to the `Declarations` source file for using this library to define an application in the project. You will see the `ctx.addApplication` method called in this file to define the `SAPLogon760` application in the following line:

```
var SAPLogon760 = ctx.addApplication('SAPLogon760',
  {"nature":"UIAUTOMATION","path":"C:\\Program Files
  (x86)\\SAP\\FrontEnd\\SapGui\\saplogon.exe"});
```

Once the application object is defined, the SAPLogon760 object of the ctx. application type is used to access the methods defined in this library. The same object is also then used to add pages to the application. The application object is used to define the methods to perform the activities that are added to the application in the **Workflow** perspective. The following source code line shows an example usage of the application to start it:

```
SAPLogon760.start();
```

- The Ctx Page class: This class provides the methods required to access and control the pages defined under an application in the **Explorer** perspective. The source code for this library can be accessed from ctx.page.js. You will see the code to add pages under an application in the **Declarations** source file. The following source line is used to define pWindowSAPLogon76 in the SAPLogon760 application:

```
SAPLogon760.pWindowSAPLogon76 =
  SAPLogon760.addPage('pWindowSAPLogon76',
    {"comment":"Window - SAP Logon 760"});
```

The preceding source line adds pWindowSAPLogon76 of the ctx.page type to the SAPLogon760 application. The UI elements are added to the SAPLogon760. pWindowSAPLogon76 page. The page object is used to define the methods to perform the activities that are added to the page in the **Workflow** perspective. An example of the usage of the page for sending a keystroke is shown in the following source line:

```
SAPLogon760.pEnterVendorInvoice.keyStroke(e.SAPScripti
  ng.key._F8_);
```

- The Ctx Item class: This class provides the methods required to access and control the UI elements added to a page. The source code for this library can be accessed from ctx.item.js. The following source code shows an example of adding UI elements to a page from the Declarations source file:

```
SAPLogon760.pWindowSAPLogon76.btLogOn =
  SAPLogon760.pWindowSAPLogon76.addItem('btLogOn');
```

The preceding source line adds the `btLogOn` control of the `ctx.item` type to the `SAPLogon760.pWindowSAPLogon76` page. Any action such as clicking or setting a value to be performed on the UI elements that are defined in the **Workflow** perspective are defined as methods on the `SAPLogon760.pWindowSAPLogon76.btLogOn` object. Example usage of the item to click is shown in the following source line:

```
SAPLogon760.pWindowSAPLogon76.btLogOn.click();
```

We have seen how the declarations in the **Explorer** perspective are converted to source code and how corresponding objects and types are used in the source code.

We will now see the SDK classes that are used to define and control the workflow.

Controlling the workflows created in the Workflow perspective

The SDK provides a `Ctx Scenario` library that includes the classes to define and control both the scenarios and the steps defined within the scenario in the **Workflow** perspective. The source code for this library can be accessed from `ctx.scenario.js`. As indicated in *Chapter 17, Generating Code*, each scenario/workflow will be converted to one corresponding source file that includes all the steps defined in the workflow.

We will first look at the classes that are used to define the workflow in the following sections.

The ctx.scenarioClass class

This class provides methods to control the order of the steps and to define the timeout for each scenario. This class also provides the functions to define the code to be executed when an error or timeout occurs while executing the scenario. We need not create an object of this type, but use the `sc` object passed as a parameter to the methods defined in the source files for each workflow. Refer to the `GLOBAL.scenario` method in the `SAPLogin.js` file generated for the `SAPLogin` workflow as an example to explore the usage of the `sc` object in the source code. You will see the method definition with the `sc` object of the `ctx.scenarioClass` type as the second parameter, as in the following screenshot:

```
24  GLOBAL.scenario({ SAPLogin: function(ev, sc) {
25      var rootData = sc.data;
26
27      sc.setMode(e.scenario.mode.clearIfRunning);
28      sc.setScenarioTimeout(600000); // Default timeout for global scenario.
29      sc.onError(function(sc, st, ex) { sc.endScenario(); }); // Default error handler.
30      sc.onTimeout(30000, function(sc, st) { sc.endScenario(); }); // Default timeout handler for each step.
31      sc.step(GLOBAL.steps.Start_SAPLogon760_1, GLOBAL.steps.pWindowSAPLogon76_man_1);
32      sc.step(GLOBAL.steps.pWindowSAPLogon76_man_1, GLOBAL.steps.pSAP_management_1);
33      sc.step(GLOBAL.steps.pSAP_management_1, null);
34  }}, ctx.dataManagers.rootData).setId('380d8cb0-426a-4d02-a0c6-b6ec2a504626') ;
```

Figure 18.2 – Code to define the SAPLogin scenario

You can see the usage of methods defined in `ctx.scenarioClass` in the code generated. For example, we can set the timeout value for the scenario with the `setScenarioTimeout` method. This method takes the value in milliseconds. The default value is set as 600000 milliseconds, meaning that if the scenario execution is not completed within 10 minutes, then the scenario will fail with a timeout. This value can be increased as required based on the time it takes to complete the execution of a scenario. You can also observe that three steps are added to `sc` using the `step` method, which takes the current step and the next step as parameters. There is also a third and optional parameter to this `sc.step`. Refer to the `SAPPostVendorInvoice.js` source file generated for the workflow to understand how the third parameter is used.

We learned about `ctx.scenarioClass` and how it is used in the generated source code for a workflow. Like `ctx.scenarioClass`, SDK provides the `ctx.stepClass` class, which is used to control the steps defined in any workflow. We will learn about this class now.

> **Note**
>
> The source code includes the functions defined as anonymous. Anonymous functions are functions without a name. You can see how this is used to set the functions to be executed for `onError` or `onTimeout` in the code. If you are not aware of the anonymous function, refer to `https://www.w3schools.com/js/js_function_definition.asp` for details.

The ctx.stepClass class

This class provides methods to control the order of the activities to be performed in each step that is defined in a workflow. Like the `ctx.scenarioClass` class, we need not create an object of this type but use the `st` object passed as a parameter to the `step` methods defined in the source file for each workflow. The third parameter to the `GLOBAL.step` method is the `sc` object, which is of the `ctx.stepClass` type. The following screenshot shows the code generated for the application start step defined in the `SAPLogin` workflow:

```
39  GLOBAL.step({ Start_SAPLogon760_1: function(ev, sc, st) {
40      var rootData = sc.data;
41      ctx.workflow('SAPLogin', '265c66bf-2258-45ac-9a4b-257b4da2c1b6') ;
42      // Starts an application.
43      SAPLogon760.start();
44      sc.endStep(); // pWindowSAPLogon76_man_1
45      return;
46  }});
```

Figure 18.3 – Code for defining the step to start the application

You can access the methods defined using the `st` object passed to this method. For example, we can define the functions to handle `onError` and `onTimeout` for a step using this object.

We have now mapped the methods in the generated source code to the scenarios, and the steps within scenarios defined in the **Workflow** perspective. These classes provide many methods that can be used on an as-required basis. You can always refer to the *Desktop SDK Reference Guide* in the *Further reading* section to know more about the methods provided by these classes. It is always a good practice to define the workflow/scenario in the **Workflow** perspective and generate the code instead of changing the code directly in the source file.

We will now see the SDK class that is used to update the context/variables.

Updating the context/variables to be used in the workflow

There will be `entities.js` in the generated code that includes all the variables declared in the **Context** panel of the **Workflow** perspective. The variables can be accessed as `ctx.dataManagers.rootData` in the source code. The following line is included in the `GLOBAL.events.START.on` method of the workflow source files used to create the object for the data to be used while executing the scenario:

```
var rootData = ctx.dataManagers.rootData.create();
```

The `rootData` object includes the complete structure created in the **Context** panel. If the `VendorNo` value is to be updated in the code, it can be accessed as follows:

```
rootData.VendorInvoiceDetails.Invoice[0].VendorNo = "100";
```

Separate data objects are created for each of the scenarios and the data objects specific to the scenario can be accessed as `sc.data`. As this is specific to a workflow, the data used in one scenario is not passed to the next scenario by default. We will learn about passing the information from one scenario to the next in *Chapter 19, SDK Extension Libraries*.

We will now look at the classes provided by SDK to work with files.

Accessing the files in the filesystem from the source code

`Framework` provides a `File System Object` library, referred to as the `FSO` library, to create, read, or update the files or to manage the folders in the filesystem. The source code for this library is available in the `fso.js` file under the `<<project folder>>\bin\lib\utils` folder. This library is accessed as `ctx.fso`. Initialization of the library is shown in the following source line as an example:

```
ctx.fso.init();
```

This library provides classes to manage the files and folders. This library also provides a class to implement the functionality to manage files available in a **File Transfer Protocol** (**FTP**) site. The classes included in this library are as follows:

- The `ctx.fso.folder` class: This class provides methods to manage the folders in the filesystem, such as creating a new folder, checking the exiting of a folder, or reading the list of files and folders under a folder.

- The `ctx.fso.file` class: This class provides methods for managing the files under a folder, including, but not limited to, creating a file, copying or moving a file to a different location, reading the content of a file, or zipping/unzipping a compressed file.

- The `ctx.fso.ftp` class: The methods provided in this class are used to download files from, or upload files to, an **FTP** site, or to get the list of files under a folder in the **FTP** site. This class must be initialized with the `init` method with the site name and the credentials' parameters as the first step in using this class.

- The `ctx.fso.drive` class: This class provides methods for managing the drives in the filesystem, such as checking for the existence of a drive or getting the name of the drive.

We have now seen the classes included in the FSO library, and we will learn more about this library and use it in *Chapter 19*, *SDK Extension Libraries*. Let's now get introduced to the classes included in SDK for working with the **XML** and **JSON** data.

Working with XML and JSON data

Framework includes a Ctx XML library that provides classes for working with **XML** and **JSON** data. The source code for this library is available in the ctx.xml.js file in the <<project folder>>\\bin\lib\ctx folder.

The methods required to work with the **XML** data are available in the ctx.xml class, while the methods required to work with the **JSON** data are available in the ctx.json class.

To convert a string to an **XML** object, you can use the following code:

```
var xmlObject = ctx.xml.parse(Stringdata);
```

Similarly, to convert an **XML** object to a **JSON** object, you can use the following code:

```
var jsonObject = ctx.xml.json2xml(xmlObject);
```

Again, there is a list of methods that are available in these classes that are very useful when working with the **XML** or **JSON** data. **Desktop Studio** provides the IntelliPrompt feature, which was discussed in *Chapter 9*, *Desktop Studio Perspectives*. This feature can be used to view the list of methods provided by each of these classes.

Here, we have learned about a few libraries and classes included in the **Desktop SDK**. Let's now get a quick list of more libraries.

Referring to other libraries and classes

There are many more libraries provided as part of the SDK that helps meet many of the automation requirements while automating a business process. The following is a list of SDK libraries for managing the network communication or system:

Library	Class	Functionality
Ctx Systray	`systray`	Adds or deletes a menu item in the system tray.
Ctx Core	`ctx.event`	Sets or manages the functional or technical events. Note that this will be passed as the parameter with the name `ev`, such as `sc` or `st`, to the methods.
Ctx Language	`ctx.registry`	Reads or sets values to the system registry.
Ctx Language	`ctx.cryptography`	Provides methods to implement cryptography.
Ctx Language	`ctx.ajax`	Includes methods to make web service calls using **HTTP/HTTPS**.
Ctx Language	`ctx.clipboard`	Manages the system clipboard.
WScript library	`ctx.wscript.shell`	Provides methods to access the system environment variables and system folders.

Table 18.1 – List of useful libraries and classes

As noted in the introduction to this chapter, the list is big and includes many libraries such as utility libraries, for managing the strings and many more. The complete and latest list of libraries can be referred from the *Desktop SDK Reference Guide* link provided in the *Further reading* section.

By now, we have learned about the most commonly used SDK libraries and the classes included in these libraries. The SDK not only includes core libraries, but also **SDK Extension** libraries to implement functional and technical requirements while automating a business process. We will learn and implement some of these extensions in the next chapter; we will now learn about one function extension called **SSO**, now provided as part of SDK.

Understanding the SSO class

The SAP Intelligent RPA provides one function extension to the SDK called the **Single Sign On** library, referred to as the **SSO** Library. This library includes the `ctx.sso` class with methods to implement the SSO for a page that allows users to enter the username and password.

Ensure that **SSO Library** is checked under the **Libraries** tab of the **Edit project** dialog to include this SSO library in the source code, as shown in the following screenshot:

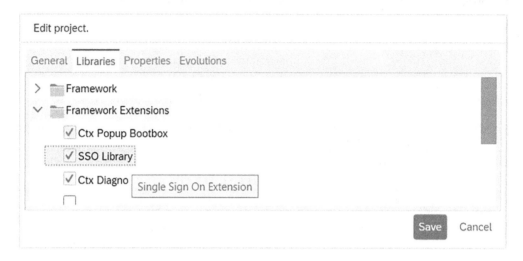

Figure 18.4 – Enabling the SSD library for the project

Once this SSO is included in the project, you will see that the `ctx.sso` class source code is included in the source under the **Framework Extensions** node in the **Scripts** panel, as shown in the following screenshot:

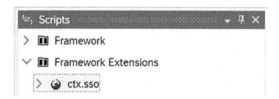

Figure 18.5 – SSD library included in the source code

The source code for this library is available in the `ctx.sso.js` file under the `<<project folder>>\\bin\lib\ctx` folder to explore the source code. As with any other library source code, this code should not be edited as the latest SDK files will always be replaced when building the project.

The SSO can be enabled for each page that accepts the username and password by calling `ctx.sso.disable` with the first parameter as a page and the second parameter is `false`. The following source line can be used to enable SSO on the `SAPLogon760.pSAP` page:

```
ctx.sso.disable( SAPLogon760.pSAP, false );
```

Change the second parameter to `true` to disable the SSO on this page. `ctx.sso.isDisabled` is used to check the status of the SSO on the page by setting the page as a parameter to this method.

The complete SSO functionality can be implemented with the `ctx.sso.setup` method that can be included at the start of the workflow that includes the page where credentials are to be captured. Some sample code is shown in the following screenshot:

```
ctx.sso.setup( SAPLogon760.pSAP.edUser, SAPLogon760.pSAP.oPassword,
  function( ev ) {
    // Functional Code to execute after entering the credentials is successful
  },
  function( ev ) {
    // Fallback Code to execute if there is an error setting up the credentials
  }
);
```

Figure 18.6 – Setting up the SSO

The first two parameters for this method are the controls captured for entering the username and password from a page. The assumption is that both the username and password are on the same page while managing the SSO. The two parameters next to this method are the functions to execute in case of success or failure when entering the values to the controls. While using this method is a simple way to manage the SSO for a page, the `ctx.sso` class provides the following additional methods to manage the credentials for the page for which the **SSO** is enabled:

- The `ctx.sso.getCredentials` method: Reads the credentials entered on a page

- The `ctx.sso.setCredentials` method: Sets the credentials when a page is loaded

- The `ctx.sso.saveCredentials` method: Captures the credentials from a page and saves them in the system registry

- The `ctx.sso.clearCredentials` method: Clears the credentials stored in the system registry for a page

The ideal place to set the credentials to the page is when the page is loaded. We will first add code to handle the SAPLogin workflow for handling the LOAD event in which we will set the credentials. Defining a handler that will be invoked when the page loads can be done by executing the following steps:

1. Open the SAPLogin.js file for editing.

2. Go to the end of the file where we want to add the handler to be invoked when the SAPLogon760.pSAP page is loaded.

3. From the context menu, select the **Select Snippet | Page | event 'on' handler** item that is shown in the following screenshot:

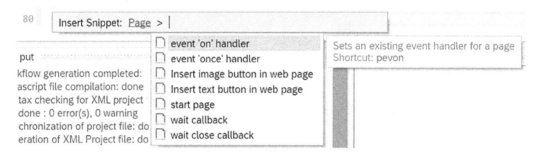

Figure 18.7 – Inserting the Page load event in the source code

4. This will add some sample code to handle the page load event in the source.

5. Change app to SAPLogon760 and page to pSAP as we want to create a handle to SAPLogon760.pSAP. The code should look like the following code block:

```
/** Description */
SAPLogon760.pSAP.events.LOAD.on(function(ev) {
    var data = {};

});
```

Figure 18.8 – Page load handler added to the source code

We have now added a handler that will be called when the SAPLogon760.pSAP page is loaded. You can call the ctx.sso methods to get from the system registry and set the values to controls here.

> **Note**
>
> The **Editor** perspective provides many code snippets that can be included in the code directly and updated as per our requirements. These code snippets are very useful for accelerating the code development time. You can explore the available code snippets directly by selecting the **Select Snippet** menu item from the context menu.

Like adding the LOAD event handler, you can also add the UNLOAD event handler to save the credentials to the registry using the saveCredential method.

We have now seen different methods provided by **Desktop SDK** to include **SSO** functionality on a page. As the credentials stored are specific to a page, you can enable SSO for as many pages as you want in the same application or project. These credentials are saved separately and will be set to the login and password controls by SAP Intelligent RPA while running the project. This class stores the credentials to the registry where the automation solution is running and, if the automation solution is deployed to a new machine, then there will be no credentials stored in the registry by default. The code must handle the scenarios when there were no credentials stored previously.

Summary

In this chapter, we learned about the most commonly used SDK core library classes and learned about the one functional extension library, which is the SSO library. The SDK core classes are very useful when developing the automation solution for any business process. You must look at these classes for available methods before writing your code to implement any functionality of a business process. For example, there are many methods provided by the ctx.string class that can be used instead of writing code to manipulate strings.

As you have understood by now, the SDK classes are included in the project source. That makes the project code complete and independent of the machine where the project is deployed for running. It is important to note that when **Desktop Studio** is upgraded, the version of the SDK is also likely to be updated to the new version. It is unlikely that the newer version of the SDK does not support code generated with the previous version of the SDK, but it is always a good practice to rebuild the project with the latest version of the SDK.

We learned about the SDK core libraries provided by the SAP Intelligent RPA, but there are extension libraries provided by SDK for handling technology-specific functionality, such as the **Microsoft Outlook Extension** for emails or **Microsoft Excel Extension** for managing Excel workbooks. We will learn about these **SDK Extension** libraries and use them in the Vendor Invoice Posting project in the next chapter.

Questions

Here are some questions for you to test your knowledge. The answers to these questions can be found at the back of the book in the section named *Assessments*:

1. Why are some libraries not showing in the code?

2. Am I allowed to change the source code of the SDK library as it is part of the source?

Further reading

- *Desktop SDK Reference Guide*: https://help.sap.com/viewer/product/IRPA/Cloud/en-US

- Link for learning about anonymous functions in JavaScript: https://www.w3schools.com/js/js_function_definition.asp

19
SDK Extension Libraries

By now, you should be familiar with the core libraries included in the **Desktop SDK**, which we discussed in *Chapter 18, An Introduction to Desktop SDK*. **SAP Intelligent RPA** also provides libraries that are extensions to the **Desktop SDK**, referred to as **Desktop SDK Extension** libraries, for working with Microsoft Office, PDF, or SAP applications. We will explore more about these libraries/classes and use them in the Vendor Invoice Posting project in this chapter.

In this chapter, we will cover the following topics to learn more about the various SDK Extension libraries:

- Using the Microsoft Office extensions
- Extracting information from PDF documents
- Learning about the technology-specific extensions

By the end of this chapter, you will have learned how to use the SDK core and Microsoft Office extension libraries in the source code that was generated for the Vendor Invoice Posting project in *Chapter 17, Generating Code*. You will have also gained knowledge on the PDF extension and the technology-specific extension for **SAPGUI** that's provided by **SAP Intelligent RPA**.

Let's start by exploring the Microsoft Office extensions and usage of these libraries in the source code.

Technical requirements

- Desktop Studio installed on your workstation

- Microsoft .NET Framework 4.7

- A source code comparison tool (KDIff3 or Beyond Compare)

- The Vendor Invoice Posting project that was built and the code that was generated in *Chapter 17, Generating Code*

Using the Microsoft Office extensions

SAP Intelligent RPA provides three extension libraries to interact with Microsoft Office products – a Microsoft Outlook extension, a Microsoft Excel extension, and a Microsoft Word extension. These three extensions are very useful for automating a business process that requires structural information as input. They process this input data by reading the structural information and then generating a result report.

Consider the vendor invoice posting business process that we implemented in *Chapter 15, Controlling Workflows and Scenarios,* as the SAPInvoicePosting workflow to post the purchase invoices. We need to post multiple purchase invoices, but how does the automation solution receive the information that's required to post a purchase invoice? One option is to gather information manually for each invoice by providing a custom dialog, as discussed in *Chapter 16, Designing Custom Pages with UI Designer*. So, asking the user to enter the required details manually is not a good way to implement a business process; instead, it is better to ask the user to send the data in a structured format that the automation solution understands. It is important to discuss and agree with the business process users on how the information that's needed to execute the business process is sent to the automation solution, as well as the standard structure of the data that the automation solution expects for a business process.

While Microsoft Excel lets you structure the data with predefined columns that the automation solution understands, Microsoft Outlook provides you with a way to send the data as an email for the automation solution to process.

> **Note**
>
> The automation solution that was developed with SAP Intelligent RPA can receive the inputs in many ways, such as by downloading the files from an FTP (`ctx.fso.ftp`), through web service (`ctx.ajax`) calls, or from a website. Similarly, SAP Intelligent RPA supports files in different formats, such as XML or JSON (`ctx.xml` and `ctx.json`). The solution should be decided on based on the business process and its automation requirements.

Going back to the vendor invoice posting business process, we will define the requirement to share the inputs via email with a specific subject; the invoice data will be attached to the email in Excel format. We will look at processing the emails in `SAPInvoicePosting` in the next section.

Reading and replying to Outlook emails

The **Outlook** library is available under the **Microsoft Office** node in the **Scripts** panel of the **Editor** perspective. If this library is not included, you need to include the library in the source code by selecting the **Outlook Integration** library under the **Microsoft Office** folder in the **Libraries** tab of the **Edit Project** dialog. This will include the **Outlook** library in the source code, as shown in the following screenshot:

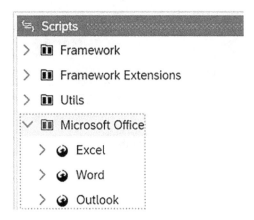

Figure 19.1 – Microsoft Office extension libraries included in the project source code

The **Outlook** library includes the functions that are used to manage the emails in Microsoft Outlook. The `outlook.js` source file for this library will be available in the `<<project folder>>\bin\lib\office` folder for reference. Like the core libraries, the instance of this library can be accessed as `ctx.outlook` in the source code. We will learn how the functions provided by this library can be used in the source code to manage emails.

Before you start using the functions provided by this library, you must initialize the library by either including the `Init Outlook` activity under the **Outlook Lib** activity group in the **Activities** panel or by calling the `init` method, as shown in the following line of code:

```
ctx.outlook.init();
```

> **Note**
>
> Most of the SDK libraries must be initialized before you can use the methods of the class/library in the source code. It is useful to check the methods in the class and if there is an `init` method, then include that in the source code before using the other methods.

The activities that are available for the **Outlook** library in the **Activities** tab of the **Workflow** perspective are shown in the following screenshot:

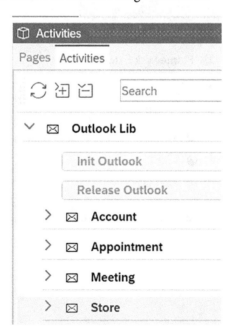

Figure 19.2 – Activities that are available for Outlook

Like calling the `init` method is mandatory before using the other methods, we need to release the Outlook resources by calling the `end` method after processing the emails. The end method, which is used to release the Outlook resources, is included in the source code, as shown in the following source line:

```
ctx.outlook.end();
```

The source code or the steps to process emails should always be between the `init` and end methods. These two methods are directly available in `ctx.outlook`, and all the methods for processing the emails can be accessed with the `ctx.outlook.mail` object.

Like the `ctx.outlook.mail` object, for processing emails, this library also includes an object for processing folders (`ctx.outlook.folder`), tasks (`ctx.outlook.task`), meetings (`ctx.outlook.meetings`), and many more. Please refer to *Figure 19.2*, where activity subgroups are included in the **Outlook Lib** activity group. It is recommended to always use these activities instead of writing the code to use the libraries in the code, which improves the clarity of the workflows. The scope of this book is limited to processing emails, though, so please refer to the *Desktop SDK Reference Guide* in the *Further reading* section to find out more about the objects and methods they provide.

Now, let's look at the methods provided by the `ctx.outlook.mail` object.

Before you start reading or retrieving the emails, you need to clear the previously read email list by calling the `resetMailCollection` method. This reset call is required for the `Outlook` library to keep the retrieved emails in a working list; the new emails will be appended to this list when the new emails are retrieved. You can include the following source line to reset the emails list before reading the new emails:

```
ctx.outlook.mail.resetMailCollection();
```

Now, let's look at the methods provided by `ctx.outlook.mail` and how they can be used in the source code.

Retrieving emails from an Outlook mailbox

Three methods need to be called in sequence to fetch the emails with specific filters. The order of execution is to search the Outlook email box for emails matching the specific criteria, then get the list of emails matching the search criteria to a list object, and finally retrieve the required email details.

First, let's understand the methods that are provided in the Outlook library to perform these three steps:

- The search or searchByCriteria method: Both methods accept the filters to search the emails as a parameter. The ctx.outlook library implements Outlook integration using the Outlook.Application ActiveX object provided by Microsoft. So, the search method accepts the filters in the format expected by the Folder.GetTable method. You can refer to the outlook.js source code of this library for more information on the format of the filters to be used for the Search method. The searchByCriteria method wraps the same functionality that the search method does but accepts the filters with defined labels so that it is developer-friendly. You are free to use any one of these methods; the searchByCriteria method will be used to implement the email reading workflow in this chapter, so let's learn more about this method.

The searchByCriteria method takes one object with search/filter criteria defined in JSON format as a parameter. You can search for and filter emails based on many parameters, such as sender email, sender name, subject, and the date when the email was received. The following code block shows an example of searching the unread emails with the subject containing the text Purchase Invoice, has an attachment, and received today:

```
var today = new Date();
try {
  ctx.outlook.mail.searchByCriteria( {
    // fromEmail : "%sender@email.com"
    subject : "%Purchase Invoice%",
    read : 0,
    hasAttachment : 1,
    date : {from : today, until : today},
    maxRow : 10
    } );
} catch (ex) {
    ctx.log("No emails pending for processing...");
}
```

Figure 19.3 – Searching emails with specific criteria

Note %, which is included in the subject. This is a wildcard character that indicates that there can be more text before and after the text Purchase Invoice in the subject. Remove % to search for the exact text. This character can be used in the fromEmail, subject, sender, and textDescription labels, where the values to be searched for are text. Please refer to *Desktop SDK Reference Guide* in the *Further reading* section or the library source code to find the complete list of filter criteria.

- The getFilteredTable method: This method returns the array of the emails matching the filter set in the Search or SearchByCriteria method. The source line to call this method looks like this:

```
var mails = ctx.outlook.mail.getFilteredTable();
```

- The retrieveMail method: Each email in the array of emails that's returned by the getFilteredTable method needs to be retrieved by calling the retrieveMail method. This method accepts a JSON object as a parameter with the EntryID and StoreID labels of the email. These values will be available in each email object of the array of the emails returned by the getFilteredTable method. So, we need to loop through the array of emails and then call this method, as shown in the following source code:

```
var mails = ctx.outlook.mail.getFilteredTable();
for (var i = 0; i < mails.length; i++) {
  try {
    ctx.outlook.mail.retrieveMail({
      EntryID : mails[i]['EntryID'],
      StoreID : mails[i]['StoreID'] });
  } catch (ex) {
    ctx.log("Could not retrieve the email");
  }
}
```

Figure 19.4 – Source code for retrieving emails

After executing these three methods in the same order as they were explained, we will have a collection of emails with complete details that are required to read the details from each email. Let's put what we've learned into practice by creating the ProcessUnreadEmails workflow in the Vendor Invoice Posting project.

Create a new workflow called `ProcessUnreadEmails` under the **GLOBAL** node in the **Workflow** panel, which can be found in the `Vendor Invoice Posting` project, and add three activities from the **Activities** panel in the following order, after the **Start** activity:

1. The **Init Outlook** activity from the **Outlook Lib** activity group. Enter the **Step name** property as `InitializeOutlook` in the **Properties** panel.

2. The **Custom** activity under the **Flow** activity group. Enter the **Step name** property as `ProcessUnreadEmails` and change the **Display name** property to `Read new purchase invoice emails`.

    A **Custom** activity is provided to allow developers to write their code as a step. The generated code includes this step method, where we can write code.

3. The **Release Outlook** activity from the **Outlook Lib** activity group. Change the **Step name** property to `ReleaseOutlook`.

Generate the code and build the project by pressing the *Ctrl + B* shortcut. This will generate the source code for the `ProcessUnreadEmails` workflow with the same name, which can be accessed from the **Scripts** panel of the **Editor** perspective.

This workflow should look as follows:

Figure 19.5 – Workflow for processing unread emails

Edit the `ProcessUnreadEmails.js` file in the **Editor** perspective to update the code that was generated for the `ProcessUnreadEmails` step with the code required to retrieve the emails by calling the `searchByCriteria`, `getFilteredTable`, and `retrieveMail` methods. The code for this step should look as follows:

```
GLOBAL.step({ ProcessUnreadEmails: function(ev, sc, st) {
    var rootData = sc.data;
    ctx.workflow('ProcessUnreadEmails', '17c1e9a1-1259-4b07-a01f-bb4b1e3f7c45') ;
    // Describe functionality to be implemented in JavaScript later in the project.
    ctx.outlook.mail.resetMailCollection();

    try {
      ctx.outlook.mail.searchByCriteria( {
        // Filter criteria
        } );
    } catch (ex) {
      ctx.log("No emails pending for processing...");
    }

    var mails = ctx.outlook.mail.getFilteredTable();
    for (var i = 0; i < mails.length; i++) {
      try {
        ctx.outlook.mail.retrieveMail({ EntryID : mails[i]['EntryID'],
                                        StoreID : mails[i]['StoreID'] });
      } catch (ex) {
        ctx.log("Could not retrieve the email");
      }
    }
    sc.endStep(); // ReleaseOutlook
    return;
}});
```

Figure 19.6 – Source code for searching and retrieving emails

You can use the same filters that are shown in *Figure 19.3* to filter unread emails with the subject containing the text `Purchase Invoice` and that were received on the same day. Save and build the project if there are errors to be corrected.

> **Tip**
> If the **IntelliPrompt** feature does not provide all the items that are available under a class or library when you're using them in the code, you can try the **Rebuild Intellisense** option from the context menu or use the *Ctrl + shift + F5* shortcut in the source editor. This will refresh the information about all the objects.

With that, we have created a new workflow and added steps to initialize Outlook, search and retrieve the emails as a custom step, and then release Outlook. But we have not read the email information or downloaded the attachment yet. Let's learn about reading emails and downloading their attachments.

Reading emails and downloading attachments

Once the emails have been filtered and retrieved, we must process the email collection. You can access individual emails using an index, such as `mails[index]`, to read the details required and download the attachments. The `ctx.outlook.mail. getCollectionLength` method returns the number of emails that match the search criteria that can be used to loop through the email collection.

Before we learn about and implement the code to read emails, we need to have context variables to store the information that we wish to read. We will proceed by updating the context to create a structure that will hold the email information in the **Context** panel of the **Workflow** perspective. Remember that we already have a context in the `Vendor Invoice Posting` project, which we created in *Chapter 12, Capturing and Declaring Applications, Pages, and Items*.

So, create a new folder called `email` under the context root; that is, `VendorInvoiceDetails`. Then, create the `SenderAddress`, `Sender`, `Subject`, `Body` items, as well as an `Attachment` folder.

You also need to create the `Index`, `AttachmentPath`, and `AttachmentName` items under `Attachment`. Both `email` and `Attachment` should be checked as arrays. This is required so that we can store multiple emails and multiple attachments for a single email. The context should look like this once you've added the necessary variables to store the email information:

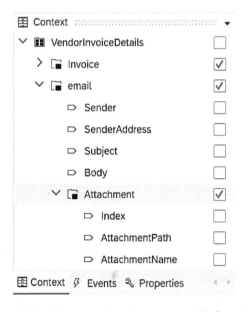

Figure 19.7 – Context updated to store email information

You need to build the project to regenerate the code for newly added variables in the context. Now that we have the context and the email collection that we need to process, let's proceed and implement the code that is required to fetch the data from each email.

Reading email data and storing it in the context

We will add a `for` loop after `retrieveMail` and before the `sc.endStep` line in the `ProcessUnreadEmails` step to process each email. There are many `get` methods available in the `ctx.outlook.mail` object, which take the index of the email as a parameter to read the email's information. We will use some of these methods to read the information and store that in the context.

The email has been defined in the context as an array, so we need to create the email object, set the item values from an item in the mail collection, and then add the new item to the array. Refer to the `Entities` script in the **Scripts** panel to understand the methods that were generated to create the items defined as folders in the **Context** panel. Each of the folders will be defined with a `create` method so that it can be used to create the object for variables defined as folders. This `create` method can be accessed using the `ctx.dataManagers` object. For example, to create the `VendorInvoiceDetails` object defined in the context, we need to use the `create` method of the `ctx.dataManagers.rootData_VendorInvoiceDetails` object. To create an email object, we need to use `ctx.dataManagers.rootData_VendorInvoiceDetails_email.create`.

We will look at the source code example after learning about the methods that we can use to download attachments from emails.

Downloading email attachments

The `ctx.outlook.mail` object provides methods for managing the email attachments for each email. These methods are as follows:

- The `getAttachmentsCount` method: This method returns the number of attachments for an email.

- The `getAttachmentsName` method: This method returns the names of the attachments for an email in an array.

- The `attachmentSave` method: This method downloads and saves the attachment in the folder. This method expects the index of the email, the folder that the attachment is to be downloaded from, and a JSON object with filters to be applied for downloading the attachment. Here, we can set `AttachmentName` or `Index` of the attachment to download. You can also set `SaveAllAttachments` to `true` to download all the attachments or filter the attachment by `ExtensionsToKeep` or `ExtensionsToSkip` with multiple values separated by a semicolon (`;`).

The following code block is an example that can be used to read an email's details and download attachments with the `.xls` or `.xlsx` extension:

```
rootData.VendorInvoiceDetails = ctx.dataManagers.rootData_VendorInvoiceDetails.create();
for (var i = 0; i < ctx.outlook.mail.getCollectionLength(); i++) {
  var email = ctx.dataManagers.rootData_VendorInvoiceDetails_email.create();
  email.Sender = mails[i]['Sender'];
  email.SenderAddress = ctx.outlook.mail.getSenderAddress(i);
  email.Subject = ctx.outlook.mail.getSubject(i);
  email.body = ctx.outlook.mail.getBody(i);
  rootData.VendorInvoiceDetails.email.push(email);
  var attachmentCount = ctx.outlook.mail.getAttachmentsCount(i);
    if (attachmentCount > 0) {
      email.attachment = [];
      var names = ctx.outlook.mail.getAttachmentsName(i);
      var path = ctx.options.path.log + "\\" + "Attachments_PuchaseInvoices";
      ctx.fso.folder.create(path);
      for (var j = 0; j < names.length; j++) {
        if(names[j].endsWith(".xlsx"||".xls")) {
          var attachment =
            ctx.dataManagers.rootData_VendorInvoiceDetails_email_Attachment.create();
          attachment['Index'] = j + 1;
          attachment.AttachmentName = names[j];
          attachment.AttachmentPath = path + '\\' + attachment.AttachmentName;
          ctx.outlook.mail.attachmentSave(i, attachment.AttachmentPath, attachment);
          email.Attachment.push(attachment);
        }
      }
    }
  ctx.outlook.mail.setUnRead(i);
}
```

Figure 19.8 – Sample source code for reading emails and downloading attachments

Let's go through the source code in the preceding screenshot. Here, we created an object of the VendorInvoiceDetails type and then created email objects in a loop for the emails. Once the values were filled in for email, we added that object to the array by calling the push method. For each email, if there is an attachment with the `.xls` or `.xlsx` extension, we download the attachment to a folder, prepare the Attachment object, and then add that to the email object. Note the usage of the ctx.fso library to create a folder using the ctx.fso.folder.create method that the attachment was downloaded in. This method creates a folder with the name given in the path variable. The path appends Attachments_PurchaseInvocie to ctx.options.path.log. ctx.options.path provides the options to access the project folders while running the project instead of hardcoding the path.

With that, we've learned about how to search and retrieve emails from Outlook, read email information, and download attachments using the `ctx.outlook` library. This code needs to be added to the `ProcessUnreadEmails` step, after the code for retrieving the emails.

Now, let's learn how to create and send emails.

Creating and sending emails

The `ctx.outlook.mail` class provides methods that can be used to create an email item, attach files to the email item, and then send the email. As we discussed in the previous section, any call to `ctx.outlook` and its classes must be after the `init` method call; we need to release Outlook by calling the `end` method once the Outlook actions are complete.

Let's look at the methods that are available in the `ctx.outlook.mail` class for creating and sending emails:

- The `create` method: This method is used to create a new email. This method accepts one JSON object as a parameter. The input JSON object can be used to set properties such as `To`, `Subject`, and `Body` for the email to be created. For the complete list of properties that can be set, please refer to the *Email item properties* page in the *Further reading* section. This method returns the index of the newly created email so that it can be used in other methods, such as `send`.

- The `attach` method: This method can be used to attach any file to the email that's created with the `create` method. You need to pass the index that was returned by the `create` method to attach files.

- The `send` method: Once the email has been created, you need to call the `send` method to send the email. Use the index that was returned by the `create` method or 0 as the parameter to send the last created email.

- The `reply` or `replyAll` method: These methods can be used to respond to an email – either to all the recipients (`replyAll`) in the email or just to the sender (`reply`). These methods will create a response email for an email by taking the index of the email to be responded to as a parameter.

These methods can be used in the Vendor Invoice Posting project to summarize the invoice's posting status. Create a new workflow called SendSummaryEmail and add a **Custom** activity to the SendSummaryEmail workflow. Enter SendEmail as the **Step name** activity property. The sample source code for creating and sending emails is shown in the following screenshot:

```javascript
GLOBAL.step({ SendEmail: function(ev, sc, st) {
    var rootData = sc.data;
    ctx.workflow('SendSummaryEmail', 'b06461b0-52a0-4121-b806-eed98740cd00') ;
    // Describe functionality to be implemented in JavaScript later in the project.
    ctx.outlook.init();
    ctx.outlook.mail.resetMailCollection();
    try {
      ctx.outlook.mail.create( {
        To : 'sender@email.com',
        Cc : 'automation@email.com',
        Subject : 'Status of the invoices posting',
        Body : 'Attached status of the purchase invoices posted today. \
              *** This is an autogenerated email, do not reply to this email ***'
      });
      ctx.outlook.mail.attach(0, "Summary file path");
      ctx.outlook.mail.send(0);
    } catch (ex) {
      ctx.log("Error sending the summary email");
    }
    ctx.outlook.end();
    sc.endStep(); // end Scenario
    return;
}});
```

Figure 19.9 – Sample source code for sending an email with an attachment

With that, we've learned about processing and writing emails with attachments. Then, we created the ProcessUnreadEmails workflow to process unread emails and the SendSummaryEmail workflow to send out an email after this processing is complete. You can invoke the ProcessUnreadEmails workflow as the first activity and the SendSummaryEmail workflow as the last activity in the SAPInvoicePosting workflow. We only downloaded the Excel attachments from unread emails in the ProcessUnreadEmails workflow; they were never used in any workflow to read information from the attachments. Now, let's learn how to work with Excel files to read purchase invoice information and write the status of the posting to an Excel file.

Processing data from an Excel file

The Microsoft Office extension library includes a class called `ctx.excel` that is used to `initialize` and end the Excel application. This class also provides the `ctx.excel.file` object for working with the Excel file, such as to create, open, or close it, and the `ctx.excel.sheet` object, which is used to read or write data to a sheet in an Excel file. Before you start processing any Excel files in your code, the library must be initialized with the `ctx.excel.initialize` method. Similarly, you need to call the `ctx.excel.end` method after processing the data in Excel files.

Activities to manage Excel files are included in the **Excel Lib** activity group or the subgroups under the **Excel Lib** activity group. It is suggested that you use the activities in the workflow. Let's look at the most used methods that are provided in this library and its classes.

The following are the methods that are available in the `ctx.excel.file` object. The activities for this object are available under the **File** subgroup in the **Excel Lib** activity group:

- The `create` method: Create a new Excel workbook. Once an empty workbook has been created, worksheets can be added with `ctx.excel.sheet.add` to write the information in Excel cells.

- The `open` method: Open an existing Excel workbook. This method takes the absolute name of the file as the first parameter. You can also send the password as the second parameter if the file to open is password protected.

- The `save`, `saveAs`, and `saveAsPDF` methods: These methods are used to save the workbook that was created or opened for the update either with the same name (`save`), with a different name (`saveAs`), or as a PDF (`saveAsPDF`).

- The `close` and `closeAll` methods: Close the workbook that was opened and saved (`close`) or close all (`closeAll`) the open Excel workbooks.

Now, let's look at the `ctx.excel.sheet` object and the methods it provides to read or write information in an Excel worksheet. These methods can be grouped into managing worksheets in a workbook, managing cell data in a worksheet, and working with ranges in a worksheet:

- **The methods to manage the worksheets in an Excel file**: The `ctx.excel.sheet` object provides a list of methods to control and manage worksheets, such as `getList` to get a list of the worksheets in an Excel workbook, `add` to add a new worksheet, `remove` or `rename` to remove or rename the existing worksheet, or `copySheet` to copy a sheet from one workbook to another workbook. Please refer to a couple of activities that are available under the **Worksheet** subgroup in the **Excel Lib** activity group to work with worksheets.

- **The methods to manage the data in a cell**: The `ctx.excel.sheet` object provides methods for reading a value from a cell (`getCell`) or setting a value for a cell (`setCell`) in a worksheet. Both these methods take the row index and the column index of the cell as the first two parameters. The `setCell` method requires passing the value to set in the cell as the third parameter. Optionally, you can specify the worksheet name as the last parameter. If the worksheet name is not set in the parameter list, then these methods work on the currently active worksheet. Please refer to the **Data** subgroup in the **Excel Lib** activity group for activities that can be used in the workflow to set or get values in a cell.

  There are also methods such as `styleAlign`, which can be used to format the alignment of the value in a cell, or `setCellBorders`, which can be used to set the border style for a cell. Please refer to the **Formatting** subgroup in the **Excel Lib** activity group for activities that can be used.

- **The methods to work with ranges in a worksheet**: Many methods are provided by the `ctx.excel.sheet` object for working with a range of cells in a worksheet. These methods include `getRange` to read all cell values in a range, `clearRange` to clear values in the range, `copyRange` and `pasteRange`. Please refer to the **Data** subgroup in the **Excel Lib** activity group for activities that can be used in the workflow to get and set values in a range.

As indicated at the start of this section, the list of complete methods that are provided in this library is not in the scope of this book. You can refer to *Desktop SDK Reference Guide* in the *Further reading* section for the complete list of objects and functions provided by this library.

So far, we've learned about the `ctx.outlook` library and the objects and methods provided by this library. Now, let's implement this learning in the `Vendor Invoice Posting` project. In the previous section, we created a workflow that reads new emails and downloads their attachments into the `Attachments_PurchaseInvocie` folder under the `ctx.options.path.log` folder. We are also storing the attachment path to the `email` context variable.

Now, let's read the downloaded Excel files by taking the path from the `email` variable in a loop, reading the invoice information from these Excel files, and preparing the invoice list in a new workflow called `ProcessExcelAttachments`. The invoice list that is created by this workflow will then be posted by the `SAPPostVendorInvoice` workflow.

You can either use the activities available in the **Excel Lib** activity group to separate the initialization and close the activities as steps in `ProcessExcelAttachments` or you can include the complete code to process the Excel attachments in a single **Custom** activity. Let's proceed and create the workflow by following these steps:

1. Create a new workflow called `ProcessExcelAttachments` under the **GLOBAL** node in the **Workflow** panel in the `Vendor Invoice Posting` project.

2. Add a **Custom** activity to the `ProcessExcelAttachments` workflow after the **Start** activity. Specify `VendorInvoiceDetails` as **Input Data Manager** in the **Properties** panel of the workflow. Also, change the **Display name** property to `ReadExcelAttachments` and the **Step name** property to `ReadExcelAttachments` for the **Custom** activity.

3. Build the project to generate the source code for the
    `ProcessExcelAttachments` workflow. You should now see that
    `ProcessExcelAttachments.js` has been generated in the **Scripts** panel.
    This file includes code for the `ReadExcelAttachments` step. Update this step
    to process the Excel attachments and prepare the invoice context with the
    following code:

```
GLOBAL.step({ ReadExcelAttachments: function(ev, sc, st) {
  var rootData_VendorInvoiceDetails = sc.data;
  ctx.workflow('ProcessExcelAttachments', 'e6e7e23f-0e85-4027-b822-618446cdf162') ;
  // Describe functionality to be implemented in JavaScript later in the project.
  ctx.excel.initialize();
  ctx.excel.application.show(true);

  for (var i = 0; i < rootData.PurchaseInvoiceEmails.emails.length; i++) {
    var email = rootData.VendorInvoiceDetails.email[i];
    if ((email.Attachment != null) && (email.Attachment.length > 0)) {
      for (var j = 0; j < email.Attachment.length; j++) {
        if (email.Attachment[j].AttachmentPath != null) {
          ctx.excel.file.open(email.Attachment[j].AttachmentPath);
          var strSheetName = (ctx.excel.sheet.getList())[0];
          var index = 0;
          while((ctx.excel.sheet.getCell(index + 2, 1, strSheetName)) != null){
            var xlsInputInvoice = ctx.dataManagers.rootData_VendorInvoiceDetails_Invoice.create();
            xlsInputInvoice.VendorNo = ctx.excel.sheet.getCell(index + 2, 1, strSheetName);
            xlsInputInvoice.InvoiceDate = ctx.excel.sheet.getCell(index + 2, 2, strSheetName);
            xlsInputInvoice.Amount = ctx.excel.sheet.getCell(index + 2, 3, strSheetName);
            xlsInputInvoice.TaxCode = ctx.excel.sheet.getCell(index+2,4, strSheetName);
            xlsInputInvoice.GLAccount = ctx.excel.sheet.getCell(index+2,5, strSheetName);
            xlsInputInvoice.GLAmount = ctx.excel.sheet.getCell(index+2,6, strSheetName);
            ctx.dataManagers.rootData.VendorInvoiceDetails.Invoice.push(xlsInputInvoice);
            index++;
          }
          ctx.excel.file.close();
        }
      }
    }
  }
  ctx.excel.end();
  sc.endStep(); // end Scenario
  return;
}});
```

Figure 19.9 – Sample source code for sending an email with an attachment

In the preceding source code for the `ReadExcelAttachments` step, we are looping through all the emails that were populated while processing the email to check if there are any attachment names in the email. If there are attachments, then we can loop through the attachment list and open the Excel attachments one by one to read them. This code assumes the order of the data as it was read in the code, starting with `VendorNo` in the first column. Data rows are assumed to start from the second row, thus leaving the first row for the headers; we are not checking these in the code.

We now have a workflow that can be invoked from the `SAPInvoicePosting` workflow after the `ProcessUnreadEmails` workflow before invoking the `SAPLogin` workflow. You can add a **Custom** activity to the `SAPPostVendorInvoice` workflow after posting all the invoices to write the invoice's information, as well as the status of the invoice posting, by creating a new Excel file and then attaching this Excel file to the summary email that will be sent in the `SendSummaryEmail` workflow.

With that, we've learned about the `ctx.excel` library and created a workflow for reading Excel attachments in emails. Just like this library can process Excel files, the Microsoft Office extension library also includes a library for processing MS Word documents. We will introduce the `ctx.word` library in the next section.

Understanding the Microsoft Word extension library

The Microsoft Office extension library includes a class called `ctx.word` that is used to `initialize` and `end` the MS Word application. This class also provides the `ctx.word.file` object for working with MS Word files, such as to create, open, or close them, as well as the `ctx.word.document` object, which is used to read or write data to an MS Word document. Before you start processing any MS Word files in the code, the library must be initialized with the `ctx.word.init` method. Similarly, you need to call the `ctx.word.end` method once you've finished working with MS Word files.

Activities that can be performed to manage MS Word files are included in the **Word Lib** activity group. Always prefer to use the activities in the workflow. Now, let's look at the most used methods that are provided in this library and its classes.

The following methods are available in the `ctx.word.file` object:

- The `create` method: Creates a new MS Word document.
- The `open` method: Opens an existing MS Word document. This method takes the absolute name of the file as the first parameter. You can also send the password as the second parameter if the file to open is password protected.

- The `save` and `saveAs` methods: These methods are used to save the document that was created or opened for the update, either with the same name (`save`) or with a different name (`saveAs`).

- The `close` method: Close the document that was created or opened. This method takes the return value of the `create` or `open` method as the first parameter. You can specify the file that needs to be saved or not before closing the document as the second parameter to this method.

Next, we will look at the `ctx.word.document` object and the methods it provides to read or write information to an MS Word document:

- **The methods to insert text into an MS Word document**: There are methods for inserting text (`insertText`), line breaks (`insertBreak`), images (`insertImage`), or another MS word document (`insertWordDocument`) into the currently open document in the `ctx.word.document` object. You can use the `goto` method to move the cursor to a specific location before using the insert methods.

- **The methods to manage bookmarks**: The `ctx.word.document` object provides methods to get the list of bookmarks (`getListBookmarks`) in a document and to set a value for a bookmark (`setBookmarkValue`). These bookmarks act like placeholders to set a specific value. These methods are very useful when an MS Word document has been prepared as a template with the values to be filled as bookmarks. You can make a copy of the document template using the `ctx.fso` library and then update the bookmarks while executing the process with the results.

- **The methods to use for formatting text**: The `ctx.word.document` object provides methods that are used to format the text, such as updating the text font (`updateFont`) or setting the margins (`margin`) in the document. Please refer to the **Formatting** subgroup in the **Word Lib** activity group for activities for formatting the text in MS Word documents.

Please refer to the *Desktop SDK Reference Guide* in the *Further reading* section for the complete list of objects and functions provided by this library.

With that, we have learned about the three libraries – that is, `ctx.outlook`, `ctx.excel`, and `ctx.word` – that are included in the SDK as Microsoft Office extensions. We have created workflows and added a **Custom** activity to write the code using the `ctx.outlook` and `ctx.excel` libraries. These extension libraries are useful for setting a communication channel as emails and the format of the input data as an Excel file for a business process. Next, we will look at another extension for PDFs that's part of the SDK.

Extracting information from PDF documents

The ctx.pdf library is the SDK extension library for extracting data from PDF documents. The ctx.pdf library only supports text-based PDF documents for extracting complete text, part of the text from a position, or searching text that matches specific criteria specified as a regular expression. Image-based PDF documents, such as scanned documents, are not supported at the time of writing.

The ctx.pdf library provides many methods that can be used to extract information from a PDF document. Developers are free to use either method in the library in the source code by adding the **Custom** activity to a workflow or the activities available under the **PDF** activity group in the **Activity** panel. To use the ctx.pdf library directly in the source code, ensure that the library is included in the project by selecting the **PDF** library under the **Framework Extensions** folder in the **Libraries** tab of the **Edit Project** dialog. Including this library manually in the project is not required if the activities under the **PDF** activity group are used as it will be enabled by **Desktop Studio** upon you adding the first **PDF** activity to the workflow.

The first step to work with PDF documents is to open the document either by calling the ctx.pdf.openPdf method in a **Custom** activity or by adding the **Open PDF** activity from the **PDF** activity group to the workflow. This method takes the PDF file path as the first parameter. The function to execute when a failure occurs when opening the PDF document is the second parameter. You can also set the password as the third parameter if the PDF document is password protected.

> **Note**
>
> The path separator, \, must be doubled when you're passing the file path and its name as a parameter to a method or when you're setting the filename property in the **Properties** panel. For example, to specify the saleOrder. pdf file in the C:\Users\Admin\files folder, you must pass the name as C:\\Users\\Admin\\files\\saleOrder.pdf.

Once the PDF document has been opened, we can use the provided methods to extract text and store the values in the context. The best practice is to call the ctx.pdf. release method or use the **Release PDF** activity from the **PDF** activity group once the information has been extracted.

Now, let's look at a few of the methods that are used to extract information from PDF documents in `ctx.pdf`:

- The `createFilter` method: Most of the text extraction methods in this library take a filter as a parameter. A filter can be created with the `createFilter` method, which takes two parameters. The first parameter is the page range, while the optional second parameter is the area within the page to extract information from. You can also use the **Create Filter** activity from the **PDF** activity group to create a filter. If no filter has been set in the parameter to get these methods, the complete PDF document will be processed.

- **The text extraction methods**: Complete text from a PDF can be extracted with the `getText` method or using the `getWordArray` method, which will extract the words in the PDF document into an array. Another option to extract text is to use the `getTextItems` method, which returns the array of text item objects. The text item object includes the word, size, and position of the word in the document. Optionally, you can limit the extraction with the `filter` parameter. Use the `getTextInArea` method to fetch the text items from a specific area.

  If you are familiar with regular expressions, then you can use the `extract` method to read the information that matches the regular expression that was passed as the first parameter to this method. Please go to `https://regex101.com/` to learn about regular expressions.

- **The methods to extract words with the index**: The `getWordAtIndex`, `getWordAfter`, and `getWordBefore` methods are used to extract a word based on the index of the word, such as in an array of the text items that's returned by the `ctx.pdf.getTextItems` method. These methods take the page number and the index as parameters.

There are also methods available in the `ctx.pdf` library to get the number of pages in the PDF document (`getPageNum`) or to search for a word (`searchWord`) that returns the array of text items that match the word specified in the parameter. Please refer to *Desktop SDK Reference Guide* in the *Further reading* section for the complete list of objects and functions provided by this library.

> **Note**
>
> Like the **Desktop SDK** is used while developing the automation solution in **Desktop Studio**, there is a **Cloud SDK** that you can use while developing the solution in **Cloud Studio**. You will learn more about **Cloud Studio** in *Chapter 24, Development Using Cloud Studio*. The **Cloud SDK** provides more activities for extracting information from PDF documents. So, try using **Cloud Studio** for any project that requires PDF extraction.

We now know that SDK provides an extension library for extracting information from text PDFs and that there are activities for reading information from PDF documents. Now, let's look at the technology-specific extensions provided by the **Desktop SDK**.

Learning about the technology-specific extensions

The Desktop SDK includes three extensions that are specific to Siebel, SAPGUI, and SAPUI5. When we're automating the applications that have been developed using these extensions, we must select the right technology to capture the applications and pages. The applications that are developed with these technologies use type controls that are specific to the technology. For example, pages in SAPGUI applications will include buttons of the GuiButton type, which work like any normal button that's added to a Windows application. Similarly, Siebel applications are web applications that use **ActiveX** objects to define the controls in a page rather than standard HTML objects.

There may be benefits or limitations regarding the actions that can be performed on the controls that have been developed with the specific technology. Developers do not need to see any difference in the controls or actions to be performed on the controls if the applications and pages are captured with the right technology. However, the technology extensions will use different techniques to perform actions or activities that have been defined in the workflow for that page. Remember that all the pages that are captured with any technology will be defined as ctx.page and that the controls in the page will be defined as ctx.item by SAP Intelligent RPA.

The following screenshot shows the additional activities that are specific to the technology while adding these activities to perform actions on the controls:

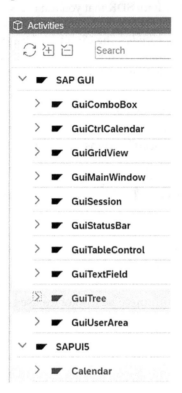

Figure 19.10 – Activities specific to pages that have been captured with a specific technology

These activities can be used on the specific control type and not on any other type of control. Please revisit SAPPostVendorInvoice, which we created in *Chapter 15, Controlling Workflows and Scenarios*, where we have an activity to get the status text from oGuiStatusbar and store it in the status variable after posting an invoice. You can alter this activity so that it uses the activities that are available in the **GUIStatusBar** subgroup under the **SAPGUI** activity group. You can explore the activities that are available for the specific control types that are provided by the technology-specific extensions by expanding each of the control types.

Summary

In this chapter, we looked at the Microsoft Office extension, PDF extension, and technology-specific extensions. These extensions provide classes and methods that can be used to filter and read emails, respond to emails, read information from Excel files or write to an Excel file, manage Word documents, or extract information in PDF documents.

Most of the methods that are provided by the SDK libraries or classes are already available as activities that can be used directly in the workflows. More activities are being added with new **SAP Intelligent RPA** releases to support the methods that can only be called with the **SDK** library in the source code. It is always better to check the latest activities list and use them in your workflows before using the object and methods directly in your code. We also looked at the **Custom** activity, which can be used to add code manually to the steps. Try creating the `ProcessUnreadEmails` and `ProcessExcelAttachments` workflows, adding the **Custom** activity, and adding the code from the sample source code screenshots provided in this chapter. Finally, build the source code using either the *Ctrl + B* or *Ctrl + Shift + B* shortcuts and correct any errors.

In the next chapter, we will learn about environment variables, the different types of environment variables, how to store them in a cloud tenant, and how to read them.

Questions

Here are some questions for you to test your knowledge of this chapter. The answers to these questions can be found at the back of this book, in the *Assessments* section:

1. Why are some methods available in the source code but there is no corresponding activity to use in the workflow?
2. How can you add custom code for a step?
3. The email list that was returned by the `ctx.outlook.mail.getFilteredTable` method includes the same email repeatedly. How can you clear the emails list?

Further reading

To learn more about the topics that were covered in this chapter, take a look at the following resources:

- *Desktop SDK Reference Guide*: `https://help.sap.com/viewer/product/IRPA/Cloud/en-US`

- *Email item properties*: `https://docs.microsoft.com/en-us/office/vba/api/outlook.mailitem`

- *Regular Expressions*: `https://regex101.com/`

20
Managing Environment Variables

We created the `SAPInvoicePosting` workflow, which orchestrates multiple workflows in the `Vendor Invoice Posting` project, in *Chapter 15, Controlling Workflows and Scenarios*. We also created workflows in *Chapter 19, SDK Extension Libraries*, to receive and process the details of the invoice by email as an Excel attachment. In that chapter, we also learned about creating and updating the context variables to process them by the other workflows. We learned about generating the code and building the projects in *Chapter 17, Generating Code*. We are almost ready to test the `Vendor Invoice Posting` project. One step remaining is to prepare the properties in the environment in which the automation solution is to run.

In this chapter, we will learn about environment variables, which are properties that can be used by automation solutions while running, in the following sections:

- Creating environment variables
- Reading environment variables

By the end of this chapter, you will understand the types of environment variables and how to create, read, and use them in a workflow.

Let's start with creating environment variables in the **SAP Intelligent RPA Cloud Factory** to use in **Desktop Studio**.

Technical requirements

- Desktop Studio installed on your workstation

- A brief understanding and access to the SAP Intelligent RPA Cloud Factory, discussed in *Chapter 2, An Overview of SAP Intelligent RPA Cloud Factory*

- The SAPInvoicePosting workflow updated as discussed in *Chapter 19, SDK Extension Libraries*

Creating environment variables

Environment variables are considered as the properties to be used by the automation solution while running. Feel free to revisit *Chapter 2, An Overview of SAP Intelligent RPA Cloud Factory*, to refresh your knowledge on creating the environments. You can create variables with the same name in multiple environments so that when a project is packaged and deployed to an environment, the variables created within that environment will be used. A package imported into multiple environments requires the same environment variables created in all those environments.

Consider a scenario where you need to access a web application in your workflow. The URL and credentials for the web application to use for development, testing, and production are different. That means that you will have three different environments to use during development, testing, and production and each environment will have different values for the URL and credentials.

You can create two different types of environment variables: one is a simple **Text** type and the second is a **Credential** type. The **Credential** type is the combination of the username and password. Cloud Factory stores the credentials encrypted so others cannot see the current values.

Let's now proceed and create SiteURL as a text variable and SiteCredentials as a credential variable in Cloud Factory:

1. Log in to Cloud Factory and go to the **Environments** tab.

2. Select an environment in which the variables are to be created. The environment is as shown in the following screenshot:

Figure 20.1 – Environments tab display in Cloud Factory

3. Click the **+ Add Variable** button in the **Variables** tile to display the **Add Variable** dialog.

4. Enter the name as `SiteURL` and set the type as **Text**. You will then be presented with a text control to enter the value for the variable.

5. Enter for **Value** your preferred URL or a dummy `https://dev.site.com` for learning. The filled-in **Add Variable** dialog looks as in the following screenshot:

Figure 20.2 – New Variable creation display for Text variable

6. You will see the **Variables** tile added to the **Environment** tab if this is the first variable created.

7. Click the **+ Add Variable** button again to display the **Add Variable** dialog. This time, we will create a **Credentials** type variable.

8. Enter the **Name** as `SiteCredentials` and select **Credential** for **Type**. You will then be displayed with options to enter a username and password.

9. You can optionally enter a **Description** for the variables.

10. Enter a username and password for the SAP. The filled-in **Add Variable** dialog looks as in the following screenshot. We will use these credentials in the **SAPLogin** workflow later, in the *Reading the environment variables* section of this chapter:

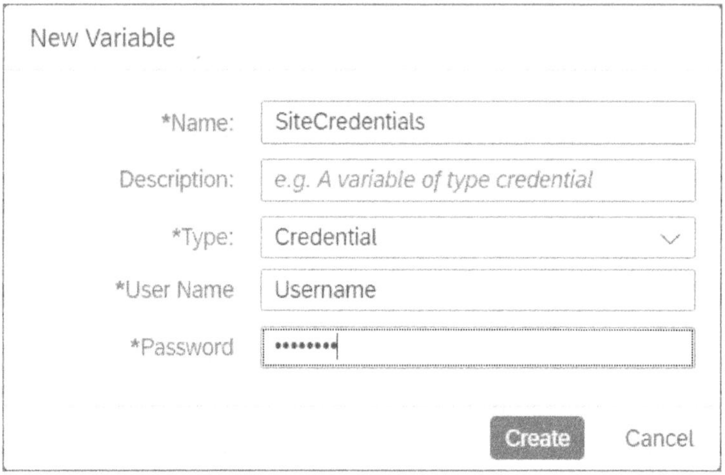

Figure 20.3 – New Variable creation display for Credential variable

We created two variables; the **Variables** tile in the **Environment** tab should display a count of 2 now. You can see the list of variables by clicking on **Desktop Studio**, as highlighted in *Figure 20.1* under the **Variables** node in the left panel.

Let's now learn how to read Desktop Studio variables from Cloud Factory and use them in a workflow.

Reading environment variables

The Desktop SDK includes two classes, `ctx.settings` to read the text variables and `ctx.cryptography.credentials` to read the credential variables. Reading the environment variables is a two-step process. In the first step, we need to declare the variable with the same name as the name used to create the variable, and the second step is to call the `get` method to read the data from Cloud Factory.

Let's first learn about reading the text variable using SiteURL as an example. Desktop Studio provides a couple of options for inserting the code to declare the variable. You can either use the **Insert | Setting | Declare Setting** option from the context menu or type setdec and then press the *Tab* key.

The following is a code example for declaring the variable:

```
ctx.setting({ SiteURL: {
    key: ctx.cryptography.keys.none,
    comment: "Site URL",
    server: true
}});
```

Figure 20.4 – Declaring the text variable in source code

The name used to create the variable is SiteURL and so the same name is used to declare the variable in the source code. Once the variable is declared, you can then use the get method to read the information from Cloud Factory using the following source code sample:

```
ctx.settings.SiteURL.get(function(code, label, setting) {
  if (code == e.error.OK) {
    // get value from setting.value
    rootData.VendorInvoiceDetails.Environment.URLToUse = setting.value;
  } else {
    // Setting not provided
    ctx.log("Cannot read SiteURL from server. Use default value...");
  }
});
```

Figure 20.5 – Sample source code to read the text variable

The shortcut to add the code snippet for getting a variable is to use the **Insert | Setting | Get Setting** option from the context menu or type setget and then press the *Tab* key.

The source sample in *Figure 20.4* assumes that there is a context variable called URLToUse already created. The information fetched from Cloud Factory is stored in the context variable for later use.

We will now look at reading the **Credential** type variable in the source code. Before that, we will create the context variables to store the variable values read from Cloud Factory, as in the following screenshot:

Figure 20.6 – Context to store the environment variable values

Then we add a **Custom** activity to the SAPLogin workflow as the first step before launching the SAPLogin application. Change the **Display name** property to Read Environment Variables and **Step name** to ReadEnvironmentVariables.

After this, we rebuild the project to regenerate the code for the newly created context and the updated SAPLogin workflow. We are ready with the step to read the environment variables and then store the values in the context variables.

Open the SAPLogin.js file for editing. As with the **Text** type, the **Credential** type variable also needs to be declared first. Add the following sample code to the method generated for the ReadEnvironmentVariables step to declare the SiteCredentials variable:

```
ctx.cryptography.credential({ SiteCredentials: {
  key: ctx.cryptography.keys.clientEncryption,
  comment: "My SAP credential",
  server: true
}});
```

Figure 20.7 – Declaring the Credential variable in source code

You can also use the **Insert | Credentials | Declare Credential** option from the context menu or type creddec and then press the *Tab* key to insert the code snippet to include in the source file.

Again, the name used to create the variable is SiteCredentials, which should be used as it declares the variable in the source code.

Observe the difference in the value set for the key. We need to set the type of encryption to use to read the credential variable to clientEncryption. Setting the key is optional; it can be set to none for **Text** variables. We declared the variable; we will now add the following code to retrieve the information after the declaration in the ReadEnvironmentVariables step:

```
ctx.cryptography.credentials.SiteCredentials.get(function(code, label, credential) {
  if (code == e.error.OK) {
    // get login/password from credential.userName and credential.password
    rootData.VendorInvoiceDetails.Environment.SAPCredentials.username =
                                                    credential.userName;
    rootData.VendorInvoiceDetails.Environment.SAPCredentials.password =
                                                    credential.password;
  } else {
    // Credential not provided
    ctx.log("Error retrieving the credentials", e.logIconType.Error);
  }
});
```

Figure 20.8 – Sample source code to read the Credential variable

The shortcut to add the code snippet for getting credentials is to use the **Insert | Credentials | Get Credential** option from the context menu or type credget and then press the *Tab* key.

The step to read the SAP credentials from Cloud Factory is complete. Remember how we hardcoded the set username and set password activities while creating the SAPLogin workflow in *Chapter 15, Controlling Workflows and Scenarios*? We can now update these activities to set the values from the context. Refer to the updated **Properties** dialog box in the following screenshot to set the username from the context:

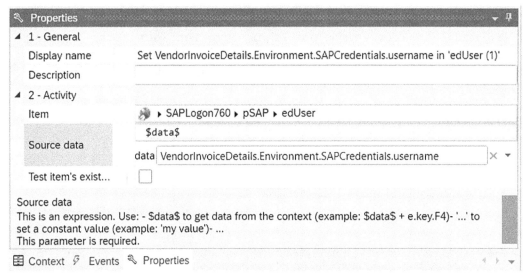

Figure 20.9 – Updated properties for the set username activity on the pSAP page

Similarly, update the set password activity properties to set the value from VendorInvoiceDetails.Environment.SAPCredentials.password.

Notes

Like the get method to read the environment variables, there is also a set method available to update the environment variables. This can be used when the values are changed, for example, to change a password that is expired.

The **Activities** panel includes the declare, get, and set activities under the **Credential** activity group. They can be used in the workflow instead of writing the code in the **Custom** activity.

The call to get the variable values from Cloud Factory is asynchronous, which means that the execution will proceed to the next step once the call is made without waiting for the response from Cloud Factory. We added `ReadEnvironmentVariables` as the first activity, so the next activity in the `SAPLogin` workflow to start the `SAPLogon760` application will be executed before the credentials are even read. The Desktop SDK provides the `ctx.polling` method, which can be used for execution to wait until a condition is true. Refer to the *Desktop Studio Developer Guide* mentioned in the *Further reading* section to understand the usage of the `ctx.polling` method.

So, we have learned about creating and reading environment variables and updated the `SAPLogin` workflow to use the SAP credentials. Rebuild the project and correct any errors, and we are ready for the next step, which is testing the project.

Summary

In this chapter, we learned about environment variables, where and how they can be created, and how to read them in the source code. We updated the `SAPLogin` workflow to read the SAP credentials from Cloud Factory and then used them to log in to the SAP server. The credentials are encrypted and stored in Cloud Factory and while reading them in Desktop Studio. However, the credentials are stored as plain text in the context, so anyone who is running the project will be able to see them. It is a best practice to have separate environments and credentials for developers, testers, and business users to use in production.

We will revisit the complete implementation of the `Vendor Invoice Posting` project and prepare for testing the project in the next chapter.

Questions

Here are some questions for you to test your knowledge. The answers to these questions can be found at the back of the book in the section named *Assessments*:

1. A call to read the environment variables is executed but the value returned is empty. What could be the reason?

2. The application URL to be used for the test environment is different from the production environment. How can the solution work without changing the code for each environment?

3. Reading the credentials information seems to be successful but the username and password are still empty. How do you wait until the read credentials from Cloud Factory are complete?

Further reading

- *Desktop Studio Developer Guide* at `https://help.sap.com/viewer/product/IRPA/Cloud/en-US`

Part 5:
Building and
Running Projects

This section is dedicated to giving a very detailed explanation of how a project can be debugged to identify the probable reasons for errors. You will learn how to check the current state of automation execution and storage. This section also covers how to make the automation solution available or release it to the testers and users once development and testing by the developers is complete..

This section comprises the following chapters:

21
Building Projects

We created the `Vendor Invoice Posting` project and learned about capturing applications, pages, and UI controls in *Chapter 12, Capturing and Declaring Applications, Pages, and Items*. The `SAPInvoicePosting` workflow orchestrates the multiple workflows that were created in *Chapter 15, Controlling Workflows and Scenarios*. We further added more workflows to receive and process the details of the invoice by email as an Excel attachment in *Chapter 19, SDK Extension Libraries*. Let's now review the complete project and the workflows before starting to test the `Vendor Invoice Posting` project.

In this chapter, we will revisit the `Vendor Invoice Posting` project and the workflows created in that project to ensure that the solution includes all the functionality required by the business process. This will be covered in the following sections:

- Revising the `Vendor Invoice Posting` project
- Preparing the environment and building the project

By the end of this chapter, you will have a fully built `Vendor Invoice Posting` project that is ready for testing and deployment.

Let's start with reviewing the `Vendor Invoice Posting` project in **Desktop Studio**.

Technical requirements

- Desktop Studio installed on your workstation

- Microsoft .NET Framework 4.7

- A source code comparison tool (KDiff3 or Beyond Compare)

- The `SAPInvoicePosting` workflow updated as discussed in *Chapter 19, SDK Extension Libraries*

Revising the Vendor Invoice Posting project

Let's first revisit the complete vendor invoice posting business process and the subprocesses that are created as separate workflows. The vendor invoice posting business process will be split into seven subprocesses and each subprocess will be automated as a separate workflow to perform certain steps, as explained in the following sections.

Processing unread emails subprocess

This will be the first subprocess that will be invoked when the automation solution execution starts. We created the `ProcessUnreadEmails` workflow for this subprocess that is used to read all the emails received on the current day and download the Excel attachments with filters, as discussed in the *Reading and replying to Outlook emails* section of *Chapter 19, SDK Extension Libraries*. The attachments are stored in the `Attachments_PurchaseInvoice` folder under the `ctx.options.path.log` folder to be processed by the next subprocess.

Processing Excel attachments subprocess

Once the emails are processed and attachments are downloaded, the next subprocess is to process Excel attachment files and prepare the context to post each invoice in a loop. This subprocess was automated in the `ProcessExcelAttachments` workflow to read the Excel files downloaded by the previous subprocess and store the information in the context variable for further processing. Once the context is updated with the invoice details to be posted, we will start the SAP application in the next subprocess. This subprocess was discussed in the *Processing data from an Excel file* section of *Chapter 19, SDK Extension Libraries*.

Logging into SAP subprocess

This subprocess is used to log in to the SAP server after starting the application. This subprocess, implemented as the SAPLogin workflow, was discussed in the *Creating SAPLogin workflow* section of *Chapter 15, Controlling Workflows and Scenarios*, to perform the following steps:

1. Read the SAP credentials from the SiteCredentials environment variable created in Cloud Factory, as discussed in *Chapter 20, Managing Environment Variables*.

2. Start the **SAP Logon** application.

3. Select an existing connection to the SAP server from the **SAP Logon** page. Then, the SAP page to enter the credentials to the SAP server is displayed.

4. Enter the credentials read from the SiteCredentials environment variable on the SAP page and log in to the SAP server. The page then will be transitioned to the **SAP Easy Access** page.

Once login to the SAP server is successful, we need to enter the FB60 transaction screens and submit the multiple invoices based on the data received in Excel attachments in the next subprocess.

Posting vendor invoice in SAP subprocess

For this subprocess, a SAPPostVendorInvoice workflow was created with steps very specific to the FB60 transaction code in the *Creating a workflow with loop and conditions* section of *Chapter 15, Controlling Workflows and Scenarios*. An additional step is required to write to Excel and send an email that was discussed in the *Creating and sending an email* section of *Chapter 19, SDK Extension Libraries*. This workflow will be invoked after the SAPLogin workflow execution is complete to perform the following steps:

1. Enter the FB60 SAP transaction code on the **SAP Easy Access** page to navigate to the **Enter Vendor Invoice** page.

2. Start the loop to post multiple vendor invoices.

3. In the **Basic data** tab of **Enter Vendor Invoice**, fill in the **Vendor, Invoice Date**, and **Amount** details.

4. Check the condition to include tax. If the tax code is available, then navigate to the **Tax** tab to enter the tax code. We will skip this step if there is no tax to be included in the vendor invoice.

5. Fill in the **G/L acct** and **Amount in doc.curr.** fields on the **Enter Vendor Invoice** page and post the invoice.

6. Read the status of the invoice posting and store it in the `Status` variable under the `Invoice` context folder.

7. Repeat *steps 1* to *6* for all the invoices.

8. Exit the **Enter Vendor Invoice** page by clicking the **Exit** button.

After the posting of all the invoices is complete, we then need to summarize the invoice posting status in Excel and send it as an email attachment in the next subprocess.

Sending process summary email subprocess

This subprocess is used for creating a summary Excel file with the invoice posting status captured and stored in the context variables in the previous step. The summary Excel file will then be sent to a designated email ID as the attachment. The subprocess automated as the `SendSummaryEmail` workflow will have the following two activities

1. A **Custom** activity to write the data stored in the `Invoice` context folder into an Excel file using the `ctx.excel` library that was discussed in the *Processing data from an Excel file* section of *Chapter 19, SDK Extension Libraries*

2. A **Custom** activity to send an email out with a summary Excel file as an attachment to a specific email ID as discussed in the *Creating and sending an email* section of *Chapter 19, SDK Extension Libraries*

With this subprocess, all the invoices are posted, and the status will be passed on to the business process users. We then carry out the clean-up tasks, such as logging off and closing the application, in the next step.

Logging off from SAP subprocess

This subprocess is to log off from the SAP server after completing the process execution. We created the `SAPLogoff` workflow in the *Creating SAPLogoff workflow* section of *Chapter 15, Controlling Workflows and Scenarios*, to perform the following steps:

1. Exit the **SAP Easy Access** page by clicking the **Log-off** button.

2. Close the **SAP Logon** application.

This step can also be used to clean up or delete the files that are downloaded from emails as they are no longer required, using the `ctx.fso` library that was discussed in the *Accessing the files in the filesystem from the source code* section of *Chapter 18, An Introduction to Desktop SDK*.

By now, we have all the workflows created. We have also created the
`SAPInvoicePosting` workflow, which invokes these workflows in a single workflow
to orchestrate the complete business process. We will review the `SAPInvoicePosting`
workflow now.

Integrating the workflows into a single workflow

We created a single workflow called `SAPInvoicePosting` in the *Reusing scenarios and
pass the data* section of *Chapter 15, Controlling Workflows and Scenarios*, which needs to
be updated to invoke the six subprocesses in the same sequence as they were discussed in
the previous section using the **Start** activity available under the **Scenario** activity group in
the **Activities** panel. Remember to update the properties of the scenario **Start** activities to
set the **Data used with the scenario** property to the context `VendorInvoiceDetails`
folder so the data created or updated in the previous step is passed to the next step.

In this section, we looked at the multiple workflows and how they are used to orchestrate
as a single business process workflow. Let's now review the project requirements and
prepare the environment required to build the project in the next section.

Preparing the environment and building the project

We've completed the development of the `Vendor Invoice Posting` project now.
We are almost ready to build the project and debug for any issues. Before we start with the
debugging and test the project, let's first check that the project dependencies are in place.

As this project uses SDK extension libraries, first we will review the libraries that are
required for the project.

Including the SDK extensions in the project

Ensure that the following libraries are checked in the **Libraries** tab of the **Edit
Project** dialog:

- **The Outlook Integration library from the Microsoft Office folder**: This library is
  required to process emails, such as reading emails, downloading attachments, and
  sending an email.

- **The Excel Integration library from the Microsoft Office folder**: This library is
  required to work with Excel files, such as reading Excel attachments or preparing
  the invoice status summary file.

- **The File System Integration library from the Utils folder**: This library is required to work with folders and files, such as creating a folder for saving the attachments.
- **The SAP GUI Scripting library from the CRM Applications folder**: This library is required to work with SAP application screens, such as capturing the SAP page or entering values into SAP controls.

You can also look at the other libraries in the **Libraries** tab of the **Edit Project** dialog that are useful to automate specific technology or utility libraries, such as **String Utilities**, which is useful for developers when manipulating strings. But for the Vendor Invoice Posting project, we need the four libraries listed.

Let's now look at the environment variable required for the project.

Creating environment variables

SAPLogin in the Vendor Invoice Posting project reads the SAP credentials from the SiteCredentials environment variable created in Cloud Factory, as discussed in *Chapter 20, Managing Environment Variables*. Ensure that the SiteCredentials environment variable is created as a credential type and the proper SAP credentials are set.

Once this environment variable is in place, we proceed with building the project.

Building the Vendor Invoice Posting project

Once the workflows are created and then code is added to the **Custom** activities in the **Editor** perspective, we need to build the project using the *Ctrl + B* shortcut key. You can also use the rebuild option to clean up previously generated code and then regenerate the code. You should see the build completed with zero errors in the **Output** panel of the **Editor** perspective. There might be errors and warnings displayed in the **Error List** panel. You can ignore any warnings displayed for the SDK libraries but all errors must be fixed and the project needs to be built again until there are zero errors.

Once the build is completed with zero errors, the source code will be available in the project folder. We will explore the project source code now.

Exploring the project source code

The structure of the project source code was discussed in the *Exploring the project structure and organization* section of *Chapter 10, Creating and Managing Projects*. The folder structure will be the same for all the projects, but the script files created for each project will be specific to the project. We also looked at the source files in the *Exploring the source code structure and source files* section of *Chapter 17, Generating Code*.

You can explore the source script files generated for the Vendor Invoice Posting project from the **Explorer** perspective. The following list of script files includes the information that was either generated or added:

- The Entities script: This file should include all the variables created in the **Context** panel. This script also includes the calls to the functions to create the folders declared in the **Context** panel.

- The Declarations script: This script includes the code to declare the SAPLogon760 application, adding the pages to the application and adding the captured controls to each page. All declarations in the **Explorer** perspective will be included in this script.

- The scripts specific to each workflow: You will see there are seven scripts generated for each of the workflows—ProcessUnreadEmails, ProcessExcelAttachments, SAPLogin, SAPLogoff, SAPPostVendorInvoice, SendSummaryEmail, *and* SAPInvoicePosting.

You can also explore the generated script files directly from the folder in the filesystem where the Vendor Invoice Posting project was created. It is suggested to always use Desktop Studio to edit the project files.

We have our project built and ready for testing and debugging.

Summary

In this chapter, we reviewed the Vendor Invoice Posting project and revisited the workflows that were created in the project. We also learned about invoking a workflow from another workflow and passing the context variable data to the invoked workflow. We prepared the environment required to run the project, to ensure that the required SDK libraries are included in the project, and created the SiteCredentials environment variable. After adding the code to the **Custom** activity, the project was built to regenerate the scripts and correct any errors in building the project by looking at them in the **Error List** panel.

Once the development is complete and the project is built successfully, we must test the project before deploying it for the business users and allowing them to use the automation solution. We will learn about testing and debugging a project in *Chapter 23, Debugging Projects*. The project needs to be packaged and imported to Cloud Factory so the package can be deployed to any Desktop Agent to run the automation solution.

We will look at packaging the project, importing it into Cloud Factory, and deploying the package in a Desktop Agent to run the automation solution in the next chapter.

Questions

Here are some questions for you to test your knowledge. The answers to these questions can be found at the back of the book in the section named *Assessments*:

1. The IntelliSense feature of the **Editor** perspective does not list the required libraries or methods. How do you get them while writing the code?

2. Why is the source code comparison tool window opened when building the code?

22
Deploying Projects

We built the **Vendor Invoice Posting** project in *Chapter 21, Building Projects*, but this project is with the developers only and is not available either for testers to test the project or business users to use the automation solution yet. After the development is complete, the project needs to be deployed in a system where the **Desktop Agent** is installed for the testers. The deployed automation solution can then be used by testers to test all known business conditions to cover normal scenarios, abnormal scenarios (error conditions), and boundary conditions (zero, one, or maximum invoices to be posted) and confirm that the automation solution meets all **functional requirements** (**FRs**) as well as **non-functional requirements** (**NFRs**) such as performance and logging. The deployment for testing should happen after the basic testing and debugging by the developers, which will be discussed in the next chapter—*Chapter 23, Debugging Projects*.

In this chapter, we will work on deploying the `Vendor Invoice Posting` project by creating an environment and agent groups, and then adding a trigger to run the project in the **Desktop Agent** in the following sections:

- Managing environments, agents, and agent groups
- Packaging and importing the project into the **Cloud Factory**
- Adding triggers for the package
- Updating the package versions

By end of this chapter, you will have the Vendor Invoice Posting project imported into the **Cloud Factory** and deployed to the **Desktop Agent**.

Let's start by learning about preparing the environment for the project deployment in the **Cloud Factory**.

Technical requirements

- Desktop Studio and Desktop Agent should be installed on your workstation.

- An internet connection.

- Desktop Agent should be registered and connected to **SAP Intelligent RPA Cloud Factory**.

- Knowledge of the Cloud Factory. Refer to *Chapter 2, An Overview of SAP Intelligent RPA Cloud Factory* to understand the Cloud Factory.

- The SAPInvoicePosting workflow should be updated, as discussed in *Chapter 21, Building Projects*.

Managing environments, agents, and agent groups

You should already be familiar with the **Cloud Factory** and creating an environment, agents, and agent groups in the **Cloud Factory**, as these topics were discussed in *Chapter 2, An Overview of SAP Intelligent RPA Cloud Factory*. We will now prepare an environment for the Vendor Invoice Posting project to be deployed in the **Cloud Factory**. Before proceeding with environment preparation, ensure that the **Desktop Agent** is installed on your system and is registered in the **Cloud Factory**, as discussed in the *Registering the Desktop Agent tenant* section of *Chapter 6, Overview of Desktop Agent*. We will now start by creating an environment to deploy the Vendor Invoice Posting project.

Creating an environment

An environment in the Cloud Factory is a logical group of related packages, agents, and triggers for the packages. The team responsible for deploying the automation solutions is free to decide on how the solutions are grouped. Ideally, automation solutions will be grouped and deployed to an environment that is specific to a **business unit** (**BU**) or functional area. The grouping could even be based on the automation target applications, with restricted access to specific systems. That said, we need an environment to deploy the Vendor Invoice Posting project. We will create an environment named Learning SAP iRPA by executing the following steps:

1. Log in to **SAP Intelligent RPA Cloud Factory**, also referred to as the *tenant*.
2. Go to the **Environments** tab in the navigation bar.
3. Click on the **New Environment** button to display the **New Environment** dialog.
4. In the **New Environment** dialog, enter the **Name** value as Learning_SAP_iRPA.
5. Select Dev for the **Type** value. The filled **New Environment** dialog will display, like this:

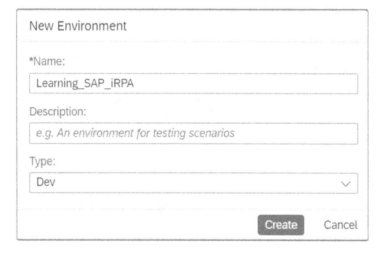

Figure 22.1 – Creating an environment

6. Click on the **Create** button. The **Cloud Factory** opens the Learning_SAP_iRPA environment page after successfully creating the environment.

We have now created an environment that can be used to add agents, deploy packages, and then create triggers. We will now add the agent group to our environment.

Managing agents and agent groups

The environment that we created allows us to link agents or agents grouped under an agent group. An agent group allows us to organize agents with agent groups as parents, and agents under that agent group as children. This will enable us to deploy packages to a single agent or a list of agents under an agent group. We must have an agent group created already so that it can be added to the environment. The creation of agent groups is discussed in the *Agents and agent groups* section of *Chapter 2, An Overview of SAP Intelligent RPA Cloud Factory*. Before an agent is used for deploying a project directly or as part of an agent group, the agent must be registered and connected to the Cloud Factory, as discussed in the *Registering the Desktop Agent tenant* section of *Chapter 6, Overview of Desktop Agent*. All the registered agents are listed in the **Agents** tab of the **Cloud Factory**.

Let's first create an agent group and add your machine to the agent group.

Creating an agent group

Assuming the **Desktop Agent** is already installed on your machine and is registered to the Cloud Factory, we will now create an agent group called SAP_iRPA_Learners and add your agent to this group by executing the following steps:

1. Go to the **Agent Groups** tab by selecting the **Agent Groups** option, displayed upon clicking the down arrow next to **Agents** in the navigation bar. This option is displayed in the following screenshot:

Figure 22.2 – Selecting the Agent Groups option

2. Click on the **New Agent Group** button to display the **Create agent group** dialog.

3. Enter the **Name** value as SAP_iRPA_Learners. Keep the **Type** value as the default Machine selection. The filled **Create agent group** dialog looks like this:

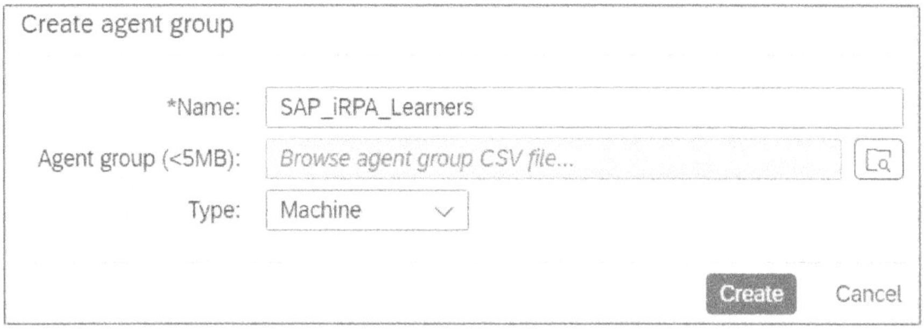

Figure 22.3 – Create agent group dialog

4. Click on the **Create** button to create a SAP_iRPA_Learners agent group. The **Cloud Factory** opens the SAP_iRPA_Learners agent group page after successful creation.

    We have now created an empty agent group. Next, we will add the machine to this agent group.

5. Click on the + button, also referred to as **Add node** button, to add your agent to this agent group.

6. The **Create node** dialog is displayed. Enter **Name** and **Label** values as your machine hostname (you can check the machine name by typing the hostname command in Command Prompt), as displayed in the following screenshot:

Figure 22.4 – Create node dialog

7. Click on the **Create** button to add your machine hostname to the agent group.

> **Note**
>
> An agent group can have subgroups specified and then add nodes to that subgroup. You can create an agent group node the same way as nodes created for an agent and then add agents to that agent group node. This feature will be useful to deploy the package to multiple agents defined under an agent group that has been added to an agent group.

8. Click on the **Save** button on the SAP_iRPA_Learners agent group page to save the agent group. You will see a success message after saving the agent group in the **Cloud Factory**.

We now have the SAP_iRPA_Learners agent group. Let's proceed and link this agent group to the Learning_SAP_iRPA environment.

Linking the agent group to the environment

We created an environment and an agent group, and we now need to link the agent group to the environment so that the packages added to the environment can be deployed to the agents.

For this, let's now link the agent under the SAP_iRPA_Learners agent group to the Learning_SAP_iRPA environment by executing the following steps:

1. Go to the Learning_SAP_iRPA environment page by clicking on the **Environments** tab and then selecting the Learning_SAP_iRPA environment from the list of environments.

2. The Learning_SAP_iRPA environment page will be displayed, with the **Overview** tab selected in the left pane. Click on the + **Add Agent** button to add an agent to the environment.

    The **Add agent** dialog provides options to select your machine name from the **Agents** tab. Then, click on the **Add Agent** button or use the **Agent Groups** tab to select an agent under an agent group. Let's try to select your agent from the **Agent Groups** tab option.

3. Select the **Agent Groups** tab in the **Add agent** dialog.

4. Select the SAP_iRPA_Learners agent group from the list of agent groups. This will display all agents or nodes added to the agent group in the right panel titled **Agent group node**, as shown in the following screenshot:

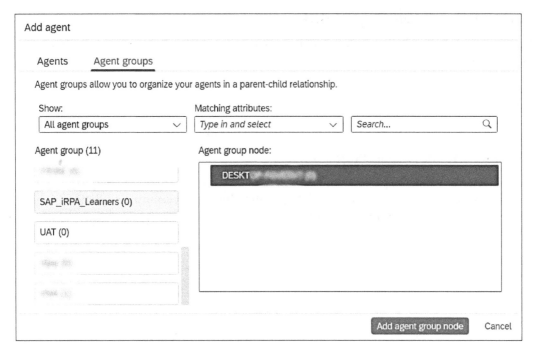

Figure 22.5 – Adding an agent to the environment

5. Select your agent hostname and then click on the **Add agent group node** button.

6. You should see an **Agent added successfully** message, and then the Learning_
    SAP_iRPA environment page will be refreshed to display the **Agents** tile with
    one agent.

We now linked your agent to the environment so that a trigger to run a package can be
added to the environment, but before creating a trigger, we need to deploy the package
to the environment. Let's now create a package for the Vendor Invoice Posting
project and then deploy the package to the environment.

Packaging and importing the project into the Cloud Factory

We now have the Learning_SAP_iRPA environment ready to add packages.
We need to export the project as a package first so that the package can be imported
into the environment. We learned about exporting projects in the *Exporting a project
for deployment into the SAP Intelligent RPA tenant* section of *Chapter 10, Creating and
Managing Projects*. Let's put that knowledge into practice to create a package for the
Vendor Invoice Posting project.

Creating a project package

A package is a `.zip` file that includes all the project source files that can be imported to an environment in the **Cloud Factory**.

Here, a package can be created by exporting the project in the Desktop Studio by executing the following steps:

1. Open the `Vendor Invoice Posting` project in the **Desktop Studio**.
2. Select the **File | Export Project** menu option.
3. Once exporting the project is completed and all the files are compressed to a `.zip` file, you will see an information dialog confirming the successful completion of the project export, as shown in the following screenshot:

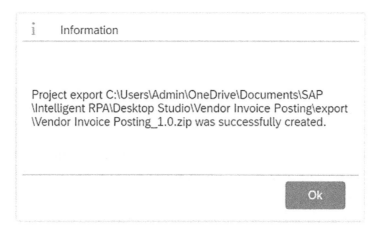

Figure 22.6 – Project export completion dialog

4. You will see the location and the package name in the confirmation dialog. Note the path and filename, as we need to specify the filename while importing the package into the **Cloud Factory**.

Our `Vendor Invoice Posting` project is now packaged as a `Vendor Invoice Posting_1.0.zip` file. The package name includes the package version. You can update the project version by editing the project, as discussed in the *Editing project details* section of *Chapter 10, Creating and Managing Projects*. Once the package version is updated, the name of the package will include the new version of the package.

Now that we have packaged the project as `Vendor Invoice Posting_1.0.zip`, we will next import this package and add it to the `Learning_SAP_iRPA` environment.

Importing the package

The package needs to be imported to the **Cloud Factory** first so that it is available to add to an environment. You can refer to the *Projects and packages* section of *Chapter 2, An Overview of SAP Intelligent RPA Cloud Factory,* to find out about importing the packages. We will import the `Vendor Invoice Posting_1.0.zip` package to the **Cloud Factory** by executing the following steps:

1. Go to the **Packages** tab in the navigation bar of the **Cloud Factory**.

2. Click on the **+ Import** button. As we created the `Vendor Invoice Posting_1.0.zip` package using the **Desktop Studio**, this is referred to as a **Desktop Package**.

3. You will see the **Import Desktop Package** dialog, which allows you to select the package from the local system, as shown in the following screenshot:

Figure 22.7 – Import Desktop Package dialog

4. Click on the **Browse** button displayed as an icon next to the textbox. That will allow you to select the package `.zip` file from the local system.

5. Select the `Vendor Invoice Posting_1.0.zip` package in the file selection dialog. The **Import Desktop Package** dialog will then display the details from the selected package, as shown in the following screenshot:

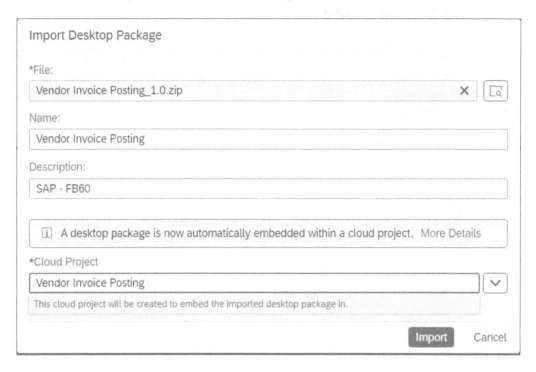

Figure 22.8 – Package details in the Import Desktop Package dialog

6. Confirm the details of the package in the dialog and click on the **Import** button.

7. After the import is complete, the package list in the **Packages** tab will be updated to include the new package. You will also see a cloud project created with the same name as the one specified in the **Cloud Project** textbox of the **Import Desktop Package** dialog. You can explore the `Vendor Invoice Posting` cloud project from the **Projects** tab of the **Cloud Factory**.

We have now imported the package, and it is available to add to the environment in the **Cloud Factory**. Let's proceed and add the package to the environment.

Adding the package to the environment

The `Vendor Invoice Posting` package version `1.0` is now imported to the **Cloud Factory**. We will now add this package to the `Learning_SAP_iRPA` environment so that it can be made available to run on the agent machines.

We need to execute the following steps to add the package to the environment:

1. Go to the `Learning_SAP_iRPA` environment page by clicking on the **Environments** tab and then selecting the `Learning_SAP_iRPA` environment from the list of environments.

2. The `Learning_SAP_iRPA` environment page will be displayed, with the **Overview** tab selected in the left pane. Click on the **+ Add Package** button to import a package to the environment.

3. You will see the **Add Package** dialog is displayed. The first step in adding the package to the environment is selecting the package, as shown in the following screenshot:

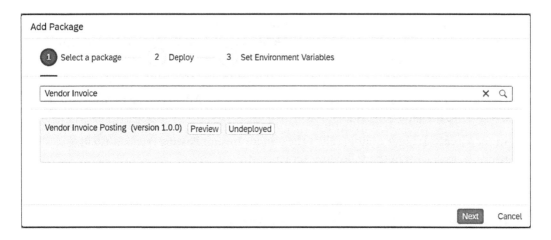

Figure 22.9 – Selecting the package to add in the Add Package dialog

4. Select the `Vendor Invoice Posting` package. The **Next** button will be enabled only after selecting the package.

5. Click on the **Next** button after it is enabled. You will notice that the dialog will move to the **Deploy** step, and then the `Learning_SAP_iRPA` environment page will be refreshed to display the **Packages** tile with one package, without a trigger.

The package is now available in the environment to add a trigger. Remember that the `Vendor Invoice Posting` project reads the SAP credentials from the `SiteCredentials` environment variable.

It is now time to create this environment variable in the `Learning_SAP_iRPA` environment, as discussed in the *Creating environment variables* section of *Chapter 20, Managing Environment Variables*. Once this environment variable is in place, we can then proceed with creating a trigger for the package.

Adding triggers for the package

A **trigger** is a mechanism provided by SAP Intelligent RPA to allow users to specify when the automation solution needs to run. An automation solution deployed as a package can be scheduled to run on agents in an unattended mode—that is, there are no manual interventions required while running the automation solution. It can also be pushed to the agent machine so that the automation solution is available to run by users in attended mode on a need basis. To create a trigger, the package must first be added to the environment, as discussed in the previous section.

You can refer to the *Triggers* section of *Chapter 2, An Overview of SAP Intelligent RPA Cloud Factory,* for details; for now, we will proceed and create a trigger for our Vendor Invoice Posting package by executing the following steps:

1. Go to the Learning_SAP_iRPA environment page by clicking on the **Environments** tab and then selecting the Learning_SAP_iRPA environment from the list of environments.

2. The Learning_SAP_iRPA environment page will be displayed, with the **Overview** tab selected in the left pane. Click on the **+ Add Trigger** button to add a trigger to the environment.

3. In the **Create Trigger** dialog, select the **Vendor Invoice Posting (version 1.0.0)** package, as shown in the following screenshot:

Figure 22.10 – Selecting the package to add a trigger

4. Click on the **Next** button. This will be enabled to allow you to click only after selecting the package.

5. You will notice that the dialog will move to the **Deploy** step and then to the **Select a trigger type** tab in the **Create Trigger** dialog.

6. Select the **Attended** radio button so that the automation solution can be run by users from the **Desktop Agent** on a need basis.

7. Click on the **Next** button. This will be enabled only after selecting the trigger type.

8. You will be presented with the **Add Attended Trigger** dialog, in which the trigger properties can be updated.

9. Update the **Name** value to `Attended_VIP` and select all weekday timeslots, as shown in the following screenshot:

Figure 22.11 – Add Attended Trigger dialog

10. You can update the **Date range** field based on the dates for this package should be available.

11. Click on the **Create** button. You will see a successful trigger creation message, and then the `Learning_SAP_iRPA` environment page will be refreshed to display the **Triggers** tile with one attended trigger. You will also observe that the **Packages** tile display is updated, and one package without a trigger is removed.

We have now created an attended trigger for the `Vendor Invoice Posting` package in the `Learning_SAP_iRPA` environment. After adding the agent, a package, an environment variable, and an attended trigger, the `Learning_SAP_iRPA` environment page should display four tiles, as shown in the following screenshot:

Packages	1	Triggers	1	Agents	1	Variables	1
Preview		Attended		Agent Groups		Desktop	
	1		1		1		1

Figure 22.12 – Tiles added to the environment

We have now successfully prepared our environment with one package and added an attended trigger for the package. The package will automatically be downloaded by the agents added to the environment so that the package can be run by users. It might take a few minutes to download the package in the **Desktop Agent**. After the latest package is downloaded to the agent machine, it should be available in the **Projects** tab of the **Desktop Agent**, as shown in the following screenshot:

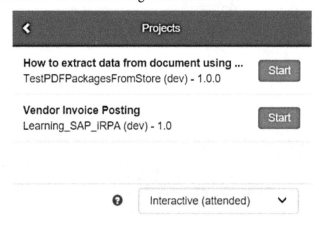

Figure 22.13 – Projects downloaded to the Desktop Agent

We have now completed packaging the `Vendor Invoice Posting` project and have created the `Learning_SAP_iRPA` environment in which the package is added. We added your machine as an agent to the environment and created a trigger for the package to run on all weekdays. The `Vendor Invoice Posting` version 1.0.0 package is now available for running from the **Desktop Agent**.

It is very common to upgrade a package version for releasing new features or for code changes based on testing observations. Let's now look at upgrading the version of the package that is already deployed.

Updating the package versions

A common practice to deliver an automation solution is to deploy the business function incrementally, selecting the features to be delivered according to the priority set by the business users. Every incremental release will have an updated version of the same package, so the previous version of the package can be restored when there are issues with the latest package.

Here, we will learn about how a package version can be updated and redeploy the latest version to the agent that is running the previous version of the same package now. To update the version of the Vendor Invoice Posting project, execute the following steps:

1. Change the **Version** value of the Vendor Invoice Posting project to 1.1 in the **Edit project** dialog, as discussed in *Chapter 10, Creating and Managing Projects.* Save all changes by pressing the *Ctrl + Shift + S* keys.

2. Select the **File | Export Project** menu option in the **Desktop Studio** after opening the Vendor Invoice Posting project. If the version update is not saved, then you will see the following **Confirmation** dialog that allows you to repackage the project with the same version or to update the version of the package:

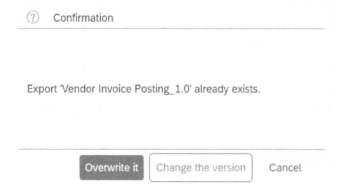

Figure 22.14 – Confirmation dialog to update the package version

3. Click on the **Change the version** button so that the **Export Project** dialog is displayed, in which you will be allowed to enter the new version for the package.

4. Change the **Version** value to 1.1 in the **Export Project** dialog.

5. Click on the **Save** button.

6. Once exporting the project is completed and all the files are compressed to a .zip file, you will see an information dialog confirming the successful completion of the project export, as shown in the following screenshot:

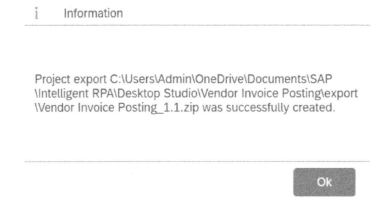

Figure 22.15 – Project export completion dialog with the updated version

7. You will see the location and the package name in the confirmation dialog. Notice the change in the filename—the new version is appended to the package filename and the new package is ready for importing into the **Cloud Factory**.

8. Go to the **Packages** tab in the **Cloud Factory** and import the new package by clicking on the **+ Import** button.

9. Select the Vendor Invoice Posting_1.0.zip package in the **Import Desktop Package** dialog.

10. Click on the **Import** button in the **Import Desktop Package** dialog after verifying the details of the package.

11. You should now see two versions of the Vendor Invoice Posting package in the **Packages** tab of the **Cloud Factory**, as shown in the following screenshot:

Packages

Date:

Filter by date Range 🗓

Items (1) | Vendor Invoice   ✕ 🔍

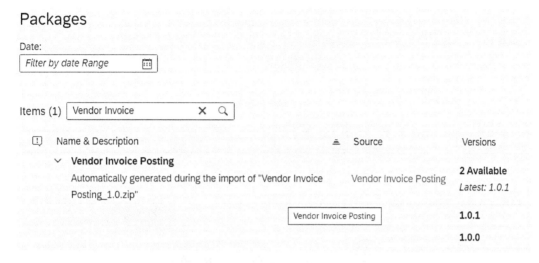

⚠	Name & Description	⚏ Source	Versions
∨	**Vendor Invoice Posting**		**2 Available**
	Automatically generated during the import of "Vendor Invoice Posting_1.0.zip"	Vendor Invoice Posting	*Latest: 1.0.1*
		Vendor Invoice Posting	**1.0.1**
			1.0.0

Figure 22.16 – Multiple versions of the same package display

12. Go to the `Learning_SAP_iRPA` environment page in the **Cloud Factory**, and then either click on the **Packages** tile or select the **Packages** tab in the left panel under **Browser**.

13. Click on the ellipsis displayed under the **Actions** column for the package, then select the **Change Package Version** option that is shown in the following screenshot:

Figure 22.17 – Changing the package version in the environment

14. In the **Change Package Version** dialog, change the **Version** value to `1.0.1`, as shown in the following screenshot:

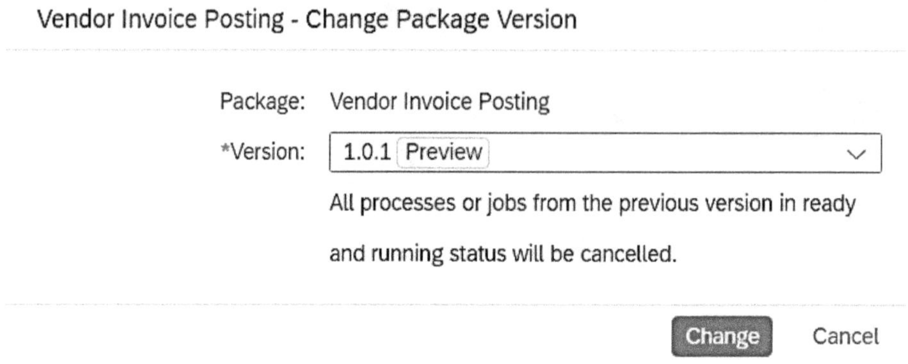

Vendor Invoice Posting - Change Package Version

Package: Vendor Invoice Posting

*Version: [1.0.1 Preview ⌄]

All processes or jobs from the previous version in ready

and running status will be cancelled.

[Change]   Cancel

Figure 22.18 – Selecting the latest package version

15. Click on the **Change** button in the **Change Package Version** dialog. You will notice the change in the package version in the **Packages** tab now.

After updating the package version of the already deployed package, the **Desktop Agent** will then download the latest version of the package. Downloading the package might take a couple of minutes to complete. Once the download is complete, the **Projects** tab of the **Desktop Agent** will include the latest version of the package available for running.

We have now completed the deployment activities for the `Vendor Invoice Posting` project by creating an environment, packaging the project, and importing it into the **Cloud Factory**, adding a package, an agent, and an environment variable to the `Learning_SAP_iRPA` environment. This package should be available for starting in the agent machine added to the environment.

Summary

In this chapter, we created a `Learning_SAP_iRPA` environment and `SAP_iRPA_Learners` agent group. We also added an agent to the agent group that is used to add an agent to the environment. We also learned to update the version of the package that is already deployed to an agent machine. We created an **SAP Intelligent RPA** learning-specific environment and added the required agent, package, environment variable, and attended trigger. The steps to deploy a project from the developer's machine to the agent machine where the project will run are the same. It is up to the business and deployment teams to decide on the exact structure of the environments to be prepared based on the business and functional needs.

We will learn to debug and test the automation solution in the next chapter.

Questions

Here are some questions for you to test your knowledge. The answers to these questions can be found at the back of the book in the section named *Assessments*:

1. A trigger to the package is added in the environment but is not available in the agent machine for running. Why?

2. How can you update the trigger for an existing package when there is a version update?

3. A package for running from the agent was available yesterday but is missing today. What could be the reason?

23
Debugging Projects

We deployed the `Vendor Invoice Posting` project in *Chapter 22, Deploying Projects*, to the `Learning_SAP_iRPA` environment so that it is available for testing by the team. In a real-time scenario, the actual deployment to the testers will happen after confirming that the automation solution is as per the agreed requirements. That means that the developers need to complete the testing of the functionality to be delivered before deploying the solution to testers. Furthermore, there could be issues/defects reported by the testers during their testing that developers need to simulate, understand the reason for the issue, apply the fix, and release the fix to the testers. A debugger such as the **Debug** perspective provided by the **Desktop Studio** will help developers to break the execution at a specific line of the code and analyze the data and context that is being used to fix the issue.

In this chapter, we will learn about debugging the `Vendor Invoice Posting` project in the Desktop Studio and learn about running the project in release mode in the following sections:

- Debugging the project in the Desktop Studio
- Running the deployed project from the **Desktop Agent**

By end of this chapter, you will understand the debugging features provided by the Desktop Studio and learn to run the deployed project from the Desktop Agent.

Let's start by reviewing the `Vendor Invoice Posting` project in the Desktop Studio.

Technical requirements

- Desktop Studio and the Desktop Agent installed on your workstation

- Microsoft .NET Framework 4.7

- Remote tools for Visual Studio 2019

- An internet connection

- The Desktop Agent registered and connected with SAP Intelligent RPA Cloud Factory

- The `SAPInvoicePosting` workflow updated, as discussed in *Chapter 19, SDK Extension Libraries*

- The `Vendor Invoice Posting` project deployed to your agent, as discussed in *Chapter 22, Deploying Projects*

Debugging the project in the Desktop Studio

Debugging a project helps developers to understand and analyze the execution flow and the data being used at each step. Debugging will enable developers to break the execution at a specific line of the code and check the status of the context, and then execute the problematic steps in the debugger to understand the actual issue. The Desktop Studio provides the **Debug** perspective that can be used by developers to test the controls and actions that can be performed on pages or controls. Developers can also set the breakpoints at a specific source line in the **Editor** perspective to analyze the data being used by source code at a specific source line while debugging the project. We will first look at the different menu options available in the Desktop Studio to run or debug the project.

You can click on the **Debug** menu option or down arrow next to the **Debug** (filled right arrow) icon in the menu bar to see the options available to run or debug the project. The menu with the **Run** and **Debug** options is shown in the following screenshot:

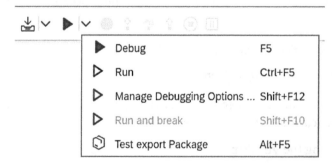

Figure 23.1 – The Debug and Run options provided by the Desktop Studio

You can use the shortcuts displayed next to each menu option for faster access to the menu options. We will be using the *F5* shortcut key to start debugging the project. The difference between **Run** and **Debug** for developers is that the **Run** option will ignore the breakpoints set in the source code and will continue executing, whereas the **Debug** option will break at the breakpoint while executing the project. There are also other options you can explore under the **Debug** menu that are enabled once the debugging of the project starts to help developers control the step-by-step execution of the project.

We will learn more about managing the debugging options in the next section.

Managing the debugging options

Before starting with debugging the project, first, let's look at the debugging options that can be updated and used. You can launch the debugging options dialog by selecting *Shift + F12*, which will allow you to define the options and behavior of the debugging in the Desktop Studio. The **Manage Debugging Options** menu is shown in the following screenshot:

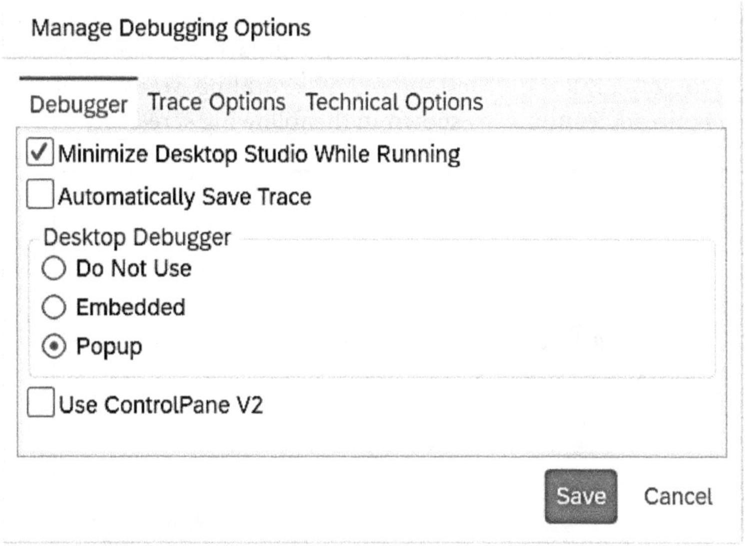

Figure 23.2 – The Manage Debugging Options menu

You can choose different options in the **Debugger** tab of this menu to control the behavior of the **Debug** perspective and the Desktop Studio. You can select to automatically minimize the Desktop Studio while running the project, specify whether the **Debug** perspective is to be embedded in the Desktop Studio or to be opened as a separate window, and choose to save the trace file automatically.

There are two more tabs in this dialog: one is **Trace Options**, which is used to control the trace level to be set for the log files generated while executing the project, and the **Technical Options** tab to set the technical information to be logged for the connectors used in the project. You need to use these options cautiously as the increase in the number of traces will affect the performance of the execution. We will leave the default options as they are and close this dialog by clicking the **Cancel** button for now. We will proceed with starting the debugger for the Vendor Invoice Posting project.

Starting the debugger

The debugging of the project can be started by entering the *F5* shortcut key, as shown in *Figure 23.1*. We will start the Vendor Invoice Posting project by executing the following steps:

1. Open the Vendor Invoice Posting project in the Desktop Studio.

2. Press the *F5* shortcut key to start the debugging. The project will be built before starting the debugger.

3. Only one instance of the Desktop Agent will run at a time in the system. So, if the Desktop Agent is not running already, then it will start in debugging mode, and you can go to *step 7*. But if the Desktop Agent is running, you will see a message that says it is already running, as shown in the following screenshot:

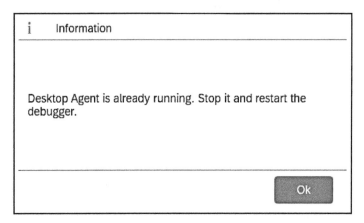

Figure 23.3 – The message when the Desktop Agent is running

4. Click on the **Ok** button.

5. Go to the Desktop Agent, click on the ellipses, and then select the **Shutdown/Restart** option, as shown in the following screenshot:

Figure 23.4 – Stopping the running instance of the Desktop Agent

6. Click on the **Shutdown** button on the confirmation message to shut down the Desktop Agent. Press *F5* in the Desktop Studio to start the debugger.

7. You should see that the **Debug** perspective is launched in the new window. You need to wait till the **LOAD** event for **POPUPS._Systray** is complete before launching the project in the **Debug** perspective, as shown in the following screenshot:

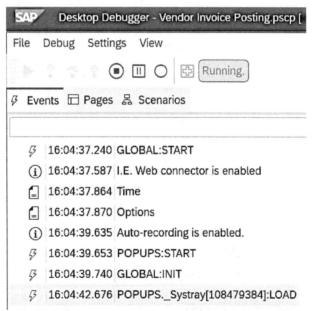

Figure 23.5 – The Debug perspective when debugging the project

You can revisit *Chapter 9*, *Desktop Studio Perspectives*, where panels included on the **Debug** perspective are explained.

8.   Go to the Desktop Agent. It should now be starting in test mode and should list all the testable workflows that are created in the Vendor Invoice Posting project, as shown in the following screenshot:

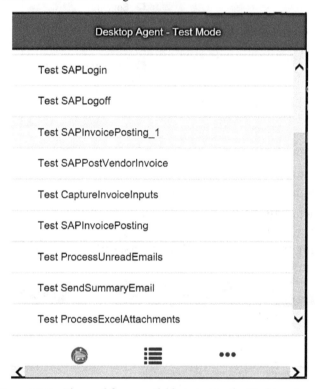

Figure 23.6 – The workflows available to test in the Desktop Agent

Once the workflows are listed in the Desktop Agent, we are ready to start debugging a specific workflow or the complete business process by selecting the appropriate list item.

Let's start with debugging the SAPLogin workflow to learn more about step-by-step debugging in the Desktop Studio.

Debugging step by step

When a workflow is selected in the Desktop Agent running in test mode, the execution of that workflow starts, and all the activities specified in the workflow will be performed. To break the execution at any specific line of code, you must insert a breakpoint at that line so that the execution will break for the verification of the data or status of the control.

Referring back to the *SAP login subprocess* section updated in *Chapter 21, Building Projects*, we will read the `SiteCredentials` environment variable, start the **SAP Logon** application, open an existing SAP connection, and enter the credentials in the SAP page to log in to the SAP server.

First, we need to set the breakpoints at source lines at which the execution needs to break. Refer to the Indicator features of the **Editor** perspective discussed in *Chapter 9, Desktop Studio Perspectives*, to know about setting and removing the breakpoints at a source line. We will set two breakpoints in the `SAPLogin` workflow source file, one at the first click activity in the `pWindowSAPLogon76` page and the next in the `pSAP` page at the first activity in the **Editor** perspective, as shown in the following screenshot:

```
83    // --------------------------------------------------------------
84    ☐GLOBAL.step({ pWindowSAPLogon76_man_1: function(ev, sc, st) {
85        var rootData = sc.data;
86        ctx.workflow('SAPLogin', '9e16813e-af36-436e-aaaf-38e2782d6e31') ;
87        // Wait until the Page loads
88    ☐   SAPLogon760.pWindowSAPLogon76.wait(function(ev) {
●   89        SAPLogon760.pWindowSAPLogon76.oDemo1.click();
90        // Clicks on an item.
91        SAPLogon760.pWindowSAPLogon76.btLogOn.click();
92        sc.endStep(); // pSAP_management_1
93        return;
94    └  });
95    └}));
96
97    // --------------------------------------------------------------
98    // Step: pSAP_management_1
99    // --------------------------------------------------------------
100   ☐GLOBAL.step({ pSAP_management_1: function(ev, sc, st) {
101       var rootData = sc.data;
102       ctx.workflow('SAPLogin', 'cc1f5579-a108-465b-9e46-e0c9b64fc1c2') ;
103       // Wait until the Page loads
104   ☐   SAPLogon760.pSAP.wait(function(ev) {
●   105       SAPLogon760.pSAP.edUser.set(rootData.VendorInvoiceDetails.Environment.SAPCredentials.username);
106       SAPLogon760.pSAP.oPassword.set(rootData.VendorInvoiceDetails.Environment.SAPCredentials.password);
107       SAPLogon760.pSAP.keyStroke(e.SAPScripting.key._Enter_);
108       sc.endStep(); // end Scenario
```

Figure 23.7 – Breakpoints set in the SAPLogin workflow

After the breakpoints are set, we can start the workflow in the Desktop Agent so that the activities in this workflow will be executed till the first breakpoint.

If the debugger has not already started, then start the debugger. Click on the **Test SAPLogin** list item shown in *Figure 23.6* to start the SAPLogin workflow. Since our first break is set after the application start step, you should see that the SAP Logon application is launched. The debugger will execute all the steps till the first breakpoint and wait for the user to continue at the first breakpoint. You will see an arrow at the line that is to be executed next in the **Editor** perspective, as shown in the following screenshot:

```
83    // -----------------------------------------------------------------
84  ⊟ GLOBAL.step({ pWindowSAPLogon76_man_1: function(ev, sc, st) {
85       var rootData = sc.data;
86       ctx.workflow('SAPLogin', '9e16813e-af36-436e-aaaf-38e2782d6e31') ;
87       // Wait until the Page loads
88  ⊟    SAPLogon760.pWindowSAPLogon76.wait(function(ev) {
⇨  89         SAPLogon760.pWindowSAPLogon76.oDemo1.click();
90         // Clicks on an item.
91         SAPLogon760.pWindowSAPLogon76.btLogOn.click();
92         sc.endStep(); // pSAP_management_1
```

Figure 23.8 – The execution waits at the first breakpoint

You can also see that there is a **LOAD** event for the pWindowSAPLogon76 page, as shown in the following screenshot:

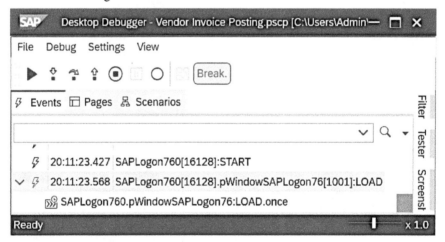

Figure 23.9 – The pWindowSAPLogon76 page load event

If there is an issue with identifying the page that is loaded, you need to verify the criteria set for the page in the **Explorer** perspective. Any mismatch in the criteria and the properties of the page loaded will result in an error to identify that the page is loaded, even if the page is launched in the application. You can recapture the page to see the differences in the captured data between the previous capture of the page and the new capture for the page.

We will now learn about using the **Tester** panel of the **Debug** perspective to test the activities that can be performed on the loaded pages.

Using the Tester panel

The **Tester** panel of the **Debug** perspective that is discussed in the *The Tester panel* section of *Chapter 9, Desktop Studio Perspectives,* can be used to test the functions or activities for the page and the UI controls that are declared in the **Explorer** perspective.

Once the page load event is completed and displayed in the **Events** tab of the **Debug** perspective, as shown in *Figure 23.9*, you will then be able to test the activities that can be performed on the page and the UI controls declared under the page.

Execute the following steps to test the activities or functions that can be performed on the page or UI controls declared under the page:

1. Click on the **Tester** tab of the **Debug** perspective after the page is loaded.

2. You should see SAPLogon760 in the loaded elements list upon clicking the filled right arrow, as shown in the following screenshot:

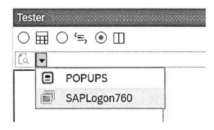

Figure 23.10 – The loaded elements list showing the application

3. Select the SAPLogon760 application and then click on the filled arrow next to the application. You will be presented with all the pages under the loaded application. Select the pWindowSAPLogon76 page, as that is the only one loaded now, as shown in the following screenshot:

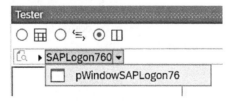

Figure 23.11 – The list of loaded pages under the application

4. The available methods list in the **Tester** panel should now display all the functions or activities that can be performed on the page. You can execute any method on the page by double-clicking on the method or selecting it and then clicking the **Execute** button. You can also select the declared UI controls under the page by clicking the filled arrow next to the page, as shown in the following screenshot:

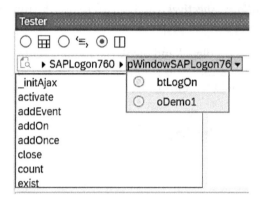

Figure 23.12 – The available methods list and the UI controls for the page

5. Select oDemo1 or btLogOn to get the available methods list updated with the methods available for the UI control.

    The reason for the failure to identify the control on the page may be because of the declared criteria for the control. If the control is visible on the page but not available for selection, compare the criteria defined for the control and the properties in the loaded page.

6. You can select any available method for the control for execution.

    All the previously executed methods are listed in the commands list, and the execution result for the last command is displayed in the **Result** sub-panel.

7. You can select one or multiple commands in the commands list and execute either by clicking the **Execute** button or pressing the *F7* shortcut key.

Once the testing of the activities for the page or UI controls is complete, you can identify the criteria mismatch and correct it in the **Explorer** perspective. The project can then be built to retest.

The **Tester** panel is used to test the activities on a page or control, and the Desktop Studio provides another useful panel in the **Editor** perspective that can be used to verify the data or the current context while debugging the project. You can use this panel while the execution breaks at a source line, as shown in *Figure 23.8*.

Go to the **Editor** perspective when the execution is waiting at a breakpoint; you will see the **Locals** panel, where the current context can be viewed. The panel is shown in the following screenshot:

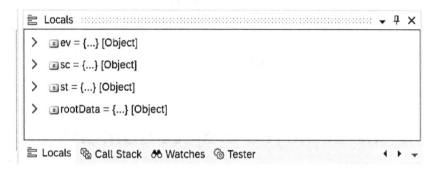

Figure 23.13 – The Locals panel of the Explorer perspective

You can verify the data and the complete context of the current execution in the **Locals** panel. This panel provides multiple tabs for the following:

- **Call Stack**: You can see the complete list of the methods executed till the breakpoint during the current debug session.

- **Watches**: This panel allows users to add the context for a focused watch of the change in the value. You can add context to a watch by selecting it in the **Code Editor** panel and then selecting the **Add Watch** option from the context menu. The following is a screenshot of **Watches** when the SAPCredentials variable from the context menu is added as an example:

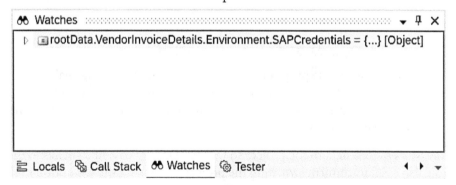

Figure 23.14 – The Watches panel of the Explorer perspective

This panel also includes the **Tester** panel, which is the same as the **Tester** panel in the **Debug** perspective that is used to test the activities on the pages or UI controls.

You can stop debugging using the *Shift + F5* shortcut key any time during the debugging. The debugging feature is very helpful for developers to identify issues with the criteria defined for the pages and UI controls, monitor the context, and ensure the expected outcome for each of the steps or the complete business process.

While debugging is used by developers using the Desktop Studio, the deployed solution needs to be executed by testers using the Desktop Agent directly, as it is normal practice to restrict testers' access to the Desktop Studio.

Next, let's learn to run the deployed project from the Desktop Agent.

Running the deployed project from the Desktop Agent

We completed the deployment of the `Vendor Invoice Posting` project in *Chapter 22, Deploying Projects*, to your agent from the `Learning_SAP_iRPA` environment. You can start the Desktop Agent on your machine to see that this project is available, as shown in the following screenshot:

Figure 23.15 – The project deployed to the agent

Remember that we deployed the project in attended mode and made it available during weekdays while adding the trigger in the *Adding triggers for the package* section of *Chapter 22, Deploying Projects*. If you are working on the weekend, this project will not be available. To make it available on weekends, you must update the trigger.

Click on the **Start** button next to the project so that the Desktop Agent switches to the project. You also need to confirm switching the project by clicking the **Ok** button in the confirmation message. You have seen that the Desktop Agent displays all the workflows to test while debugging, but now you will see no workflow to test; that is, the workflow list will be empty in the Desktop Agent, even after switching to the project, as shown in the following screenshot:

Figure 23.16 – An empty workflow list to test

This is because the code to add the menu item to systray will be executed only if the project is running in debug mode.

So next, we will learn to enable the workflow execution in release mode.

Enabling a workflow to run in release mode

The systray menu items needed to run a workflow are, by default, added only when the project is running in debug mode in the generated code. We need to modify the GLOBAL. events.START.on method in each workflow that we want to allow users to run from the Desktop Agent. The default code for this method looks like the following source code screenshot:

```
4    // ------------------------------------------------------------
5    ⊟ GLOBAL.events.START.on(function (ev) {
6          if (ctx.options.isDebug) {
7              // Add item in systray menu.
8    ⊡        systray.addMenu('', 'SAPLogin', 'Test SAPLogin', '', function (ev) {});
14         }
15   });
```

Figure 23.17 – The generated code for the START event

Observe that the systray.addMenu method call is added under the ctx.options. isDebug condition. Because of this condition, we will see the option to test the workflow while running the project in debug mode, but it will not be available for testers by default. To enable the option to run the workflow in release mode, that is, from the Desktop Agent, we need to change this code. We need to comment out this condition in the source code of a workflow, which we want to enable the testers or users to run from the Desktop Agent.

We will change the method code for the `SAPLogin` and `SAPInvoicePosting` workflows so that the testers can run those only. The updated code in line 6 and the corresponding closing bracket in line 14 are shown in the following source code screenshot:

```
5   GLOBAL.events.START.on(function (ev) {
6      // if (ctx.options.isDebug) {
7         // Add item in systray menu.
8      systray.addMenu('', 'SAPLogin', 'Test SAPLogin', '', function (ev) {});
14     // }
15   });
```

Figure 23.18 – The updated source code to run the workflow

Once the source code is changed for both `SAPLogin` and `SAPInvoicePosting` workflows, we need to redeploy the project. You can follow the *Updating the package versions* section of *Chapter 22, Deploying Projects*, to deploy version 1.2 of the `Vendor Invoice Posting` package. Once the new version of the package is imported to the **Cloud Factory** and the package version is updated in the `Learning_SAP_iRPA` environment, you need to wait till the Desktop Agent downloads the latest package, as it might take a couple of minutes to complete.

After the Desktop Agent is refreshed with the new package, you will see that the two workflows are now available to run in attended mode, as shown in the following screenshot:

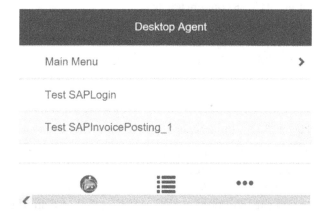

Figure 23.19 – Two workflows enabled to run in the Desktop Agent

The testers or users for which the Vendor Invoice Posting package version 1.2 is installed will now be able to select the workflow to test in attended mode and confirm that the automation solution meets all the business or functional requirements.

We need to deploy the project in multiple agents and get them tested before releasing the automation solution to the business users. Each agent machine must meet the requirements to run the project; for instance, it must have all the software or applications installed locally and must have access to the sites that will be used by the automation solution.

In this section, we learned how to enable any workflow to run in release mode for the testers; the general practice is that they will be given the option to run the complete workflow, that is, the SAPInvoicePosting workflow only, instead of allowing them to run the workflows created for subprocesses.

Summary

In this chapter, we learned about running the Vendor Invoice Posting project in both debug mode and release mode. Debugging is the most useful feature for developers to simulate errors and verify the status of context or data at one point of the execution. The Desktop Studio provides the **Tester** panel that is used by developers to test the activities on a page or UI control once the page is loaded. This also helps developers to identify whether there are any mismatches in the criteria defined for the page or UI control from the page or control while running. We also learned that there are more panels in the **Editor** perspective, such as **Locals** and **Watches**, in which context and data can be verified while debugging the solution.

In the next chapter, we will learn about the **Cloud Studio**, which is an alternative to the Desktop Studio, provided by SAP Intelligent RPA.

Questions

Here are some questions for you to test your knowledge. The answers to these questions can be found at the back of this book in the *Assessments* section:

1. The updated version of a project is deployed to the environment, but the Desktop Agent still displays the old version of the project. How do you get the latest version of the package to the Desktop Agent?

2. Is there any option to run the package in debug mode from the Desktop Agent?

3. An application is started and a page is loaded, but SAP Intelligent RPA does not recognize the page or the controls on the page. What could be the reason?

Part 6: Orchestrating Workflows with Cloud Studio

This section will provide a detailed explanation of creating, importing, and using the components in Cloud Studio. It also focuses on the reusability of the automation components or building blocks and accelerated automation solution development using the process recorder.

This section comprises the following chapters:

- *Chapter 24, Development Using Cloud Studio*
- *Chapter 25, Reusability of Packages across Multiple Solutions*
- *Chapter 26, An Introduction to Process Recorder*

24
Development Using Cloud Studio

For a long time, when a business needed a new application, there were only two routes to address those application needs – first, building the application from scratch, and second, buying a ready-made app and customizing it to meet the requirements as closely as possible. While developing a custom application guaranteed to meet all the needs, this route was lengthy and expensive. Success depended upon the availability of skilled developers for development and, crucially, post-production support. Buying a ready-made app provided a quick turnaround, but customization options were limited.

Recently, a new breed of **Low-Code/No-Code (LC/NC)** development platforms has appeared that offers the best of both worlds. Using these platforms, organizations can rapidly create bespoke applications without the need for deep technical skills while still meeting all their requirements.

We will discuss the following topics in the sections that follow:

- An overview of Cloud Studio
- Capturing and declaring applications
- Designing automation
- **Software Development Kit (SDK)** packages and custom script development

Cloud Studio is the LC/NC development platform for SAP Intelligent RPA, and we will learn about development using this platform in this chapter.

Let's begin by getting an overview of Cloud Studio.

Technical requirements

- An internet connection and a web browser

- System administrator rights on your computer

- Completed installation of the SAP Intelligent RPA on-premise components from the previous chapters

- Access to the SAP Business Technology Platform trial system (`https://www.sap.com/cmp/td/sap-cloud-platform-trial.html`)

- Subscription to the SAP Intelligent RPA trial version (`https://help.sap.com/viewer/82d5a2499d8449dda691bb4d5b3d7949/Cloud/en-US`)

- Access to the SAP Intelligent RPA Store for reusable packages (optional)

An overview of Cloud Studio

Before beginning the first section, we'd like to acknowledge the limitation of the book format to cover every tiny nuance and evolving nature of Cloud Studio. At the time of writing, we will cover the major functionality of Cloud Studio here. However, once you have read this chapter, we highly recommend you go visit the following resources to gain a deeper understanding of Cloud Studio:

- *Enter Next-Level Bot Building with SAP Intelligent RPA 2.0*: `https://open.sap.com/courses/rpa5`

- *What's New with Bot Building in SAP Intelligent RPA 2.0*: `https://open.sap.com/courses/rpa6`

- *SAP Intelligent RPA Cloud Studio User Guide*: `https://help.sap.com/doc/464781c43f264b8fb956c6e1594cd723/Cloud/en-US/29e8302075ea4c75a5952d44625ce508.pdf`

As discussed earlier, Cloud Studio is the LC/NC development platform for SAP Intelligent RPA. You will need to navigate to your SAP Intelligent RPA factory instance to use Cloud Studio.

The following is the URL format to the factory instance. Please replace <Your tenant information> in the URL format with your tenant information.

```
https://<Your tenant information>.hana.ondmand.com/#/home
```

Once in the SAP Intelligent RPA factory, select **Projects** (**1**) from the main menu and then select **New Project** (**2**) or open an existing project (**3**) if you created one earlier:

Figure 24.1 – Using Cloud Studio

As soon as you create the project, SAP Intelligent RPA imports two SDKs –irpa_core and irpa_excel – to the project. You can find these SDKs under dependencies. We will discuss the SDKs in the *SDK packages and custom script development* section in detail.

As shown in the following screenshot, you can create and import several artifacts with Cloud Studio:

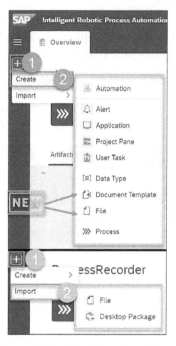

Figure 24.2 – Cloud Studio artifacts

We discussed most of these artifacts in *Chapter 7, An Overview of Cloud Studio*, and will use several of these artifacts in this and the next chapter.

The **File** and **Document Template** artifacts are new. We did not touch upon them earlier, so let's discuss them briefly before moving forward. In the next chapter, we will extensively discuss the **Desktop Package** artifact.

- **File**: In Cloud Studio, you can create files of four types: Text, YAML, XML, and JSON. Once created, you can operate on a file in your automation using usual file operations such as **Read File**.

- **Document Template**: The SAP **Business Technology Platform** (**BTP**) Document Information Extraction service has been in development for some time and is now available for use from directly within SAP Intelligent RPA Cloud Studio. You can use this service to extract information from various business documents such as invoices, payment advice, or purchase orders without using a template. However, a **Document Template** artifact can help you improve the quality of data extracted from pre-trained models and extract data from custom document types.

Now that we know about them, let's see how to use some of these artifacts.

Capturing and declaring applications

We use an **Application** artifact to capture applications running on our workstation and recognize UI elements from these applications for later use in automation. As you will know from your experience with Desktop Studio so far, capturing an application results in getting the elements that make up the application and having them available to you for the next step, which is for declaration. As a productive application will have hundreds if not thousands of elements, you will choose the elements you want to work with and declare only those in the declaration step.

Let's understand each process in brief in the following subsections.

Capturing applications

Capturing an application is a multi-step process in the **Application** editor of Cloud Studio, and it starts with capturing one of the application screens.

To capture an application screen, navigate to Cloud Studio and create a project as discussed in the previous section, *An overview of Cloud Studio*.

As shown in the following screenshot, once your project opens, click the + sign and then **Create**, followed by **Application**:

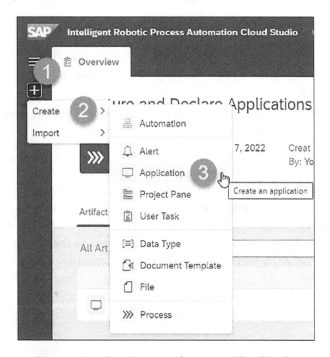

Figure 24.3 – Creating an application in Cloud Studio

You will see the application editor, similar to the following screenshot:

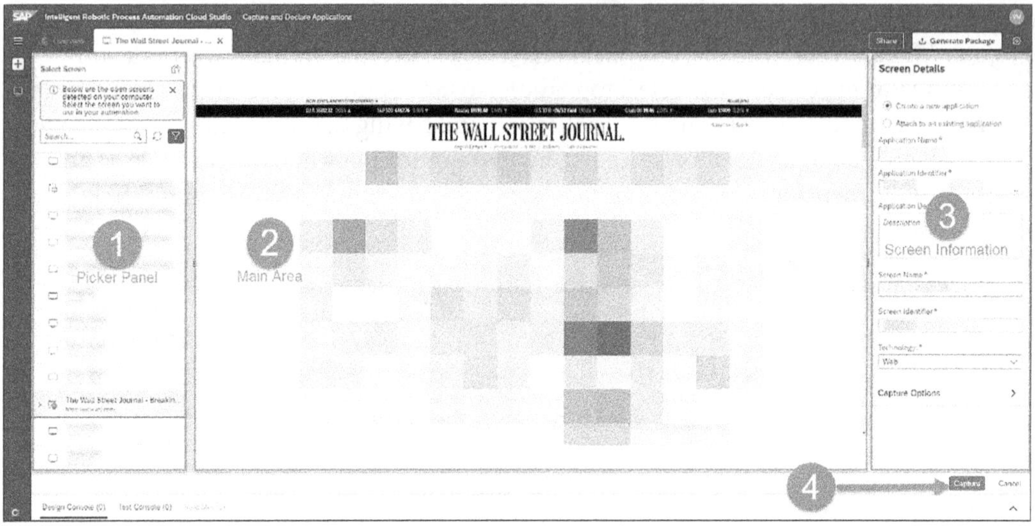

Figure 24.4 – Capturing applications in Cloud Studio

While the picker panel on the left will list all open screens, the remaining two areas will be empty till you select an application, as we have done.

Let's understand these three distinct areas in the **Application** editor.

1. **Picker Panel**: This panel lists all the open screens and will show a list of all available screens as soon as your new application opens. To begin, you should select the screen to capture.

2. **Main Area**: This area will start empty but will fill up with the preview of the selected screen as soon as you select a screen in the picker panel.

3. **Screen Information**: Once you have selected a screen in the picker panel, relevant information such as the application name, the screen name, and technology for that screen will load in this area. Please realize that on the capture of the first screen, you will provide an application name that can be reused for subsequent screen captures. However, should you create another application in the existing project, you will see an option of attaching the captured screen to the new application or an existing one. Also, while you can choose the technology for screen capture, we recommended sticking to the detected technology unless there is a particular reason to do otherwise.

Once you click the **Capture** button (**4**), the application and screen will save the recognition criteria, which are automatically filled – for example, as shown in the following screenshot, two recognition criteria are automatically filled. If needed, you can delete or update these pre-filled criteria or add a new one from the **Captured Data** area (**3**):

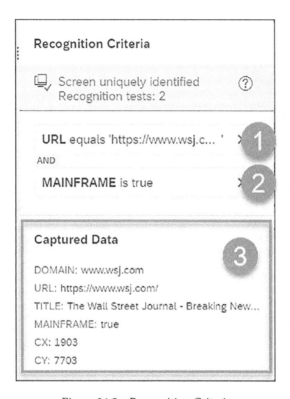

Figure 24.5 – Recognition Criteria

Setting **MAINFRAME is true** is mandatory on the main page of a web application to enable the capture of its sub-elements. You may also need to set the **MAINFRAME** property to **true** for iFrames, but we will not discuss this topic in detail and invite you to explore this topic in the referenced resources in the *An overview of Cloud Studio* section of this chapter. However, as shown in the following screenshot, you are unlikely to find this property for applications captured using other technologies such as UI automation:

Figure 24.6 – Variation in recognition criteria for technologies

Before you start capturing a screen, you can choose the capture options, which vary between technologies, to limit certain aspects of the application screen. As shown in the following screenshot, the capture options for **Web** and **UI Automation** have some similarities and some differences. The differences are highlighted here:

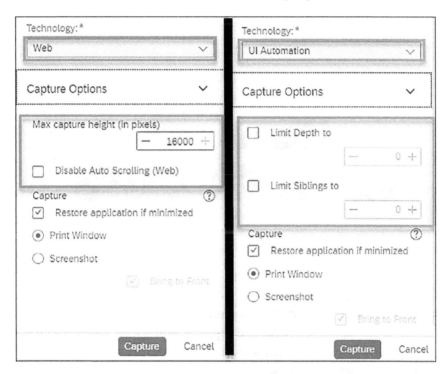

Figure 24.7 – Variation in capture options for technologies

Once you have selected the first screen, depending upon your use case, you can add other screens to the application or another capture of the first screen if you want to show elements such as popups.

Now, let's capture one application and a few screens before moving to the next section. We will capture a web application through www.tesla.com and three screens about **Model S**, **Model X**, and **Solar Panels** for this small exercise:

1. Navigate to Tesla.com in Chrome, as it works best with Chrome.

2. As explained earlier in the *An overview to Cloud Studio* section, create a new project or open an existing one in Cloud Studio.

3. As explained at the beginning of this section, create an **Application** artifact in your project and select the Tesla web page. You will see the following screen:

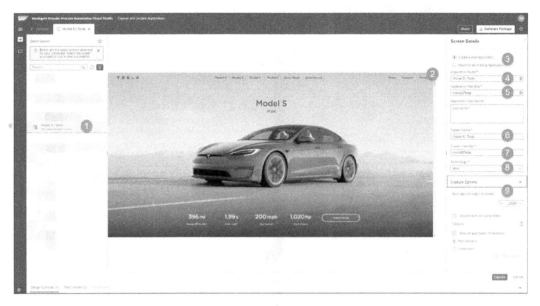

Figure 24.8 – Application capture

(**1**) is the selected screen, (**2**) shows a preview of the screen, (**3**) shows the options to create a new application or attach the captured screen to an existing application, (**4**) and (**5**) show the application name and application identifier, (**6**) and (**7**) show the screen name and screen identifier, (**8**) shows the identified capture technology, and (**9**) shows all the capture options.

We will change **Application Name** to Application_Tesla and **Screen Name** to Page_Tesla_Landing. Since this is a very long web page and we do not need any elements not shown on the current screenshot, we will limit **Max capture height (in pixels)** to **2000** and select **Disable Auto Scrolling (Web) Capture**.

4. Click **Capture** and keep the proposed recognition criteria.

5. Now, click on **Model X** on the Tesla web page in Chrome.

6. As shown in the following screenshot, click on the ellipsis beside the application name and select **Add Screen**:

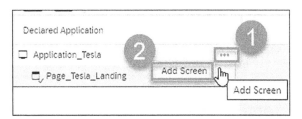

Figure 24.9 – Add Screen

7. Provide a screen name, adjust the capture parameters as discussed in step 3, and press **Capture**. Follow similar steps to capture screens for **Solar Panels** too.

8. Once done, you should see something similar to the following screenshot:

Figure 24.10 – Multiple screens captured

Now that we have captured an application with multiple screens, let's see how to declare the desired elements.

Declaring applications

As mentioned earlier, declaration defines the identification criteria for application and its subcomponents. The declaration needs to occur at the three levels of **Application**, **Screen**, and **Elements**. As we have already seen the process of defining **Recognition Criteria** for applications and screens in the previous section, we will touch upon these elements briefly. However, our focus will be on the declaration of elements in this section.

As shown in the following screenshot, we accepted the proposed recognition criteria of **DOMAIN equals 'www.tesla.com'** for our web application. We had various other criteria listed under the **Captured Data** section available to add to the recognition criteria, but it was unnecessary, as the application was identified with the proposed criterion:

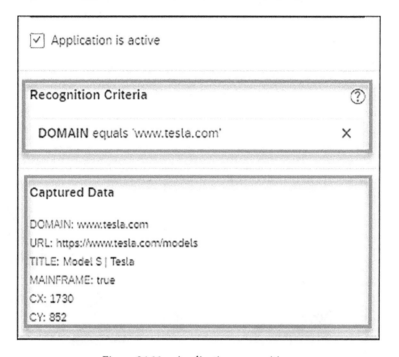

Figure 24.11 – Application recognition

For the **Model X** screen, we again accepted the proposed recognition criteria of **URL equals 'https:/www.tesla.com/modelx'**. As with our application, we can tweak this recognition criterion (**1**) or choose other recognition options (**2**) from the **Captured Data** section, but we did not exercise these options:

Figure 24.12 – Screen recognition

Now, let's focus on element recognition on identified screens.

We will declare the link to **Model X** on the landing page to build automation where the bot clicks on this link. As shown in the following screenshot, let's perform these steps:

1. We will click on the **Page_tesla_Landing** (**1**) screen name, which will load the captured screen in the main panel.

2. Here, we will click on the **Model X** (**2**) link. This action will load the **Name**, **Identifier**, and **Element Class** (**3**) options of this element, the confirmation of element identification (**4**), and the proposed recognition criteria (**5**) in the screen information panel.

   You will also see other available recognition criteria under the **Captured Data** (**6**) section.

Once you click on **Declare Element** (7), the name of the declared element will appear in the left panel under the **Declared Elements** section.

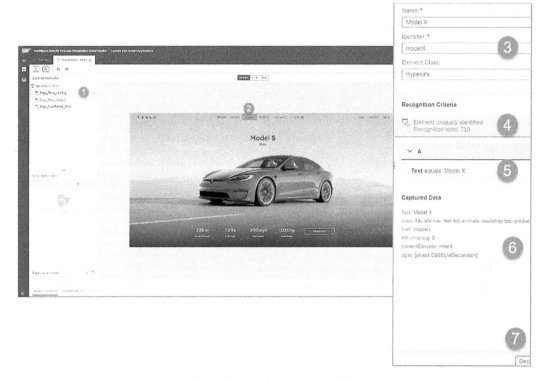

Figure 24.13 – Element recognition

You should follow a similar approach to declare various other elements on your screens. However, you are bound to come across several nuances in doing so. We will discuss them here briefly, but you need to pursue the recommended resources mentioned at the beginning of the *An overview to Cloud Studio* section for a complete understanding.

The following screenshot lists some of the options available to you during element capture:

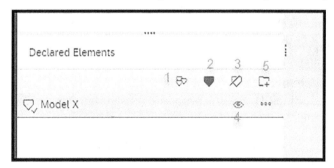

Figure 24.14 – The element capture options

Let's understand each of these:

1. **Collection of elements**: Sometimes, several elements, for example, several search results of a Google search, will have similar identification criteria. In such scenarios, you should declare all these elements as a collection and iterate through these in the automation.

2. **Must exist element**: Some elements must exist on a screen to identify that screen positively. You can mark such elements as must-exist.

3. **Must not exist element**: Some elements must not exist on a screen. You can mark such elements as must-not-exist.

4. **Ignore element on current capture**: You can ignore an element on the capture by selecting this option.

5. **Group elements**: If you need to organize your elements better, you can group some elements based upon your defined needs.

Now that we know how to capture and declare applications and their components, let's understand how to build automation using them.

Designing automation

Automation is a sequence of activities that carry out the task you want to automate. Automation comprises several steps, and each step can act upon applications and screens running on a computer. You can execute automation on your desktop using your local desktop agent manually or per a defined schedule. Automations are the Cloud Studio counterpart of scenarios in Desktop Studio.

As shown in the following screenshot, we design **Automation** by creating an automation artifact:

1. To create an automation artifact, go to + | **Create** | **Automation**:

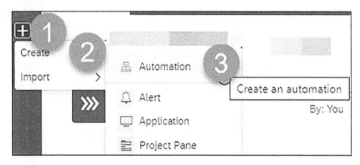

Figure 24.15 – Creating automation

2. Choose the desired agent version, click **Confirm**, and fill in a name for your automation – for example, we named our automation `book_automation`. We are presented with the following screen. You can see the automation name (**1**), the automation template (**2**), and a list of tools (**3**) available to build your automation:

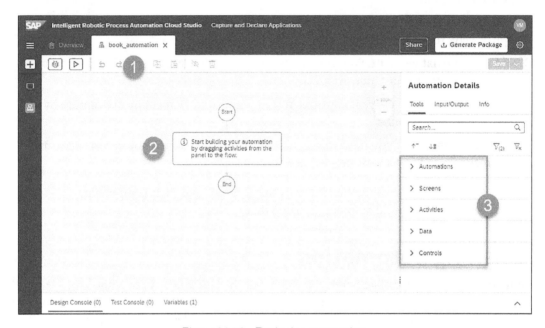

Figure 24.16 – Designing automation

As shown in the following screenshot, these tools are available for designing your automation:

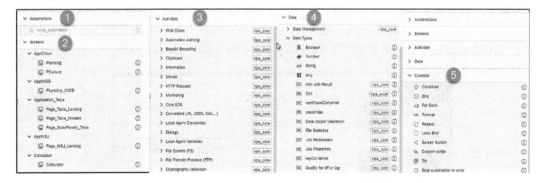

Figure 24.17 – Tools for automation

Here is a detailed explanation of the tools that are available for designing your automation:

1. Automations available in the project, meaning that an automation can include another automation

2. All screens

3. Various activities available under the default `irpa_core` and `irpa_excel` SDKs

4. Data management capabilities and data types available under the default SDKs

5. Several controls such as conditions, loops, and scripts to regulate the flow of automation.

Besides tools, we have two other tabs named **Input/Output** and **Info** in the right panel. The **Input/Output** parameters are variables that you can pass between automation, SDKs, and controls to exchange required data.

Let's now build a simple automation using all three screens of our **Application_Tesla** application:

1. We will start by launching the landing page, **Page_Tesla_Landing**, and then click on the **Model X** link to navigate to the second screen.

2. After that, we will return to the landing page and finally navigate to the third screen, **Page_SolarPanels_Tesla**. The final automation will look like the following screenshot where (**1**) is our automation, (**2**) shows the properties of a **Click** event, and (**3**) shows the test panel to test our automation:

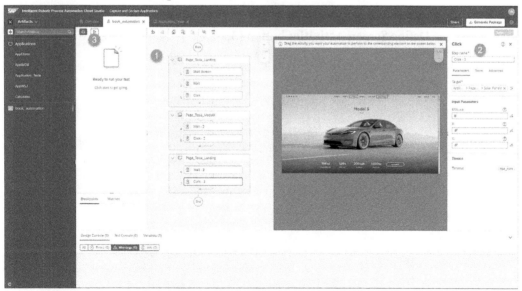

Figure 24.18 – Building a simple automation

To build this automation, follow the following steps:

- Open the **book_automation** automation.

- From the **Screen** list in the right panel, drag and drop the **Page_Tesla_Landing** screen between **Start** and **End**, creating a screen instance in the workflow.

- As shown in the following screenshot, click on this screen instance (**1**) to open the **Screen** panel with a small preview (**2**) of the screen:

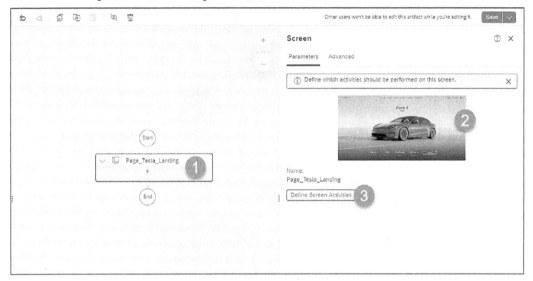

Figure 24.19 – Add the screen instance to the automation

- Click the **Define Screen Activities** button (**3**).

3. As shown in the following screenshot, a screen preview becomes visible in the main panel (**4**):

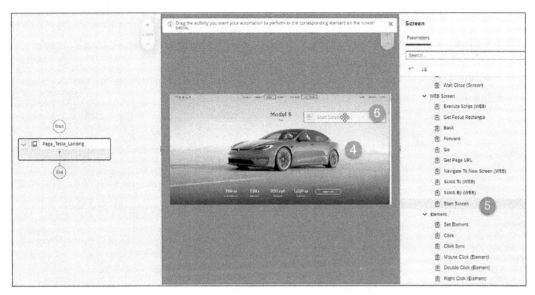

Figure 24.20 – Add activities to the automation

4. Navigate to the **Start Screen** activity (**5**) in the right panel under the **WEB Screen** group, under the **Activities** tool, and drag this activity over the screen preview (**6**) in the main panel.

5. As shown in the following screenshot, the **Start Screen** activity appears within the screen instance of **Page_Tesla_Landing** and is marked as activity **1** (**7**). Next, search for the `Wait` and `Click` activities under the **Tools** section. You will find several options for both searches. Choose **Wait (Screen)** to ensure that you see the screen load before the click event happens and the screen changes. For the `Click` search, choose the one under **Element**. To understand the difference between various options for both searches, click on the information icon indicated with arrows (**8**). Click the **Save** button at the top right to save automation:

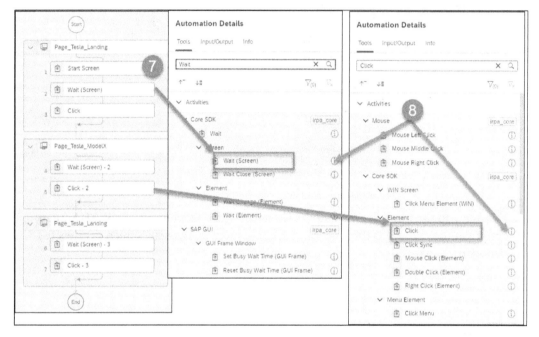

Figure 24.21 – Adding activities to the automation

6. Our automation is now ready, and we can test it by pressing the **Test** button, as shown in the following screenshot:

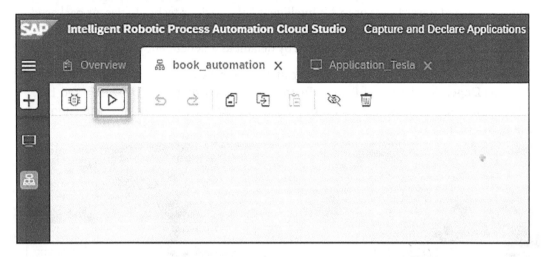

Figure 24.22 – Test automation

With this, although we are at the end of the section, we have barely touched the surface of the available tools for designing automation. To build any production-worthy applications, please ensure you go through the recommended material listed under the initial paragraphs of the *An overview of Cloud Studio* section.

SDK packages and Custom script development

An SDK is a collection of functionalities or tools provided by various software vendors such as SAP. SDKs can be required or optional. For example, the **Java Development Kit (JDK)** is required for Java development, and the iOS SDK is needed for iOS application development. Similarly, SAP has provided several SDKs for SAP Intelligent RPA. While one SDK, `irpa_core`, is necessary for development, other SDKs are optional and can be added as needed.

While SDKs provide a large set of functionalities to enable the development of SAP Intelligent RPA applications, sometimes you will encounter a requirement where the SDKs either won't offer an in-built functionality or won't meet your needs completely. In those circumstances, you have the option of writing your code using a control *custom script*.

Let's understand SDKs and custom script development in this section.

SDK packages

In SAP Intelligent RPA parlance, an **Software Development Kit** (**SDK**) is a collection of activities targeted toward the core SAP Intelligent RPA, various technologies, or packaged solutions. As discussed earlier, every time you create a project in Cloud Studio, two SDKs, `irpa_core` and `irpa_excel`, are added by default as a dependency.

As shown in the following screenshot, you can check for the existence of these SDKs under the **Dependencies** tab of **Project Properties** by following three steps (marked **1**, **2**, and **3**). To add more SDKs or available packages, click **Add Dependency** (**4**) and choose packages or SDKs:

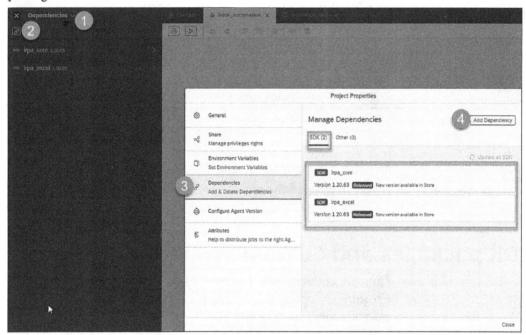

Figure 24.23 – The SDK packages as dependencies

> **Note**
>
> As of writing this chapter, SAP provides 12 SDKs that are mentioned here: `https://help.sap.com/viewer/8e71b41b9ea043c8bccee01a10d6ba72/Cloud/en-US/c53b9d35aafd42ef96c7089c24a3141e.html`.

Custom script development

While working in Desktop Studio, you might have used custom JavaScript code for some activities. As shown in the following screenshot, using the **Custom script** activity, you can also use the custom JavaScript in Cloud Studio:

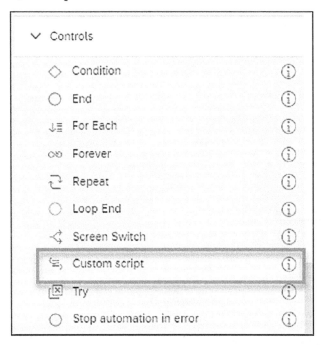

Figure 24.24 – Custom script

SAP recommends using the **Custom script** activity only when a built-in SDK activity is unavailable, and avoid calling SDK activities from your custom code.

As shown in the following screenshot, to write your custom code, click on the **Custom script** step (**1**) in the workflow after adding it, and select **Edit Script** (**2**):

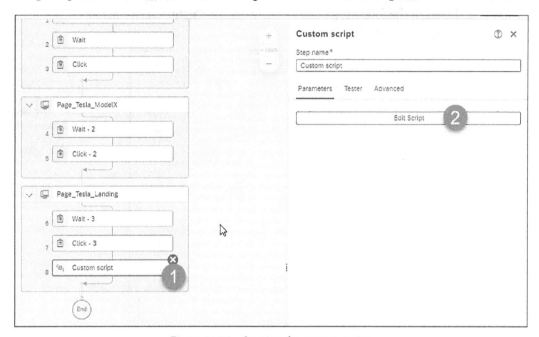

Figure 24.25 – Starting the custom script

Then, you can access the code editor in the central panel (**3**) and **Input parameters** and **Output parameters** (**4** and **5**) in the right panel:

Figure 24.26 – Writing custom script

In code, you can reference input and output parameters, applications (`$.application_ Tesla.start`), application screens (`$.application_Tesla.screens. page_Tesla_Landing`), and various SDK activities (`irpa _core.dialog. openInputDialog`) from your custom code.

We have reached the end of this chapter with this short discussion about **Custom script** development. Let's summarize what we have learned in this chapter.

Summary

At SAP Intelligent RPA's launch in 2018, Desktop Studio was the only available development platform; now, Cloud Studio is the new and recommended platform for new SAP Intelligent RPA bot developments. Therefore, we started with an overview before delving into capturing and declaring applications using Cloud Studio. Finally, we discussed designing automation using the captured applications and the functionalities of the available SDK packages. We also briefly discussed writing custom code within our automation when the available SDKs won't provide the necessary functionality.

All this learning will enable you to write basic automation, but to become proficient, you must follow the recommended material from the initial section of this chapter. Investing time and actively staying aware of the regular updates of SAP Intelligent RPA will help you become and remain a knowledgeable developer in no time.

In the next chapter, we will continue our discussion of Cloud Studio, but the focus will shift to the reusability of packages across multiple solutions.

Questions

Here are some questions for you to test your knowledge. The answers to these questions can be found at the back of the book in the section named *Assessments*:

1. How many SDKs has SAP made available to SAP Intelligent RPA customers, and which SDKs become part of projects by default?

2. What is the difference between capturing and declaring applications?

3. Can you use an existing automation in the new automation that you are developing?

25
Reusability of Packages Across Multiple Solutions

The English idiom *reinventing the wheel* translates roughly to duplicating something basic that others have already optimized. Reinventing the wheel is usually unproductive as it uses up the precious time that we could otherwise devote to developing sophisticated ideas or things based upon already existing ideas. Thus, society must learn to reuse its predecessors' core ideas or solutions to move forward.

A similar concept exists in the software world, where intelligent developers must learn when to reuse the work done by their predecessors or peers to move ahead quickly. In the SAP Intelligent RPA world, this concept translates to reusing existing packages across multiple solutions.

To understand this concept well, we will discuss the following topics:

- Reusing packages developed by Desktop Studio
- Exporting projects from Cloud Studio
- Deploying projects developed in Cloud Studio

Let's begin with understanding how to reuse packages.

Technical requirements

- An internet connection and a web browser

- System administrator rights on your computer (optional)

- The completed installation of SAP Intelligent RPA on-premises components from the previous chapter (optional)

- Access to the SAP Business Technology Platform trial system (`https://www.sap.com/cmp/td/sap-cloud-platform-trial.html`)

- A subscription to the SAP Intelligent RPA trial version (`https://help.sap.com/viewer/82d5a2499d8449dda691bb4d5b3d7949/Cloud/en-US`)

- Access to the Intelligent RPA store for reusable packages

Reusing packages developed by Desktop Studio

You have learned by now that we use Desktop Studio to create scenarios that automate the identified repetitive activities. We can then compile and export a project containing one or many scenarios as a desktop package. As a refresher, here is how the project export process appears:

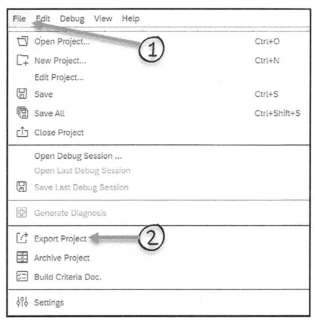

Figure 25.1 – Desktop project export

This exported package would become available as a `.zip` archive under the **Export** folder in the project directory. Once you have exported a desktop package, importing this package into Cloud Studio is simple.

You can import a desktop package from the **Packages** tab on the **Automation Factory** toolbar or from within an existing project. The URL to your factory tenant would be in the format `https://<YOUR-TENANT>.hana.ondemand.com/#/home`, where `<YOUR-TENANT>` will be your unique tenant name. The import process remains the same for both options.

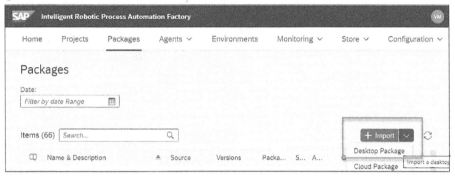

Figure 25.2 – Desktop Package import

When importing from the **Packages** tab, Cloud Factory will automatically create a cloud project to embed the imported desktop package, as shown in the following screenshot:

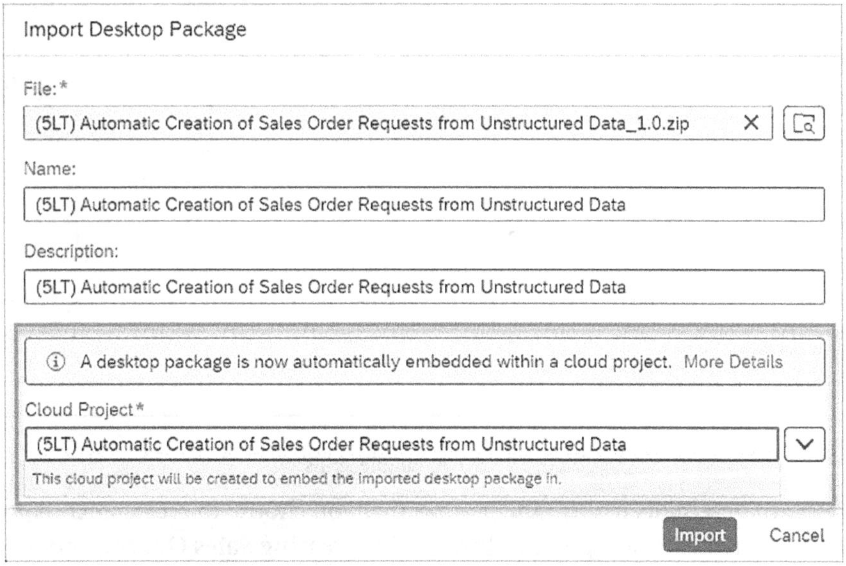

Figure 25.3 – Automatic creation of a cloud project

Once you have successfully imported the desktop package into a project, all the artifacts from the project will become available to you. We see one desktop package (**1**) and two data types (**2** and **3**) in the following screenshot:

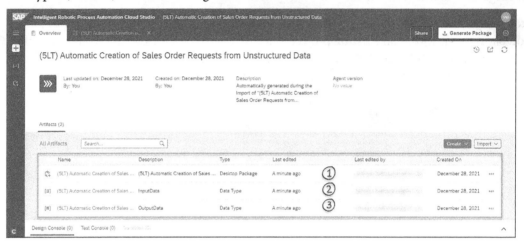

Figure 25.4 – Available artifacts

Click on **Desktop Package** to see the list of available skills, as shown in the following screenshot:

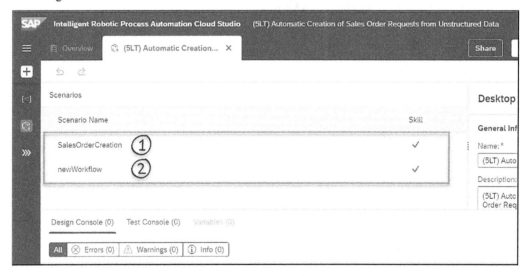

Figure 25.5 – Available skills

You can use both these skills in any new process that you choose to create next. For example, we have created a new process, **Process for creating Sales Orders**, and used both **Skills**, as shown in the following screenshot:

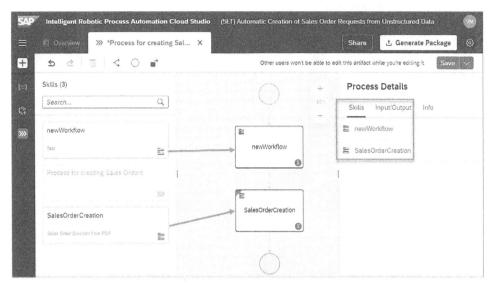

Figure 25.6 – Using available skills

If you have created custom data types in your Desktop project, you can create these data types while importing the scenarios as part of the desktop package. You will recall that two out of the three artifacts imported into our imported package were data types.

To achieve this feat, you need to create such data types under a unique folder with two sub-folders for input and output data structures in the relevant context.

In the following screenshot, our unique folder is named IO, while the input and output folders are called InputData and OutputData, respectively. While both these folders serve as the data types, you can have multiple sub-folders under InputData and OutputData if there is more than one custom data type.

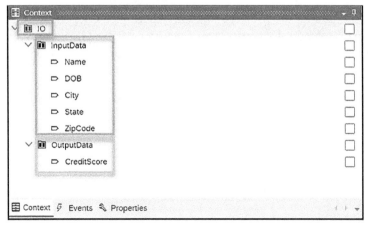

Figure 25.7 – Folder structure for custom data types

The next step is to mark these folders as **Input** and **Output** folders under the **Properties** | **Activity** section.

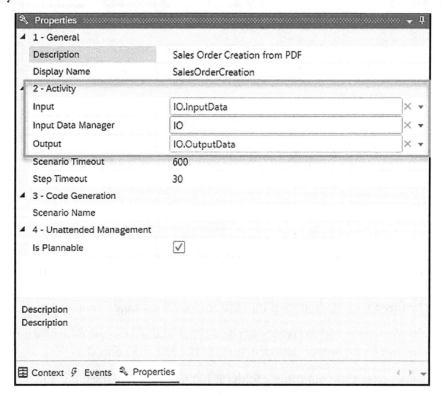

Figure 25.8 – Marking folders as input and output

This step concludes our discussion about reusing packages developed by Desktop Studio.

Studio in another Cloud Studio project using the structure of a dependency. From our discussion in *Chapter 24*, *Development Using Cloud Studio*, you can recall that while some SDKs are added to each cloud project as dependencies by default, you can add more SDKs or packages as a dependency as required.

When you add a package as a dependency, you can use artifacts automation, environment variables, alerts, applications, and data types of the added package in the host project.

As shown in the following screenshot, to add a package as a dependency, ensure that the package is shared with the **Read** authorization with **Anyone**:

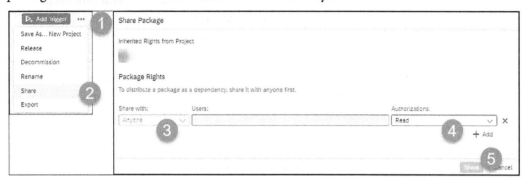

Figure 25.9 Share package

Then, to import this package as a dependency, as shown in the following screenshot, click on the gear icon (**1**), select **Dependencies** (**2**), and click on **Add Dependency**. Then, follow the prompts to select a **Package**, **Version**, and **Alias** to have the package artifacts available in your project.

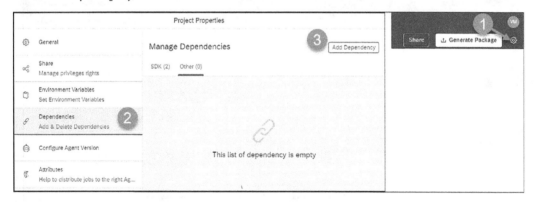

Figure 25.10 Add a package as a dependency

As SAP introduced Desktop Studio with the launch of SAP iRPA, there are many desktop packages that you may find helpful to import into Cloud Studio and use for your processes. Now, let's focus on exporting projects from Cloud Studio.

Exporting projects from Cloud Studio

Organizations running SAP usually have three physical systems tasked with functional responsibilities: development, test, and production. All development work takes place in the development system before being moved to the test system for testing and then to the production system.

SAP Intelligent RPA customers have a choice to either run three environments in the same tenant or three separate tenants. To transport your project to another environment or tenant, you can export a project from Cloud Studio and import it into another environment or tenant. While this approach is feasible and may be required in some scenarios, to ensure that all changes are made only in DEV, we recommend only exporting and importing generated packages when moving your work from DEV to QA, or from QA to Production.

Let's see how the project export process works from Cloud Studio once you click the **Export** button (**1**), as shown in the following screenshot:

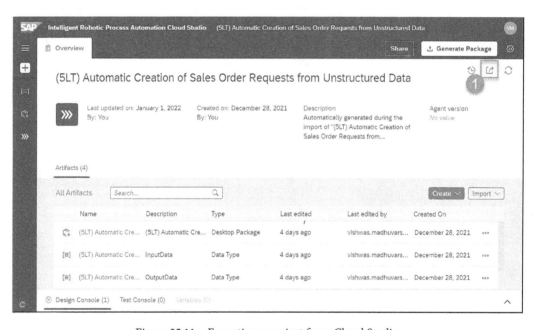

Figure 25.11 – Exporting a project from Cloud Studio

Upon doing this, a warning about exporting project dependencies will appear, as shown in the following screenshot:

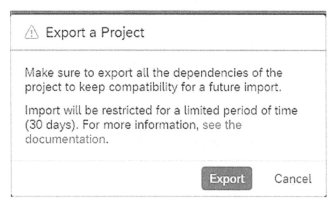

Figure 25.12 – Dependency warning

Click **Export** and the exported package will download to your laptop's downloads folder in ZIP format. You can import the project into another tenant or environment from this folder.

Now that we understand how to export projects from Cloud Studio, let's find out how to deploy the projects developed in Cloud Studio.

Deploying projects developed in Cloud Studio

Once you complete the development and testing of your project, the next step is to make this project available in your target environment for the production run. To do so, you generate a package that becomes available in Cloud Factory automatically.

To generate the package, navigate to your project and click on the **Generate Package** button, as shown in the following screenshot:

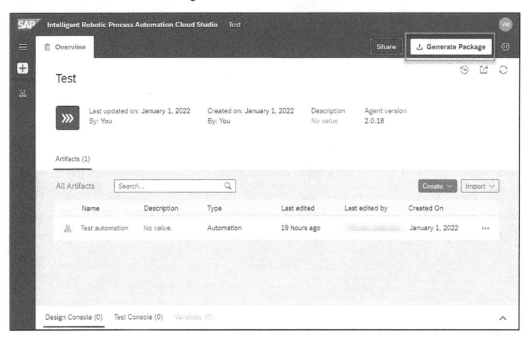

Figure 25.13 – Generate Package button

You will see a pop-up window open where you can fill in the package's **Name** and **Description** fields, while **Version Number** is generated automatically:

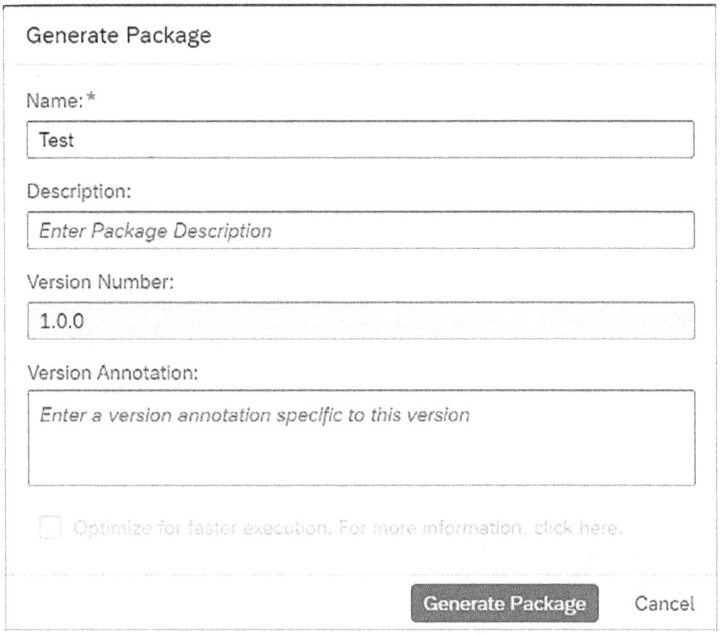

Generate Package

Name: *

Test

Description:

Enter Package Description

Version Number:

1.0.0

Version Annotation:

Enter a version annotation specific to this version

Optimize for faster execution. For more information, click here.

Generate Package   Cancel

Figure 25.14 – Package generation details

Once the package is generated, it becomes available in the factory for use in an environment of your choice. Once you click on **Add Trigger**, you will be asked to select the environment. Deployment will take place automatically, an option for environment variables may or may not show up, and finally, you will select the trigger type.

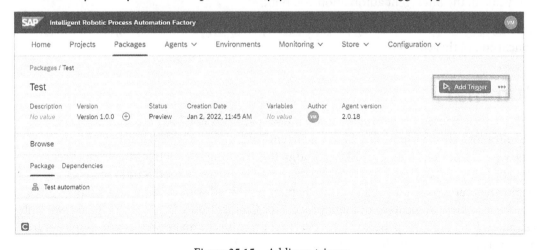

Figure 25.15 – Adding a trigger

The following screenshot shows the steps of adding a trigger. You will see that the attended trigger is not available to us because we did not create a project pane or add a desktop package to our project. In your case, you may have this option available.

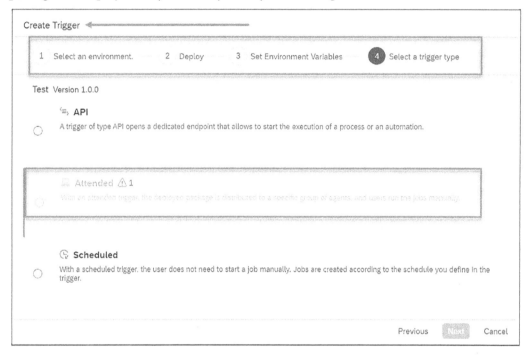

Figure 25.16 – Selecting a trigger type

Once you create a trigger and set a schedule, your package will run as per the plan and carry out all the intelligent automation you built.

This discussion about deploying projects developed in Cloud Studio brings us to the conclusion of this chapter.

Summary

This chapter focused on reusing Desktop Studio packages in Cloud Studio. As several organizations that started using SAP Intelligent RPA in the years 2018 and 2019 have developed numerous bots in Desktop Studio, this learning is vital to ensure that those investments do not go to waste. We also discussed exporting Cloud Studio projects and deploying them to Cloud Factory. This chapter, combined with the previous chapter, gives us a holistic view of the development process for Cloud Studio. In the next chapter, we will see an exciting tool, the **process Recorder**, that promises to make SAP application capture as easy as running the application itself.

Questions

Here are some questions for you to test your knowledge. The answers to these questions can be found at the back of the book in the section named *Assessments*:

1. Where will you find the package you have exported from Desktop Studio?

2. From which areas in Cloud Factory can you import a desktop package?

3. While exporting projects from Cloud Studio, how do we ensure that all the dependencies are also exported?

4. While generating a package, a version number is created automatically. What happens to this version number when you subsequently generate the package from the same project?

26
An Introduction to Process Recorder

At this point, you understand that developing automation involves three core steps – capturing applications, declaring applications, and designing automation. It usually takes a technically savvy developer to carry out these steps manually and linearly to develop any significant automation. However, as we discussed in *Chapter 24, Development Using Cloud Studio*, the scarcity of skilled developers has become a concern for enterprises, and several **low-code/no-code** (**LCNC**) development platforms have offered alternate development options.

Process Recorder is a no-code approach to developing automation. With this approach, a business user goes through the application to automate, as they usually do, while the application is captured and declared and any automation is designed in the background.

However, this doesn't mean that only business users can use process Recorder effectively. On the contrary, process Recorder can significantly reduce the automation development time for a technically savvy developer. Due to this, you should know about process Recorder intricately so that you can get the best **return on investment** (**ROI**) on your development time.

In this chapter, we will cover only the following topic:

- Introducing process Recorder

Technical requirements

- An internet connection and a web browser.
- The SAP Intelligent RPA on-premise components from the previous chapters must be installed.
- Access to the SAP Business Technology Platform trial system (`https://www.sap.com/cmp/td/sap-cloud-platform-trial.html`).
- A subscription for the SAP Intelligent RPA trial version (`https://help.sap.com/viewer/82d5a2499d8449dda691bb4d5b3d7949/Cloud/en-US`).
- Access to release 2105 or higher of SAP Intelligent Robotic Process Automation.
- All the SAP listed requirements for enabling process Recorder for WebGUI and WinGUI under the *Prerequisites* section at `https://help.sap.com/doc/464781c43f264b8fb956c6e1594cd723/Cloud/en-US/29e8302075ea4c75a5952d44625ce508.pdf`.

Introducing process Recorder

Once you have fulfilled all the prerequisites mentioned in the *Technical requirements* section, you can start using process Recorder by choosing the application you wish to capture, clicking the **Launch Recorder** (**1**) button, and then clicking the **Record** button (**2**):

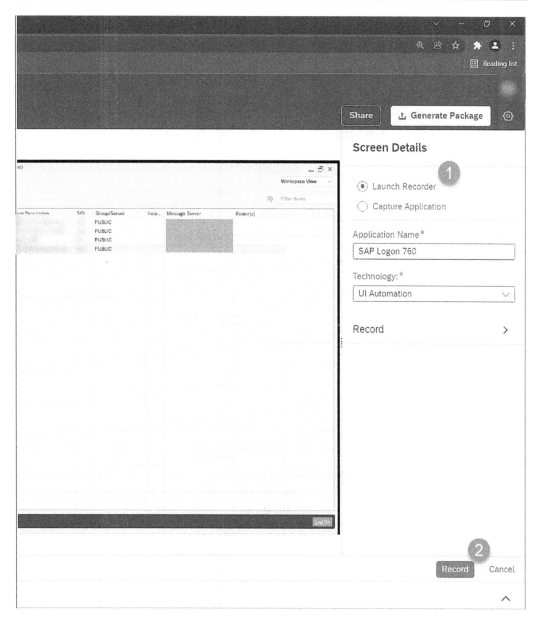

Figure 26.1 – Launch Recorder

As soon as you click the **Record** button, process Recorder will appear, as shown in the following screenshot:

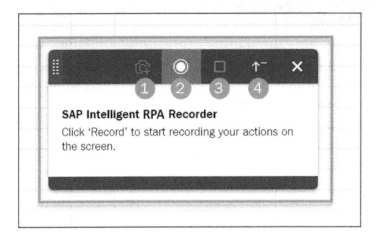

Figure 26.2 – process Recorder buttons

Let's discuss the various buttons/functionalities available here:

1. **The Screen Capture button**: When you're recording an application, you need to press this button every time a screen change occurs. A new screen can be a new application screen, a modal dialog, a pop-up, value help, UI elements such as control, a table, a hierarchical list, and so on. Unless you click the screen capture button, the recording will continue under the previous screen and this may need to be corrected manually.

2. **The Record/Resume/Pause button**: This button works based on the state of the recording. Initially, we can use this button to start recording a new application. While recording is in progress, this button will take the shape of a pause button. When recording has been paused, we can resume recording with the same button.

3. **The Stop button**: Once we have finished recording the application, we can press the **Stop** button to stop recording. Once you've pressed this button, the application will stop recording and the **Export** button will become available.

4. **The Expand/Collapse button**: This button expands or collapses the list of all screen activities.

Once you've captured all the necessary activities and pressed the stop button, as shown in the following screenshot, the status of process Recorder will change to **Stopped**:

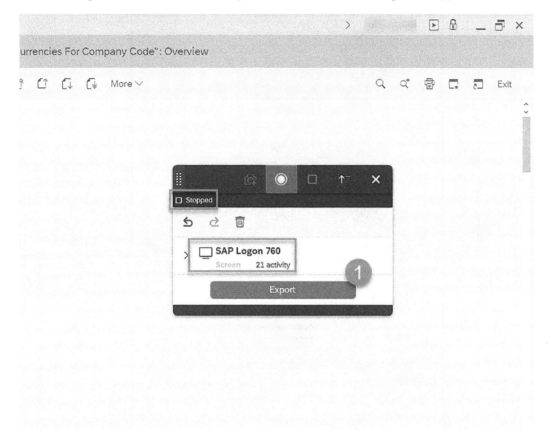

Figure 26.3 – Finished recording

Before you click the **Export** button to send all the recorded activities to Cloud Studio, ensure that you have not been logged out of Cloud Studio due to inactivity. Once started, the export process will take some time, and your computer's CPU and memory utilization will become high during this period.

As shown in the following screenshot, all the recorded activities will appear in Cloud Studio once the export process completes:

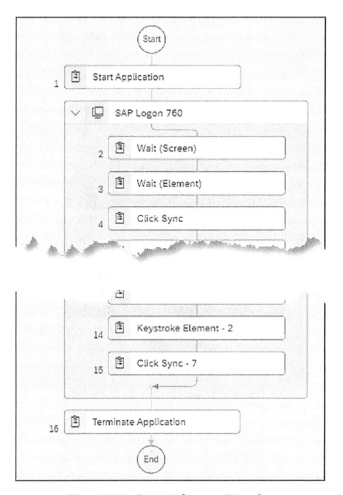

Figure 26.4 – Output of process Recorder

You can add to, change, update, or delete these activities as needed. Once you have made all the necessary changes, you can test the automation and generate the package.

At the time of writing, process Recorder does not support all application types but is an excellent time-saving tool for the applications that it works with. Use it as often as possible, and keep an eye on SAP's announcements about the newer versions of Intelligent Robotic Process Automation at `https://help.sap.com/viewer/0f258aabfbdb476b9bebbc636a1ca5cc/Cloud/en-US`.

Summary

Across organizations, as the development demands exceed supply, intelligent developers should know what help is available to them to deal with the ever-growing requests for their time. This chapter discussed one such tool, the SAP Intelligent Robotic Process Automation process Recorder, and showed you how it works. In the next chapter, we will discuss a platform that offers pre-built bots to SAP customers.

We suggest that you understand these tools thoroughly and make the best use of them so that you can serve your customers well.

Questions

Here are some questions for you to test your knowledge of this chapter. The answers to these questions can be found at the back of this book, in the *Assessments* section:

1. You want to use process Recorder to record a supported application but do not see the option to use it. What should you do to troubleshoot this issue?

2. You have recorded an application with three screens, but all the activities show under one screen. Why has this inconsistency occurred?

Part 7: SAP Intelligent RPA Store, Roadmap, and SAP BTP Automation Services

SAP Intelligent RPA Store includes predefined solutions built by SAP and is available to all registered SAP tenants. This provides a list of solutions suggested as best practices and can be used as a reference to increase productivity while automating the business processes.

This section comprises the following chapters:

27
SAP Intelligent RPA Store

SAP acquired Contextor in November 2018 and rebranded it to SAP Intelligent RPA soon after. At the time of acquisition, SAP also planned to automate half of the SAP ERP business processes. You can read more about this announcement here, `https://news.sap.com/2018/11/sap-acquires-contextor-robotic-process-automation/`.

To achieve this lofty goal, SAP took two parallel paths. One was educating SAP partners on using SAP Intelligent RPA effectively to automate business processes. The other was rolling out pre-built SAP Intelligent RPA packages to its partners at no charge.

Initially, SAP delivered these packages through the best practices route and, as shown in the following screenshot, you can still find Intelligent RPA packages listed under SAP Best Practices Explorer at `https://rapid.sap.com/bp/`.

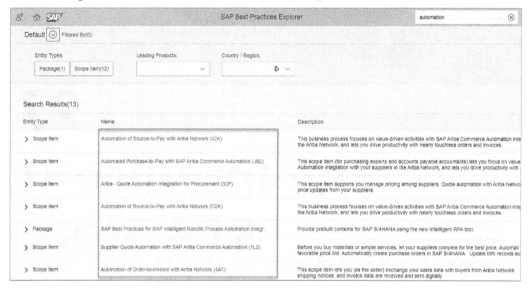

Figure 27.1 – Intelligent RPA packages in SAP Best Practices Explorer

However, as the number of packages increased, it became tough for customers to find the required packages. At that time, SAP launched the SAP Intelligent RPA Store with a search and segmentation facility to help customers easily find their desired package.

We will discuss the following topics and how to access the SAP Intelligent RPA Store in the following sections:

- Getting a package from the Store
- Deploying the Store package
- Downloading and modifying the Store package

Let's begin with getting a package from the Store.

Technical requirements

- An internet connection and a web browser
- System administrator rights on your computer
- Completed installation of SAP Intelligent RPA on-premises components from the previous chapters

- Access to the SAP Business Technology Platform trial system (`https://www.sap.com/cmp/td/sap-cloud-platform-trial.html`)

- Subscription to the SAP Intelligent RPA trial version (`https://help.sap.com/viewer/82d5a2499d8449dda691bb4d5b3d7949/Cloud/en-US`)

Getting a package from the Store

Before you can get a package from the Store, you need to access the Store from the **Store** (**1**) menu of SAP Intelligent RPA Factory, as shown in the following screenshot:

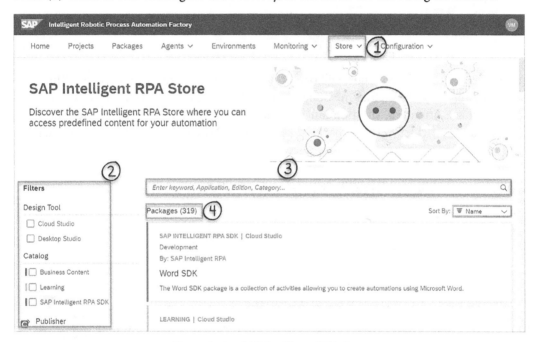

Figure 27.2 – SAP Intelligent RPA Store

Once in the Store, you can use various filters (**2**), such as **Design Tool**, **Catalog**, **Publisher**, and **Category**, on the left and a keyword-based search (**3**) to find the desired packages. As shown in the previous screenshot (**4**), the Store currently has **319** packages.

Once you identify the desired package, click on the package to open the package details. For now, we have chosen the **Create Purchase Requisitions from Excel (48M)** package for acquisition.

Figure 27.3 – Getting a package from the Store

Once selected, the package details will open up, and the **Get** button will be visible. The following screenshot shows that the design tool (**1**) for this package is Cloud Studio. The package can use **Attended**, **Unattended/Scheduled**, and **API** triggers (**2**), the **Get** button (**3**), documents provided with the package (**4**), the test script for the package (**5**), as well as the content of the package (**6**), as shown here:

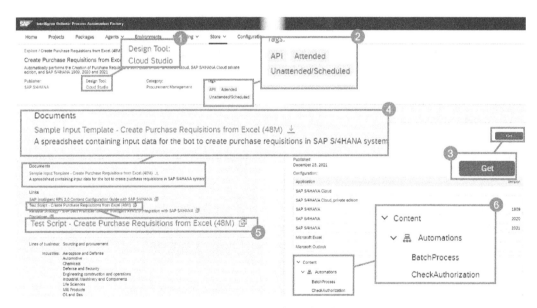

Figure 27.4 – Package details

Now, you can click on the **Get** button to get the package from the Store. Once the acquisition is complete, you will see the package under **Store-Acquisitions**. Be aware that if you or someone from your team have already acquired the package, you will see either **Acquired** or **Update** in place of **Get**. Also, if the package comes from a partner instead of SAP, you will see **Purchase in SAP Store** at that exact location.

Now that we know various ways of getting a package from the Store, let's understand how to deploy these packages after acquisition.

Deploying the Store package

Once you have acquired a package from the Store, there are two ways of deploying it. In this section, we will go through each of them:

- **Deploying the package from the Environments tab**: If you want to deploy a package without assigning a trigger, as shown in the following screenshot, navigate to **Environments** (**1**) of your choice, select **Add Package** (**2**), find the package to deploy (**3**), and click **Next** (**4**). This process will deploy the package without assigning a trigger (**5**):

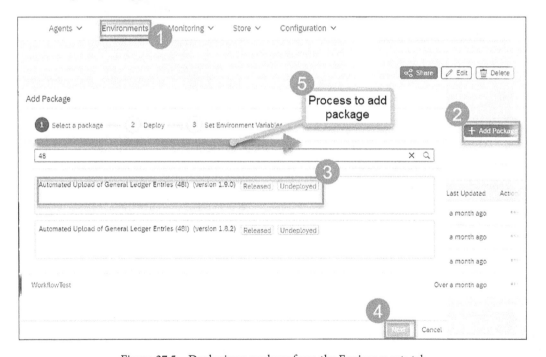

Figure 27.5 – Deploying a package from the Environments tab

- **Deploying from the Packages tab**: When you deploy a package from the **Packages** tab, you start by clicking on the **Add Trigger** button, and then a similar process as seen earlier but with the addition of a trigger follows. See the following screenshot for a stepwise approach:

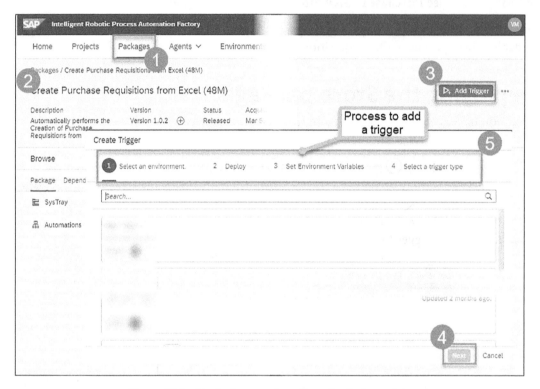

Figure 27.6 – Deploying a package from the Packages tab

Once you deploy the package, the added trigger will be visible under **Triggers** for the selected environment.

Figure 27.7 – Added trigger

Now that we have understood the process of package deployment, let's see how we can download and modify Store packages as needed.

Downloading and modifying the Store package

While it is conceivable to use a Store package as is for your projects, there will be times when you may need to alter some of the functionality of the Store package. There are two ways to go about such a requirement depending on the design tool used to develop the package.

Let's look at them in the following sections.

Modifying packages created using Desktop Studio

To modify packages created using Desktop Studio, we work in two steps:

1. Acquire the desired package, as described in the *Getting a package from the Store* section. Once you have acquired the package, go to the **Packages** tab (**1**) and select the acquired package. Then, under **Package** (**2**), select the relevant archive file (.zip) to download and click the **Download** button (**3**), as shown in this screenshot:

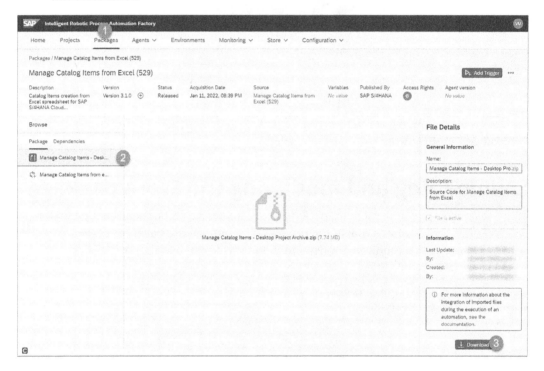

Figure 27.8 – Download package

2. The next step is to extract the contents of the downloaded archive file and open the project (.pspc) file.

Now you can make all necessary changes to the project and reuse this package in your cloud project, as discussed in *Chapter 25, Reusability of Packages Across Multiple Solutions*.

Packages created using Cloud Studio

To modify packages created using Cloud Studio, the first step is still to acquire the desired package. Once you have acquired the package, go to the **Packages** tab (**1**) and select the acquired package. Then, click the ellipses next to the **Add Trigger** button (**2**), and select the **Save as… New Project** option (**3**):

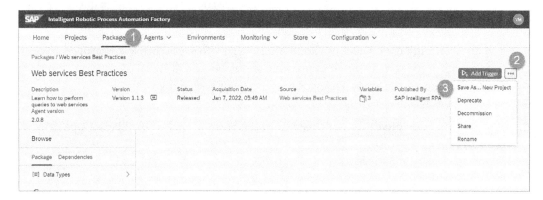

Figure 27.9 – Create a new project from an existing package

Provide a project name and click **Save**. A new project with all the original artifacts will become available to you for modification. Update the project as desired and use it as described in *Chapter 25, Reusability of Packages Across Multiple Solutions*.

This concludes our discussion of modifying the packages developed using Desktop Studio and Cloud Studio.

Summary

In this chapter, we discussed getting a package from the SAP Intelligent RPA Store, deploying this package, and modifying it.

Early in their careers, good developers learn to reuse the stellar work shared by their peers and predecessors. SAP Intelligent RPA Store is the standard delivery platform for SAP and partners for delivering all pre-built content for SAP Intelligent RPA. Therefore, exploring the SAP Intelligent RPA Store will benefit you immensely before starting any new project, as doing so is likely to save you countless hours of rework.

In his 1676 letter to Robert Hooke, Isaac Newton said, *"If I have seen a little further it is by standing on the shoulders of giants."* We hope that the SAP Intelligent RPA Store helps you see a little further in your SAP Intelligent RPA development journey.

In the next chapter, we will discuss the future roadmap of SAP Intelligent RPA and the automation-related service.

Questions

Here are some questions for you to test your knowledge. The answers to these questions can be found at the back of the book in the section named *Assessments*:

1. You are working on a project in Cloud Studio that involves complex Microsoft Excel functionality. To learn as much as possible about Microsoft Excel usage, you would like to find out all the Store packages that use MS Excel. How would you find all the relevant packages?

2. We discussed downloading a package from the Store. Can we also upload a package to the Store?

28
SAP Intelligent RPA – Future Roadmap and Automation-Related Services

Since SAP acquired Contextor and renamed it **SAP Intelligent RPA (SAP IRPA)** in 2018, the product has grown continuously. We have looked at the launch of IRPA 2.0, a built-in PDF reader OCR and text detector, the bot store, and, recently, Process Recorder. While we expect this growth to continue, it will help to know SAP's plans so that we can schedule our development effort accordingly. There is no point in developing something bespoke if SAP plans to launch that feature soon. Therefore, we will devote this chapter to understanding SAP's plans for future developments of SAP IRPA.

SAP IRPA is a service that runs on the SAP **Business Technology Platform** (**BTP**). Therefore, we will also take a quick look at SAP BTP, its primary constructs, and some of the essential services you should know as a SAP IRPA developer.

In this chapter, we will cover the following topics:

- New and upcoming features in SAP IRPA
- SAP Business Technology Platform overview
- Complementary automation services for SAP IRPA in SAP BTP

Let's begin by understanding the basic and new features of SAP IRPA.

Technical requirements

- An internet connection and a web browser
- Access to the SAP Business Technology Platform trial system (`https://www.sap.com/cmp/td/sap-cloud-platform-trial.html`)

New and upcoming features in SAP IRPA

Every quarter, SAP releases new features in SAP IRPA and many other services that run on BTP. As shown in the following screenshot, you can find the schedule and the upcoming features in SAP's roadmaps at `https://roadmaps.sap.com/board?range=2022Q2-2022Q4&PRODUCT=73554900100800002142#Q3%20 2022`:

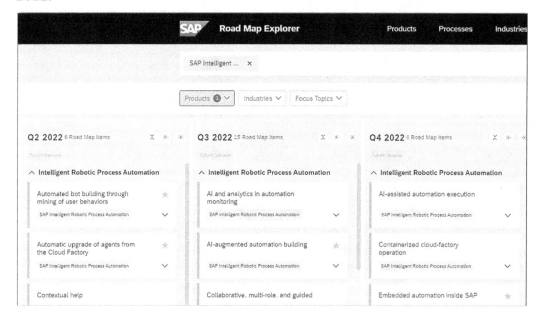

Figure 28.1 – SAP Road Map Explorer

SAP plans to release 28 additions or upgrades in its quarterly updates for 2022. Here are a few important updates that you should be aware of:

- **External connectors for Microsoft Office 365 and Google Office Suite**: While we can easily connect with desktop-based Microsoft Office products using the relevant SDKs, the external connectors promise to provide easy connectivity with Office 365 and Google Office Suite. This feature is planned for Q2 of 2022.

- **AI-augmented automation building**: This is one of the most awaited features for bot building. Based on our understanding of SAP, this update should be able to mine the behavior of a user group in SAP systems, analyze it, and generate automation templates. Expect this feature in Q3 of 2022.

- **Embedded automation inside SAP S/4HANA and other cloud LoB products**: SAP has been working to include automation at the process level and has announced the launch of embedded automation. While the details are not available yet, we expect in-built automation within the business processes that use SAP Intelligent RPA, Workflows, Situation Handling, and Embedded AI. Watch out for this feature in Q4 of 2022.

While we have discussed a few updates here, please bookmark the SAP roadmap for SAP IRPA and check it regularly to remain aware of any upcoming features. Now, let's discuss the foundation of SAP IRPA – the SAP Business Technology Platform.

SAP Business Technology Platform overview

Technology is a vital contributor to the success and failure of businesses today. A business's ability to integrate its heterogeneous technology landscape seamlessly, derive value from its enormous data, and innovate quickly defines its odds of survival.

SAP BTP is a platform that offers the tools and products to address the core enterprise needs of integration, innovation, and generating value from data. The following screenshot shows that SAP BTP offers these possibilities through four core pillars:

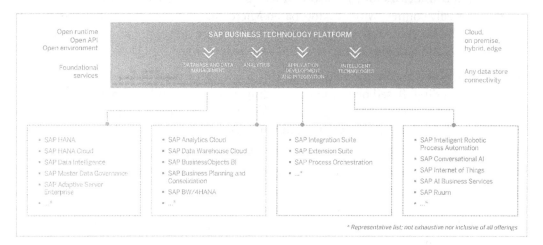

Figure 28.2 – SAP BTP (https://news.sap.com/2021/03/part-two-unified-technology-platform-partners-enable-customer-success/)

Let's understand each of these in brief:

- **DATABASE AND DATA MANAGEMENT**: These solutions enable enterprises to securely access and manage continuously growing organization data stored in various locations, with the end goal of providing a single source of truth to the organization.

- **ANALYTICS**: Various solutions under the analytics portfolio help businesses derive insights from the vast amount of data.

- **APPLICATION DEVELOPMENT AND INTEGRATION**: These solutions address the crucial need to integrate heterogeneous solutions seamlessly and extend the platform's capabilities while keeping the core clean.

- **INTELLIGENT TECHNOLOGIES**: The solutions that are clubbed under this pillar address the need for the rapid innovation cycles that are demanded by enterprises worldwide. SAP IRPA is part of these solutions, along with several others.

> **Note**
>
> Please visit the following link to learn more about SAP BTP:
>
> ```
> https://www.sap.com/products/business-technology-
> platform.html
> ```

Now that we understand the role of SAP BTP, let's look at some of the services that are offered through the SAP BTP that may enhance your automation.

Complementary automation services for SAP IRPA in SAP BTP

Gartner coined the term **hyperautomation** in 2019 to define an approach and a collection of technologies that let organizations identify, evaluate, and automate business processes at scale. The following diagram shows that the hyperautomation toolchain contains technologies such as **robotic process automation** (**RPA**), workflow and business rules management, chatbots, low-code/no-code development, process discovery and mining, **natural language processing** (**NLP**), integration platforms, **artificial intelligence** (**AI**), and **machine learning** (**ML**):

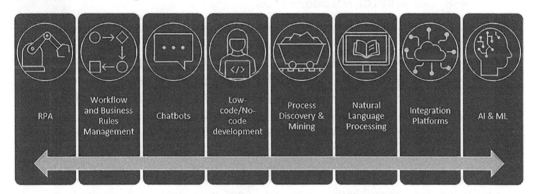

Figure 28.3 – The hyperautomation toolchain

While SAP IRPA addresses the RPA component of the hyperautomation toolchain, SAP BTP offers many other services that address the other components of the toolchain. While these services are not essential for you to be a successful SAP IRPA developer, we recommend that you understand these services well. There are usually several ways you can solve an automation problem, and awareness of these services can come in handy while you're deciding on the optimal solution to a business problem.

Let's have a quick look at some of these services:

- **SAP Workflow Management** allows you to create, run, and manage workflows using a low-code approach. Business rules management is also part of this service. You can also use pre-built workflow management and business rules packages to speed up your automation. You may recall that Cloud Studio offers a **Process** artifact that combines SAP IRPA and Workflow artifacts. So, you can use the workflows you've created here and any automation that's you've designed in Cloud Studio to create processes that work across the boundaries of multiple systems. You can learn more about this service at `https://help.sap.com/viewer/product/WORKFLOW_MANAGEMENT/Cloud/en-US?task=discover_task`. At the time of writing, SAP has launched a new service, **SAP Process Automation** that combines SAP Intelligent RPA and SAP Workflow Management. You can read more about this service at `https://help.sap.com/viewer/product/PROCESS_AUTOMATION/Cloud/en-US`.

- **SAP Conversational AI** lets you build, train, test, deploy, and monitor chatbots with a low-code approach. In addition, you can easily connect these chatbots to all popular messaging channels, such as Amazon Alexa, Slack, Telegram, Twitter, and others. This service comes with an NLP engine to help your bots understand intent, expressions, and sentiments. Furthermore, SAP Conversational AI bots can integrate with SAP IRPA bots bidirectionally to exchange messages and act on them. Read more about this service can be found at `https://help.sap.com/viewer/product/SAP_CONVERSATIONAL_AI/latest/en-US`.

- **SAP AppGyver** provides a no-code application development platform to create applications for web and native mobile use. AppGyver comes with hundreds of pre-built building blocks, and you can use these blocks to develop apps using drag-and-drop functionality quickly. You can learn more about this service at `https://www.appgyver.com/`.

- **SAP Business Process Intelligence** is an umbrella term for various services. It includes SAP Process Insights, SAP Signavio Process Manager, SAP Signavio Process Intelligence, SAP Signavio Journey Modeler, SAP Signavio Process Collaboration Hub, and SAP Signavio Process Governance. These services help customers understand the actual business processes or design, simulate, and share new ones. You can learn more about these services at `https://www.sap.com/products/business-process-intelligence.html`.

- • **The SAP AI and machine learning services** are a collection of various business services and development platforms. Business services such as **Business Entity Recognition**, **Data Attribute Recommendation**, and **Document Classification** have been trained to offer a single business functionality. On the other hand, development platforms such as **Conversational AI** and **SAP AI Core** let you develop or carry out various AI operations. While you can consume some AI services from within SAP IRPA bots today, starting with the Q3 2022 release, SAP promises to make using SAP and non-SAP AI and machine learning services even easier. You can learn more about the SAP AI and machine learning services at `https://discovery-center.cloud.sap/viewServices?provider=all&regions=all&category=ai-and-machinelearning`.

With that, we have finished discussing the complimentary automation services that are available through SAP BPT.

Summary

SAP IRPA is a rapidly evolving platform, and it will help you remain aware of any new features as they are released so that you can use them to your team's benefit. SAP's roadmaps provide you with a view of the upcoming features and may help you avoid reinventing the wheel. The SAP BTP is not only the platform for SAP's Intelligent Enterprise but it is also the de facto technology foundation for all SAP applications. SAP IRPA runs on the SAP BTP, and so do several services that can complement your SAP IRPA bots. We suggest that you understand the SAP BTP and its complementary services well enough to help your customers choose the right services.

We hope this book has helped you get started as a SAP IRPA developer. We wish you all the best with learning and progressing on your chosen path.

Questions

Here are some questions for you to test your knowledge of this chapter. The answers to these questions can be found at the back of this book, in the *Assessments* section:

1. How often does SAP release new features for SAP IRPA?
2. Can you name the four core pillars of the SAP BTP and some leading products from each pillar?

Assessments

Chapter 1:

1. Cloud Studio.
2. Mail and Cloud ALM (this question will have required some exploration on your part. If you were unable to answer it from the chapter, that is understandable).
3. Cloud Studio.

Chapter 2:

1. A project is a design-time object, while a package is an immutable deployable entity created from a project.
2. Attended, scheduled, and API.
3. You have not signed in from the agent.
4. Text and credential.
5. Job's monthly consumption for the past 13 months.
6. Jobs, agents, triggers, **CALM** (**Cloud Application Lifecycle Management**).

Chapter 3:

1. Only Microsoft Windows.
2. Webview control of MS Internet Explorer 11 is required for the desktop agent. This requirement will soon become obsolete with the upcoming updates, but until then, install both IE11 and either Google Chrome or Microsoft Edge.
3. Yes. English, German, and French are supported by default, but you can add other languages too.

Chapter 4:

1. The part of the URL after `hana.ondemand.com/` needs to be removed.

2. You need to allow access to file URLs in the Google Chrome setup.

3. There is no straightforward answer to this question, and it would have taken you some research. There are two other options for the project template – `v3` and `v2`. It would be best if you never used these options as these are intended for older versions of projects from the legacy Contextor technology.

Chapter 5:

1. The **Explorer** perspective.

2. Go to **Menu** | **Debug** button or *F5*.

3. Unlikely, as the unattended automations are run without a user and the UI is unlikely to be used.

4. To connect the captured applications.

5. This is a subjective answer and would be unique to your understanding.

Chapter 6:

1. Trick question. You cannot yet install the desktop agent on any other OS besides Windows.

2. A dedicated API connector.

3. No.

Chapter 7:

1. No, an active internet connection is required to use Cloud Studio.

2. Yes, you can use APIs to interact with many SAP BTP services from Desktop Studio.

3. Besides the automation developed within a project, you can use scenarios, user tasks, and other processes as skills.

4. Most complex projects are likely to have multiple scenarios to break down the automation into manageable parts.

Chapter 8:

1. Only the production server, and not even a copy of the production server.

2. No. A spotlight report shows automation opportunities addressable using INTELLIGENT RPA, Fiori, machine learning, and situation handling.

3. A user with the SAP administrator role.

4. SAP Process Manager by Signavio, SAP Process Intelligence by Signavio, SAP Workflow Accelerator by Signavio, and SAP Process Collaboration Hub by Signavio.

Chapter 9:

1. The Debug perspective can be launched by clicking the filled right arrow button in the menu bar.

2. If the criteria are not defined or if there are any conflicts with other controls in the page.

3. The UI Designer perspective can be used to create custom pop-up dialogs, and these dialogs or popups can be used in the workflow in the same way as any application pages.

4. The **Find and Replace** panel, and the **Properties** panel.

Chapter 10:

1. Users can create a new project, update an existing project, archive a project for sharing the source with other developers, and export the project for deployment

2. Project dependencies can be updated by editing the project.

3. Once the project is deployed, if there are any additional features to be added or fixes to be applied, then the project version needs to be updated. Updating the project version helps to revoke the update to the previous version in case of any issues.

4. Exporting a project is required to deploy the project to SAP Intelligent RPA Cloud Factory, whereas archiving is used for zipping the source and sharing it with other developers.

Chapter 11:

1. Some of the technology connectors are extensions to other connectors, for example, the SAP GUI connector is an extension to the UI Automation connector, and the SAPUI5 connector is an extension to the web connector. The extensions are available while capturing the pages and not while capturing the applications.

2. Ensure that the page or application being captured is in the foreground and visible while capturing. Only the page that is being displayed in the active tab of the browser will be available for capture.

3. SAP Intelligent RPA reads the complete DOM structure of the page. The time it takes to complete the capture depends on the number of visible and invisible controls present on the page.

Chapter 12:

1. The **Explorer** perspective identifies controls or pages that have conflicting criteria. This means that the criteria set for the control are not unique. Refer to the **Captured Data** panel to identify unique properties that can be used.

2. The invisible controls can be declared by navigating to the source of the control from the **Source Tree** panel

3. SAP Intelligent RPA reads the complete DOM structure of the page. The time it takes to capture the page depends on the size of the page or the number of controls, both visible and non-visible, present on the page.

Chapter 13:

1. These activities are specific to controls and are available for selection when the page is opened in the workflow.

2. The **Keystroke** activity under the **Item - Set** activity group is used to send a key sequence to a control. The **Keystroke** activity under the **Page** activity group is used to send the key sequence to a page.

Chapter 14:

1. `https://www.packtpub.com/`: To use the **Ancestor** parameter, the control must be declared first, whereas we can add the parent hierarchy to the criteria without defining the parent control. Application of one of the options is up to the developers. However, if more than one control under the same parent is to be captured, you can use the **Ancestor** parameter. The preferred option for capturing the array of controls is to declare the hierarchy in the **Criteria** panel.

2. The parameters available for the controls are in context with the technology used to capture the page. Not all parameters are available for all technologies, meaning the **Labelled By** parameter is not available for the controls on the pages captured with the **Web** connector.

3. You can use the **Item - Get** activity to like any normal control. You need to define the context variable as an array.

4. If there is more than one control with the same matching criteria on the page, SAP Intelligent RPA will recognize the first control that matches the criteria. If **Occurs** is used, then it will recognize all the controls matching the criteria.

Chapter 15:

1. The **if (else)** activity must be preceded by an **if (start)** activity and should be defined under the **if (start)** activity hierarchy.

2. The **Switches Output** activity supports a maximum of 11 conditional flows based on the number of connections possible from this activity.

3. `$data$` is used to select the context variables in the **Properties** panel.
   `$item$` is used to select the defined controls on the page in the **Properties** panel.

Chapter 16:

1. We can use the **Wait click** activity under the **Item – Wait** activity group.

2. A custom page must be captured by clicking on the **Capture** button in the **Designer View** panel to make it available for use in any workflow.

Chapter 17:

1. The **Build** option is used to incrementally generate the code, whereas **Rebuild** is used to clean the already generated code and then build it.

2. The changes made in the code are not reflected in the workflow. Any changes required to the workflow can be made in the **Workflow** perspective and then the code can be regenerated.

3. Include them in the **Libraries** tab of the **Edit Project...** dialog.

Chapter 18:

1. Those libraries are likely not included in the project. Go to the **Libraries** tab of the **Edit Project** dialog and select the required library.

2. No, the source code of the SDK library should only be used as a reference. This code should not be edited.

Chapter 19:

1. Activities are increasing with every product release to support the methods that are available in the SDK library.

2. Use the **Custom** activity to create a step and add the code to the method defined for that step.

3. Make sure you include the `ctx.outlook.mail.resetMailCollection` method before calling the `search` method. The `ctx.outlook.mail.resetMailCollection` method clears the working mails list.

Chapter 20:

1. The calls to read the environment variables are asynchronous. You need to have enough time to use them after reading. You can implement the steps, such as launching the application and going to the login page, after the read steps.

2. You can create an environment variable with the same name in multiple environments. The project deployed to an environment will use the variable from that specific environment.

3. The calls to get the values from environment variables are asynchronous, and so execution will continue to the next step even before the values are fetched. Either the value is to be read much before its actual use, or use `ctx.polling` to wait until the values are fetched.

Chapter 21:

1. First, we need to ensure that the required library is included in the project by editing the project. You can also try the **Rebuild IntelliSense** option from the context menu in the **Source Editor** panel, or use the *CTRL + Shift + F5* shortcut key.

2. Desktop Studio opens the source comparison tool to merge the source code manually If there are conflicts in the source code and Desktop Studio cannot decide which source to use while building the project. This often happens when a new step is added to the workflow before an exiting step for which the source code was already generated. You need to merge the source manually and save it so the build can proceed.

Chapter 22:

1. Ensure that the agent hostname specified in the environment is correct. It generally takes a couple of minutes to download the package to the agent's machine. If it is not available even after a few minutes, restart the agent.

2. The triggers are created for the package, and updating the package version in the environment will be sufficient to change the package in the agent's machine. Once created, the trigger need not be updated for the package version.

3. Check the date range specified while creating the trigger. The package is not available after the date range specified. You can update the trigger to specify the new date range.

Chapter 23:

1. Downloading the latest package might take a long time based on the size of the package and network speed. You can force a package refresh by restarting Desktop Agent.

2. The testers or users can only run the workflows from Desktop Agent. Debugging the project is only possible from Desktop Studio. General practice is that the test will only have Desktop Agent installed and not Desktop Studio.

3. The only reason SAP Intelligent RPA does not recognize the loaded page or the controls is the criteria declared for the page or control. You need to redefine the criteria to make it match the page or control.

Chapter 24:

1. SAP has made 12 SDKs available. Of these 12, two SDKs, `iRPA_core` and `iRPA_excel`, are added by default as a dependency to every new project.

2. Capturing an application gets all the elements that make up an application. At the same time, a declaration helps us set the recognition criteria for the application, applications screens, and only the chosen elements that we want to work with.

3. Yes, automations are among the five tools you can use in your automation. The other four are screens, activities, data, and controls.

Chapter 25:

1. You will find the exported package as a ZIP archive under the `export` folder in the `project` directory.

2. You can import a **Desktop Package** from the **Packages** tab on the **Automation Factory** toolbar or within an existing project. The cloud factory would automatically create a cloud project to embed the imported desktop package while importing from the **Packages** tab.

3. By default, the exported project would not include the contents of dependencies. You will also see a warning to this effect during the export process. You must export the dependency packages separately, except if they are from the store.

4. Packages follow the semantic versioning in the format `MAJOR.MINOR.PATCH`. When recreating a package, you will be given an option to choose the upgrade level, and accordingly, a new version will be created. To learn more, see `https://semver.org/`.

Chapter 26:

1. Ensure that you are using the correct version of SAP Intelligent RPA and that your basis team has fulfilled all the necessary prerequisites.

2. You forgot to click the screen capture button when the screens changed. The recorder will often warn you about the screen change, but sometimes it won't, and you have to pay attention.

Chapter 27:

1. In SAP Intelligent RPA Store, select **Cloud Studio** under **Design Tool** and **Microsoft Excel** under **Application**. Optionally, choose **Learning** under **Catalog** to target only example applications.

2. Yes, while submitting a package to the store is possible, the functionality is restricted to SAP partners and may not be available to all developers.

Chapter 28:

1. SAP releases new features in SAP Intelligent RPA, and many other services running on BTP, every quarter. However, some releases may not have any new features or updates, as was the case for Q1, Q2, and Q3 releases for 2021.

2. The four pillars of SAP Business Technology Platform and their leading products are as follows:

   - Database and data management – SAP HANA Cloud, SAP Data Intelligence

   - Analytics – SAP Analytics Cloud

   - Application development and integration – SAP Integration Suite, Business Application Studio, SAP AppGyver

   - Intelligent technologies – SAP Intelligent RPA, Workflow Management

Index

F

G

Packt.com

Subscribe to our online digital library for full access to over 7,000 books and videos, as well as industry leading tools to help you plan your personal development and advance your career. For more information, please visit our website.

Why subscribe?

- Spend less time learning and more time coding with practical eBooks and Videos from over 4,000 industry professionals

- Improve your learning with Skill Plans built especially for you

- Get a free eBook or video every month

- Fully searchable for easy access to vital information

- Copy and paste, print, and bookmark content

Did you know that Packt offers eBook versions of every book published, with PDF and ePub files available? You can upgrade to the eBook version at packt.com and as a print book customer, you are entitled to a discount on the eBook copy. Get in touch with us at customercare@packtpub.com for more details.

At www.packt.com, you can also read a collection of free technical articles, sign up for a range of free newsletters, and receive exclusive discounts and offers on Packt books and eBooks.

Other Books You May Enjoy

If you enjoyed this book, you may be interested in these other books by Packt:

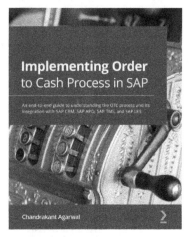

Implementing Order to Cash Process in SAP

Chandrakant Agarwal

ISBN: 9781801076104

- Discover master data in different SAP environments

- Find out how different sales processes, such as quotations, contracts, and order management, work in SAP CRM

- Become well-versed with the steps involved in order fulfillment, such as basic and advanced ATP checks in SAP APO

- Get up and running with transportation requirement and planning and freight settlement with SAP TMS

- Explore warehouse management with SAP LES to ensure high transparency and predictability of processes

- Understand how to process customer invoicing with SAP ECC

Robotic Process Automation Projects

NandanMullakara, Arun Kumar Asokan

ISBN: 9781839217357

- Explore RPA principles, techniques, and tools using an example-driven approach
- Understand the basics of UiPath by building a helpdesk ticket generation system
- Automate read and write operations from Excel in a CRM system using UiPath
- Build an AI-based social media moderator platform using Google Cloud Vision API with UiPath
- Explore how to use Automation Anywhere by building a simple sales order processing system
- Build an automated employee emergency reporting system using Automation Anywhere
- Test your knowledge of building an automated workflow through fun exercises

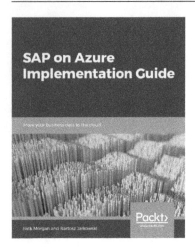

SAP on Azure Implementation Guide

Nick Morgan, Bartosz Jarkowski

ISBN: 9781838983987

- Successfully migrate your SAP infrastructure to Azure
- Understand the security benefits of Azure
- See how Azure can scale to meet the most demanding of business needs
- Ensure your SAP infrastructure maintains high availability
- Increase business agility through cloud capabilities
- Leverage cloud-native capabilities to enhance SAP

Packt is searching for authors like you

If you're interested in becoming an author for Packt, please visit `authors.packtpub.com` and apply today. We have worked with thousands of developers and tech professionals, just like you, to help them share their insight with the global tech community. You can make a general application, apply for a specific hot topic that we are recruiting an author for, or submit your own idea.

Share Your Thoughts

Now you've finished *SAP Intelligent RPA for Developers*, we'd love to hear your thoughts! Scan the QR code below to go straight to the Amazon review page for this book and share your feedback or leave a review on the site that you purchased it from.

`https://packt.link/r/1801079196`

Your review is important to us and the tech community and will help us make sure we're delivering excellent quality content.